Pentium Pro
and
Pentium II
System
Architecture

Second Edition

Pentium Pro and Pentium II System Architecture

Second Edition

MINDSHARE, INC.
Tom Shanley

ADDISON–WESLEY

Boston • San Francisco • New York • Toronto • Montreal
London • Munich • Paris • Madrid
Capetown • Sydney • Tokyo • Singapore • Mexico City

Many of the designations used by manufacturers and sellers to distinguish their products are claimed as trademarks. Where those designations appear in this book, and we were aware of a trademark claim, the designations have been printed in initial capital letters or in all capitals.

The author and publisher have taken care in the preparation of this book, but make no expressed or implied warranty of any kind and assume no responsibility for errors or omissions. No liability is assumed for incidental or consequential damages in connection with or arising out of the use of the information or programs contained herein.

The publisher offers discounts on this book when ordered in quantity for special sales. For more information, please contact:

Pearson Education Corporate Sales Division
One Lake Street
Upper Saddle River, NJ 07458
(800) 382-3419
corpsales@pearsontechgroup.com

Visit AW on the Web: www.awl.com/cseng/mindshare/

Library of Congress Cataloging-in-Publication Data

Shanley, Tom.
    Pentium Pro and Pentium II system architecture / Mindhsare, Inc;
Tom Shanley.
        p.   cm. — (PC system architecture series)
    ISBN 0-201-30973-4 (alk. paper)
    1. Pentium (Microprocessor) I. Mindshare, Inc.   II. Title.
III. Series.
QA76.8.P46S48   1997
004.165—dc21   97-39010
                                                    CIP

Set in 10 point Palatino by MindShare, Inc.

ISBN 0-201-30973-4
Text printed on recycled paper
5 6 7 8 9 10—MA—0403020100
Fifth printing, August 2000

PC System Architecture Series

MindShare, Inc.

Please see our web site (http://www.awl.com/cseng/series/mindshare) for more information on these titles.

CardBus System Architecture
0-201-40997-6

80486 System Architecture: Third Edition
0-201-40994-1

FireWire® System Architecture
0-201-69470-0

ISA System Architecture: Third Edition
0-201-40996-8

PCI System Architecture: Third Edition
0-201-40993-3

PCMCIA System Architecture: Second Edition
0-201-40991-7

Pentium® Pro and Pentium® II System Architecture: Second Edition
0-201-30973-4

Pentium® Processor System Architecture: Second Edition
0-201-40992-5

Plug and Play System Architecture
0-201-41013-3

Power PC System Architecture
0-201-40990-9

Protected Mode Software Architecture
0-201-55447-X

Universal Serial Bus System Architecture
0-201-46137-4

To my daughter Jennifer—I love you and I'm very proud of you.

Contents

About This Book

Part 1: System Overview

Chapter 1: System Overview

Contents

Part 2: Processor's Hardware Characteristics

Hardware Section 1: The Processor

Chapter 2: *Processor Overview*

Chapter 3: *Processor Power-On Configuration*

Contents

Chapter 4: *Processor Startup*

Contents

Chapter 5: *The Fetch, Decode, Execute Engine*

Contents

Chapter 6: *Rules of Conduct*

Contents

Chapter 7: *The Processor Caches*

Contents

Hardware Section 2: Bus Intro and Arbitration

Chapter 8: *Bus Electrical Characteristics*

Contents

Chapter 9: *Bus Basics*

Chapter 10: *Obtaining Bus Ownership*

Contents

Contents

Hardware Section 3: The Transaction Phases

Chapter 11: *The Request and Error Phases*

Chapter 12: *The Snoop Phase*

Contents

Chapter 13: *The Response and Data Phases*

Contents

Hardware Section 4: **Other Bus Topics**

Chapter 14: *Transaction Deferral*

Chapter 15: *IO Transactions*

Contents

Chapter 16: *Central Agent Transactions*

Chapter 17: *Other Signals*

Contents

Contents

Part 4: Processor's Software Characteristics

Chapter 19: *Instruction Set Enhancements*

Contents

Chapter 20: *Register Set Enhancements*

Chapter 21: *BIOS Update Feature*

Chapter 22: *Paging Enhancements*

Contents

Chapter 23: *Interrupt Enhancements*

Chapter 24: *Machine Check Architecture*

Contents

Chapter 25: *Performance Monitoring and Timestamp*

Chapter 26: *MMX: Matrix Math Extensions*

Contents

Contents

Chapter 28: *440FX Chipset*

Appendix A: The MTRR Registers

Figures

Figures

Figures

Figures

Tables

Tables

Acknowledgments

I would like to acknowledge my co-workers for their collective hard work in teaching our Pentium Pro/Pentium II class from this book. In my experience, it's extremely difficult to teach a class based on a book authored by someone else. You have to devote an immense amount of time to research in order to verify that the author is on target. If not, you might inadvertantly tell a lie. You also have to figure out a way to make the subject matter your own—put your own spin on it and add your own anecdotal information. It's not easy. My respects to John Swindle, Dave Dzatko, Ravi Budruk and Don Anderson.

About This Book

The MindShare Architecture Series

The MindShare Architecture book series includes: *ISA System Architecture, EISA System Architecture, 80486 System Architecture, PCI System Architecture, Pentium System Architecture, PCMCIA System Architecture, PowerPC System Architecture, Plug-and-Play System Architecture, CardBus System Architecture, Protected Mode Software Architecture, USB System Architecture, Pentium Pro and Pentium II System Architecture, and FireWire System Architecture: IEEE 1394.* The book series is published by Addison-Wesley.

Rather than duplicating common information in each book, the series uses the building-block approach. *ISA System Architecture* is the core book upon which most of the others build. The figure below illustrates the relationship of the books to each other.

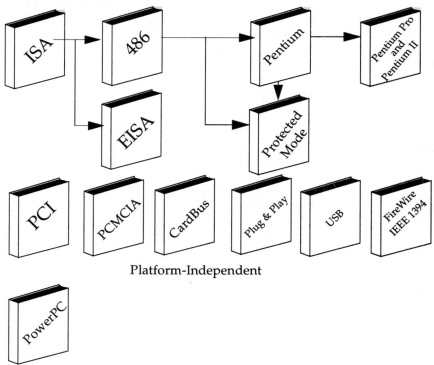

Platform-Independent

Cautionary Note

The reader should keep in mind that MindShare's book series often deals with rapidly-evolving technologies. This being the case, it should be recognized that each book is a "snapshot" of the state of the targeted technology at the time that the book was completed. We attempt to update each book on a timely basis to reflect changes in the targeted technology, but, due to various factors (waiting for the next version of the spec to be "frozen," the time necessary to make the changes, and the time to produce the books and get them out to the distribution channels), there will always be a delay.

What This Book Covers

The purpose of this book is to provide a detailed description of the Pentium Pro and Pentium II processors both from the hardware and the software perspectives. As with our other x86 processor books, this book builds upon and does not duplicate information provided in our books on the previous generation processors. As an example, our *Pentium Processor System Architecture* book provided a detailed description of the APIC module, while this book only describes differences between the two implementations.

What this Book Does not Cover

This book does not describe the x86 instruction repertoire. There are a host of books on the market that already provide this information. It does, however, describe the new instructions added to the instruction set.

Organization of This Book

Pentium Pro and Pentium II System Architecture extends MindShare's coverage of x86 processor architecture to the Pentium Pro and Pentium II processors. The author considers this book to be a companion to the MindShare books entitled *80486 System Architecture, Pentium Processor System Architecture, and Protected Mode Software Architecture* (all published by Addison-Wesley). The book is organized as follows:

Pentium Pro and Pentium II System Architecture

Who this Book is For

This book is intended for use by hardware and software design and support personnel. Due to the clear, concise explanatory methods used to describe each subject, personnel outside of the design field may also find the text useful.

Prerequisite Knowledge

It is highly recommended that the reader have a good knowledge of x86 processor architecture. Detailed descriptions of the 286 and 386 processors can be found in the MindShare book entitled *ISA System Architecture*. Detailed descriptions of the 486 and Pentium processors can be found in the MindShare books entitled *80486 System Architecture* and *Pentium Processor System Architecture*, respectively. Detailed descriptions of both real and protected mode operation can be found in the MindShare book entitled *Protected Mode Software Architecture*. All of these books are published by Addison-Wesley.

Documentation Conventions

This document utilizes the following documentation conventions for numeric values.

Hexadecimal Notation

All hex numbers are followed by an "h." Examples:

```
9A4Eh
0100h
```

Binary Notation

All binary numbers are followed by a "b." Examples:

```
0001 0101b
01b
```

Decimal Notation

Numbers without any suffix are decimal. When required for clarity, decimal numbers are followed by a "d." The following examples each represent a decimal number:

```
16
255
256d
128d
```

Signal Name Representation

Each signal that assumes the logic low state when asserted is followed by a pound sign (#). As an example, the HITM# signal is asserted low when a snoop agent has a hit on a modified line in its caches.

Signals that are not followed by a pound sign are asserted when they assume the logic high state.

Warning

The majority of the processor's signal pins are active low signals (e.g., all of the pins involved in a transaction). All tables in the Intel *Pentium Pro Volume One* data book, however, represent an asserted signal (in other words, in the electrically low state) with a one, while deasserted signals (electrically high) are represented by a zero in table entries. In other words, a "logical" one in a table indicates that the respective signal pin is asserted (in the electrically low state).

As an example, when a table entry indicates a one for the HITM# signal state, this indicates that it is asserted (electrically low).

Identification of Bit Fields (logical groups of bits or signals)

All bit fields are designated in little-endian bit ordering as follows:

[X:Y],

where "X" is the most-significant bit and "Y" is the least-significant bit of the field. As an example, the IOPL field in the EFLAGS register consists of bits [13:12], where bit 13 is the most-significant and bit 12 the least-significant bit of the field.

Register Field References

Bit fields in registers are frequently referred to using the form **Reg[field name]**. As an example, the reference CR4[DE] refers to the Debug Extensions bit in Control Register 4.

Resources

The Intel Developers' web site contains many documents available for download that provide excellent reference materials. We have a hot-link to their web site on our web site (see next section).

Visit Our Web Site

Our Web site contains a listing of all of our courses and books. In addition, it contains errata for a number of the books, a hot link to our publisher's web site, course outlines, and hot links to other useful web sites.

www.mindshare.com

Our publisher's web page contains a listing of our currently-available books and includes pricing and ordering information. Their MindShare page is accessible at:

www.awl.com/cseng/mindshare/

We Want Your Feedback

MindShare values your comments and suggestions. You can contact us via mail, phone, fax or internet email.

Phone: (972) 231-2216 and, in the U.S., (800) 633-1440
Fax: (972) 783-4715
E-mail: tshanley@interserv.com

For information on MindShare seminars, books, book errata, etc., check our web site.

Mailing Address:

MindShare, Inc.
2202 Buttercup Drive
Richardson, Texas 75082

Part 1: System Overview

This Part

Part 1 of the book presents a basic description of a typical server's architecture, describing the relationships of the processors, caches, main memory, host/PCI bridges, PCI masters and targets, and E/ISA masters and targets. This subject is covered first to provide a backdrop for the subjects covered in the remainder of the book.

The Next Part

Part 2 of the book focuses on the hardware aspects of the processor's internal operation as well as its bus structure and protocol.

1 *System Overview*

This Chapter

This chapter provides a basic description of a typical server's architecture, describing the relationships of the processors, caches, main memory, host/PCI bridges, PCI masters and targets, and E/ISA masters and targets. This subject is covered first to provide a backdrop for the subjects covered in the remainder of the book.

The Next Chapter

The next chapter provides a brief introduction to the internal architecture of the processor.

Introduction

Rather than launching into a detailed discussion of the Pentium Pro processor, it would be useful to provide some background regarding the processor's relationship to the other devices in the system. Figure 1-1 on page 12 illustrates a typical PC server based on the Pentium Pro processor and a typical Pentium Pro chipset. As noted in the figure, the major components have been labelled with the nomenclature of the Intel 450GX chipset (originally called the "Orion" chipset). An overview of this chipset as well as the 450KX and 440FX may be found in the chapters entitled "450GX and KX Chipsets" on page 523 and "440FX Chipset" on page 559.

Figure 1-1: Block Diagram of a Typical Server

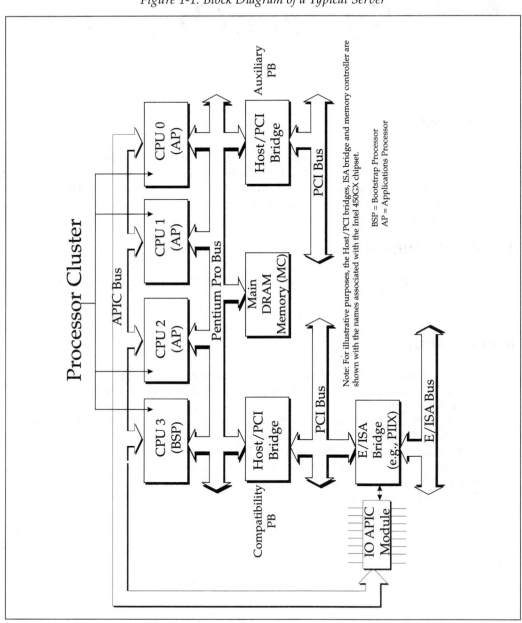

What is a Cluster?

The term cluster refers to the processors that reside on the Pentium Pro processor bus. It can consists of anywhere from one to four processors.

What Is a Quad or 4-Way System?

A Pentium Pro system with four processors on the processor bus is frequently referred to as a quad, or 4-way system.

Bootstrap Processor

Which processor begins fetching and executing the power-on self-test (POST) when reset is removed from the processors? It should be fairly obvious that all of them aren't going to execute the POST. In fact, one processor will execute the POST, configure the system board devices and enable them, detect the presence of the other processors and perform the boot to read the OS into memory and pass control to it.

This processor is referred to as the bootstrap processor, or BSP. The processors negotiate amongst themselves before the first instruction is fetched from memory to determine which will be the BSP. This negotiation is not performed on the host processor bus. Rather, it is performed over the APIC (Advanced Programmable Interrupt Controller) bus. This negotiation process is described in the chapter entitled "Processor Startup" on page 51.

Starting Up Other Processors

According to the Intel-authored Multiprocessing Specification (available for download on the Intel web site), the code executing on the BSP (i.e., the POST/BIOS code) is responsible for detecting the presence of the other processors. This information is then stored in non-volatile memory in the form of a table (the MP, or multiprocessing, table). An MP (Multi-Processing) OS uses this information to determine the available processors, their types and features. An OS that is not MP-aware (e.g., DOS) only makes use of the BSP. The other processors remain dormant (in other words, they're useless).

Assuming that it is an MP OS, it assigns a task to a processor in the following manner:

- Typically, it instructs a bus mastering disk controller to load a task into memory.
- Once the task is in memory, the OS kernel, executing on the BSP, causes the BSP's internal APIC to issue a Startup IPI (Inter-Processor Interrupt, or message) to one of the other processors over the APIC bus. Supplied in this message packet is the start address of the program just placed in memory.
- Upon receipt of the Startup IPI, the target processor leaves the wait-for-IPI state and begins to fetch and execute the task in memory.

Relationship of Processors to Main Memory

Each of the processors contains an L2 cache as well as L1 data and code caches. Once software enables a processor's caches and tells the processor which areas of memory it's safe to cache from (via the processor's Memory Type and Range Registers, or MTRRs), the caches begin to make copies of information from main memory (the processors are typically permitted to cache information from main memory, but not from memory on the PCI and other buses). When making a copy of memory information in the cache, the processor always copies 32-byte blocks into the cache. Each block is referred to as a line.

Each line of information in the processor's L2 cache and L1 data cache may be stored in four possible states (referred to as the MESI cache protocol):

- **I state**. Indicates that the line is invalid (i.e., the cache doesn' t have a copy).
- **E state**. Indicates that this processor's cache has a copy of the line, that it is still the same as the copy in memory, and that no other processor's cache has a copy of the same data.
- **S state**. Indicates that this processor's cache has a copy of the line, that it is still the same as memory, and that at least one other processor's cache has a copy of the same data (and it is also still the same as the copy in memory).
- **M state**. Indicates that this processor has a copy of the line, that no other processor has a copy in its cache, and that one or more of the bytes within this copy have been updated by writes from the processor core since it was read from memory. The copy in memory is stale (i.e., out-of-date).

Lines in the L1 code cache are marked either I (Invalid) or S (Shared, or valid).

Processors' Relationships to Each Other

As stated in the previous section, the processors read lines of information from main memory into their caches. After getting a line of data into the cache, the programmer may perform memory writes to update bytes within the line. The line is then different then memory. If the MTRRs designate the area of memory as a write-back area (covered later), the processor absorbs the new bytes into the line and marks the line modified (i.e., places it in the M state). The update is not performed on the bus, however, so the line in memory is not updated.

When a device performs a memory read or write transaction on the processor bus, all of the processors must snoop the address in their caches and report the state of their copies to the initiator of the transaction and to the main memory controller. The initiator must do the right thing based on the snoop result. As an example, if other caches report that they have a copy of the line in the E or S state, the processor reading the line from memory must place the new line in its cache in the S state. Likewise, if a snooper had a copy in the E state, it would have to change its state from E to S as a result of watching the other processor reading the same line. Table 1-1 on page 15 contains some additional examples.

Table 1-1: Example Cache State Transitions

Stimulus	Effect on Initiator	Effect on Snoopers
Memory read initiated due to a cache miss that misses all other caches.	When read is complete, store line in E state.	None.
Memory read initiated due to a cache miss that hits on an E line in one other cache.	When read is complete, store line in S state.	The cache with the E copy must transition the state of its copy from E to S.
Memory read initiated due to a cache miss that hits on an S line in two or more other caches.	When read is complete, store line in S state.	None.
Memory read initiated due to a cache miss that hits on an M line in one other cache.	After receiving the line from the snoop agent that has the M copy, the requestor places line in S state.	Modified line is supplied directly from snooper to requestor. Memory is also updated with the fresh line. Snooper changes state of its copy from M to S.

Table 1-1: Example Cache State Transitions (Continued)

Stimulus	Effect on Initiator	Effect on Snoopers
Memory write of less than 32 bytes initiated due to a cache hit (cache line is updated) or miss in an area of memory defined as write-through memory by the MTRRs. Misses all other caches. Memory is updated.	If cache hit in initiating processor, copy is updated.	None.
Memory write of less than 32 bytes initiated due to a cache hit (cache line is updated) or miss in an area of memory defined as write-through memory by the MTRRs. Hits on E copy in one cache or an S copy in more than one cache.	If cache hit in initiating processor, copy is updated.	Snoopers transition the state of their copies from E->I or S->I (because they can't snarf the write data as it flies by on its way to memory).
Memory read and invalidate of 0 bytes initiated due to a store hit on a line in the S state in a write-back area of memory. Hits on S copy in one or more caches.	After the memory read and invalidate for 0 bytes completes, initiator then stores into its copy and transitions it from S to M.	Snoopers transition state of their copies to I state.
Memory read and invalidate of 32 bytes initiated due to a store miss in a write-back area of memory. Hits on E copy in one other cache or an S copy in two or more.	After the memory read and invalidate for 0 bytes completes, initiator then stores into its copy and transitions it from I to M.	Snoopers transition state of their copies to I state.

Table 1-1: Example Cache State Transitions (Continued)

Stimulus	Effect on Initiator	Effect on Snoopers
Memory read and invalidate of 32 bytes initiated due to a store miss in a write-back area of memory. Hits on M copy in one other cache.	Upon receipt of the line from the snooper's cache, requestor immediately stores into line and transitions from I to M. Memory controller accepts line as it is written from the snooper. Alternately, realizing that it's a read and invalidate, the memory controller may choose to accept the data written by the snooper, but not actually waste time writing it into memory (because initiator immediately stores into it and marks it modified).	Snooper supplies requested line directly from its cache and then invalidates its copy.

Host/PCI Bridges

Bridges' Relationship to Processors

The host/PCI bridge is a bridge between the processor bus and a PCI bus. When a processor initiates a transaction, the bridge must handle the scenarios defined in Table 1-2 on page 17.

Table 1-2: Processor-Initiated Transactions

Processor Action	Bridge Action
Processor is performing a memory read or write that targets main memory.	Ignore (because main memory is on the processor bus).

Table 1-2: Processor-Initiated Transactions (Continued)

Processor Action	Bridge Action
Processor is performing a memory read or write with a PCI memory target.	If the processor is targeting a PCI (or ISA or EISA) memory target that resides behind the bridge, the bridge must act as the surrogate target of the processor's transaction. To do this, bridge must know the memory ranges associated with the entire community of memory targets that reside behind it (including those that may reside behind PCI-to-PCI bridges). It arbitrates for ownership of the PCI bus and reinitiates the transaction on the PCI bus. If it's a read transaction, it must return the data to the requesting processor when it receives it from the target.
Processor accesses PCI IO target.	Same actions as for processor-initiated memory access to PCI memory target. Bridge must know the IO ranges associated with the entire community IO targets that reside behind it (including those that may reside behind PCI-to-PCI bridges).
Processor accesses PCI device configuration register.	Bridge must compare target PCI bus number to the range of PCI buses that exists beyond the bridge. If the target bus is directly behind the bridge, initiate a type 0 PCI configuration transaction. If the target bus is beyond the bridge but isn't the one directly behind it, initiate a type 1 PCI configuration transaction. If the target bus isn't within the range of buses beyond the bridge, ignore the transaction. If the processor is targeting the bridge's internal configuration registers, act as the target but do not pass the transaction onto the PCI bus.
Processor initiates an interrupt acknowledge transaction.	If the 8259A interrupt controller is behind the bridge, initiate a PCI interrupt acknowledge transaction to obtain the interrupt vector from the controller.
Processor initiates a special transaction.	If the message encoded on the processor's byte enables is one that the PCI devices must receive, the bridge must initiate a PCI special cycle transaction to pass the processor's message to the PCI bus. If the message is one that the bridge itself must respond to, the bridge acts as the target of the transaction, but doesn't pass it to the PCI bus.

Bridges' Relationship to PCI Masters and Main Memory

When a PCI master initiates a transaction on the PCI bus directly behind the bridge, the bridge must act as indicated in Table 1-3 on page 19.

Table 1-3: PCI Master-Initiated Transactions

PCI Master Action	Bridge Action
PCI master initiates a memory read or write.	If the transaction targets main memory, arbitrate for ownership of the processor bus and access main memory. If a read, return the requested data to the master. The bridge must know the address range of main memory.
PCI master initiates an IO read or write.	The action taken by the bridge is bridge-specific. If there are no IO ports behind the bridge that are accessible by PCI masters, ignore (e.g., the Intel 450GX/KX chipset). If the bridge permits PCI masters to pass IO transactions onto the processor bus, the bridge arbitrates for the processor bus and passes the transaction through.
PCI master initiates a dual-address (i.e., 64-bit memory address) command.	If the transaction targets main memory, arbitrate for ownership of the host bus and access main memory. If a read, return the requested data to the master. The bridge must know the address range of main memory.

Bridges' Relationship to PCI Targets

The bridge must know the memory and IO ranges associated with the entire community of memory and IO targets that reside behind the bridge, including those that reside behind PCI-to-PCI bridges.

Bridges' Relationship to EISA or ISA Targets

The bridge must know if the EISA or ISA bus is located behind it. If it is, the bridge must act as the target when a processor transaction targets a memory or IO address that may be for an EISA or ISA target.

Bridges' Relationship to Each Other

If there are two host/PCI bridges, they both share access to the BPRI# signal to request processor bus ownership. Only one device is permitted to use this signal at a time. If the two bridges both require access to main memory, they must arbitrate amongst themselves for ownership of the BPRI# signal. In the 450GX chipset, two sideband signals, IOREQ# and IOGNT#, are used for this purpose. The compatibility PB (i.e., the bridge with the ISA or EISA bridge behind it) has higher priority than the aux PB (when both bridges simultaneously require access to main memory).

Bridge's Relationship to EISA and ISA Masters and DMA

When an EISA master, an ISA master, or a DMA channel in the EISA or ISA bridge requires access to main memory, the EISA or ISA bridge initiates a memory access on the PCI bus. The host/PCI bridge between the EISA or ISA bridge and main memory must arbitrate for ownership of the processor bus and access main memory. Because EISA and ISA masters and DMA channels are frequently sensitive to memory access time, the host/bridge between them and main memory is typically assigned higher processor bus priority than the other host/PCI bridge. This feature is typically referred to as GAT (Guaranteed Access Time).

Part 2: Processor's Hardware Characteristics

The Previous Part

Part 1 provided a basic description of a typical server's architecture, describing the relationships of the processors, caches, main memory, host/PCI bridges, PCI masters and targets, and E/ISA masters and targets. This subject was covered first to provide a backdrop for the subjects covered in the remainder of the book.

This Part

Part 2 provides a description of the processor's internal and external hardware characteristics. It is divided into the following sections, each consisting of one or more chapters:

- "Hardware Section 1: The Processor" on page 23.
- "Hardware Section 2: Bus Intro and Arbitration" on page 197.
- "Hardware Section 3: The Transaction Phases" on page 259.

The Next Part

Part 3 provides a description of the Pentium II processor and how it differs from the Pentium Pro processor.

Hardware
Section 1:
The Processor

This Section

Part 1, Section 1 focuses on the processor's internal operation. The chapters that comprise this section are:

- "Processor Overview" on page 25.
- "Processor Power-On Configuration" on page 35.
- "Processor Startup" on page 51.
- "The Fetch, Decode, Execute Engine" on page 75.
- "Rules of Conduct" on page 133.
- "The Processor Caches" on page 149.

The Next Section

The chapters that comprise Part 1, Section 2 introduce the processor's bus and transaction protocol.

Warning

The majority of the processor's signal pins are active low signals (e.g., all of the pins involved in a transaction). All tables in the Intel *Pentium Pro Volume One* data book, however, represent an asserted signal (in other words, in the electrically low state) with a one, while deasserted signals (electrically high) are represented by a zero in table entries. In other words, a "logical" one in a table indicates that the respective signal pin is asserted (in the electrically low state).

As an example, when a table entry indicates a one for the HITM# signal state, this indicates that it is asserted (electrically low).

2 *Processor Overview*

The Previous Chapter

The previous chapter provided a basic description of a typical server's architecture, describing the relationships of the processors, caches, main memory, host/PCI bridges, PCI masters and targets, and E/ISA masters and targets. This subject was covered first to provide a backdrop for the subjects covered in the remainder of the book.

This Chapter

This chapter provides a brief introduction to the internal architecture of the processor.

The Next Chapter

The next chapter describes the manner in which the processor automatically configures some of its operational characteristics at power up time upon the removal of reset. In addition, it describes some of the basic processor features that may be enabled or disabled by the programmer.

Two Bus Interfaces

Refer to Figure 2-1 on page 26. The current implementations of the processor package consist of two tightly-coupled dies (set in a dual-cavity package), one containing the processor itself, while the other contains the L2 cache. The processor is connected to the L2 die over a dedicated bus (frequently referred to as the backside bus) consisting of a 36-bit address bus and a 64-bit data bus. In addition, the processor's bus interface unit is connected to the external world via the external bus. In the event of a miss on the L1 data or code cache, the L2 cache can be accessed via the backside bus at the same time that the processor (or an another bus agent) is using the external bus. Later versions of the processor (e.g., the Pentium II) eliminate the L2 die from the package. Instead, the processor core is mounted on a card that also contains the L2 cache. The core interfaces to the L2 cache via the backside bus and to the external world via the card-edge connector.

Figure 2-1: Two Bus Interfaces

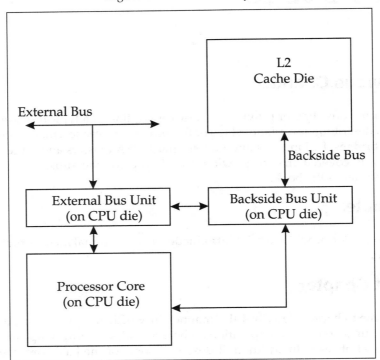

External Bus

Bus on Earlier Processors Inefficient for Multiprocessing

The processor's external bus is significantly different than that found on the earlier processors. The older buses were designed to be used by one initiator at a time. Each transaction consisted of an address and a data phase. When a processor gained ownership of the bus, it owned the entire bus and no other processor could use the bus until the transaction in progress completed.

Pentium Bus has Limited Transaction Pipelining Capability

It should be noted that a small degree of transaction overlap is possible on the Pentium bus (see Figure 2-2 on page 28). If the target of the transaction (e.g., the external L2 cache) supports transaction pipelining, it asserts NA# (Next Access) to the processor, thereby granting it permission to initiate another transaction before the data transfer for the current transaction is completed. In a dual-processor Pentium configuration, either the same processor that initiated the first transaction or the other processor in the pair can then initiate the address phase of a new transaction. However, the processor that initiated the second transaction (or the target, if a read) cannot transfer data over the data bus until the data transfer for the first transaction completes. The Pentium processor can only keep track of up to two currently-outstanding (i.e., pipelined) transactions.

Many target devices are extremely slow to provide read data or to accept write data. A classic example is a host/PCI bridge. Before it can supply a processor with read data from a PCI device, it must first arbitrate for PCI bus ownership. This can take quite a while if the PCI bus is currently in use by another PCI master. In addition, other masters may also be requesting PCI bus ownership and it may be their turn rather than the host/PCI bridge's. Once PCI ownership is acquired, the bridge then must wait for the target device to supply the read data. It's possible that the read may have to traverse a PCI-to-PCI bridge to get to the target. The net result can be a very lengthy delay before the read data is presented to the processor that requested the data. The Pentium's data bus would be tied up until the data is presented and BRDY# is asserted. Only then can the processor read the data and end the transaction.

The Pentium processor and bus have the following drawbacks:

- Processor can only keep track of up to two transactions currently-outstanding on the bus.
- Targets have no way of issuing a retry to a processor if they cannot handle a transaction immediately. The bus remains busy until the data transfer finally takes place.
- A very slow access target cannot memorize a transaction, disconnect from the initiator, process the transaction off-line, and reconnect with the initiator when finally ready to transfer data. This is called transaction deferral.

This approach is fine for a single-processor environment, but terrible for an environment that incorporates multiple processors on the host bus.

Figure 2-2: Pentium Transaction Pipelining

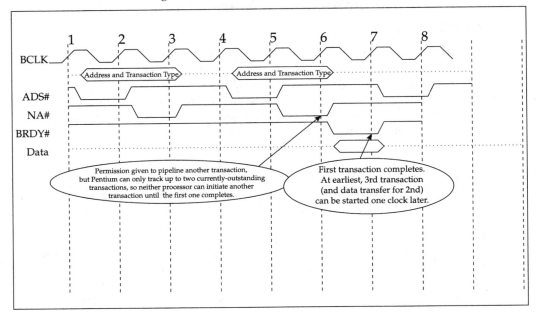

Pentium Pro Bus Tuned for Multiprocessing

The Pentium Pro bus protocol prevents bus stalls in three basic ways:

- In a typical Pentium Pro bus environment, up to eight transactions can be currently outstanding at various stages of completion.
- If the target of the transaction cannot deal with the transaction right now, rather than tie up the processor bus by inserting wait states, it will issue a retry to the initiator. This causes the initiator to wait a little while and try the transaction again at a later time. This frees up the processor bus for other initiators.
- If the target of a read or write transaction realizes that it will take a fairly long time to complete the data transfer (i.e., provide read data or accept write data), it can instruct the initiator to break the connection and the target will initiate a transaction later to complete the transaction. This is referred to as transaction deferral.

These mechanisms prevent any properly-designed bus agent from tying up the processor bus for extended periods of time. A detailed description of the processor's bus is presented later in the book.

IA = Legacy

With the advent of the Pentium Pro, Intel refers to the x86 instruction and register sets as the Intel Architecture ("IA" for short) instruction and register sets. In essence, IA refers to the legacy architecture inherited by the designers of the Pentium Pro and subsequent generations of the processor family. The IA instructions are complex, requiring a number of resources for execution, and the register set is quite small.

Instruction Set

IA Instructions Vary in Length and are Complex

Many IA instructions are complex in nature, requiring extensive decode and execution logic. Many of them require a number of execution resources in order to complete. As an example, one IA instruction may entail one or more memory reads, one or more computations, and one or more memory writes. In addition, an IA instruction may be anywhere from one to 15 bytes in length. This presents the processor designer with a formidable obstacle with regard to dispatching and executing more than one instruction simultaneously (i.e., designing a superscalar processor). The processor has to pre-scan the instruction stream (i.e., the prefetched instructions) in order to determine where one instruction ends and another begins. Only then could the processor logic decode the instructions and determine whether or not they can be executed simultaneously. The instructions that comprise a sequence of IA instructions are frequently very co-dependent on each other, thereby making it very difficult to execute the instructions in parallel with each other.

Pentium Pro Translates IA Instructions into RISC Instructions

Instructions are prefetched from memory and are placed into the L2 cache and the L1 code cache. The code cache feeds the instruction pipeline in the processor core. As blocks of instructions are obtained from the cache, the processor core parses them to identify the boundaries between instructions. It then decodes the variable-length IA instructions into fixed length RISC instructions referred to as micro-ops (or uops). The micro-ops are then passed along to an instruction pool where they await dispatch and execution. The dispatch logic can see all 40 entries in the pool and can dispatch any instruction for execution if the appropriate execution unit and the data operands it requires are available.

In-Order Front End

Instructions are prefetched, decoded and placed into the instruction pool in strict program order (i.e., the order in which the programmer expects them to be executed).

Out-of-Order Middle

Once the micro-ops are placed into the instruction pool, however, they can be executed out-of-order (i.e., not in the original program order). In other words, the dispatch logic does not have to wait for all instructions that precede an instruction to complete execution before executing the instruction. It will dispatch any instruction for execution if the appropriate execution unit and the data operands the instruction requires are available. It should be noted that a copy of the micro-op remains in the pool until the instruction is retired (explained in the text that follows). The results of the speculatively-executed instruction are stored in the instruction's pool entry rather than in the processor's register set, however.

The instruction may have been executed before a conditional branch that resides earlier in the program flow. Only when it is certain that all upstream branches have been resolved and that the instruction should have been executed, is it marked as ready for retirement. If it turns out that the instruction should not have been executed, the micro-op and its results are discarded from the pool.

In-Order Rear End

In order to have the program appear to execute in the order intended by the programmer, the processor core retires the instructions from the pool and commits their results from the pool locations to the processor's real register set in original program order.

A detailed description of the processor core can be found in the chapter entitled "The Fetch, Decode, Execute Engine" on page 75.

Register Set

IA Register Set is Small

The IA register set implemented in earlier x86 processors is extremely small. The small number of registers permits the processor (and the programmer) to keep only a small number of data operands close to the execution units where they can access them quickly. Rather, the programmer is frequently forced to write back the contents of one or more of the processor's registers to memory when he or she needs to read additional data operands from memory to be operated on. Later, when the programmer requires access to the original set of data operands, they must again be read from memory (perhaps after first storing the current contents of the registers). This juggling of data between the register set and memory takes time and exacts a penalty (perhaps severe) on the performance of the program. Figure 2-3 on page 31 illustrates the IA general register set.

Figure 2-3: IA General Register Set

	31	23	15	8 7	0
EAX			AH	AX	AL
EBX			BH	BX	BL
ECX			CH	CX	CL
EDX			DH	DX	DL
EBP				BP	
ESI				SI	
EDI				DI	
ESP				SP	

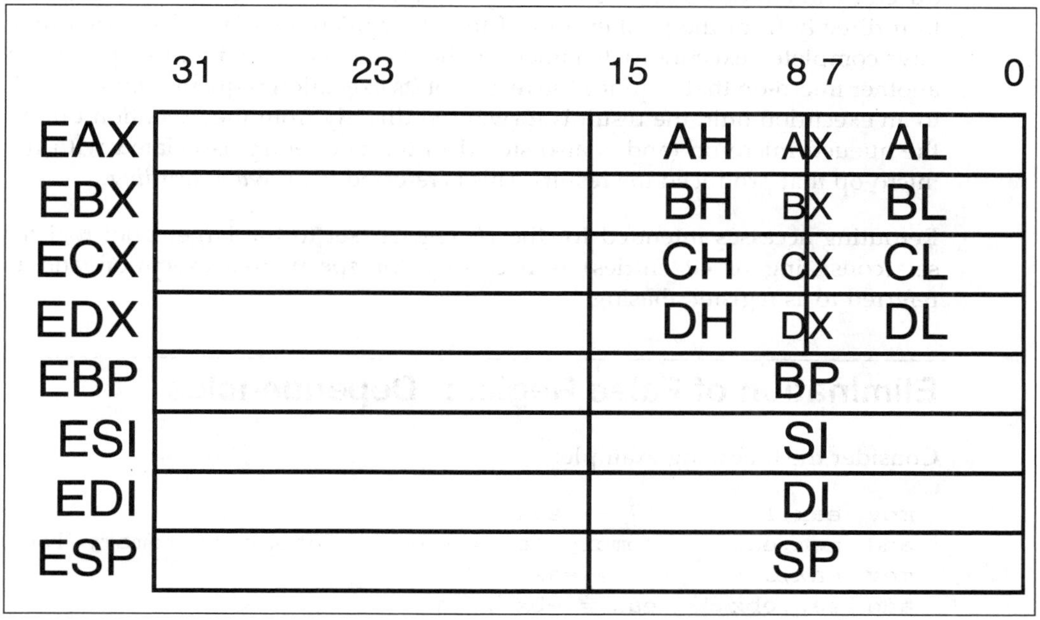

Pentium Pro has 40 General-Purpose Registers

Rather than the extremely limited register set pictured in Figure 2-3 on page 31, the Pentium Pro has 40 registers. As described earlier, IA instructions are translated into fixed-length micro-ops prior to being executed. When executed, the micro-op may:

- have to place a value into one of the IA general registers.
- have to read a value (from an IA register) that was placed into it by an instruction that was executed earlier.
- when executed, change the contents of the EFLAGS or FPU status register.

Remember that the processor core permits instructions to be executed out-of-order (referred to as speculative execution). Imagine what might happen if the results of the instruction's execution were immediately committed to the processor's register set. Values in registers would be changed and condition bits in the EFLAGS and FPU status registers would be updated, perhaps erroneously and certainly not in the expected order.

Rather than immediate commitment of instruction results to the real register set, the processor stores the result of an instruction's execution in the instruction's pool entry. If, when executed, another micro-op requires the result produced by micro-ops that precede it in program flow, the result(s) are forwarded to it directly from the pool entries of the other micro-ops (assuming that they have completed execution). If a micro-op has been dispatched for execution and another micro-op that requires the results of its execution is queued for dispatch to an execution unit, the result is forwarded directly from the execution unit to the queued micro-op (and is also stored in the pool entry associated with the micro-op that produced the result). This is referred to as *feed forwarding*.

Rerouting accesses intended for the IA register set to the larger pool register set (consisting of 40 entries) is necessary for speculative execution and is referred to as register aliasing.

Elimination of False Register Dependencies

Consider the following example:

```
mov  eax,17     ;17 -> eax
add  mem,eax    ;memory loc.= eax + content of memory loc.
mov  eax,3      ;3 -> eax
add  eax,ebx    ;eax = ebx + eax
```

In earlier x86 processors, these instructions would have to be executed one at a timein sequence, in order to yield the correct results. The processor couldn't execute the third and fourth instructions before the 1st and 2nd had completed (because the 2nd instruction must use the value placed into eax before the 3rd instruction can place a new value into eax).

The Pentium Pro processor recognizes that the eax register needn't be loaded with the value 17. Rather, the same result can be produced by just adding 17 to the memory location. Likewise, eax doesn't need to be loaded with the value 3. Instead, the value 3 can just be added to ebx and the result stored in eax. The processor can execute instructions 1 and 3 simultaneously, placing the values 17 and 3 into the pool entries for these two micro-ops. Likewise, instructions 2 and 4 can then be executed in parallel, obtaining the values 17 and 3 from the pool entries associated with micro-ops 1 and 3.

Introduction to the Internal Architecture

Refer to Figure 2-4 on page 34. The Pentium Pro processor consists of the following basic elements:

- **External bus unit**. Performs bus transactions when requested to do so by the L2 cache or the processor core.
- **Backside bus unit**. Interfaces the processor core to the unified L2 cache.
- **Unified L2 cache**. Services misses on the L1 data and code caches. When necessary, issues requests to the external bus unit.
- **L1 data cache**. Services data load and store requests issued by the load and store execution units. When a miss occurs, forwards request to the L2 cache.
- **L1 code cache**. Services instruction fetch requests issued by the instruction prefetcher.
- **Processor core**. The processor logic responsible for the following:
  - Instruction fetch.
  - Branch prediction.
  - Parsing of IA instruction stream.
  - Decoding of IA instructions into RISC instructions (referred to as micro-ops, or uops).
  - Mapping accesses for IA register set to a larger physical register set.
  - Dispatch, execution and retirement of micro-ops.
- **Local APIC unit**. Responsible for receiving interrupt requests from other processors, the processor local interrupt pins, the APIC timer, APIC error conditions, performance monitor logic, and the IO APIC module. These requests are then prioritized and forwarded to the processor core for execution.

Pentium Pro and Pentium II System Architecture

A detailed description of the processor's internal operation can be found in subsequent chapters.

Figure 2-4: Simplified Processor Block Diagram

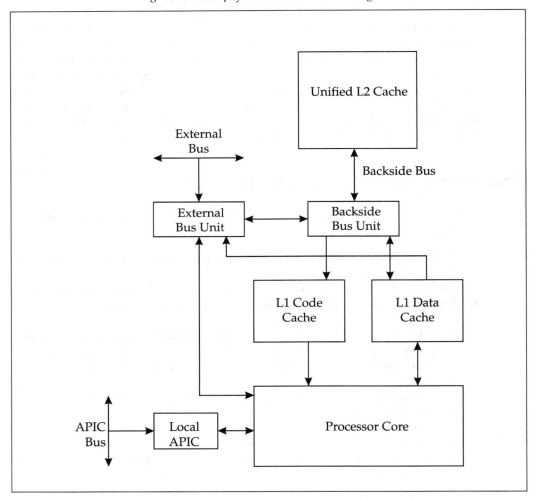

3 *Processor Power-On Configuration*

The Previous Chapter

The previous chapter provided a brief introduction to the internal architecture of the processor.

This Chapter

This chapter describes the manner in which the processor automatically configures some of its operational characteristics at power up time upon the removal of reset. In addition, it describes some of the basic processor features that may be enabled or disabled by the programmer.

The Next Chapter

The next chapter describes the processor state at startup time. It also describes the process that the processors engage in to select the processor that will fetch and execute the power-on self-test (POST), as well as how, after it has been loaded, an MP OS can detect the additional processors and assign tasks for them to execute.

Automatically Configured Features

The processor samples a subset of its signal pins on the trailing-edge of reset to configure certain of its operational characteristics. Figure 3-1 on page 36 illustrates the signals that are sampled and the features associated with each. The sections that follow describe each of these selections and the pins sampled to determine the selection.

Figure 3-1: Automatic Feature Determination

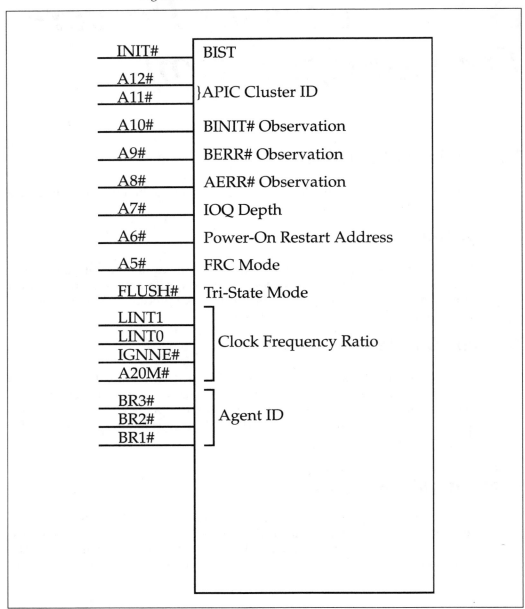

Chapter 3: Processor Power-On Configuration

Example of Captured Configuration Information

Figure 3-2 on page 38 is a screen shot of configuration information captured on the removal of RESET#. It was captured using the HP Pentium Pro/Pentium II bus preprocessor. In this example, the power-on configuration has the following effects:

- Output tristate mode, execution of the BIST, AERR#, BERR# and BINIT# observation, and FRC mode are disabled.
- The IOQ depth is set to 8.
- The power-on restart address is set to FFFFFFF0h.
- The APIC cluster ID is set to cluster zero.

In addition, each agent on the Pentium Pro bus that is capable of initiating bus transactions has a mutually-exclusive agent ID assigned to it.

Figure 3-2: Captured Power-On Configuration Information

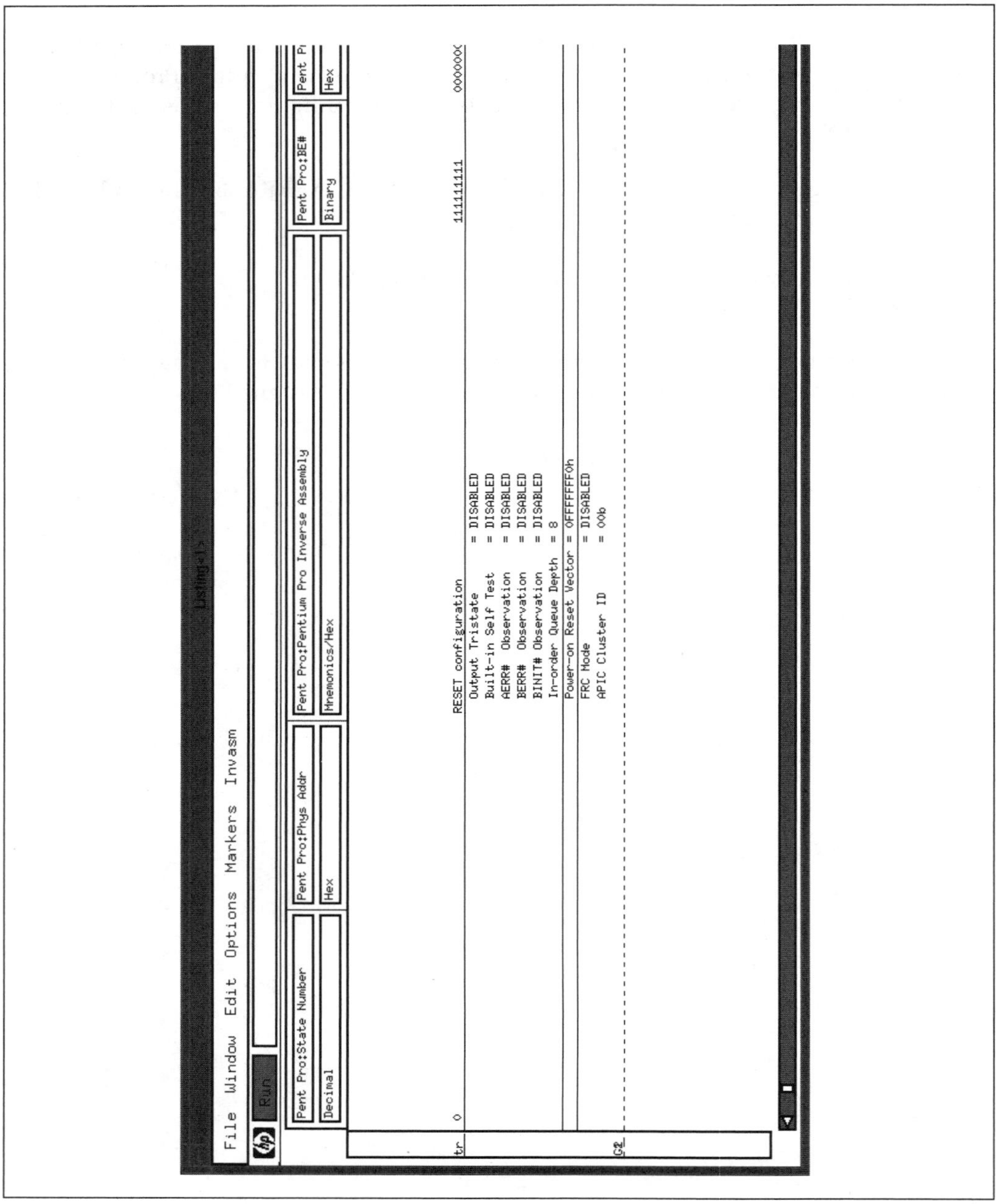

Setup and Hold Time Requirements

In order to reliably sample the values presented on its pins on the trailing-edge of the reset signal, the following setup and hold times must be met:

- the signal must be in the appropriate state for at least four bus clocks before the trailing-edge of RESET#. This is the setup time requirement.
- signal must be held in that state for at least two but not greater than 20 bus clocks after RESET# is deasserted. This is the hold time requirement.

Run BIST Option

If the INIT# pin is sampled in the low state at the trailing-edge of RESET#, the processor will execute its internal Built-In Self-Test prior to initiation of program fetch and execution. This takes approximately 5.5 million processor clock cycles to complete on the Pentium Pro processor, but it should be noted that the exact clock count is processor-specific and can change. If the BIST completes successfully, EAX contains zero. If an error is incurred during the BIST, however, EAX contains a non-zero error code. Intel does not provide a breakdown of the error codes. When the BIST is not invoked, EAX contains zero when program execution is initiated after reset's removal. In either case, the programmer should check to ensure that EAX is clear at the start of the Power-On Self-Test and not proceed with the POST if it contains a non-zero value.

Error Observation Options

The processor (actually, any bus agent) may be configured to monitor or to ignore three of its error inputs that are used to signal errors during bus transactions. Those three inputs are:

- **AERR#** (Address Error). Sampling A8# low at the trailing-edge of reset configures the processor to sample AERR# at the end of the error phase of transactions initiated by itself or by other bus agents. Sampling A8# high configures the processor to ignore AERR#. This is referred to as the processor's *AERR# observation policy*. A detailed discussion of AERR# may be found in the section entitled "Error Phase" on page 273.
- **BERR#** (Bus Error). Sampling A9# low at the trailing-edge of reset configures the processor to monitor BERR#. Sampling A9# high configures the processor to ignore BERR#. This is referred to as the processor's *BERR#*

observation policy. A detailed discussion of BERR# may be found in the chapter entitled "Other Signals" on page 365. *It should be noted that, although other bus agents may be configured to do so, the Pentium Pro processor does not support BERR# sampling.*

- **BINIT#** (Bus Initialization). Sampling A10# low at the trailing-edge of reset configures the processor to sample BINIT#. Sampling A10# high configures the processor to ignore BINIT#. This is referred to as the processor's *BINIT# observation policy*. A detailed discussion of BINIT# may be found in the chapter entitled "Other Signals" on page 365.

In-Order Queue Depth Selection

If the processor samples its A7# pin low at the trailing-edge of reset, it configures the depth of its In-Order Queue (IOQ) to one. Sampling A7# high configures its queue depth to eight. The IOQ is described in subsequent chapters.

Power-On Restart Address Selection

Sampling A6# low configures the processor to initiate program execution at memory address 0000FFFF0h (the PC-compatible POST entry point 16 locations from the top of the first MB).

Sampling A6# high configures the processor to initiate program execution at memory address 0FFFFFFF0h (16 locations from the top of the first 4GB).

FRC Mode Enable/Disable

Sampling A5# low configures a processor pair to act as a Functional Redundant Checker (FRC) pair. A detailed discussion of FRC mode can be found in "Processor's Agent and APIC ID Assignment" on page 42.

Sampling A5# high configures the processor to act normally after reset is removed (i.e., begin program execution).

APIC ID Selection

Each processor contains a local APIC module. This module must be assigned two addresses at startup time:

Chapter 3: Processor Power-On Configuration

- **Cluster ID**. Identifies what cluster of processors the processor (and therefore its encapsulated APIC) belong to. The processor may be assigned a cluster number of 0, 1, 2, or 3. A[12:11]# are sampled at the trailing-edge of reset to determine the cluster ID (the following binary values are sampled electrical values): 00b = 3, 01b = 2, 10b = 1, and 11b = 0.
- **APIC ID**. Identifies the number of the processor (and therefore that of its encapsulated APIC) within its cluster. At the trailing-edge of reset, the processor is assigned a processor number of 0, 1, 2, or 3 when it samples the value present on its BR[3:1]# inputs. A description of this process can be found in this chapter under the heading "Processor's Agent and APIC ID Assignment" on page 42.

Selecting Tri-State Mode

In a test environment, the processor can be configured to disconnect from (i.e., to tri-state its output drivers) all of its output pins. This permits an external board tester to drive all of the signal traces (normally driven by the processor) to known values. Using a bed-of-nails fixture that permits probing of all system board nodes, the board tester can then verify that all of these signal traces are properly connected to all of the appropriate nodes on the board.

The processor is configured to tri-state all of its output drivers when it samples a low on its FLUSH# pin at the trailing-edge of reset.

Processor Core Speed Selection

The processor's bus clock (BCLK) is supplied directly to its bus interface by an external clock connected to its BCLK input pin. The processor's internal clock is supplied by an internal phase-locked loop (PLL) that multiplies the BCLK by a value determined at startup time to yield the internal processor clock (PCLK).

The processor determines the PLL multiplication factor by sampling the values supplied on its A20M#, IGNNE#, LINT1, and LINT0 pins during reset. Specifically, it starts sampling these pins when reset is first asserted and continues to sample them throughout the reset assertion period. It latches the value on the trailing-edge of reset and uses the latched value as the PLL multiplication factor for the entire power up session. Table 3-1 on page 42 defines the available selections (note that all multipliers are not supported by all processor variants).

The setup time for these four pins must be at least 1ms prior to reset deassertion and the values presented must remain stable throughout this period and for at least two additional BCLKs after reset is removed (in other words, the hold time for them is 2 BCLKs).

Table 3-1: Core Speed Selection (values shown are electrical)

Multiplier	LINT1	LINT0	IGNNE#	A20M#
2	0	0	0	0
3	0	0	1	0
4	0	0	0	1
5/2	0	1	0	0
7/2	0	1	1	0
Reserved	0011b, 0101b, 0111b - 1110b			
2	1	1	1	1

Processor's Agent and APIC ID Assignment

Each of the processors in the cluster is assigned an agent ID at power up time. This value is also loaded into the processor's APIC ID register. When a processor needs the bus to initiate a transaction, it must first request bus ownership. The processor's agent ID is used during the bus arbitration process (a detailed description of processor bus arbitration may be found in the chapter entitled "Obtaining Bus Ownership" on page 221). The processor's APIC ID is used as an address by the IO APIC module and the local APICs in other processors to transmit messages to a specific processor over the APIC bus.

Refer to Figure 3-3 on page 44 and Table 3-2 on page 43. A processor determines its agent and APIC IDs at power up time by sampling the state of its BR[3:1]# pins on the trailing-edge of reset. The system board designer ensures that each of the processors within the cluster is assigned a unique ID by asserting the BREQ0# signal line. BREQ0# must be asserted for at least four BCLKs prior to the trailing edge of reset and must be held asserted for an additional two BCLKs.

Each processor also samples its A5# pin on reset's trailing-edge to determine whether it is to operate as a master (i.e., normal operation) or a checker (in FRC mode). For a detailed description of FRC mode, refer to "FRC Mode" on page 44. If the processor that would normally be designated as agent 1 samples a low on A5#, it is assigned an agent ID of 0 and will act as the checker for agent

0. Likewise, if the processor that would normally be designated as agent 3 samples a low on A5#, it is assigned an agent ID of 2 and will act the checker for agent 2.

Table 3-2: Processor Agent ID Assignment (values shown are electrical)

BR1#	BR2#	BR3#	A5#	Agent ID
FRC mode disabled (A5# = 1)				
1	1	1	1	Agent ID = 0 and processor operates as a master.
1	1	0	1	Agent ID = 1 and processor operates as a master.
1	0	1	1	Agent ID = 2 and processor operates as a master.
0	1	1	1	Agent ID = 3 and processor operates as a master.
FRC mode enabled (A5# = 0)				
1	1	1	0	Agent ID = 0 and processor operates as a master.
1	1	0	0	Agent ID = 0 and processor operates as a checker for agent 0 (see previous row).
1	0	1	0	Agent ID = 2 and processor operates as a master.
0	1	1	0	Agent ID = 2 and processor operates as a checker for agent 2 (see previous row).

Figure 3-3: Processor Agent ID Assignment

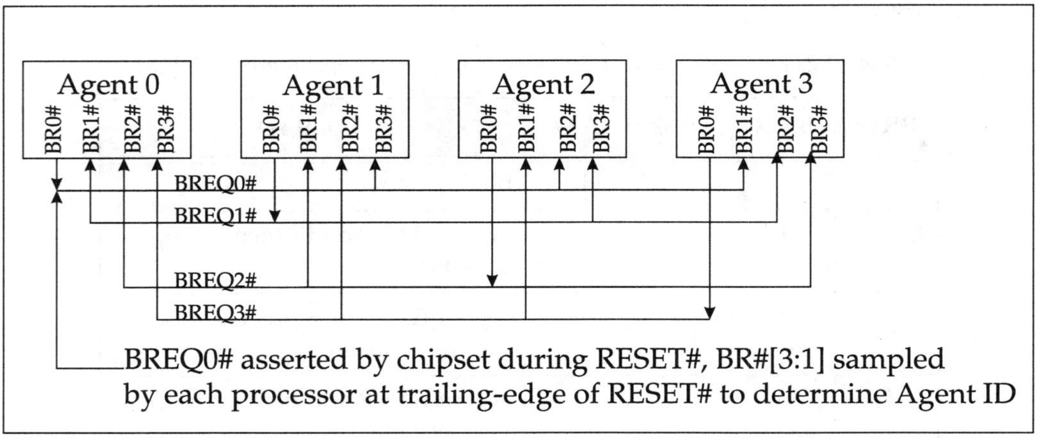

BREQ0# asserted by chipset during RESET#, BR#[3:1] sampled
by each processor at trailing-edge of RESET# to determine Agent ID

FRC Mode

When a pair of processors (processors 0 and 1, or 2 and 3) are setup as a master/checker pair, the checker is assigned the same agent ID as the master it is paired with. From that point forward, the checker takes the following actions:

- It never drives the bus.
- Whenever it sees its partner initiate a memory code read transaction, it accepts the code read from memory at the same time that its partner does.
- It decodes the instructions that are fetched and executes them in synchronism with its partner (they are sync'd to the same clock).
- It watches the bus to see that its partner, executing the same code stream, does everything that it would do, clock-by-clock.
- If, in any BCLK, it sees its partner do anything that it wouldn't do, it asserts its FRCERR output to inform the system board logic that a miscompare has occurred.

To exit FRC mode, reset must be reasserted, the value of A5# changed, and reset is then removed.

Chapter 3: Processor Power-On Configuration

Program-Accessible Startup Features

One of the processor's MSRs (model-specific registers) provides the programmer with two capabilities:

- the ability to determine the state of the features that were automatically enabled or disabled on the trailing-edge of reset (when the processor sampled a subset of its pins).
- the ability to programmatically select other processor features.

The EBL_CR_POWERON MSR (external bus logic poweron configuration register) contains a series of read-only bits used to indicate the automatic selections, as well as a series of read/write bits used to programmatically enable/disable other features. This register is accessed using the RDMSR and WRMSR instructions (described in the chapter entitled "Instruction Set Enhancements" on page 409). The EBL_CR_POWERON register is pictured in Figure 3-4 on page 49 and described in Table 3-3 on page 45.

Table 3-3: Bit Assignment of EBL_CR_POWERON MSR

Bit	Read/ Write	Description
0	X	Reserved.
1	R/W	0 = disable **data bus ECC error checking**. 1 = enable data bus ECC error checking.
2	R/W	0 = disable **response bus parity checking**. 1 = enable response bus parity checking. For additional information, refer to "Response Phase Signal Group" on page 298.
3	R/W	0 = disable processor's **ability to assert AERR#** upon detection of bad request information received from another initiator. 1 = enable. For additional information, refer to the section on the Error Phase in the chapter entitled "Error Phase" on page 273.

Table 3-3: Bit Assignment of EBL_CR_POWERON MSR (Continued)

Bit	Read/ Write	Description
4	R/W	0 = disable processor's **ability to assert BERR#** when it is acting as the initiator and observes an unrecoverable error. 1 = enable processor's ability to assert BERR# when it is acting as the initiator and observes an unrecoverable error. For a detailed description of BERR#, refer to the chapter entitled "Other Signals" on page 365.
5	x	Reserved
6	R/W	0 = disable processor's **ability to assert BERR#** (along with IERR#) when an internal error occurs. 1 = enable processor's ability to assert BERR# (along with IERR#) when an internal error occurs. For a detailed description of BERR#, refer to the chapter entitled "Other Signals" on page 365.
7	R/W	0 = disable processor's **ability to assert BINIT#** if the processor has lost track of the transactions currently outstanding on the bus. 1 = enable processor's ability to assert BINIT# if the processor has lost track of the transactions currently outstanding on the bus. For a detailed description of BINIT#, refer to the chapter entitled "Other Signals" on page 365.
8	R	1 = **Output tri-state mode** enabled. 0 = Output tri-state mode disabled. This option was automatically set on the trailing-edge of reset when FLUSH# was sampled. For more information, refer to "Selecting Tri-State Mode" on page 41.
9	R	1 = **BIST** enabled. 0 = BIST disabled. This option was automatically set on the trailing-edge of reset when INIT# was sampled. For more information, refer to "Run BIST Option" on page 39.

Table 3-3: Bit Assignment of EBL_CR_POWERON MSR (Continued)

Bit	Read/ Write	Description
10	R	1 = **AERR# observation** enabled. 0 = AERR# observation disabled. This option was automatically set on the trailing-edge of reset when A8# was sampled. For more information refer to "Error Observation Options" on page 39, and to the section on the Error Phase in the chapter entitled "Error Phase" on page 273.
11	X	Reserved
12	R	1 = **BINIT# observation** enabled. 0 = BINIT# observation disabled. This option was automatically set on the trailing-edge of reset when A10# was sampled. For more information on BINIT#, refer to the chapter entitled "Other Signals" on page 365 and to "Error Observation Options" on page 39.
13	R	1 = **IOQ depth** of 1. 0 = IOQ depth of 8. This option was automatically set on the trailing-edge of reset when A7# was sampled. For more information on the IOQ depth selection, refer to "In-Order Queue Depth Selection" on page 40.
14	R	1 = **Poweron restart address** is 0000FFFF0h (1MB - 16d). 0 = Poweron restart address is 0FFFFFFF0h (4GB - 16d). This option was automatically set on the trailing-edge of reset when A6# was sampled. For more information, refer to "Power-On Restart Address Selection" on page 40.
15	R	1 = **FRC mode** enabled. 0 = FRC mode disabled. This option was automatically set on the trailing-edge of reset when A5# was sampled. For more information, refer to "FRC Mode Enable/Disable" on page 40.
17:16	R	**APIC cluster ID**. This ID was automatically set on the trailing-edge of reset when A[12:11]# were sampled. For more information, refer to "APIC ID Selection" on page 40.
19:18	X	Reserved

Table 3-3: Bit Assignment of EBL_CR_POWERON MSR (Continued)

Bit	Read/Write	Description
21:20	R	**Symmetric arbitration ID**. Also referred to as the processor's agent or CPU ID. This option was automatically set on the trailing-edge of reset when BR[3:1]# were sampled. For more information, refer to "Processor's Agent and APIC ID Assignment" on page 42, and to the chapter entitled "Obtaining Bus Ownership" on page 221.
24:22	R	**Clock frequency ratio**. This option was automatically set on the trailing-edge of reset when LINT[1:0]#, IGNNE# and A20M# were sampled. For more information, refer to "Processor Core Speed Selection" on page 41.
25	X	Reserved
26	R/W	**Low power enable**. The Intel Pentium Pro documentation provides no explanation of this bit. However, it is obvious that it is used to enable (when set to one) or disable (when cleared to zero) the processor's power conservation features. The Pentium Pro processor only implements one power conservation feature, the STPCLK# pin. For more information, refer to "STPCLK#" on page 375.
63:27	X	Reserved

Figure 3-4: EBL_CR_POWERON MSR

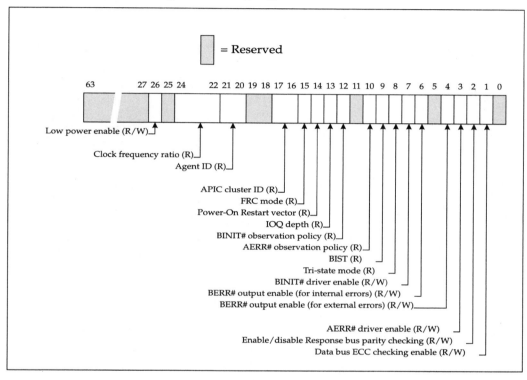

4 *Processor Startup*

The Previous Chapter

The previous chapter described the manner in which the processor automatically configures some of its operational characteristics at power up time upon the removal of reset. In addition, it described some of the basic processor features that may be enabled or disabled by the programmer.

This Chapter

This chapter describes the processor state at startup time. It also describes the process that the processors engage in to select the processor that will fetch and execute the power-on self-test (POST), as well as how, after it has been loaded, an MP OS can detect the additional processors and assign tasks for them to execute.

The Next Chapter

The next chapter provides a detailed description of the processor logic responsible for instruction fetch, decode, and execution.

Selection of Processor's Agent and APIC IDs

At the trailing-edge of reset, the processor samples its BR[3:1]# inputs to determine its agent ID. The agent ID also serves as its APIC ID and as its APIC's startup arbitration ID (when arbitrating for ownership of the APIC bus). Refer to "Processor's Agent and APIC ID Assignment" on page 42 and to the chapter entitled "Obtaining Bus Ownership" on page 221 for additional information regarding processor agent ID assignment.

Processor's State After Reset

The assertion of the processor's RESET# input has the effects indicated in table Table 4-1 on page 52.

Table 4-1: Effects of Reset on CPU

Effect	Result
L2 cache	All entries in the L2 Cache are invalidated.
L1 code cache	All entries in the L1 code cache are invalidated.
L1 data cache	All entries in the L1 data cache are invalidated.
Branch Target Buffer (BTB)	All entries in the BTB are invalidated, causing all initial branches to predicted by the static, rather than dynamic, branch prediction units. For additional information, refer to the sections on branch prediction in the chapter entitled "The Fetch, Decode, Execute Engine" on page 75.
Prefetch queue	The prefetch queue is cleared, so there are no instructions available to the instruction pipeline.
Instruction decode queue	The instruction decode queue is invalidated, so there are no micro-ops available to be placed in the instruction pool for execution.
Instruction pool	The instruction pool is cleared, so there are no micro-ops available for execution.
CR0	Contains 60000010h. The processor is in real mode with paging disabled.
CR4	**Software Features register.** Contains 00000000h. All post-486 (Pentium and Pentium Pro) software features are disabled.

Table 4-1: Effects of Reset on CPU (Continued)

Effect	Result
DTLB and ITLB	**Data and Instruction Translation Lookaside Buffers**. All DTLB and ITLB entries are invalidated. This has no initial effect because paging is disabled.
APIC	**Advanced Programmable Interrupt Controller**. Has been assigned an ID (see the section "Selection of Processor's Agent and APIC IDs" on page 51) and begins (after the BIST, if the BIST has been enabled) to negotiate with the APICs in the other processors to select the bootstrap processor (see "Selection of Bootstrap Processor (BSP)" on page 56). Recognition of all external interrupts is disabled. The local APIC is in Virtual-Wire Mode (aka 8259A mode).
EFLAGS register	Contains 00000002h. Recognition of external interrupts is disabled.
EIP	**Extended Instruction Pointer register**. Contains 0000FFF0h.
CS	**Code Segment register**. The visible part of the CS register contains F000h. The invisible part contains the following: base = FFFF0000h; limit = FFFFh; AR = present, R/W, accessed.
CR2	**Page Fault Address register**. Contains 00000000h. No effect.
CR3	**Page Directory Base Address register**. Contains 00000000h. No effect (because paging is disabled).
SS, DS, ES, FS, GS	**Stack and data segment registers**. Contain 00000000h.

Table 4-1: Effects of Reset on CPU (Continued)

Effect	Result
EDX	Contains 000006xxh, where xx can be any 2 hex digits (see "EDX Contains Processor Identification Info" on page 55 for additional information).
EAX	Contains 00000000h if BIST not performed, and BIST result if BIST performed. See "Run BIST Option" on page 39.
EBX, ECX, ESI, EDI, EBP, ESP	Contain 00000000h.
LDTR	**Local Descriptor Table Register**. Visible part contains 0000h. Invisible part contains: base = 00000000h; limit = FFFFh. No effect (because processor is in real mode).
GDTR and IDTR	**Global and Interrupt Descriptor Table Registers**. Base = 00000000h. Limit = FFFFh. Access rights = present and R/W. GDTR contents has no effect because processor is in real mode. IDTR contents places real mode interrupt table at memory location 000000000h.
DR0 through DR3	**Debug Breakpoint Address Registers**. Contain 00000000h.
DR6	**Debug Status Register**. Contains FFFF0FF0h.
DR7	**Debug Control register**. Contains 000000400h. All four breakpoints are disabled.
Time Stamp Counter (TSC)	Contains 0000000000000000h. After removal of reset, incremented once for each processor clock.
Performance Counter registers and Event Select registers	Cleared to zero. Counting of Performance Events is disabled.
Other Model-Specific Registers (MSRs)	Undefined.

Table 4-1: Effects of Reset on CPU (Continued)

Effect	Result
Memory Type and Range Registers (MTRRs)	Disabled, causing all 4GB of memory space to be treated as UC (UnCacheable) memory.
Machine Check Architecture (MCA)	In undefined state.

EDX Contains Processor Identification Info

After reset, the EDX register contains 000006xxh, where xx can be any 2 hex digits. Figure 4-1 on page 55 illustrates the EDX contents.

Figure 4-1: EDX Contents after Reset

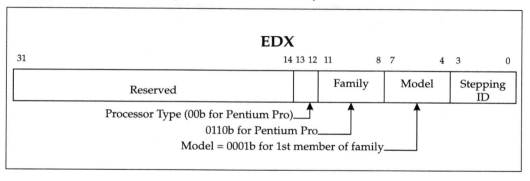

State of Caches and Processor's Ability to Cache

Reset's setting of the CR0[CD] and CR0[NW] bits disables the processor's ability to cache. Although this bit setting permits it to perform lookups in the caches, all lookups result in misses (because the caches were cleared by reset).

The instruction streaming buffer (i.e., the prefetch queue), instruction decode queue, and instruction pool are empty, resulting in total starvation for the processor's fetch, decode and execute engines. The processor must therefore immediately begin fetching instructions from external memory.

Selection of Bootstrap Processor (BSP)

Introduction

Refer to Figure 4-2 on page 57. Upon the deassertion of reset (and the completion of a processor's BIST, if started), the processors within the cluster must negotiate amongst themselves to select the processor that will wake up and start fetching, decoding and executing the POST code from ROM memory. This processor is referred to as the BootStrap Processor, or BSP. After the BSP is identified, the other processors, referred to as the applications processors, or APs, remain dormant (in the halt state) until they receive a startup message (via the APIC bus) from the BSP. The following section provides a detailed description of the BSP selection process. For a detailed discussion of the APIC, refer to the APIC section in MindShare's *Pentium Processor System Architecture* book (published by Addison-Wesley).

Figure 4-2: System Block Diagram

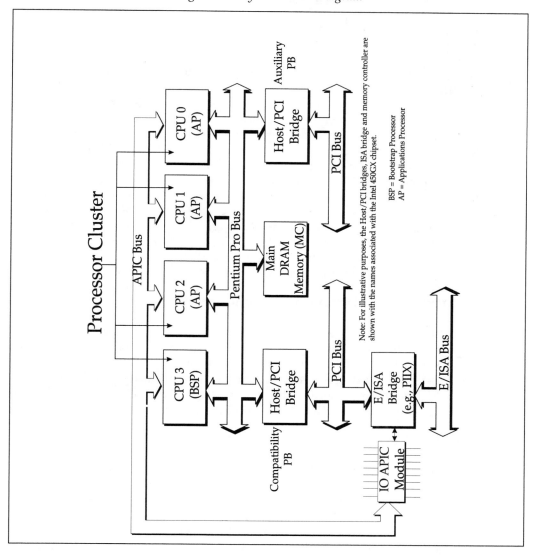

BSP Selection Process

APIC Arbitration Background

During output of any message on the APIC bus, as a preamble the local APIC's 4-bit ID is inverted and driven onto APIC data bus line one (PICD1) serially, msb first. It's important to note that PICD[1:0] have pullups on them. Multiple processors may start driving messages simultaneously. In this case, as each inverted bit of the arbitration ID is driven onto the bus, msb first, an electrical zero beats an electrical one (think of it as a card game). If a local APIC's current bit is a one, it doesn't actually drive PICD1 to a one. Rather, it depends on the pullup to keep a one on the PICD1 signal line. When a processor with an electrical one detects an electrical zero on the line, it realizes that it has lost the arbitration and ceases to attempt transmission of its message. It waits until the current message transmission completes and then reattempts transmission of its message. The winner of the arbitration sends its message and then changes its APIC arbitration ID to the lowest value (i.e., 1111b). The losers each upgrade their priority by inverting their current arbitration ID, adding one to it and then reinverting it.

Startup APIC Arbitration ID Assignment

On the trailing-edge of reset, each processor's local APIC arbitration ID is set to the invert of its processor's agent ID. At start-up time, the net result is that the processor with an APIC arbitration priority ID of Fh has the lowest APIC arbitration priority and the processor with highest numerical agent ID has the highest APIC arbitration priority. The final result is that the processor with the numerically highest agent ID will be the BSP (as described in the next section).

BSP Selection Process

1. After each processor's BIST completes (if it was started), the local APICs in all processors simultaneously attempt to send their BIPI (Bootstrap Inter-Processor Interrupt) message to all processors (including themselves) over the APIC bus.
2. The processor with the highest APIC arbitration priority (i.e., inverted agent ID) wins the arbitration and sends the first BIPI message to all of the processors (including itself). The processors that lose the arbitration must wait until the winner finishes issuing its BIPI message before they reattempt issuance of their BIPI messages.
3. The arbitration winner's BIPI message is received by all of the processors and the APIC ID field of the message (lower 4 bits of the 8-bit vector field) is

compared to each of the receiving processors' APIC ID. The processor with a match sets the BSP bit in its APICBASE register. This identifies it as the bootstrap processor. All of the losers clear this bit in their respective APICBASE registers, thereby identifying themselves as the applications processors, or APs (note that some Intel documentation refers to them as the auxiliary processors).

4. The winner (i.e., the BSP) changes its rotating APIC priority level to Fh (the lowest APIC priority) and attempts to issue the FIPI (Final Inter-Processor Interrupt) message to all processors (including itself). The losers of the first competition each upgrade their priority by inverting their current arbitration ID, adding one to it and then reinverting it.

5. All of the processors that lost the first competition (the APs) attempt once again to transmit their BIPI messages and the winner of the first arbitration (the BSP) attempts to transmit its FIPI message.

6. Because the BSP set its arbitration priority level to the lowest, it is guaranteed to lose the competition. One of the other processors will win (the one with the highest arbitration ID).

7. As each of the APs is successful in acquiring APIC bus ownership and transmitting its BIPI message, it then sets its arbitration ID to Fh, to make itself the least important.

8. As each of the application processors (APs) in succession wins the bus and finishes broadcasting its BIPI, it then remains in the halt state until it subsequently receives a SIPI (Startup Inter-Processor Interrupt message) from the BSP at a later time (see "AP Detection by the POST/BIOS" on page 70).

9. After all of the APs have broadcast their BIPIs, the BSP will be successful in re-acquiring APIC bus ownership and will then broadcast its FIPI to announce to the system that it will now begin to fetch code using the Pentium Pro bus. Upon receiving its own FIPI, the BSP then begins fetching the POST code.

Once the BSP selection process has completed, the BSP initiates fetch, decode and execution of the ROM POST code starting at the power-on restart address selected at the trailing edge of reset (see "Power-On Restart Address Selection" on page 40).

Example of APIC Bus Traffic Captured during BSP Selection

Figure 4-3 on page 61 illustrates the APIC bus traffic that is generated by the processors immediately after reset is deasserted. The example system is a four processor system. The information was captured using the HP APIC bus preprocessor. The messaging sequence is as follows:

1. Starting in state 136, processor three issues its BIPI (bootstrap inter-processor interrupt) message to all processors including itself (destination field = Fh indicates this). 43h in the vector field indicates that the BIPI was issued by processor three (the upper-digit is 4, indicating that this is a Pentium Pro BIPI message).

2. When all of the processors receive this message, processor three has a compare on its processor number (its agent ID, assigned on the trailing-edge of reset, is three and the 3 of 43h indicates that the message just received was sent by it), indicating that it won the arbitration for the APIC bus and broadcast its BIPI message successfully. Processor three therefore sets the BSP bit in one of its internal APIC registers, marking it as the BSP. Conversely, when processors zero, one and two receive the message and compare the vector to their agent IDs, they realize that a processor other than themselves successfully broadcast the first BIPI message and is therefore the BSP processor. The BSP bit in their respective APIC registers remains cleared to zero (it's state after reset).

3. Starting in state 138, processor two sends its BIPI message.

4. Starting in state 140, processor one sends its BIPI message.

5. Starting in state 142, processor zero sends its BIPI message.

6. Starting in state 144, the BSP (processor three) broadcasts its FIPI (final IPI) message), after which it begins fetching code (see "Initial BSP Memory Accesses" on page 62). The vector is 13h, with the upper digit, "1" indicating it is the FIPI message and the lower digit, "3" indicating that it was issued by processor three.

Figure 4-3: APIC Bus Traffic during BSP Selection

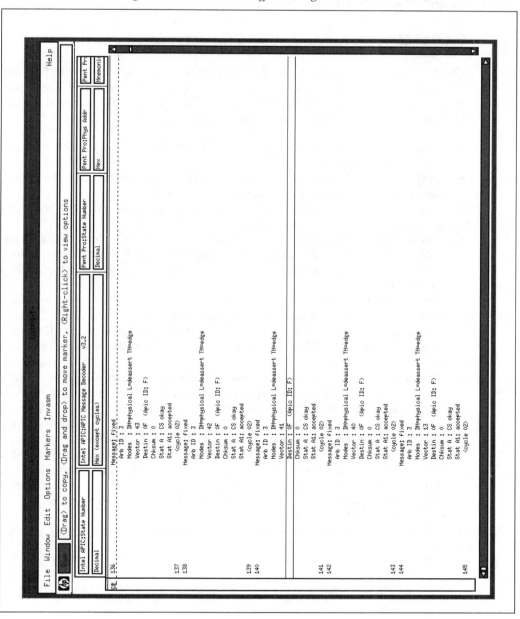

Initial BSP Memory Accesses

General

The following description refers to bus transactions using the State Number field illustrated in Figure 4-4 on page 68 and Figure 4-5 on page 69. This information was captured using the HP Pentium Pro/Pentium II bus preprocessor. Here are some general notes regarding these screen shots:

- The **State Number** represents the BCLK (relative to the trigger point) in which a transaction was initiated.
- In the **Inverse Assembly** column, the entries that are not indented represent instructions that were decoded and executed.
- In the **Inverse Assembly** column, the entries that are indented represent information about the transaction.
- **Branch trace messaging** (for more information, refer to "Branch Trace Message Transaction Used for Program Debug" on page 360) has been enabled. This causes the processor to broadcast a message whenever a branch is taken when executed.
- The indented entries that are associated with a branch trace message transaction display the *Causing* and *Target* addresses. The **Causing address** points to the location that immediately follows the branch being executed, while the **Target address** identifies the address being branched to.
- The indented entries marked *mem rd code* are shown in blocks of four each and represent the four quadwords read, critical quadword first, in toggle mode order (for more information, refer to "Toggle Mode Transfer Order" on page 189). The **Phys Addr** column displays the address of the quadwords being read from memory. The two columns of hex code immediately to the right of the quadword addresses represent the eight bytes of data read from each of the quadwords. The data is presented in little-endian order, showing the byte read from the lowest location within the quadword on the right and the byte read from the highest location on the left.
- The BSP, Symmetric agent 3 (**sym3**), performed each of these transactions.

When Caching Disabled, Prefetcher Always Does 32-byte Code Reads

It should be noted that when reset is removed, the cache enable bits in CR0 (CR0[CD] and CR0[NW]) contain 11b, disabling all caching. The initial code fetched by the processor is therefore not cached in the L1 code and the L2 caches. The processor performs a full line read to fetch each individual instruction from memory. *This is true even for instructions that reside within the same line and within the same quadword.*

State 2: 1st Line Read (and jump at FFFFFFF0h executed)

In state 2, processor 3 (the BSP) initiates a 32-byte memory code read starting at quadword address FFFFFFF0h, the power-on restart address. Although the attribute field (for more information, refer to "Contents of Request Packet B" on page 269) is not illustrated in Figure 4-4 on page 68, the processor indicates that this is an uncacheable access by outputting the UC code (for more information, refer to "Memory Types" on page 138) on the ATTRIB[7:0]# signals during packet B of the request phase.

Whenever a jump is executed, the processor starts the four-quadword read at the quadword within which the instruction starts (i.e., the quadword consisting of locations FFFFFFF0h through FFFFFFF7h). The first access is, in effect, a jump (caused by the deassertion of reset) to FFFFFFF0h. As illustrated in state 2 (and the three lines that follow it), the processor fetches the critical quadword first, followed by the other three quadwords that comprise the line in toggle mode order: i.e., the quadword that starts at FFFFFFF0h, followed by quadwords starting at FFFFFFF8h, FFFFFFE0h, and FFFFFFE8h. The actual hex code fetched is illustrated in the left two columns under the Inverse Assembly heading and is repeated here:

```
FFFFFFF000E05BEA
FFFFFFFFFFFFFFFF
FFFFFFFFFFFFFFFF
4505FFFFFFFFFFFF
```

The line immediately following these four lines displays the far jump instruction that starts at FFFFFFF0h. The machine language instruction is EA5BE000F0, representing a JMP F000:E05B. The code beyond that point (all Fs) is not executed because this is an unconditional far jump.

State 10: Branch Trace Message for Jump at FFFFFFF0h

The far jump (fetched from FFFFFFF0h) is predicted taken by the branch prediction logic (for more information, refer to "Description of Branch Prediction" on page 122) , so the processor issues a request for the line containing the target address (the line consisting of locations 000FE40h through 000FE5Fh). Prior to issuing this request, however, the processor issues a branch trace message transaction (starting in state 10) to inform the HP preprocessor that the branch is being taken. The *causing* address driven onto the bus consists of the EIP value (which currently points to the location immediately following the jump instruction executed). The *target* address is 000FE05Bh, the physical address of the instruction being branched to.

The line immediately following the branch trace message transaction is the instruction being branched to, JMP FC00:2060.

State 16: Branch Target Line Read (and 2nd jump executed)

Starting in state 16, the line that contains the target instruction is fetched. This line consists of locations 000FE040h through 000FE05Fh. Notice that execution of the first far jump caused the processor to cease asserting address lines above A[19]#, thereby permitting the processor to fetch code only below the 1MB address boundary.

Quadword 000FE058h is fetched first, followed by the remaining three quadwords in toggle mode order. Quadword 000FE058h contains the start byte of the target instruction that starts in location 000FE05Bh. When the first quadword has been fetched, the first instruction, another unconditional jump (JMP FC00:2060), is decoded. The processor issues a branch trace message transaction indicating to the HP preprocessor that that this branch is being taken.

State 26: Branch Trace Message for 2nd Jump

In state 26, the branch trace message transaction is initiated, indicating to the preprocessor that the branch instruction whose last byte resides at location 000FE060h minus one is being executed and that it is branching to location 000FE060h.

State 32: CLI Fetched and Executed

When the branch trace message transaction has been issued, the processor initiates a read for the line containing the branch target address (000FE060h). This line consists of locations 000FE060h through 000FE07Fh. The quadword that contains the start location of the target instruction is 000FE060h through 000FE067h. It is fetched first, followed by the remaining three quadwords in toggle mode order: 000FE068h, 000FE070h, and 000FE078h. When the instruction that starts at location 000FE060h is decoded, it is a CLI and is one byte in length. Since this is a non-jump instruction, the next sequential instruction is executed next.

State 42: CLD Fetched and Executed

The next instruction also starts in quadword 000FE060h (at location 000FE061h), so the processor again fetches the same line in toggle mode order starting at the same quadword. When decoded, it is a one byte CLD instruction. It is a non-jump instruction, so the next sequential instruction is fetched.

State 50: JMP Rel/Fwd Fetched and Executed

The next instruction also starts in quadword 000FE060h (at location 000FE062h), so the processor again fetches the same line in toggle mode order starting at the same quadword. When decoded, it is an unconditional three byte forward relative JMP to EIP + 0B7Fh (i.e., target address is 000FEBE4h).

State 58: Branch Trace Message for JMP Rel/Fwd

When the jump from location 000FE062h is executed, the processor generates (in state 26) the branch trace message transaction indicating to the preprocessor that the branch instruction whose last byte resides at location 000FE065h minus one is being executed and that it is branching to location 000FEBE4h.

State 64: SHL EDX,10h Fetched and Executed

Starting in state 64, the processor performs a line read to fetch the line containing the instruction (SHL EDX,10h) that resides at the branch target address, 000FEBE4h. The line consists of locations 000FEBE0h through 000FEBFFh and the quadword containing the branch target address is 000FEBE0h. The line is fetched in toggle mode order. When executed, the SHL instruction does not alter code flow (i.e., it isn't a branch), so the next instruction is then fetched.

State 74: MOV DX,048Bh Fetched and Executed

This transaction starts at the bottom of Figure 4-4 on page 68 and is continued in Figure 4-5 on page 69. The previous instruction did not alter code flow, so the next instruction, MOV DX,048Bh, is fetched. It starts at location 000FEBE8h, so quadword 000FEBE8h is fetched first, followed by the remaining three quadwords in toggle mode order.

State 82: AND Fetched and Executed

The previous instruction did not alter code flow, so the next instruction, AND EAX, FFFCFFFBh, is fetched. It starts at location 000FEBEBh, so quadword 000FEBE8h is fetched first, followed by the remaining three quadwords in toggle mode order.

State 90: OUT Fetched and Executed

The previous instruction did not alter code flow, so the next instruction, OUT DX,AL, is fetched. It starts at location 000FEBF1h, so quadword 000FEBF0h is fetched first, followed by the remaining three quadwords in toggle mode order.

State 98: IO Write to 48Bh

Starting in state 98, the processor performs the IO write transaction caused by the execution of the OUT instruction.

State 106: OR Fetched and Executed

After issuing the IO write transaction, the processor performs a line read to fetch the line that contains the next instruction, OR EAX,EAX. This instruction starts at location 000FEBF2, so the processor fetches quadword 000FEBF0h followed by the remaining three quadwords in toggle mode order.

State 114: MOV BX,CS Fetched and Executed

The previous instruction did not alter code flow, so the next instruction, MOV BX,CS, is fetched. It starts at location 000FEBF5h, so quadword 000FEBF0h is fetched first, followed by the remaining three quadwords in toggle mode order.

State 122: MOV SS,BX Fetched and Executed

The previous instruction did not alter code flow, so the next instruction, MOV SS,BX, is fetched. It starts at location 000FEBF7h, so quadword 000FEBF0h is fetched first, followed by the remaining three quadwords in toggle mode order.

State 130: JE Fetched and Executed

The previous instruction did not alter code flow, so the next instruction, JE EIP + 9, is fetched. It starts at location 000FEBF9h, so quadword 000FEBF8h is fetched first, followed by the remaining three quadwords in toggle mode order. The EFLAGS[ZF] bit is set, so the EQUAL condition is met and the branch is taken (to location 000FEC04h).

State 138: Branch Trace Message for JE

The processor executes the JE instruction, the condition is met (EFLAGS[ZF] = 1) and the branch is therefore taken. The processor generates the branch trace message transaction indicating to the preprocessor that the branch instruction that ends at location 000FEBFB minus one has been taken to the target location 000FEC04h. This ends the analysis of the example startup code fetches.

Figure 4-4: Code Accesses Immediately after BSP Issues FIPI Message

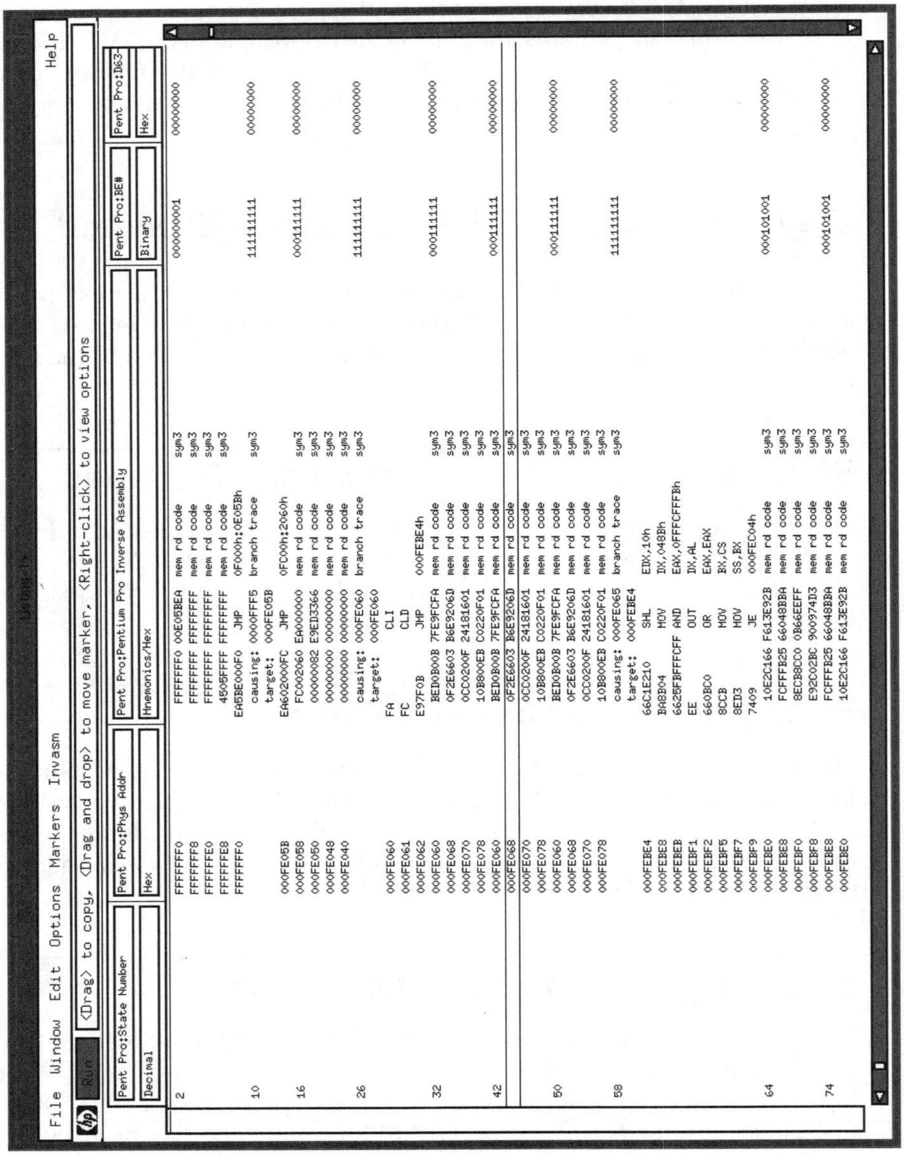

Figure 4-5: Initial Code Accesses, continued

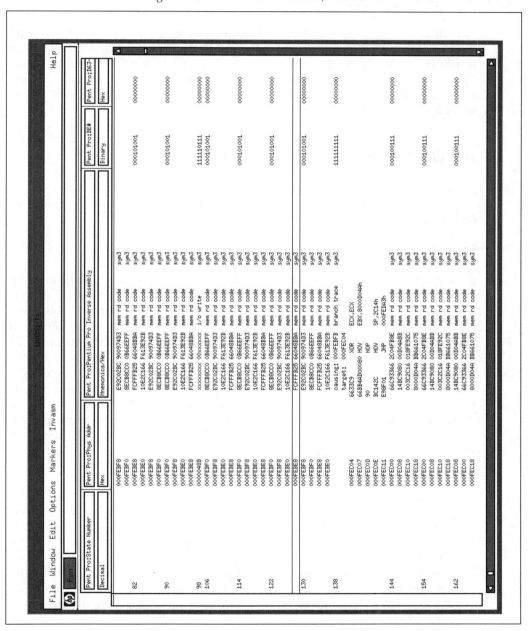

How APs are Started

The Intel Multiprocessing specification (available for download at the Intel developers' web site) dictates that the startup code executed by the BSP is responsible for detecting the presence of processors other than the BSP. When the available AP processors have been detected, the startup code stores this information as a table in non-volatile memory (for the MP OS to consult when it is loaded and takes over).

AP Detection by the POST/BIOS

According to the Multiprocessor Specification, the BIOS/POST code is responsible for detecting the presence of and initializing the APs. Intel recommends that this be accomplished in the following manner.

Introduction

A startup message will be broadcast to all of the APs (assuming any are present). The vector field in this message selects a slot in the interrupt table that points to the FindAndInitAllCPUs routine. Upon receipt of this message, all of the APs will simultaneously request ownership of the Pentium Pro bus to begin fetching and executing the FindAndInitAllCPUs routine. To prevent all of the processors from simultaneously executing the body of this routine, a semaphore will be tested upon entry into the routine to determine if the body may be executed. The first AP processor that is successful in testing and setting the semaphore can execute the body of the routine, while the other APs will go into a program spin loop waiting for the winning processor to clear the semaphore. In this way, each of the processors in succession will get to execute the body of the routine.

The POST/BIOS Code

1. The POST/BIOS code executing on the BSP initializes a pre-defined RAM location to 1h (to represent the fact that one processor, the BSP, is known to be present and functioning). This location is referred to as the CPU counter.
2. The POST/BIOS code executing on the BSP clears a memory semaphore location to 00h to permit one of the APs to execute the body of the FindAndInitAllCPUs routine (See "The FindAndInitAllCPUs Routine" on page 72.).

3. The POST/BIOS code executing on the BSP broadcast a startup message to all of the APs (assuming any are present). The vector field in this message selects a slot in the interrupt table that points to the FindAndInitAllCPUs routine.

4. Upon receipt of this message, all of the APs simultaneously request ownership of the Pentium Pro bus to begin fetching and executing the FindAndInitAllCPUs routine.

5. The POST/BIOS code executing on the BSP then waits for all of the APs that may be present to complete execution of the FindAndInitAllCPUs routine. The wait loop can be implemented using a long, software-enforced delay, the chipset's Timer 0 (refer to the MindShare book entitled *ISA System Architecture*, published by Addison-Wesley), or using the timer built into the BSP's local APIC. Alternately, the following wait procedure can be used:

    • Using a locked read, the POST/BIOS code executing on the BSP examines the CPU counter RAM location every two seconds and compares the counter value read with that read two seconds ago. If the value has not changed (i.e., been incremented), all AP processors have completed their execution of the FindAndInitAllCPUs routine. This assumes that an AP takes less than two seconds to complete execution of the routine.

    • The counter value at the end of the wait (in other words, when two seconds have passed without a change of the counter value) indicates the total number of processors in the system (including the BSP).

6. Once the all of the APs have completed execution of the FindAndInitAllCPUs routine, they have all made entries in the MP (i.e., multiprocessor) table in CMOS memory. In addition, all of their MTRR register sets have been initialized identically, so that they will all treat the various regions of memory in the same manner (regarding cacheability, read/writability, etc.).

7. The POST/BIOS code executing on the BSP reads the user-selected setup parameters from CMOS to determine how many of the available processors to utilize during this OS session. The POST/BIOS code then completes building the MP table in CMOS, removing or disabling the entries associated with the processors not to be used in this session. A new checksum value is computed for the adjusted MP table and its length and number of entries fields are completed.

8. As each of the APs completed execution of the FindAndInitAllCPUs routine, they either halted or entered a program loop. The POST/BIOS instructs the BSP's local APIC to broadcast an INIT message to the APs. This causes them to enter (or remain) in the halted state and await

receipt of a startup message that will be issued by the MP OS once it has been loaded and control is passed to it.

The FindAndInitAllCPUs Routine

Upon receipt of the startup message issued by the BSP's local APIC under the control of the POST/BIOS code, each of the APs simultaneously begin to fetch and execute the FindAndInitAllCPUs routine. This routine performs the following functions:

1. The first AP that executes the semaphore test at the start of the FindAndInitAllCPUs routine will discover that the semaphore is clear (the POST/BIOS code cleared it to 00h before issuance of the startup message). It sets the semaphore to FFh, thereby indicating that it and no other AP will execute the body of the FindAndInitAllCPUs routine (see step 2 in the previous section) until it completes its execution and clears the semaphore. The following is an example of the semaphore test and set routine (note that an x86 processor automatically asserts LOCK# when performing the memory read and write transactions associated with an exchange instruction):

```
                    mov   al,FFh
      TestLock:
                    xchg  byte ptr [Semaphore],al;read and set semaphore
                    cmp   al,FFh                  ;test value read
                    jz    TestLock                ;spin if already set
      ;execute body of FindAndInitAllCPUs routine (see next step)
```

2. Increment the CPU counter RAM location.
3. Initialize the AP's MTRR registers to the same values as the BSP's MTRRs.
4. Execute the CPUID instruction to obtain AP processor's ID and feature information.
5. The AP constructs its entry in the CMOS-based MP table using its local APIC ID and the ID information returned by its execution of the CPUID instruction.
6. If necessary, load a BIOS (i.e., microcode) update into the AP processor. For more information, refer to "BIOS Update Feature" on page 431.
7. Upon completing the MP table entry and processor initialization, release the semaphore so that another AP can exit its spin loop and execute the body of the FindAndInitAllCPUs routine. The following is an example of the semaphore clear routine:

```
      ReleaseLock:
                    mov   al,00h
                    xchg  byte ptr[Semaphore],al;clear semaphore to 00h
      ;go to next step
```

8. At the end of the routine, the AP goes into a loop.

The OS is Loaded and Control is Passed to It

When the BSP has completed execution of the POST/BIOS code and has configured and enabled the devices necessary to read the OS from a mass storage device, it executes the OS boot to begin the process of reading the OS into memory and, after doing so, passes control to the OS startup code.

Once the OS startup code has been read into memory, the boot program jumps to and starts executing it. The OS startup code is responsible for reading the remainder of the OS into memory.

Uni-Processor OS

If the OS (e.g., DOS) is not capable of recognizing the existence of the APs, they remain dormant and are never used (in other words, they suck power and are a waste of money).

MP OS

If the OS is a Multi-Processing, or MP, OS, it must:

- consult the MP table built in CMOS memory to determine the presence (or abscence) of the other processors (the APs).
- place tasks in memory for them to execute
- Using a startup message, pass the start address of these programs to each of them.

5 The Fetch, Decode, Execute Engine

The Previous Chapter

The previous chapter described the processor state at startup time. It also described the process that the processors engage in to select the processor that will fetch and execute the power-on self-test (POST), as well as how, after it has been loaded, an MP OS can detect the additional processors and assign tasks for them to execute.

This Chapter

This chapter provides a detailed description of the processor logic responsible for instruction fetch, decode and execution.

The Next Chapter

In preparation for the discussion of the processor's caches, the next chapter introduces the register set that tells the processor its rules of conduct within various areas of memory. The Memory Type and Range Registers, or MTRRs, must be programmed after startup to define the various regions of memory within the 4GB memory space and how the processor core and caches must behave when performing accesses within each region. A detailed description of the MTRRs may be found in the appendix entitled "The MTRR Registers" on page 567.

Please Note

This chapter discusses the internal architecture of the Pentium Pro processor. It must be stressed that this information is based on the information released by Intel to the general development community. Since Intel is not in the business of giving away their intellectual property, it stands to reason that they haven't revealed every detail of the processor's operation. The author has made every effort to faithfully describe the processor's operation within the bounds of the information released by Intel.

Introduction

Throughout this chapter, refer to the overall processor block diagram pictured in Figure 5-1 on page 77. Figure 26-7 on page 520 illustrates the block diagram with the MMX excution units added in.

At the heart of the processor are the execution units that execute instructions. The processor includes a fetch engine that attempts to properly predict the path of program execution and generates an on-going series of memory read operations to fetch the desired instructions.

If the processor didn't include an instruction cache, each of these memory read requests would have to be issued (on the processor's external bus) to external memory. The processor would suffer severe performance degradation for two reasons:

- The clock rate at which the processor generates external bus transactions is a fraction of the internal clock rate. This results in a relatively low-speed memory read to fetch the instructions.
- Secondly, the access time of main DRAM memory is typically even slower than the bus speed. In other words, the memory injects wait states into the bus transaction until it has the requested information available.

The high-speed (e.g., 150 or 200MHz) processor execution engine would then be bound by the speed of external memory accesses. It should be obvious that it is extremely advantageous to include a very high-speed cache memory on board the processor to keep copies of recently used (and, hopefully, frequently used) information (both code and data). Memory read requests generated by the processor core are first submitted to the cache for a lookup before being propagated to the external bus (in the event of a cache miss).

The Pentium Pro processor includes both a code and a data cache (the level one, or L1, caches). In addition, it includes an L2 cache tightly coupled to the processor core via a private bus. The processor's caches are disabled at powerup time, however. In order to realize the processor's full potential, the caches must be enabled. The following section describes the enabling of the caches.

Figure 5-1: Overall Processor Block Diagram

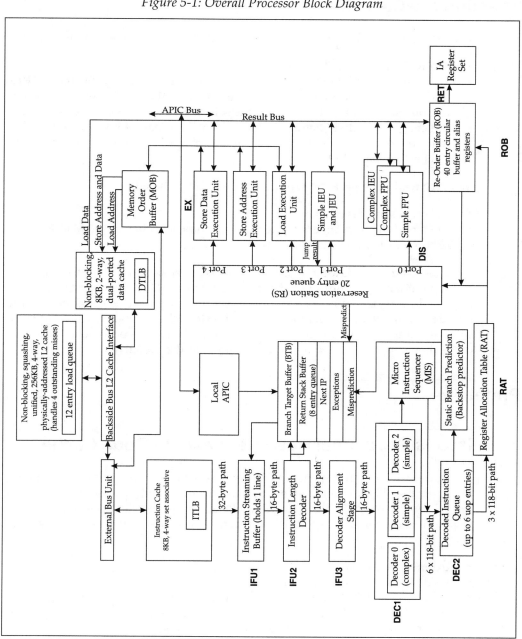

Enabling the Caches

The processor's caches are disabled at startup (by reset) and are enabled when:

- CR0[CD] and CR0[NW] = 00b,
- and the targeted memory area is designated as cacheable by the MTRRs (memory type and range registers, described in the chapter entitled "Rules of Conduct" on page 133) and/or the selected page table entry (described in the chapter entitled "Paging Enhancements" on page 439). For more information on cache enabling, refer to the chapter entitled "The Processor Caches" on page 149.

Memory read requests are not issued to the code cache when:

- the caches are disabled or
- the target memory area is designated as non-cacheable by the MTRRs and/or the selected Page Table entry.

The following sections assume that the caches are enabled (via CR0) and the targeted memory area is designated cacheable (via the MTRRs and/or the selected page table entry). In this case, all code memory read requests generated by the instruction prefetcher are submitted to the code cache for a lookup. This discussion also assumes that the request results in a hit on the code cache. The code cache then supplies the requested information to the prefetcher.

Prefetcher

Issues Sequential Read Requests to Code Cache

In Figure 5-1 on page 77, the prefetcher interacts with the prefetch streaming buffer in the IFU1 pipeline stage. Although not directly pictured, it is represented by the Next IP block in the picture. The prefetcher continues issuing sequential access requests to the code cache unless one of the following events occurs:

- external interrupt.
- software exception condition.
- previously-fetched branch instruction results in a hit on the Branch Target Buffer (BTB) and the branch is predicted taken, or that static branch prediction results in a prediction of a branch to be taken.

Chapter 5: The Fetch, Decode, Execute Engine

- when executed, a branch instruction is determined to have been mispredicted. The instruction pipeline is flushed and fetching is re-initiated at the correct address.

In Intel's Pentium Pro documentation, the prefetch queue is referred to as the prefetch streaming buffer. The prefetch streaming buffer can hold 32 bytes of code (Please note that Intel's documentation states that it holds two 16-byte lines. In reality, it holds one line divided into two 16-byte blocks.). Assuming that caching is enabled, the prefetcher attempts to always keep the buffer full by issuing read requests to the code cache whenever the buffer becomes empty.

From the prefetch streaming buffer, the instructions enter the instruction pipeline. The series of stages that an instruction passes through from fetch to completion is referred to as the pipeline. The prefetch stage is the first stage of the pipeline.

Introduction to Prefetcher Operation

Figure 5-2 on page 80 illustrates a 64-byte area of memory (from memory location 0h through 3Fh) that contains a series of program instructions (for the time being, ignore the "S" and "C" designations). Notice that the length of the instructions vary. Some are one byte in length, some two bytes, etc. Assume that the processor's branch prediction logic predicts a branch to instruction one (the first instruction represented in grey). The prefetcher issues a request to the code cache for the line (consisting of memory locations 0-1Fh) that contains the first byte of the target instruction. These 32 bytes are loaded into the processor's prefetch streaming buffer (see Figure 5-3 on page 80).

In this example, the first 25-bytes (those that precede the branch target address) are unwanted instruction bytes and are discarded by the prefetcher. It should be noted that although the figures illustrate the boundary between each instruction, in reality the boundaries are not marked in the prefetch streaming buffer. At this point, this is just a "raw" code stream. The boundaries will be determined and marked at a later stage of the pipeline (see "Decode Stages" on page 88).

These "raw" instructions are fed to the instruction pipeline 16-bytes at a time. Until another branch is predicted, the prefetcher requests the next sequential line from the code cache each time that the streaming buffer is emptied by the processor core.

Figure 5-2: Example Instructions in Memory

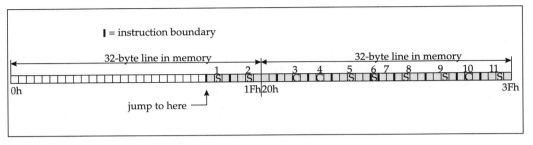

Figure 5-3: Contents of Prefetch Streaming Buffer Immediately after Line Fetched

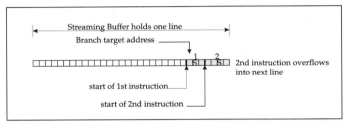

In the example pictured in Figure 5-3 on page 80, the first 16-byte block is discarded, as are the first nine bytes of the second 16-byte block. Only instruction one is passed to the complex decoder (see Figure 5-5 on page 87) in the current clock. The complex decoder is referred to as decoder zero, while the two simple decoders are decoders one and two.

The second instruction cannot be passed to a decoder yet because it overflows into the next line. In the next clock, the next line is accessed, supplying the remainder of instruction two. The pipeline can pass up to three instructions to decoders zero, one and two (in the same clock). A detailed description of the passing of IA instructions to the three decoders can be found in the section entitled "IFU3 Stage: Align Instructions for Delivery to Decoders" on page 85.

Brief Description of Pentium Pro Processor

The processor:

1. Fetches IA instructions from memory in strict program order.
2. Decodes, or translates, them (in strict program order) into one or more

fixed-length RISC instructions known as micro-ops, or uops.

3. Places the micro-ops into an instruction pool in strict program order.
4. Until this point, the instructions have been kept in original program order. This part of the pipeline is known as the in-order front end. The processor then executes the micro-ops in any order possible as the data and execution units required for each micro-op become available. This is known as the out-of-order (OOO) portion of the pipeline.
5. Finally, the processor commits the results of each micro-op execution to the processor's register set in the order of the original program flow. This is the in-order rear-end.

Beginning, Middle and End

In-Order Front End

In the first seven stages of the instruction pipeline (the prefetch, decode, RAT and ROB stages), the instructions are kept in strict program order. The instructions are fetched, decoded into micro-ops, stored in the instruction decode queue and are then moved into the ROB in strict program order.

Out-of-Order (OOO) Middle

Once the micro-ops are placed in the instruction pool (i.e., the ROB) in strict program order, they are executed out-of-order, one or more at a time (up to five instructions can be dispatched and start execution simultaneously) as data and execution units for each micro-op become available. As each micro-op in the instruction pool completes execution, it is marked as ready for retirement and its results are retained in the micro-op's entry in the instruction pool. Intel has implemented features that permit the processor to execute instructions out-of-order:

*   **Register aliasing**. Eliminates false dependencies created by the small IA register set.
*   **Non-blocking data and L2 caches**. Permits the processor to continue to make progress when cache misses occur.
*   **Feed forwarding**. Result of one micro-op's execution are immediately made available to other micro-ops that require the results in order to proceed with their own execution.

In-Order Rear End

The retirement unit (in the RET1 and RET2 stages) is constantly testing the three oldest micro-ops in the instruction pool to determine when they have completed execution and can be retired in original program order. As each group of three micro-ops is retired, the results of their execution is "committed" to the processor's IA register set. The micro-ops are then deleted from the pool and the pool entries become available for assignment to other micro-ops.

Intro to the Instruction Pipeline

Figure 5-4 on page 82 illustrates the main instruction pipeline. Table 5-1 on page 82 provides a basic description of each stage, while the sections that follow the table provide a detailed description of each.

Figure 5-4: Instruction Pipeline

Table 5-1: Pipeline Stages

Stage	Description
IFU1	**Instruction Fetch Unit stage 1.** Load a 32-byte line from the code cache into the prefetch streaming buffer.
IFU2	**Instruction Fetch Unit stage 2.** Mark instruction boundaries. In the IFU2 stage, two operations are performed simultaneously: • The boundaries between instructions within a 16-byte block are identified. Intel documents frequently refer to this as a line of information, but the term line is typically applied to the size of a block of information in a cache. To avoid possible confusion, the author therefore has decided not to refer to this as a line. • If any of the instructions within the 16-byte block are branches, the memory addresses that they were fetched from are presented to the BTB (Branch Target Buffer) for branch prediction. Refer to "Description of Branch Prediction" on page 122.
IFU3	**Instruction Fetch Unit stage 3.** Align the instructions for presentation to the appropriate decoders (see Figure 5-5 on page 87) in the next stage.

Chapter 5: The Fetch, Decode, Execute Engine

Table 5-1: Pipeline Stages (Continued)

Stage	Description
DEC1	**Decode stage 1.** Translate (i.e., decode) the instructions into the corresponding micro-op(s). Up to three instructions can be decoded simultaneously (if they are aligned with a decoder that can handle the instruction; see Figure 5-5 on page 87).
DEC2	**Decode Stage 2.** Pass the micro-ops to the decoded instruction queue. Since some IA instructions (e.g., string operations) translate into rather large streams of micro-ops and the decoded instruction queue can only accept six micro-ops per clock, it should be noted that this stage may have to be repeated a number of times (i.e, it may last for a number of processor clock ticks).
RAT	**Register Alias Table and Allocator stage.** The processor determines if a micro-op references any source operands. If it does, the processor determines if the source operand should be taken from a real IA register or from an entry in the ROB. The latter case will be true if a micro-op previously placed in the ROB (from earlier in the code stream) will, when executed, produce the result required as a source operand by this micro-op. In this case, the source field in this micro-op is adjusted to point to the respective ROB entry. As an example, a micro-op earlier in the code stream may, when executed, place a value in the EAX register. In reality, when the processor executes this micro-op, it places the value, not in the EAX register, but rather in the ROB entry occupied by the micro-op. A micro-op later in the code stream that requires the contents of EAX as a source would be adjusted in the RAT stage to point to the result field of the ROB entry occupied by the earlier micro-op, rather than to the real EAX register.
ROB	**ReOrder Buffer (ROB) stage.** Move micro-ops from the RAT/Allocator stage to the next sequential three ROB entries at the rate of three per clock. If all of the data required for execution of a micro-op is available and an entry is available in the RS (Reservation Station) queue, also pass a copy of the micro-op to the RS. The micro-op then awaits the availability of the appropriate execution unit.
DIS	**Dispatch stage.** If not already done in the previous stage (because all of the data required by the micro-op was not available or an entry wasn't available in the RS), copy the micro-op from the ROB to the RS, and then dispatch it to the appropriate execution unit for execution.

Table 5-1: Pipeline Stages (Continued)

Stage	Description
EX	**Execution stage**. Execute micro-op. The number of clocks that an instruction takes to complete execution is instruction dependent. Most micro-ops can be executed in one clock.
RET1	**Retirement stage 1**. When a micro-op in the ROB has completed execution, all conditional branches earlier in the code stream have been resolved and it is determined that the micro-op should have been executed, it is marked as ready for retirement.
RET2	**Retirement stage 2. Retire instruction**. When the previous IA instruction has been retired and all of the micro-ops associated with the next IA instruction have completed execution, the real IA register(s) affected by the IA instruction's execution are updated with the instruction's execution result (this is also referred to as "committing" the results to the machine state) and the micro-op is deleted (i.e., retired) from ROB. Up to three micro-ops are retired per clock in strict program order.

In-Order Front End

Instruction Fetch Stages

The first three stages of the instruction pipeline are the instruction fetch stages. The Intel documentation states that this takes 2.5 clock periods, but it doesn't define which clock edges within that 2.5 clock period define the boundaries between the three stages.

IFU1 Stage: 32-Byte Line Fetched from Code Cache

The instruction pipeline feeds from the bottom end of the prefetch streaming buffer, requesting 16 bytes at a time. When the buffer is emptied, the prefetch logic issues a request (during the IFU1 stage) to the code cache for the next sequential line. The prefetcher issues a 32-byte-aligned linear address to the code cache and a 32-byte block of "raw" code (the next sequential line) is loaded into the prefetch streaming buffer by the code cache.

Chapter 5: The Fetch, Decode, Execute Engine

IFU2 Stage: Marking Boundaries and Dynamic Branch Prediction

During the IFU2 stage, the boundaries between instructions within the first 16-byte block are identified and marked. In addition, if any of the instructions are branches, the memory addresses that they were fetched from (for up to four branches within the 16-byte block) are presented to the branch target buffer (BTB) for branch prediction. For a discussion of dynamic branch prediction, refer to the section entitled "Description of Branch Prediction" on page 122. Assuming that none of the instructions are branches or that none of the branches are predicted taken, code fetching will continue along the same sequential memory path.

IFU3 Stage: Align Instructions for Delivery to Decoders

Refer to Figure 5-5 on page 87. The processor implements three decoders that are used to translate the variable-length IA instructions into fixed-length RISC instructions referred to as micro-ops. Each micro-op is 118 bits in length and is referred to as a triadic micro-op because it includes three elements (in addition to the RISC instruction itself):

- two sources
- one destination

Intel does not document the format of the micro-ops.

The first of the three decoders (decoder 0) is classified as a complex decoder and can translate any IA instruction that translates into between one and four micro-ops. The second and third decoders (decoders 1 and 2) are classified as simple decoders and can only translate IA instructions that translate into single micro-ops (note that most of the IA instructions translate into one micro-op). In general:

- Simple IA instructions of the register-register form convert to a single micro-op.
- Load instructions (i.e., memory data reads) convert to a single micro-op.
- Store instructions (i.e., memory data writes) convert to two micro-ops.
- Simple read/modify instructions convert into two micro-ops.
- Simple instructions of the register-memory form convert into two or three micro-ops.
- MMX instructions are simple (note that MMX is implemented in the Pentium II, but not in the Pentium Pro).
- Simple read/modify/write instructions convert into four micro-ops.

Appendix D of Intel Application Note AP-526 (order Number 242816) contains the number of micro-ops that each IA instruction converts to.

Using the instruction boundary markers inserted into the 16-byte block in the IFU2 stage, the IFU3 stage rotates the next three sequential IA instructions to optimize their alignment with the three decoders (decoders 0, 1, and 2). If the three instructions consist of three simple instructions, no rotation is necessary and they are submitted to the three decoders in strict program order. If, on the other hand, the three IA instructions consists of two simple instructions and a complex instruction (in any order), the IFU3 stage rotation logic rotates the instructions to align the complex instruction with decoder 0 (the complex decoder) and the two simple instructions with decoders 1 and 2. In the next clock (the DEC2 stage), the micro-ops produced by the decoders are placed in the ID Queue in strict program order. If the series of three IA instructions contains more than one complex instruction, decoder throughput will not be optimal. Table 5-2 on page 86 describes the various scenarios.

Table 5-2: Decoder Throughput Table

Composition of Next 3 IA Instructions	Instructions Decoded	Description
simple,simple,simple	3	Throughput optimized. No rotation necessary. In the DEC1 stage, all three decoders are simultaneously passed simple IA instructions to decode.
simple,simple,complex	3	Throughput optimized. Rotation performed to correctly align the three IA instructions with the three decoders. In the DEC1 stage, all three decoders are simultaneously passed IA instructions to decode.
simple,complex,simple	3	Throughput optimized. Rotation performed to correctly align the three IA instructions with the three decoders. In the DEC1 stage all three decoders are simultaneously passed IA instructions to decode.

Table 5-2: Decoder Throughput Table (Continued)

Composition of Next 3 IA Instructions	Instructions Decoded	Description
simple,complex,complex	2	The first two IA instructions are rotated and passed to decoders 0 and 1.
complex,simple,simple	3	Throughput optimized. No rotation necessary to correctly align the three IA instructions with the three decoders. In the DEC1 stage, all three decoders are simultaneously passed IA instructions to decode.
complex,simple,complex	2	The first two IA instructions are passed to decoders 0 and 1.
complex,complex,simple	1	Just the first IA instruction is submitted to decoder 0.
complex,complex,complex	1	Just the first IA instruction is submitted to decoder 0.

Figure 5-5: The Three Instruction Decoders

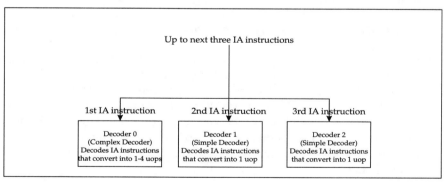

Decode Stages

After the IA instructions are aligned with the three decoders, they are submitted to one or more of the decoders (see "IFU3 Stage: Align Instructions for Delivery to Decoders" on page 85). There are two decode pipeline stages, DEC1 and DEC2, taking a total of 2.5 clocks to complete. The following sections discuss these two stages.

DEC1 Stage: Translate IA Instructions into Micro-Ops

In the DEC1 stage, between one and three IA instructions are submitted to decoders 0 through 2 for translation into micro-ops. The complex decoder can decode any IA instruction that is not greater than seven bytes in length and that translates into no more than four micro-ops. The simple decoders can decode any IA instruction that is not greater than seven bytes in length and that translates into a single micro-op. Most IA instructions are categorized as simple.

The best case throughput scenario is when a complex instruction is presented to decoder 0, and two simple instructions are simultaneously submitted to decoders 1 and 2. In this case, up to six micro-ops can be created in one clock (up to four from the complex instruction and one each for the two simple instructions). In the DEC2 stage (see "DEC2 Stage: Move Micro-Ops to ID Queue" on page 89), the micro-ops created are placed into the ID (instruction decode) queue in the same order as the IA instructions that they were translated from (i.e., in program order).

Micro Instruction Sequencer (MIS)

Refer to Figure 5-6 on page 89. Some IA instructions translate into more than four micro-ops and therefore cannot be handled by decoder 0. These instructions are submitted to the micro instruction sequencer (MIS) for translation. Essentially, the MIS is a microcode ROM that contains the series of micro-ops (five or more) associated with each very complex IA instruction. Some instructions (e.g., string operations) may translate into extremely large, repetitive micro-op sequences. The micro-ops produced are placed into the ID queue in the DEC2 stage.

Figure 5-6: Decoders and the Micro Instruction Sequencer (MIS)

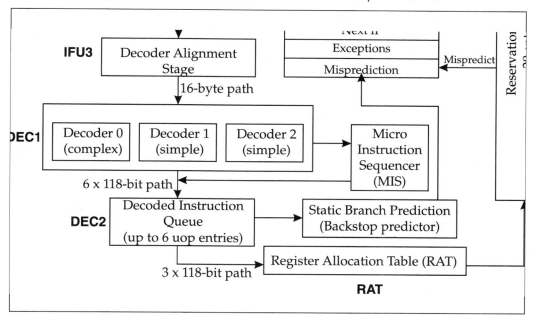

DEC2 Stage: Move Micro-Ops to ID Queue

Two operations occur in the decode 2 stage:

1. The micro-ops produced by the decoders (or by the MIS) are placed in the ID queue in original program order. The best-case scenario is one where, in the DEC1 stage, the complex decoder is presented with an IA instruction that translates into four micro-ops and the two simple decoders are simultaneously presented with simple IA instructions that each create a single micro-op. In this case, six micro-ops are the loaded into the ID queue simultaneously (note that a micro-op consists of 118 bits and the path between the DEC1 and DEC2 stages is 6 x 118-bits wide).

2. If any of the micro-ops in the ID queue represent branches, static branch prediction (for more information, refer to "Static Branch Prediction" on page 126) is applied to predict if the branch will be taken when executed or not.

Queue Micro-Ops for Placement in Pool. In the DEC2 stage, the micro-ops created by the three decoders or by the MIS are stored in the ID queue in original program order. The ID queue can hold up to six micro-ops and is pictured in Figure 5-6 on page 89.

Second Chance for Branch Prediction. As the micro-ops are deposited in the ID queue, the processor checks to see if any are branches. If any are, the processor's static branch prediction algorithm is applied to predict whether, when executed, the branch will be taken. For a detailed discussion of static branch prediction, refer to the section entitled "Static Branch Prediction" on page 126.

RAT Stage: Overcoming the Small IA Register Set

The IA register set only includes 16 registers that can be used to store data. They are the eight floating-point registers (FP0 through FP7) and the EAX, EBX, ECX, EDX, ESI, EDI, EBP, and ESP registers. The small number of IA registers restricts the programmer to keeping a very small number of data variables close at hand in the registers. When these registers are all in use and the programmer needs to retrieve another data variable from memory, the programmer is forced to first copy the current contents of one of the IA registers back to memory before loading that register with new data from another area of memory. As an example, the following code fragment saves off the data in EAX before loading a new value into EAX:

```
mov   [mem1],  EAX
mov   EAX, [mem2]
```

Due to the small register set, this sequence is very common in x86 programs. Ordinarily, the processor could not execute these two instructions simultaneously (because EAX must first be saved before it can be loaded with the new value). This is commonly referred to as a false register dependency that prevents the simultaneous execution of the two instructions.

However, the processor is designed to use another, hidden register as the register to be written by the second instruction and can therefore execute both instructions simultaneously. In other words, at the same time that the first instruction is reading the value from EAX to write into memory, the second instruction can read from memory and write into a hidden register rather than the real EAX register. The value in the hidden EAX can be copied into the actual EAX at a later time.

As another example, consider the following code fragment:

```
mov   eax,17
add   mem,eax
mov   eax,3
add   eax,ebx
```

Chapter 5: The Fetch, Decode, Execute Engine

Ordinarily, these four instructions would have to be executed in serial fashion, one after the other. The Pentium Pro can execute the first and the third instructions simultaneously, moving the values into two, separate hidden registers rather than into the EAX register. Likewise, the second and the fourth instructions can then be executed simultaneously. The EAX reference in the second instruction is changed to point to the hidden register that was loaded with the value 17 by the first instruction. The EAX reference in the fourth instruction is changed to point to the hidden register that was loaded with the value 3 by the third instruction.

The processor includes a set of 40 hidden registers that can be used in lieu of any of the eight general purpose registers or any of the eight floating-point registers. This eliminates many false dependencies between instructions, thereby permitting simultaneous execution and resulting in better performance. During the register alias table (RAT) stage, the processor selects which of the 40 surrogate registers will actually be used by the micro-op when it is executed. The surrogate registers reside in the ROB (discussed in the next section).

ReOrder Buffer (ROB) Stage

After the micro-ops are produced by the decoders and have had their source fields adjusted in the RAT stage, they are placed in the 40-deep ROB in strict program order, at the rate of up to three per clock. Once placed in this instruction pool, the RS (reservation station) can copy multiple micro-ops from the pool (up to five simultaneously) and queue them up for delivery to the appropriate execution units. When micro-ops in the ROB have completed execution and are retired (described later), they are deleted from the ROB. These ROB entries are then available to move new micro-ops to the ROB from the ID queue. The sections that follow provide a detailed description of the ROB.

Instruction Pool (ROB) is a Circular Buffer

Refer to Figure 5-7 on page 93. During each clock, between one and three micro-ops (depending on how many micro-ops are currently in the ID queue) are moved from the top three locations (zero through two) of the ID queue to the Register Alias Table (RAT) stage. As stated earlier (see "RAT Stage: Overcoming the Small IA Register Set" on page 90), the processor adjusts the micro-ops' source fields to point to the correct registers (i.e., one of the real IA registers, or one of the 40 hidden registers in the ROB).

The ROB is implemented as a circular buffer with 40 entries. A micro-op and, after it has completed execution, the result of its execution are stored in each ROB entry. Initially, the ROB is empty and the start-of-buffer pointer and the end-of-buffer pointer both point to entry 0. As IA instructions are decoded into micro-ops, the micro-ops (up to three per clock) are placed in the ROB starting at entry 0 in strict program order. As additional micro-ops are produced by the decoders, the end-of-buffer pointer is incremented once for each micro-op. At a given instant in time, the end-of-buffer pointer points to where the next micro-op decoded will be stored, while the start-of-buffer pointer points to the oldest micro-op in the buffer (corresponding to the earliest instruction in the program).

Later, in the retirement stage, the retirement logic will retire (remove) the three oldest micro-ops from the pool and will increment the start-of-buffer pointer by three. The three pool entries that were occupied by the three micro-ops just retired are then available for new micro-ops.

To summarize, the logic is always adding new micro-ops to the end-of-buffer, incrementing the end-of-buffer pointer, and is also removing the oldest micro-ops from the start-of-buffer and incrementing the start-of-buffer pointer.

Figure 5-7: The ROB, the RS and the Execution Units

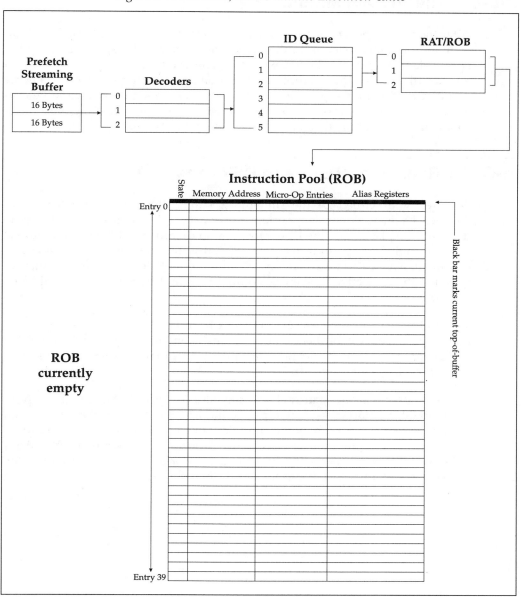

Out-of-Order (OOO) Middle

After the micro-ops are placed in the instruction pool (i.e., the ROB), the RS can copy multiple micro-ops from the pool in any order and dispatch them to the appropriate execution units for execution. The criteria for selecting a micro-op for execution is that the appropriate execution unit and all necessary data items required by the micro-op are available—the micro-ops do not have to be executed in any particular order. Once executed, the results of the micro-op's execution are stored in the ROB entry occupied by the micro-op.

In-Order Rear End (RET1 and RET2 Stages)

As already described in the previous sections, the processor fetches and decodes IA instructions in program order. The micro-ops produced by the decoders are placed into the ID queue in program order and are moved into the ROB in original program order. Once placed in the ROB, however, the micro-ops are dispatched and executed in any order possible. The execution results are stored in the respective ROB entries (rather than in the processor's actual register set).

When all upstream (i.e., earlier) branches have been resolved (i.e., executed) and it has been established that a downstream micro-op that has already completed execution should have been executed, that micro-op is marked as ready for retirement (in the RET1 stage).

The retirement logic constantly checks the status of the oldest three micro-ops in the ROB (at the start-of-buffer) to determine when all three of them have been marked as ready for retirement. The micro-ops are then retired (in the RET2 stage), three at a time in original program order. As each is retired, the micro-op's execution result is copied into the processor's real register set from the ROB entry and the respective ROB entry is then deleted.

Chapter 5: The Fetch, Decode, Execute Engine

Three Scenarios

To explain the relationship of—

- the prefetch streaming buffer,
- the decoders,
- the ID queue,
- the RAT,
- the ROB,
- the reservation station (RS),
- and the execution units,

the following sections have been included. They describe three example scenarios:

- The first assumes that reset has just been removed from the processor.
- The second assumes that the processor's caches have just been enabled.
- The third assumes that the processor's caches have been enabled for some time and the code cache contains lines of code previously fetched from memory.

Scenario One: Reset Just Removed

Immediately after reset is removed, the following conditions exist:

- Code cache and L2 cache are empty and caching is disabled.
- Prefetch streaming buffer is empty.
- ID queue is empty.
- ROB is empty.
- Reservation station (RS) is empty.
- All execution units are idle.
- The CS:IP registers are pointing to memory location FFFFFFF0h.

Starvation!

The ROB and the RS are empty, so the processor's execution units have no instructions to execute.

First Instruction Fetch

Because caching is disabled (CR0[CD] and CR0[NW] are set to 11b), the prefetcher bypasses the L1 code cache and the L2 cache and submits its memory read request directly to the external bus interface (this occurs in the IFU1 stage). This read request has the following characteristics:

- Memory address is FFFFFFF0h, identifying the quadword (group of eight locations) consisting of memory locations FFFFFFF0h through FFFFFFF7h.
- When caching is disabled, the prefetcher always requests 32 bytes of information, but doesn't cache the line. It only uses the data originally requested and discards the remainder of the line.

First Memory Read Bus Transaction

In response to this 32-byte memory read request, the external bus interface arbitrates for ownership of the external bus and then initiates a 32-byte memory read. *Please note that, even though caching is disabled, the current implementations of the Pentium Pro processor initiates a 32-byte rather than an 8-byte read. The critical quadword (in this example, the one that starts at 0FFFFFFF0h) is returned by the boot ROM, followed by the remaining three quadwords that comprise the line. The processor passes the first quadword into the prefetch streaming buffer and discards the remaining three quadwords. When the prefetcher issues the request for the next sequential 8-bytes, the processor initiates another 32-byte read for the same line, keeps the first quadword and discards the next three returned. Whether or not future versions of x86 processors will also indulge in this behavior is unknown at this time. The author believes that this was done for simplicity of design.*

During this period of time, the processor core starvation continues (because the instructions have not percolated down through the instruction pipeline stages to be decoded and executed).

Eight Bytes Placed in Prefetch Streaming Buffer

Refer to Figure 5-8 on page 97. The addressed memory device presents the eight bytes back to the processor. The processor latches the data and places it in the first eight locations of the prefetch streaming buffer. The prefetcher immediately issues a request for the next sequential group of eight memory locations, FFFFFFF8h through FFFFFFFFh and the bus interface initiates another external bus transaction.

Figure 5-8: Scenario One Example—Reset Just Removed

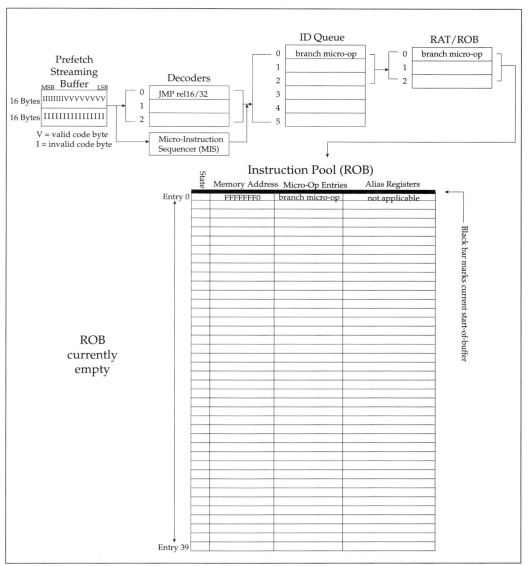

Instruction Boundaries Marked and BTB Checked

Refer to Figure 5-9 on page 98. In the IFU2 stage, the instruction boundaries within the eight-byte block are marked. In addition, if any of the instructions are branches (up to four of them), the memory address that it was fetched from is submitted to the BTB for a lookup. The BTB, a cache, was cleared by reset, so the lookup results in a BTB miss. In other words, the BTB has no history on the branch and therefore cannot predict whether or not it will be taken when it arrives at the jump execution unit (JEU) and is executed. Sequential fetching continues.

Realistically speaking, the first instruction fetched from the power-on restart address (FFFFFFF0h) is almost always an unconditional branch to an address lower in memory (because FFFFFFF0h is only 16 locations from the top of memory space).

Figure 5-9: The IFU2 Stage

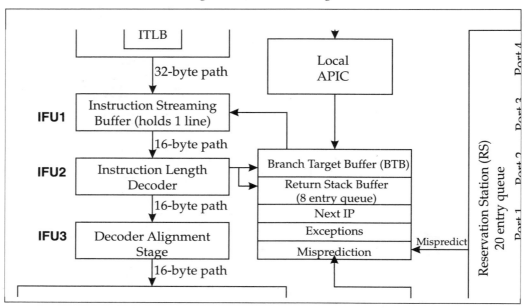

Between One and Three Instructions Decoded into Micro-Ops

Refer to Figure 5-10 on page 100 and to Figure 5-8 on page 97. In the DEC1 stage, the first three IA instructions (assuming that there are three embedded within the first eight bytes) are submitted to the three decoders for translation into micro-ops. The best case throughput scenario would be a simple/simple/simple or a complex/simple/simple sequence. This would produce between three and six micro-ops in one clock cycle.

In the DEC2 stage, the micro-ops are forwarded to the ID queue. In addition, if any of the micro-ops are branches, the static branch prediction logic decides whether or not to alter the fetch stream (i.e., to predict whether or not the branch will be taken when it arrives at the jump execution unit (JEU) and is executed).

As mentioned earlier, the first instruction fetched after power-up is almost always an unconditional branch to an address lower in memory (the entry point of the system's power-on self-test, or POST). If this is the case, the static branch prediction logic predicts whether the branch will be taken when it is executed by the JEU (for more information, refer to "Static Branch Prediction" on page 126).

Assuming that the first instruction is an unconditional branch, it is predicted as taken (in the DEC2 stage). This has the following effects:

- The instructions in the IFU1 through DEC2 stages (i.e., in the prefetch streaming buffer and the ID queue) are flushed (the unconditional branch remains in the ID queue, however). The flushing of the instructions in the first five stages causes a "bubble" in the pipeline, resulting in a temporary decrease in performance.
- The branch target address is supplied to the prefetcher and is used to fetch the next instruction.
- Both the predicted branch target address and the fall-through address accompany the branch until it is executed by the JEU.

Figure 5-10: Decoders and the Micro Instruction Sequencer (MIS)

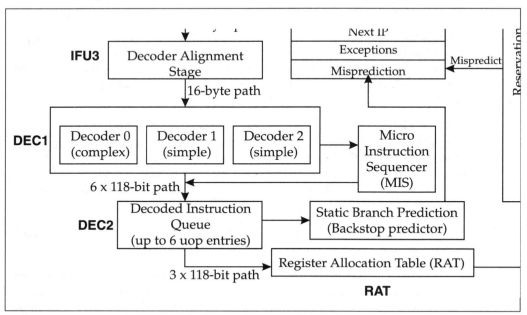

Source Operand Location Selected (RAT)

Refer to Figure 5-10 on page 100 and to Figure 5-8 on page 97. The branch instruction advances to the RAT stage where the processor determines if the micro-op references any source operands. If it does, the processor determines if the source operand should be supplied from a real IA register or from an entry in the ROB. The latter case will be true if a micro-op previously placed in the ROB (from earlier in the code stream) will, when executed, produce the result required as a source operand for this micro-op. In this case, the source field in this micro-op is adjusted to point to the respective ROB entry.

As an example, a micro-op earlier in the code stream may, when executed, place a value in the EAX register. In reality, when the processor executes this micro-op, it places the value, not in the EAX register, but rather in the ROB entry occupied by the micro-op. A micro-op later in the code stream that requires the contents of EAX as a source would be adjusted in the RAT stage to point to the result field of the ROB entry occupied by the earlier micro-op.

Chapter 5: The Fetch, Decode, Execute Engine

Micro-Ops Advanced to ROB and RS

Refer to Figure 5-11 on page 101. The reservation station (RS) is the gateway to the processor's execution units (see "The ROB, the RS and the Execution Units" on page 93). Basically, it is a queuing mechanism that, according to the Intel documentation, can queue up to 20 micro-ops to be forwarded to execution units as they become available. The documents don't define whether it is implemented as one 20-entry queue common to all five execution ports or as five separate queues (one for each execution port) each with four entries.

In the ROB stage, up to three micro-ops per clock are moved from the ID queue to the ROB in strict program order and are placed in the next three available ROB entries. In this example scenario, the branch micro-op in the ID queue is simultaneously moved to ROB entry zero and to the RS (because the RS has queue space available). In the event that there are no open RS queue entries, the micro-op is moved from the RAT to the ROB, but is not copied into the RS from the ROB until room becomes available (as the respective execution unit completes the execution of another micro-op).

Figure 5-11: The ReOrder Buffer (ROB) and The Reservation Station (RS)

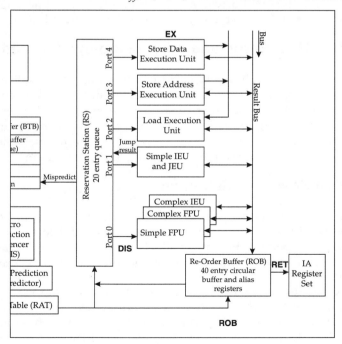

Micro-Ops Dispatched for Execution

Refer to Figure 5-11 on page 101. The JEU is currently idle, so the branch micro-op is immediately dispatched from the RS to the JEU for execution during the EX (execution) stage and begins execution. In ROB entry zero, the branch micro-op is marked as executing (see Figure 5-8 on page 97).

Micro-Ops Executed

In this example, the micro-op is an unconditional branch, so the branch is taken when executed. The RS provides this feedback to the BTB where an entry is made indicating that the branch should be predicted taken the next time that is fetched. In addition, the branch target address is also stored in the BTB entry so that it will know where to branch to.

Since the branch was correctly predicted (by the static branch prediction logic during the DEC2 stage) and prefetching altered accordingly, the correct stream of instructions are behind the branch in the pipeline (albeit with a bubble in between). If the branch had been incorrectly predicted, the instructions that were prefetched after the branch, translated and placed in the ROB would be incorrect and must be flushed, along with those in pipeline stages earlier than the ROB (i.e., the RAT, ID queue, and prefetch streaming buffer).

Result to ROB Entry (and other micro-ops if necessary)

The branch micro-op has completed execution and its result is stored in the same ROB entry as the micro-op. The micro-op is marked completed in its respective ROB entry. Another micro-op currently awaiting execution in the ROB or RS may require the result produced by this micro-op. In this case, the result produced by the just-completed micro-op is now available to the stalled micro-op. That micro-op can then be scheduled for execution.

Micro-op Ready for Retirement?

It must be noted that micro-ops in the ROB are executed out-of-order (i.e., not in the original IA instruction order) as the required execution unit and any required data operands become available. A micro-op later in the program can therefore complete execution before instructions earlier in the program flow.

Consider the situation where there is a branch micro-op in the ROB from earlier in the program flow that has not yet been executed. When that branch is executed it may or may not alter the program flow. If it branches to a different area of memory, the micro-ops currently in the ROB that were prefetched from the other path should not have been fetched, decoded and executed. Any micro-op already executed from the mispredicted path must therefore be deleted along with any results that it produced (in other words, as if it had never been executed).

A micro-op is not ready for retirement until it is certain that no branches from earlier in the program are currently in the ROB that, when executed, might result in a branch that would preclude the execution of this micro-op. When this condition is met, the branch micro-op in ROB entry zero is marked (in the RET1 stage) as ready for retirement.

Micro-Op Retired

In order to have the program execute in the order originally intended by the programmer, micro-ops must be retired (i.e., commited to the real register set) in original program order. In other words, a micro-op that has completed execution and been marked as ready for retirement cannot be retired until all micro-ops that precede it in the program have been retired.

Retiring a micro-op means to permit its execution result to affect the processor's state (i.e., the contents of its real register set). Consider the following example:

```
add   edx,ebx
mov   eax,[0100]
cmp   eax,edx
jne   loop
```

The instructions that comprise this code fragment must alter and/or observe the processor's real register set in the following order:

1. EDX must be changed to reflect the result of the addition.
2. EAX must then be loaded with the four bytes from memory locations 00000100h through 00000103h in the data segment.
3. The values in EDX and EAX are then compared, altering the appropriate condition bits in the processor's EFLAGS register.
4. The conditional jump instruction then checks the EFLAGS[EQUAL] bit to determine whether or not to branch.

The process of retiring a micro-op involves:

*   Permitting its result (currently stored only in the ROB entry) to be copied to the processor's real register set.
*   Deleting the micro-op from the ROB
*   The ROB entry then becomes available to accept another micro-op.

The processor is capable of retiring up to three micro-ops per clock during the RET2 stage.

Scenario Two: Processor's Caches Just Enabled

Assuming that the processor's caches have just been enabled (by clearing both CR0[CD] and CR0[NW] to zero), the caches are currently empty. Also assume that the processor's MTRR registers have been set up to define one or more memory ranges as cacheable. When the prefetcher requests the next quadword, the quadword address (assuming it falls within a region defined as cacheable) is submitted to the code cache for a lookup. This results in a miss and the code cache issues a read request to the L2 cache (see Figure 5-12 on page 104) for the 32-byte code line that contains the requested quadword. This results in an L2 cache miss and the cache line request is issued to the processor's bus interface unit. The bus interface arbitrates for ownership of the external bus and initiates a 32-byte memory read request from main memory. The 32-byte line is returned to the processor in toggle-mode order (see "Toggle Mode Transfer Order" on page 189). The line is placed in the L2 cache and is also passed to the code cache where another copy is made. In addition, the line is immediately passed from the code cache to the prefetch streaming buffer. From this point, the processing of the code proceeds as already discussed starting in the section entitled "Instruction Boundaries Marked and BTB Checked" on page 98.

Figure 5-12: Code Cache and L2 Cache Miss

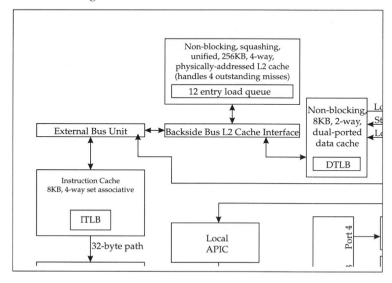

Chapter 5: The Fetch, Decode, Execute Engine

Scenario Three: Caches Enabled for Some Time

In this scenario, the processor's caches have been enabled for some time and the processor's instruction pipeline, including the ID queue, the ROB and the RS currently contain a stream of micro-ops in various stages of completion. Refer to Figure 5-13 on page 106 during this discussion.

Micro-ops (such as those illustrated in Figure 5-13 on page 106) are always placed in the ROB in original program order. The instruction in ROB entry 13 is the oldest instruction currently in the ROB, while the instruction in entry eight is the youngest. Instructions must be retired in strict program order, from oldest to youngest. The basic format of an entry (note that Intel does not provide this level of information, so this table is based on hopefully intelligent speculation) is introduced in Table 5-3 on page 107, while an entry-by-entry description is provided in Table 5-4 on page 108. Note that the micro-ops in Table 5-4 on page 108 are listed in original program order.

Figure 5-13: Scenario Three

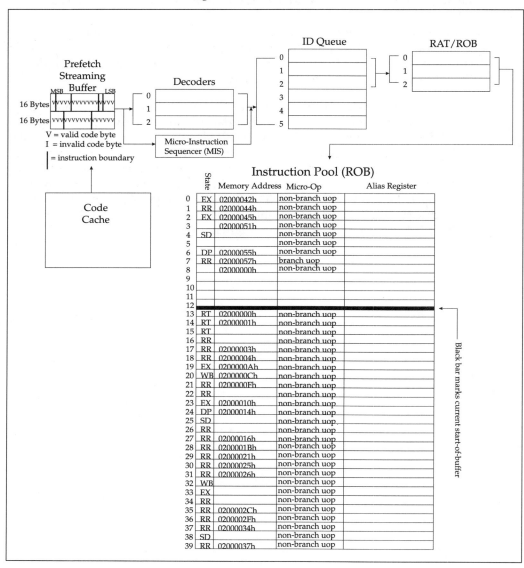

Table 5-3: Basic Composition of a ROB Entry

Element	Description
State	A micro-op in the ROB can be in one of the following states: • **SD**: scheduled for execution. Indicates that the micro-op has been queued in the RS, but has not yet been dispatched to an execution unit. • **DP**: indicates that the micro-op is at the head of the RS dispatch queue for its respective execution port and is being dispatched to the respective execution unit for execution. • **EX**: the micro-op is currently being executed by its respective execution unit. • **WB**: the micro-op has completed execution and its results are being written back to the micro-op's ROB entry. In addition, if any other micro-ops are stalled waiting for the result, the result is forwarded to the stalled micro-op(s). • **RR**: the micro-op is ready for retirement. • **RT**: the micro-op is being retired.
Memory address	Indicates the start memory address of the IA instruction that generated the micro-op(s).
Micro-op	The micro-op is either a branch or a non-branch instruction.
Alias register	If a micro-op references one of the IA registers, the reference is re-directed to one of the 40 registers contained within the ROB (each ROB entry contains a register field that can store a value up to 80-bits wide (a floating-point value would be 80-bits wide, while integer values may be one, two, or four bytes wide).

Table 5-4: Description of Figure 5-13 on page 106 ROB Entries

Entry	Explanation
13	This is the oldest micro-op in the ROB and, along with the next two micro-ops, is being retired in the current clock. The new start-of-buffer will then be 16 and entries 13, 14 and 15 will be available for new micro-ops (see Figure 5-14 on page 116). Entry 13 was the only micro-op decoded from the 1-byte IA instruction that was fetched from memory address 02000000h. It is not a branch micro-op, so it did not alter program flow. The next IA instruction was fetched from memory address 02000001h (see entry 14).
14	This micro-op (and those in entries 15 and 16) was decoded from the 2-byte IA instruction that was fetched from memory locations 02000001h and 02000002h. Along with entries 13 and 15, it is being retired in the current clock. It is not a branch micro-op, so it did not alter program flow. The next IA instruction was fetched from memory address 02000003h (see entry 17).
15	This micro-op (and those in entries 14 and 16) was decoded from the 2-byte IA instruction that was fetched from memory locations 02000001h and 02000002h. Along with entries 13 and 14, it is being retired in the current clock. It is not a branch micro-op, so it did not alter program flow. The next IA instruction was fetched from memory address 02000003h (see entry 17).
16	This micro-op (and those in entries 14 and 15) was decoded from the 2-byte IA instruction that was fetched from memory locations 02000001h and 02000002h. It is ready for retirement and will be retired in the next clock (see Figure 5-15 on page 117) along with entries 17 and 18. The new start-of-buffer will then be 19 and entries 16, 17 and 18 will be available for new micro-ops. Entry 16 is not a branch micro-op, so it did not alter program flow. The next IA instruction was fetched from memory address 02000003h (see entry 17).
17	This micro-op was the only one decoded from the 1-byte IA instruction that was fetched from memory location 02000003h. It is ready for retirement (see Figure 5-15 on page 117) and will be retired in the next clock along with entries 16 and 18. It is not a branch micro-op, so it did not alter program flow. The next IA instruction was fetched from memory address 02000004h (see entry 18).
18	This micro-op was the only one decoded from the 6-byte IA instruction that was fetched from memory locations 02000004h through 02000009h. It is ready for retirement (see Figure 5-15 on page 117) and will be retired in the next clock along with entries 16 and 17. It is not a branch micro-op, so it did not alter program flow. The next IA instruction was fetched from memory address 0200000Ah (see entry 19).

Table 5-4: Description of Figure 5-13 on page 106 ROB Entries (Continued)

Entry	Explanation
19	This micro-op was the only one decoded from the 2-byte IA instruction that was fetched from memory locations 0200000Ah and 0200000Bh. It is currently being executed and, depending on the type of micro-op, may take one or more clocks to complete execution. When it completes execution, its state will change from EX to RR. It will be retired when: • it has completed execution • its results have been written back to entry 19 • it and the micro-ops in entries 20 and 21 are ready for retirement • the micro-ops in entries 13 through 18 have been retired It is not a branch micro-op, so it did not alter program flow. The next IA instruction was fetched from memory address 0200000Ch (see entry 20).
20	This micro-op was the only one decoded from the 3-byte IA instruction that was fetched from memory locations 0200000Ch through 0200000Eh. It has completed execution and its results are currently being written back to entry 20 (the micro-op is currently in the writeback stage). It will then be ready for retirement, but will not be retired until entries 19 and 21 are also ready for retirement (see entry 19). At that point, entries 19 through 21 will be retired. It is not a branch micro-op, so it did not alter program flow. The next IA instruction was fetched from memory address 0200000Fh (see entry 21).
21	This micro-op (and the one in entry 22) was decoded from the one-byte IA instruction that was fetched from memory location 0200000Fh. It is ready for retirement, but will not be retired until entries 19 and 20 are also ready for retirement (see entry 19). At that point, entries 19 through 21 will be retired. It is not a branch micro-op, so it did not alter program flow. The next IA instruction was fetched from memory address 02000010h (see entry 23).
22	This micro-op (and the one in entry 21) was decoded from the one-byte IA instruction that was fetched from memory location 0200000Fh. It will be retired when: • it has completed execution • its results have been written back to entry 22 • it and the micro-ops in entries 23 and 24 are ready for retirement • the micro-ops in entries 13 through 21 have been retired It is not a branch micro-op, so it did not alter program flow. The next IA instruction was fetched from memory address 02000010h (see entry 23).
23	This micro-op was the only one decoded from the 4-byte IA instruction that was fetched from memory locations 02000010h through 02000013h. It is still executing (and it may take more than one clock). After execution, it will enter the writeback stage where its execution results will be written back to entry 23. It will then be ready for retirement, but will not be retired until entries 22 and 24 are also ready for retirement (see entry 22). At that point, entries 22 through 24 will be retired. It is not a branch micro-op, so it did not alter program flow. The next IA instruction was fetched from memory address 02000014h (see entry 24).

Table 5-4: Description of Figure 5-13 on page 106 ROB Entries (Continued)

Entry	Explanation
24	This micro-op and the ones in entries 25 and 26 were decoded from the 2-byte IA instruction that was fetched from memory locations 02000014h and 02000015h. It is currently being dispatched to its respective execution unit and will begin execution in the next clock. After execution, it will enter the writeback stage where its execution results will be written back to entry 24. It will then be ready for retirement, but will not be retired until entries 22 and 23 are also ready for retirement (see entry 22). At that point, entries 22 through 24 will be retired. It is not a branch micro-op, so it did not alter program flow. The next IA instruction was fetched from memory address 02000016h (see entry 27).
25	This micro-op and the ones in entries 24 and 26 were decoded from the 2-byte IA instruction that was fetched from memory locations 02000014h and 02000015h. It is currently in the RS and is scheduled for dispatch to its respective execution unit. After execution, it will enter the writeback stage where its execution results will be written back to entry 25. It will be retired when: • it has completed execution • its results have been written back to entry 25 • it and the micro-ops in entries 26 and 27 are ready for retirement • the micro-ops in entries 13 through 24 have been retired It is not a branch micro-op, so it did not alter program flow. The next IA instruction was fetched from memory address 02000016h (see entry 27).
26	This micro-op and the ones in entries 24 and 25 were decoded from the 2-byte IA instruction that was fetched from memory locations 02000014h and 02000015h. It is ready for retirement, but will not be retired until entries 25 and 27 are also ready for retirement (see entry 25). At that point, entries 25 through 27 will be retired. It is not a branch micro-op, so it did not alter program flow. The next IA instruction was fetched from memory address 02000016h (see entry 27).
27	This micro-op was the only one decoded from the 5-byte IA instruction that was fetched from memory locations 02000016h through 0200001Ah. It is ready for retirement, but will not be retired until entries 25 and 26 are also ready for retirement (see entry 25). At that point, entries 25 through 27 will be retired. It is not a branch micro-op, so it did not alter program flow. The next IA instruction was fetched from memory address 0200001Bh (see entry 28).
28	This micro-op was the only one decoded from the 6-byte IA instruction that was fetched from memory locations 0200001Bh through 02000020h. It is ready for retirement, as are those in entries 29 and 30. It will be retired after the micro-ops in entries 13 through 27 have been retired. It is not a branch micro-op and therefore did not alter program flow. The next IA instruction was fetched from memory address 02000021h (see entry 29).
29	This micro-op was the only one decoded from the 4-byte IA instruction that was fetched from memory locations 02000021h through 02000024h. It is ready for retirement, as are those in entries 28 and 30. It will be retired after the micro-ops in entries 13 through 27 have been retired. It is not a branch micro-op and therefore did not alter program flow. The next IA instruction was fetched from memory address 02000025h (see entry 30).

Table 5-4: Description of Figure 5-13 on page 106 ROB Entries (Continued)

Entry	Explanation
30	This micro-op was the only one decoded from the 1-byte IA instruction that was fetched from memory location 02000025h. It is ready for retirement, as are those in entries 28 and 29. It will be retired after the micro-ops in entries 13 through 27 have been retired. It is not a branch micro-op and therefore did not alter program flow. The next IA instruction was fetched from memory address 02000026h (see entry 31).
31	This micro-op (and those in entries 32 through 34) was decoded from the 6-byte IA instruction that was fetched from memory locations 02000026h through 0200002Bh. It is ready for retirement and will be retired when: • the micro-op in entry 32 has written back its results to entry 32 and is ready for retirement • the micro-op in entry 33 has completed execution, has written its results back to entry 33 and is ready for retirement • the micro-ops in entries 13 through 30 have been retired. It is not a branch micro-op and therefore did not alter program flow. The next IA instruction was fetched from memory address 0200002Ch (see entry 35).
32	This micro-op (and those in entries 31, 33 and 34) was decoded from the 6-byte IA instruction that was fetched from memory locations 02000026h through 0200002Bh. It is writing its results back to entry 32 during the current clock and will be retired when: • it has written back its results to entry 32 and is ready for retirement • the micro-op in entry 33 has completed execution, has written its results back to entry 33 and is ready for retirement • the micro-ops in entries 13 through 30 have been retired. It is not a branch micro-op and therefore did not alter program flow. The next IA instruction was fetched from memory address 0200002Ch (see entry 35).
33	This micro-op (and those in entries 31, 32 and 34) was decoded from the 6-byte IA instruction that was fetched from memory locations 02000026h through 0200002Bh. It is executing and will be retired when: • It has completed execution and has written back its results to entry 33 and is ready for retirement • the micro-op in entry 32 has written its results back to entry 32 and is ready for retirement • the micro-ops in entries 13 through 30 have been retired. It is not a branch micro-op and therefore did not alter program flow. The next IA instruction was fetched from memory address 0200002Ch (see entry 35).
34	This micro-op (and those in entries 31, 32 and 33) was decoded from the 6-byte IA instruction that was fetched from memory locations 02000026h through 0200002Bh. It is ready for retirement, as are the micro-ops in entries 35 and 36. It will be retired when the micro-ops in entries 13 through 33 have been retired. It is not a branch micro-op and therefore did not alter program flow. The next IA instruction was fetched from memory address 0200002Ch (see entry 35).

Table 5-4: Description of Figure 5-13 on page 106 ROB Entries (Continued)

Entry	Explanation
35	This micro-op was decoded from the 3-byte IA instruction that was fetched from memory locations 0200002Ch through 0200002Eh. It is ready for retirement, as are the micro-ops in entries 34 and 36. It will be retired when the micro-ops in entries 13 through 33 have been retired. It is not a branch micro-op and therefore did not alter program flow. The next IA instruction was fetched from memory address 0200002Fh (see entry 36).
36	This micro-op was decoded from the 5-byte IA instruction that was fetched from memory locations 0200002Fh through 02000033h. It is ready for retirement, as are the micro-ops in entries 34 and 35. It will be retired when the micro-ops in entries 13 through 33 have been retired. It is not a branch micro-op and therefore did not alter program flow. The next IA instruction was fetched from memory address 02000034h (see entry 37).
37	This micro-op (and the one in entry 38) was decoded from the 3-byte IA instruction that was fetched from memory locations 02000034h through 02000036h. It is ready for retirement and will be retired (along with entries 38 and 39) when: • the micro-op in entry 38 has been dispatched, executed, its results have been written back to entry 37 and it's ready for retirement. • the micro-ops in entries 13 through 36 have been retired. It is not a branch micro-op and therefore did not alter program flow. The next IA instruction was fetched from memory address 02000037h (see entry 39).
38	This micro-op (and the one in entry 37) was decoded from the 3-byte IA instruction that was fetched from memory locations 02000034h through 02000036h. It is currently scheduled for dispatch to its respective execution unit. It will be retired (along with entries 37 and 39) when: • it has been dispatched, executed, its results have been written back to entry 37 and it's ready for retirement. • the micro-ops in entries 13 through 36 have been retired. It is not a branch micro-op and therefore did not alter program flow. The next IA instruction was fetched from memory address 02000037h (see entry 39).
39	This micro-op was decoded from the 11-byte IA instruction that was fetched from memory locations 02000037h through 02000041h. It is ready for retirement and will be retired (along with entries 37 and 38) when: • entry 38 has been dispatched, executed, its results have been written back to entry 38and it's ready for retirement. • the micro-ops in entries 13 through 36 have been retired. It is not a branch micro-op and therefore did not alter program flow. The next IA instruction was fetched from memory address 02000042h (see entry 0).

Table 5-4: Description of Figure 5-13 on page 106 ROB Entries (Continued)

Entry	Explanation
0	This micro-op was decoded from the 2-byte IA instruction that was fetched from memory locations 02000042h through 02000043h. It is currently executing and will be retired (along with entries 1 and 2) when:
	• it has completed execution, its results have been written back to entry 0 and it's ready for retirement.
	• the micro-op in entry 2 has completed execution, its results have been written back to entry 2 and it's ready for retirement
	• the micro-ops in entries 13 through 39 have been retired.
	It is not a branch micro-op and therefore did not alter program flow. The next IA instruction was fetched from memory address 02000044h (see entry 1).
1	This micro-op was decoded from the 1-byte IA instruction that was fetched from memory location 02000044h. It is ready for retirement and will be retired (along with entries 0 and 2) when:
	• the micro-op in entry 0 has completed execution, its results have been written back to entry 0 and it's ready for retirement.
	• the micro-op in entry 2 has completed execution, its results have been written back to entry 2 and it's ready for retirement
	• the micro-ops in entries 13 through 39 have been retired.
	It is not a branch micro-op and therefore did not alter program flow. The next IA instruction was fetched from memory address 02000045h (see entry 2).
2	This micro-op was decoded from the 12-byte IA instruction that was fetched from memory locations 02000045h through 02000050h. It is currently executing and will be retired (along with entries 0 and 1) when:
	• the micro-op in entry 0 has completed execution, its results have been written back to entry 0 and it's ready for retirement.
	• the micro-op in entry 2 has completed execution, its results have been written back to entry 2 and it's ready for retirement
	• the micro-ops in entries 13 through 39 have been retired.
	It is not a branch micro-op and therefore did not alter program flow. The next IA instruction was fetched from memory address 02000051h (see entry 3).

Table 5-4: Description of Figure 5-13 on page 106 ROB Entries (Continued)

Entry	Explanation
3	This micro-op (and the ones in entries 4 and 5) was decoded from the 4-byte IA instruction that was fetched from memory locations 02000051h through 02000054h. It is has not yet entered the RS and will be retired (along with entries 4 and 5) when: • the micro-op in entry 3 has been scheduled for dispatch (i.e., it has entered the RS), dispatched, executed, its results have been written back to entry 3 and it's ready for retirement. • the micro-op in entry 4 has dispatched, executed, its results have been written back to entry 4 and it's ready for retirement • the micro-op in entry 5 has been scheduled for dispatch, dispatched, executed, its results have been written back to entry 5 and it's ready for retirement. • the micro-ops in entries 13 through 2 have been retired. It is not a branch micro-op and therefore did not alter program flow. The next IA instruction was fetched from memory address 02000055h (see entry 6).
4	This micro-op (and the ones in entries 3 and 5) was decoded from the 4-byte IA instruction that was fetched from memory locations 02000051h through 02000054h. It is currently in the RS and has been scheduled for dispatch to its respective execution unit. It will be retired (along with entries 3 and 5) when: • the micro-op in entry 3 has been scheduled for dispatch, dispatched, executed, its results have been written back to entry 3 and it's ready for retirement. • the micro-op in entry 4 has dispatched, executed, its results have been written back to entry 4 and it's ready for retirement • the micro-op in entry 5 has been scheduled for dispatch, dispatched, executed, its results have been written back to entry 5 and it's ready for retirement. • the micro-ops in entries 13 through 2 have been retired. It is not a branch micro-op and therefore did not alter program flow. The next IA instruction was fetched from memory address 02000055h (see entry 6).
5	This micro-op (and the ones in entries 3 and 4) was decoded from the 4-byte IA instruction that was fetched from memory locations 02000051h through 02000054h. It is has not yet entered the RS and will be retired (along with entries 3 and 4) when: • the micro-op in entry 3 has been scheduled for dispatch, dispatched, executed, its results have been written back to entry 3 and it's ready for retirement. • the micro-op in entry 4 has dispatched, executed, its results have been written back to entry 4 and it's ready for retirement • the micro-op in entry 5 has been scheduled for dispatch, dispatched, executed, its results have been written back to entry 5 and it's ready for retirement. • the micro-ops in entries 13 through 2 have been retired. It is not a branch micro-op and therefore did not alter program flow. The next IA instruction was fetched from memory address 02000055h (see entry 6).

Table 5-4: Description of Figure 5-13 on page 106 ROB Entries (Continued)

Entry	Explanation
6	This micro-op was decoded from the 2-byte IA instruction that was fetched from memory locations 02000055h and 02000056h. It is being dispatched to its respective execution unit. It will be retired (along with entries 7 and 8) when: • the micro-op in entry 6 has been executed, its results have been written back to entry 6 and it's ready for retirement. • the micro-op in entry 8 has been scheduled for dispatch, dispatched, executed, its results have been written back to entry 8 and it's ready for retirement. • the micro-ops in entries 13 through 5 have been retired. It is not a branch micro-op and therefore did not alter program flow. The next IA instruction was fetched from memory address 02000057h (see entry 7).
7	This branch micro-op was decoded from the IA instruction that was fetched from memory starting at location 02000057h. It will be retired (along with entries 6 and 8) when: • the micro-op in entry 6 has been executed, its results have been written back to entry 6 and it's ready for retirement. • the micro-op in entry 8 has been scheduled for dispatch, dispatched, executed, its results have been written back to entry 8 and it's ready for retirement. • the micro-ops in entries 13 through 5 have been retired. It is a branch micro-op, was predicted taken and therefore altered program flow. The next IA instruction was fetched from memory address 02000000h (see entry 8).
8	This was the only micro-op decoded from the 1-byte IA instruction that was fetched from memory address 02000000h. It is not a branch micro-op, so it did not alter program flow. The next IA instruction was fetched from memory address 02000001h.
9	empty
10	empty
11	empty
12	empty

Figure 5-14: Micro-Ops in Entries 13, 14 and 15 Have Been Retired

Instruction Pool (ROB)

	State	Memory Address	Micro-Op	Alias Register
0	EX	02000042h	non-branch uop	
1	RR	02000044h	non-branch uop	
2	EX	02000045h	non-branch uop	
3		02000051h	non-branch uop	
4	SD		non-branch uop	
5			non-branch uop	
6	DP	02000055h	non-branch uop	
7	RR	02000057h	branch uop	
8		02000000h	non-branch uop	
9				
10				
11				
12				
13				
14				
15				
16	RR		non-branch uop	
17	RR	02000003h	non-branch uop	
18	RR	02000004h	non-branch uop	
19	EX	0200000Ah	non-branch uop	
20	WB	0200000Ch	non-branch uop	
21	RR	0200000Fh	non-branch uop	
22	RR		non-branch uop	
23	EX	02000010h	non-branch uop	
24	DP	02000014h	non-branch uop	
25	SD		non-branch uop	
26	RR		non-branch uop	
27	RR	02000016h	non-branch uop	
28	RR	0200001Bh	non-branch uop	
29	RR	02000021h	non-branch uop	
30	RR	02000025h	non-branch uop	
31	RR	02000026h	non-branch uop	
32	WB		non-branch uop	
33	EX		non-branch uop	
34	RR		non-branch uop	
35	RR	0200002Ch	non-branch uop	
36	RR	0200002Fh	non-branch uop	
37	RR	02000034h	non-branch uop	
38	SD		non-branch uop	
39	RR	02000037h	non-branch uop	

Black bar marks current start-of-buffer

Figure 5-15: Micro-Ops in Entries 16, 17 and 18 Have Been Retired

Instruction Pool (ROB)

	State	Memory Address	Micro-Op	Alias Register
0	EX	02000042h	non-branch uop	
1	RR	02000044h	non-branch uop	
2	EX	02000045h	non-branch uop	
3		02000051h	non-branch uop	
4	SD		non-branch uop	
5			non-branch uop	
6	DP	02000055h	non-branch uop	
7	RR	02000057h	branch uop	
8		02000000h	non-branch uop	
9				
10				
11				
12				
13				
14				
15				
16				
17				
18				
19	EX	0200000Ah	non-branch uop	
20	WB	0200000Ch	non-branch uop	
21	RR	0200000Fh	non-branch uop	
22	RR		non-branch uop	
23	EX	02000010h	non-branch uop	
24	DP	02000014h	non-branch uop	
25	SD		non-branch uop	
26	RR		non-branch uop	
27	RR	02000016h	non-branch uop	
28	RR	0200001Bh	non-branch uop	
29	RR	02000021h	non-branch uop	
30	RR	02000025h	non-branch uop	
31	RR	02000026h	non-branch uop	
32	WB		non-branch uop	
33	EX		non-branch uop	
34	RR		non-branch uop	
35	RR	0200002Ch	non-branch uop	
36	RR	0200002Fh	non-branch uop	
37	RR	02000034h	non-branch uop	
38	SD		non-branch uop	
39	RR	02000037h	non-branch uop	

Black bar marks current start-of-buffer

Memory Data Accesses—Loads and Stores

During the course of a program's execution, a number of memory data reads (i.e., loads) and memory data writes (i.e., stores) may be performed.

Handling Loads

Refer to Figure 5-16 on page 119. An IA load instruction decodes into a single load micro-op that specifies the address to be read from and the number of bytes to read from memory starting at that address. The load (i.e., a memory data read) micro-op is executed by the load execution unit (connected to port 2 on the RS). Unless prevented from doing so (by defining an area of memory such that speculative execution is not permitted; for more information see "Rules of Conduct" on page 133), loads can be executed speculatively in any order. In other words, a load micro-op from later in the program flow can be executed before one that occurs earlier in the program flow. A load instruction flows through the normal instruction pipeline until it is dispatched to the load execution unit. It has then entered the load pipeline stages. They are illustrated in Figure 5-17 on page 119 and detailed in Table 5-5 on page 120.

When executed, the load address is always compared to those of stores currently-posted in the posted-write buffer. If any of the stores in the posted-write buffer occur earlier in the program flow then the load and the store has updated the data to be read by the load, then the store buffer supplies the data for the read. This is referred to as store, or feed, forwarding. For more information about loads, refer to "L1 Data Cache" on page 160.

Figure 5-16: Load and Store Execution Units

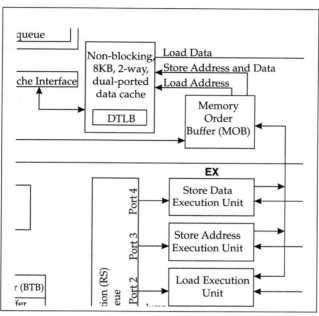

Figure 5-17: Load Pipeline Stages

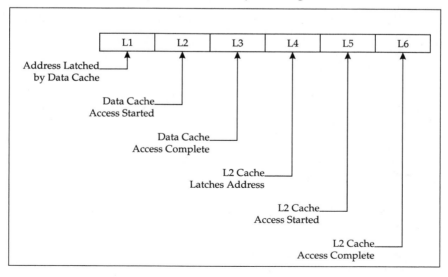

Table 5-5: Load Pipeline Stages

Stage(s)	Description
L1	During the L1 stage, the memory address for the load is translated from the linear to the physical address by the data TLB at the front end of the data cache.
L2-L3	During the L2 and L3 stages, the L1 data cache is accessed. • If this results in a hit on the L1 data cache, the data is supplied to the RS and the micro-op's ROB entry in the L3 stage. The micro-op then proceeds to the RR stage (see RR entry in this table). • If there is a miss on the L1 data cache, the instruction enters the L4 stage (see next entry).
L4-L6	In the event that the load misses the L1 data cache, the load proceeds to the L4, L5 and L6 stages where the L2 cache lookup is performed. • In the event of an L2 cache hit, the data is delivered to the RS and the micro-op's ROB entry in L6 and the micro-op proceeds to the RR stage (see RR entry in this table). • If there is a miss on the L2 cache, the load is forwarded to the bus interface unit for an access to main memory and the micro-op stalls until it has fulfillment. Because the L1 and L2 caches are non-blocking, however, subsequent loads that hit on L1 or L2 can complete before the stalled load.
RR	Ready for retirement. When it has been established that there is no chance of a branch occurring earlier in the program flow that would preclude execution of the load instruction, the load micro-op is marked RR in the ROB.
RT	Retirement stage. Data returned by the load is copied to the real target register from the ROB entry and the ROB entry becomes available for a new micro-op.

Handling Stores

An IA store (i.e., memory data write) instruction decodes into two micro-ops. When executed,

• one generates the address to be stored to.
• the other generates the data to be stored .

They can both be dispatched and executed simultaneously because the processor implements two separate execution units for handling stores:

- Store address execution unit generates the address to be stored to.
- Store data execution unit generates the data to be written.

Relative to other stores, the processor always performs stores in strict program order. A store cannot be executed until all earlier program stores have been performed. This is necessary in order to ensure proper operation of memory devices that are sensitive to the order in which write data is delivered to them. In addition, stores are never speculatively executed. All upstream conditional branches must have been resolved before stores are executed.

When executed, all stores are handled in the following manner:

- If the store is within **UC memory**, it is posted in the posted-write buffer and, when the posted writes are performed on the bus, will be performed in strict program order relative to other stores. For a description of UC memory, refer to "Uncacheable (UC) Memory" on page 138.
- If the store is within **WC memory**, it is posted in a WC (write-combining) buffer to be written to memory later. When the WC buffers are written to memory, the write may not occur in the order specified by the program relative to other writes. For a description of WC memory, refer to "Write-Combining (WC) Memory" on page 138.
- If the store is within **WT memory** and it's a hit on the data or L2 caches, the cache line is updated and the write is also posted in the posted-write buffer. If the store is a cache miss, it has no effect on the caches, but is posted in the posted-write buffer. When the posted writes are performed on the bus, it will be performed in strict program order relative to other stores. For a description of WT memory, refer to "Write-Through (WT) Memory" on page 139.
- If the store is in **WP memory**, it has no effect on the caches, but is posted in the posted-write buffer. When the posted writes are performed on the bus, it will be performed in strict program order relative to other stores. For a description of WP memory, refer to "Write-Protect (WP) Memory" on page 140.
- If the store is in **WB memory** and it's a hit on the data or L2 cache, the write is absorbed into the cache line and is posted in neither the posted-write nor WC buffers. For a description of operation within WB memory, refer to "Relationship of L2 and L1 Caches" on page 163 and to "Write-Back (WB) Memory" on page 141.

The Intel documentation does not specify the depth of the posted-write buffer.

Description of Branch Prediction

486 Branch Handling

The 486 processor does not implement any form of branch prediction. The instruction decode logic does not differentiate branches from other instruction types and therefore does not alter prefetching. In other words, instruction prefetching always continues past a branch to the next sequential instruction. If the branch is taken when it is executed, the instructions in the prefetch queue and those in the D1 and D2 stages are flushed. This creates a relatively minor bubble in the instruction pipeline (minor because the pipeline has so few stages).

Pentium Branch Prediction

The Pentium processor implements dynamic branch prediction using a very simple mechanism that yields a typical 85% hit rate. As each prefetched instruction is passed into the dual instruction pipelines, the memory address it was fetched from is used to perform a lookup in the BTB (branch target buffer). The BTB is implemented as a high-speed, look-aside cache. If there's a branch and it misses the BTB, it is predicted as not taken and the prefetch path is not altered. If it hits in the BTB, the state of the BTB entry's history bits is used to determine whether the branch should be predicted as taken or not taken. When the branch is executed, its results (whether it was taken or not and, if taken, the branch target address) are used to update the BTB. If the branch is incorrectly predicted, the instructions in the two pipelines and those in the currently-active prefetch queue must be flushed. This doesn't cause a terrible performance hit because the Pentium has relatively shallow instruction pipelines. For a more detailed discussion of the Pentium's branch prediction algorithm, refer to the MindShare book entitled *Pentium Processor System Architecture* (published by Addison-Wesley).

Pentium Pro Branch Prediction

Mispredicted Branches are VERY Costly!

The Pentium Pro processor's instruction pipeline is deep (i.e., it consists of many stages). Close to the beginning of the pipeline (in the IFU2 stage; see Figure 5-18 on page 124), the address of a branch instruction is submitted to the dynamic branch prediction logic for a lookup and, if a hit, a prediction is made on whether or not the branch will be taken when the branch instruction is finally executed by the JEU. The BTB only makes predictions on branches that it has seen taken previously. Based on this prediction, the branch prediction logic takes one of two actions:

- If the branch is predicted taken, the instructions that were fetched from memory locations along the fall-through path of execution are flushed from the 16-byte block of code that is currently in the IFU2 stage. The instructions currently in the prefetch streaming buffer are also flushed. The branch prediction logic provides the branch target address to the IFU1 stage and the prefetcher begins to refill the streaming buffer with instructions from the predicted path.
- If the branch is predicted as not taken, the branch prediction logic does not flush the instructions that come after the branch in the 16-byte code block currently in the IFU2 stage. It also does not flush the streaming buffer and the prefetcher continues fetching code along the fall-through path.

The branch instruction migrates through the pre-ROB pipeline stages, is placed in the ROB and, ultimately, is executed by the JEU (jump execution unit). The series of instructions from the predicted path followed along behind it in the pipeline and were also placed in the ROB. Due to the processor's out-of-order execution engine, by the time the branch is executed a number of the instructions that come after the branch in the program flow may have already completed execution.

When the branch is finally executed, all is well if the prediction was correct. However, if the prediction is incorrect:

- all instructions currently in the ROB that came after the branch must be flushed from the ROB (along with their execution results if any of them had already been executed).
- all of the instructions that come after the branch that are currently in the RS or are currently being executed must be flushed.
- all instructions in the earlier pipeline stages must be flushed.
- the streaming buffer must be flushed.
- the prefetcher must then issue a request for code starting at the correct address. This is supplied by the BTB which always keeps a record of the branch target address as well as the fall through address.

Because of the large performance hit that results from a mispredicted branch, the designers of the processor incorporate two forms of branch prediction: dynamic and static branch prediction, and implemented a more robust dynamic branch prediction algorithm than that used in the Pentium processor. The sections that follow describe the static and dynamic branch prediction mechanisms.

Figure 5-18: Fetch/Decode/Execute Engine

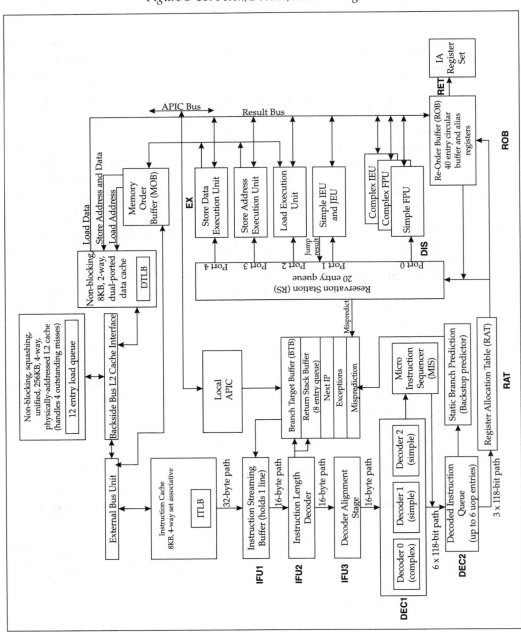

Chapter 5: The Fetch, Decode, Execute Engine

Dynamic Branch Prediction

General. Refer to Figure 5-18 on page 124. The Pentium Pro processor's BTB implements a two-level, adaptive dynamic branch prediction algorithm. *Please note that the following initial discussion temporarily ignores the static branch prediction mechanism.* In the IFU2 pipeline stage, the address of any conditional branch instruction (up to four simultaneously) that resides within the 16-byte code block is submitted to the BTB for a lookup (in other words, the BTB can make up to four branch predictions simultaneously). The first time that a branch is seen by the BTB, it results in a BTB miss (the BTB has no history on how it will execute). When the branch finally arrives at the JEU (jump execution unit) and is executed, an entry is made in the BTB. The entry records:

- the address that the branch was fetched from.
- whether or not the branch was taken and, if so, the branch target address.

The size and organization of the BTB is processor design-specific. The current implementations have a 4-way set-associate BTB with a total of 512 entries (double the Pentium BTB's size).

Yeh's Prediction Algorithm. Unlike the Pentium's BTB, which uses a simple counting mechanism (a variant on the Smith algorithm: a 2-bit counter that increments each time the branch is taken and decrements each time it's not; either of the higher two values indicate a taken prediction, while the lower two values indicate a not taken prediction), the Pentium Pro processor's BTB is capable of recognizing behavior patterns such as taken, taken, not taken. The algorithm used is referred to as Yeh's algorithm and is a two-level, adaptive algorithm. Each BTB entry uses 4-bits to maintain history on the branch's behavior the last four times that it was executed. There are many ways in which this algorithm can be implemented, but Intel has declined to describe the Pentium Pro's implementation. For additional information on Yeh's algorithm, refer to a very good article in the 3/27/95 issue of Microprocessor Report (Volume 9, Number 4). It is estimated that this algorithm can achieve accuracy of approximately 90-95% on SPECint92 and better on SPECfp92.

Return Stack Buffer (RSB)

The programmer calls a subroutine by executing a call instruction, explicitly citing the address to jump to. In other words, a call instruction is an unconditional branch and is therefore always correctly predicted as taken. When the call is executed, the address of the instruction that immediately follows the call is automatically pushed onto the stack by the processor. The programmer always ends the called routine with a return instruction. The return instruction pops the previously-pushed address off the stack and jumps to the instruction it points to in order to resume execution of the program that called the routine. In other words, the return instruction is also an unconditional branch and can always be predicted as taken. While this is true, it doesn't address the question of where it will branch to.

Previous x86 processor implementations kept no record of the address pushed onto the stack and therefore, although it could be predicted that the branch is taken, it could not "remember" where the branch would be taken to.

When a CALL instruction is executed, the return address is pushed into stack memory and is also pushed onto the RSB. The next RET instruction subsequently seen by the IFU2 stage causes the processor to access the top (i.e., most-recent) entry in the RSB. The branch prediction logic predicts a branch to the return address recorded in the selected RSB entry. In the event that the called routine alters the return address entry in stack memory, this will result in a misprediction.

The Intel documentation is unclear as to the size of the RSB, but the author has seen sizes of 4 and 8 entries quoted.

Static Branch Prediction

The static branch predictor is also referred to as the backstop mechanism because it provides a backup to the dynamic branch prediction logic. Branches are submitted to the static branch prediction logic in the DEC2 stage (see Figure 5-20 on page 128). The static branch prediction decision tree is illustrated in Figure 5-19 on page 127.

For the most part, the static branch predictor handles branches that miss the BTB. However, in the case of an unconditional IP-relative branch, the static branch predictor always forces the prediction to the taken state (and updates the BTB if there was a disagreement).

Figure 5-19: Static Branch Prediction Algorithm

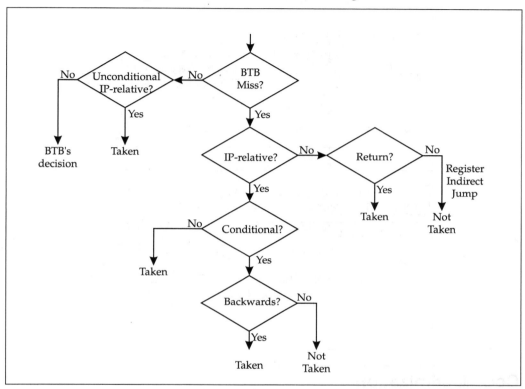

Figure 5-20: Static Branch Prediction Logic

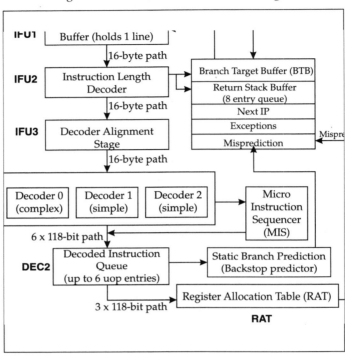

Code Optimization

General

This section highlights some of the code optimizations recommended by Intel to yield the best processor performance.

Reduce Number of Branches

As described in "Pentium Pro Branch Prediction" on page 122, mispredicted branches cause a severe performance penalty. Wherever possible, eliminate branches. One excellent way to do this is by using the CMOV and FCMOV instructions (see "Conditional Move (CMOV) Eliminates Branches" on page 417 and "Conditional FP Move (FCMOV) Eliminates Branches" on page 418).

Follow Static Branch Prediction Algorithm

In order to optimize performance for branches that miss the BTB, craft branches to take advantage of the static branch prediction mechanism (see "Static Branch Prediction" on page 126).

Identify and Improve Unpredictable Branches

Indirect branches, such as switch statements, computed GOTOs, or calls through pointers can branch to an arbitrary number of target addresses. When the branch goes to a specific target address a large amount of the time, the dynamic branch predictor will handle it quite well. However, if the target address is fairly random, the branch prediction may not have a very good rate of success. It would be better to replace the switch, etc., with a set of conditional branches that the branch prediction logic can handle well.

Don't Intermingle Code and Data

Don't intermingle code and data within the same cache line. The line can then end up residing in both the code and data caches. If the data is modified, the processor treats this as if it is self-modifying code (see "Self-Modifying Code and Self-Snooping" on page 191), resulting in poor performance.

Align Data

Data objects should be placed in memory aligned within a dword wherever possible. A data object (consisting of 2 or 4 bytes) that straddles a dword boundary may cause a lengthy delay to read or write the object. The worst-case scenario would be a data object that straddles a page (i.e., a 4KB) address boundary and causes two page fault exceptions (because neither page is currently in memory). This would result in a stall of the current program until both pages had been read from mass storage into memory.

Avoid Serializing Instructions

See "CPUID is a Serializing Instruction" on page 416. Serializing instructions such as CPUID restrain the processor from performing speculative code execution and have a serious impact on program execution. Sometimes they must be used to achieve a specific goal, but should be used as sparingly as possible. The following instructions cause execution serialization:

- Privileged instructions—MOV to control register, MOV to debug register, WRMSR, INVD, INVLPG, WBINVD, LGDT, LLDT, LIDT, and LTR.
- Non-privileged instructions—CPUID, IRET, and RSM.

Where Possible, Do Context Switches in Software

When the processor hardware is used to perform a task switch (by jumping through a task gate descriptor), the bulk of the processor's register set is automatically saved to the TSS (task state segment) for the program being suspended, and the register set is then reloaded with the register image from the TSS associated with the program being started (or resumed). This save and reload takes quite a bit of time. It may be possible to suspend the current task by saving a smaller subset of the register set (rather than the entire register set), and it may be possible to start (or resume) the new task by loading just a few of the registers. In this case, performance would be aided if the programmer performs the state save and reload using software.

Eliminate Partial Stalls: Small Write Followed by Full-Register Read

If a full register (EAX, EBX, ECX, or EDX) is read (e.g.— mov ebx, eax) after part of the register is written to (e.g.— mov al, 5), the processor experiences a stall of at least 7 clocks (and maybe much longer). The micro-op that reads from the full register is stalled until the partial write is retired, writing the data to the subset of the real IA register. Only then is the value read from the full, real IA register. In addition, none of the micro-ops that follow the full register read micro-op will be executed until the full register read completes.

Since 16-bit code performs partial register writes a lot, the processor suffers poor performance when executing 16-bit code.

Data Segment Register Changes Serialize Execution

16-bit code frequently changes the contents of data segment registers (DS, ES, FS, and GS). Unlike the processor's general-purpose registers, the data segment registers are currently not aliased. A write to the register immediately changes the value in the real, IA data segment register. Micro-ops that reside downstream from the micro-op that changes the register may perform accesses (loads or stores) within the affected data segment. If the processor were permitted to speculatively execute instructions beyond the one that changes the data segment register before that micro-op had completed execution, they would be using the old, stale contents of the segment register and would address the wrong location.

For this reason, the processor will not execute any instructions beyond the segment register load until the load has completed. The processor's performance degrades because it is restrained from out-of-order execution. *Since 16-bit code changes the contents of the data segment registers a lot, the processor suffers poor performance when executing 16-bit code.*

Intel has fixed this problem in the Pentium II processor by aliasing the data segment registers to micro-op entries in the ROB (as is already done for the general-purpose registers).

6 *Rules of Conduct*

The Previous Chapter

The previous chapter provided a detailed description of the processor logic responsible for instruction fetch, decode, and execution.

This Chapter

In preparation for the next chapter's discussion of the processor's caches, this chapter introduces the register set that tells the processor its rules of conduct within various areas of memory. The Memory Type and Range Registers, or MTRRs, must be programmed by the BIOS after startup to define the various regions of memory within the 64GB's of memory space and how the processor core and caches must behave when performing accesses within each region. A more detailed description of the MTRRs may be found in the appendix entitled "The MTRR Registers" on page 567.

The Next Chapter

The next chapter provides a detailed description of the processor's L2, L1 data, and L1 code caches.

The Problem

General

The overall memory space that the processor may read and write can be populated with many different types of devices. The operational characteristics of a device must dictate how the processor (and its caches) behaves when performing accesses within the memory range assigned to a device. Not following the correct "rules of conduct" when performing accesses within the device's range can lead to a confused device and improper operation.

A Memory-Mapped IO Example

As an example, if a memory range is populated by one or more memory-mapped IO devices and the processor were to perform speculative, out-of-order reads from or were to cache from that memory range, the memory-mapped IO devices would be hopelessly confused. The programmer might perform a read of a single location to read a device's status port and, without the programmer's knowledge, the processor performs a cache line fill to obtain the requested byte plus the other 31 locations that occupy the same line. The read of the other 31 locations might read data from FIFO buffers and status from other status registers within the same or other memory-mapped IO devices. The device(s), thinking that the data and/or status had been read, would move new data into the FIFO locations, and might clear status bits that had been set in the status ports. In other words, the device(s) would be left in a very different state than the programmer expects and would no longer function as expected.

Pentium Solution

The only Pentium mechanism available to the programmer to define the rules of conduct within a specific memory range are the PCD and PWT bits in a page table entry. This gives the OS programmer the ability to define the rules of conduct with 4KB granularity. Unfortunately, the OS is typically not platform-specific and doesn't necessarily have an accurate view of the denizens that occupy various areas of memory space. This means that although the OS may have informed the processor (via the two bits in the page table entry) that the memory area being accessed is cacheable, the platform-specific hardware may have been configured (by the BIOS code) with a more accurate view of the map and who lives where.

When the Pentium initiates a memory access, it projects the rules of conduct obtained from a page table entry on its PCD and PWT output pins. If it considers the memory region cacheable, it asserts its CACHE# output to request the entire line. Before proceeding with the data transfer, however, it first samples its KEN# input to see if the chipset has examined the memory address and agrees that is cacheable. If the processor is attempting a cache line fill, but KEN# is sampled deasserted, too bad. The chipset will only return the data indicated by the byte enables, not the whole line.

Pentium Pro Solution

The Pentium Pro processor includes a set of registers that the platform-specific software (e.g., the BIOS or the OS HAL) sets up to define the rules of conduct throughout memory space. The Memory Type and Range Registers, or MTRRs, are implemented as model-specific registers and are accessed using the RDMSR and WRMSR instructions (see the chapter entitled "Instruction Set Enhancements" on page 409).

The MTRR register set is divided into fixed-range and variable-range registers. The fixed-range registers define the processor's rules of conduct within the first MB of memory. If present (they are optional) and enabled, the fixed-range MTRRs divide the first MB into 88 regions, with a memory type assigned to each (illustrated in Figure 6-1 on page 136). Each of the variable-range registers can be programmed with a start and end address and the rules of conduct within the programmer-defined range. A detailed description of the MTRRs can be found in the appendix entitled "The MTRR Registers" on page 567.

Figure 6-1: Fixed-Range MTRRs Define Rules of Conduct within First MB of Memory Space

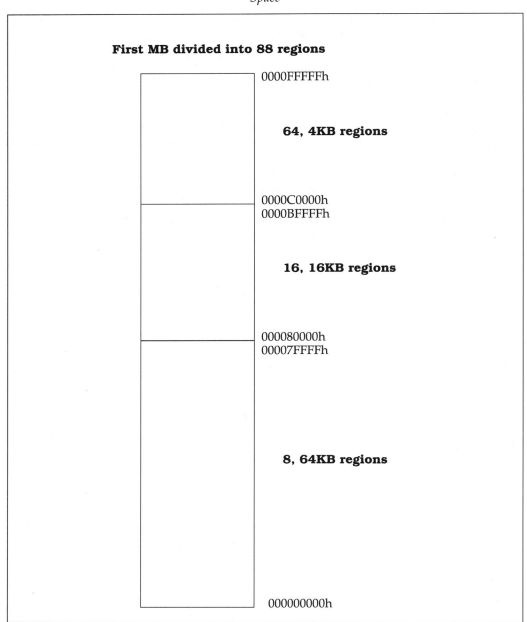

First MB divided into 88 regions

0000FFFFFh

64, 4KB regions

0000C0000h
0000BFFFFh

16, 16KB regions

000080000h
00007FFFFh

8, 64KB regions

000000000h

State of the MTRRs after Reset

Reset disables all of the MTRRs by clearing the MTRRdefType register (MTRR default type; see Figure 6-2 on page 137), setting all of memory space to the uncacheable (UC) memory type. After the processor starts executing the POST, the programmer can change the default rules of conduct by changing the value in the register's TYPE field. The MTRRdefType register is implemented as a Model-Specific Register, or MSR, and is accessed using the RDMSR and WRMSR instructions (see the chapter entitled "Instruction Set Enhancements" on page 409). Once the MTRRs are enabled, the rules of conduct (i.e., the memory type) specified in the MTRRdefType register are used for any accesses within ranges not covered by the MTRRs.

Figure 6-2: MTRRdefType Register

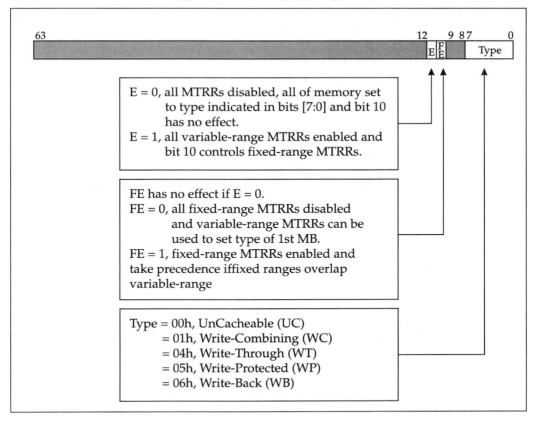

Memory Types

Using the MTRRdefType register or the individual fixed-length and/or variable range MTRRs, the programmer can define each memory range as one of five types (note that they are listed in order of agressiveness: UC yields very low performance while WB yields the best overall performance):

- Uncacheable, or UC.
- Write-Combining, or WC.
- Write-Through, or WT.
- Write-Protect, or WP.
- Write-Back, or WB.

The rules of conduct within the five types of memory areas are defined in the sections that follow. *The Pentium Pro processor never performs speculative writes (because there is no way to "undo" the write if it is later discovered that the write should not have been done).*

Uncacheable (UC) Memory

The rules that the processor follows when performing memory reads and writes in a memory range designated as UC are as follows:

- Cache lookups are not performed.
- Read requests are not turned into line reads from memory. They are performed as is. The data returned is routed directly to the requestor and is not placed in any cache.
- Memory writes are first posted in the processor's posted-write buffer and later performed on the bus in original program order.
- Speculative reads are not performed.

In other words, the processor is very well-behaved within a UC memory. For this reason, the UC type is well-suited to memory regions populated by memory-mapped IO devices. On the negative side, accesses within UC memory yield low performance due to lack of caching and speculative read constraining.

Write-Combining (WC) Memory

Note that the programmer must check the WC bit in the MTRRcap (see "The MTRR Registers" on page 567) register to determine if the WC memory type is supported. The rules that the processor follows when performing memory reads and writes in a memory range designated as WC are as follows:

- Cache lookups are not performed.
- Read requests are not turned into line reads from memory. They are performed as is. The data returned is routed directly to the requestor and is not placed in any cache.
- Speculative reads permitted.
- When one or more bytes are to be written to memory, a 32-byte Write Combining Buffer (WCB) memorizes the 32-byte aligned start address of the block the bytes are to be written to as well as the bytes to be written within the block.
- The contents of the WCB are written to memory under the following conditions:
    - If any additional writes within WC memory are performed to a different 32-byte area and all of the WCBs are in use, the processor will flush one of the WCBs to memory. The empty WCB will then be available to record the new 32-byte aligned start address and the bytes to be written to that 32-byte block.
    - Execution of a serializing instruction (e.g., CPUID, IRET, RSM), an IO instruction, or a locked operation causes the processor to flush all write buffers to memory before proceeding to the next instruction.

When flushing a WCB to memory, the processor will take one of two courses of action:

- If the WCB is full (i.e., all 32 bytes have been posted), the processor will perform a single 32-byte write transaction to write the entire line to memory.
- If all bytes in the WCB are not valid, the processor will perform the appropriate number of quadword or partial-quadword write transactions to write the updates to memory. As an example, if there are five bytes to be written to the first quadword and three to be written to the third quadword of the 32-byte block, the processor will perform two separate write transactions: one using the start address of the first quadword with five byte enables asserted; and the other using the start address of the third quadword with three byte enables asserted.

It should be noted that when these writes appear on the bus, the byte enables may or may not be contiguous, depending on the bytes to be written within the quadword. The WC memory type is useful for linear video frame buffers.

Write-Through (WT) Memory

The rules that the processor follows when performing memory reads and writes in a memory range designated as WT are as follows:

- Cache lookups are performed.
- On a cache read miss, the entire line is fetched from memory and placed in the cache.
- On a cache read hit, the requested data is supplied by the cache and a bus transaction does not take place.
- On a cache write miss, the data is posted in the processor's posted-write buffer to be written to memory later.
- On a cache write hit, the cache line is updated (but the line is not marked modified) and the data is posted in the processor's posted-write buffer to be written to memory later.
- Lines are never marked modified. They may only be in the S or I states.
- Speculative reads allowed.
- A write updates the L1 data cache, but invalidates the L2 and L1 code caches on a hit (see the section on self-modifying code in the chapter entitled "The Processor Caches" on page 149).

Write-Protect (WP) Memory

The rules that the processor follows when performing memory reads and writes in a memory range designated as WP are as follows:

- Cache lookups are performed.
- On a cache read miss, the entire line is fetched from memory and placed in the cache.
- On a cache read hit, the requested data is supplied by the cache and a bus transaction does not take place.
- On a cache write miss, the data is posted in the processor's posted-write buffer to be written to memory later.
- On a cache write hit, the cache line is *not* updated and the data is posted in the processor's posted-write buffer to be written to memory later.
- Lines are never marked modified. They may only be in the S or I states.

The WP memory type is useful for shadow RAM that contains ROM code. It may be cached for good performance, but cannot be changed in the cache (thereby simulating ROM memory). It should be noted that writes, although not performed in the cache, are performed to main memory. It is the memory controller's responsibility to ignore the memory write (note that the memory controller can examine the ATTRIB[7:0]# bits in the transaction request to determine the memory type).

Write-Back (WB) Memory

The rules that the processor follows when performing memory reads and writes in a memory range designated as WB are as follows:

- Cache lookups are performed.
- On a read cache miss, the entire line is fetched from memory and placed in the cache (in the E or S state).
- On a read cache hit, the requested data is supplied by the cache and a bus transaction does not take place.
- On a cache write miss, the entire line is read from memory using the read and invalidate transaction type. This is referred to as an *allocate-on-write miss policy.* Any other cache that has a snoop hit on a line in the E or S state must invalidate its copy (i.e., E->I, or S->I). Any other cache with a snoop hit on a line in the M state must source the 32-byte modified line to the requesting processor and to memory and invalidate its copy (i.e., M->I). When the requesting processor receives the line, it places it into the cache, writes into it and marks it as M.
- On a cache write hit, the cache line is updated. If the line was in the E state, it is changed to the M state (E->M). If it was in the M state, it stays in the M state (M->M). In either case, no bus transaction takes place and main memory is not updated. If the line was in the S state, the processor performs a memory read and invalidate transaction on the external bus to kill copies of the line in the caches of other processors. When the transaction has been completed, the line accepts the write data and transitions from the S to the M state.
- Speculative reads permitted.

The WB memory type yields the best overall performance. Reads and writes can be serviced solely in the cache without performing bus transactions, so bus traffic is greatly diminished. Ideally, most of main memory should be designated as the WB memory type.

Rules as Defined by MTRRs

Assuming that the MTRRs are enabled and have been set up by the programmer, the processor interrogates the MTRRs for any memory access to determine its rules of conduct. The determination is made as indicated in Table 6-1 on page 142.

Table 6-1: Memory Type Determination Using MTRRs

Scenario	Resulting Memory Type
Memory address within first MB, fixed-range MTRRs present and enabled, and address not within range defined by any of the variable-length MTRRS.	Type defined by the fixed-length MTRR for the range.
Address within first MB, fixed-length MTRRs disabled (or not present), and address not within a range defined by variable-length MTRRs.	Type defined by TYPE field in the MTRRdefType register.
Address within first MB, fixed-length MTRRs disabled (or not present), and address within a range defined by one variable-length MTRR.	Type defined by the variable-length MTRR for the range.
Address within first MB, fixed-length MTRRs disabled (or not present), and address within a range defined by more than one variable-length MTRR.	• If all of the respective variable-length MTRRs define the range identically, then the type is that defined by them. • If the respective variable-length MTRRs define the range as UC and any other memory type, then the type is UC. • If the respective variable-length MTRRs define the range as WT and WB, then the type is WT. • If the respective variable-length MTRRs are different and define combinations other than those defined above, then the behavior of the processor is undefined.
Address not within first MB, but not within a range defined by any of the variable-length MTRRs.	Type defined by TYPE field in the MTRRdefType register.
Address not within first MB and within a range defined by one of the variable-length MTRRs.	Type defined by TYPE field in a variable-range MTRR register.

Table 6-1: Memory Type Determination Using MTRRs (Continued)

Scenario	Resulting Memory Type
Address not within first MB and within ranges defined by more than one variable-length MTRRs.	• If all of the respective variable-length MTRRs define the range as UC, then the type is UC. • If the respective variable-length MTRRs define the range as UC and WB, then the type is UC. • If the respective variable-length MTRRs define the range as other than UC and WB, then the behavior of the processor is undefined.

Rules of Conduct Provided in Bus Transaction

Whenever the processor performs a memory read or write bus transaction, it outputs the memory type on the ATTRIB[7:0]# signals as part of the transaction request. In this manner, the memory controller and an L3 cache (if present) are also informed of the rules of conduct within the addressed memory area.

MTRRs and Paging: When Worlds Collide

Table 6-2 on page 143 and Table 6-3 on page 144 define the resulting rules of conduct when the MTTRs and page table entries agree or disagree on the memory type. Basically, when the target address of the memory access is covered by both a page table entry and an MTRR, the resulting memory type is the more conservative (i.e., the safer) of the two.

Table 6-2: Basic Relationship of the MTRRs to Paging

MTRR State	Paging State	Resulting Rules of Conduct
MTRRs disabled (MTRRdefType register = 0).	Paging disabled (CR0[PG] = 0).	MTRRdefType register's TYPE field defines default memory type.

Table 6-2: Basic Relationship of the MTRRs to Paging (Continued)

MTRR State	Paging State	Resulting Rules of Conduct
MTRRs enabled.	Paging disabled.	MTRR for target memory range defines memory type.
MTRRs disabled.	Paging enabled (CR0[PG] = 1).	PCD and PWT bits in selected page table entry define memory type as uncacheable, cacheable write-through, or cacheable write-back.
MTRRs enabled.	Paging enabled.	and target address is covered by both...see Table 6-3 on page 144.

Table 6-3: Type if Paging and MTRRs enabled and Address Covered by Both

MTRR Type	PCD	PWT	Resulting Memory Type	Notes
UC	x	x	UC	Memory is treated as uncacheable regardless of PCD/PWT setting because MTRR setting indicates uncacheable and that's more conservative than any other setting.

Table 6-3: Type if Paging and MTRRs enabled and Address Covered by Both (Continued)

MTRR Type	PCD	PWT	Resulting Memory Type	Notes
WC	0	0	WC	The PCD/PWT settings indicate cacheable writeback, but the MTRR WC setting is more conservative.
	0	1	WC	The PCD/PWT settings indicate cacheable writethrough, but the MTRR WC setting is more conservative.
	1	0	WC	PCD/PWT indicates memory cannot be cached but writes don't need to be propagated through to memory immediately (i.e., PWT indicates that it's not write through memory). Since the MTRR WC setting is basically in agreement with this, the memory is treated as WC.
	1	1	UC	PCD/PWT indicates memory cannot be cached but writes need to be propagated through to memory immediately (PWT indicates that it's writethrough memory). Although the MTRR WC setting also defines the memory as uncacheable, it permits a delay of writes to memory (they wouldn't occur until the WC buffer was dumped to memory), the memory is treated as UC. This forces the writes to memory to take place immediately.

Table 6-3: Type if Paging and MTRRs enabled and Address Covered by Both (Continued)

MTRR Type	PCD	PWT	Resulting Memory Type	Notes
WT	0	x	WT	The MTRR setting indicates that it's cacheable writethrough memory and the PCD setting agrees that it's cacheable. However, if the PWT bit indicates that it's writeback memory (writes to memory can be delayed), writethrough is more conservative (writes to memory cannot be delayed), so the memory type is WT.
	1	x	UC	While the MTRR indicates the memory is cacheable writethrough, the PCD setting indicates that its uncacheable, so it's treated as UC memory.
WP	0	0	WP	While the PCD/PWT setting indicates cacheable writeback memory, the WP setting is more conservative (because writes to memory must be performed immediately), so it's treated as WP.
	0	1	WP	While the PCD/PWT setting indicates cacheable, writethrough memory, the WP setting is more conservative (because , although writes to memory must be performed immediately, they are not permitted to update the cache in the event of a cache hit), so it's treated as WP.
	1	0	UC	While the MTRR WP setting indicates that its cacheable memory, the PCD setting indicates that it's not, so the memory type is UC.
	1	1	UC	While the MTRR WP setting indicates that its cacheable memory, the PCD setting indicates that it's not, so the memory type is UC.

Table 6-3: Type if Paging and MTRRs enabled and Address Covered by Both (Continued)

MTRR Type	PCD	PWT	Resulting Memory Type	Notes
WB	0	0	WB	Both settings agree, so the memory is WB.
	0	1	WT	While the MTRR WB setting indicates that it's cacheable writeback memory (writes to memory can be delayed), the PCD/PWT setting indicates writes cannot be delayed, so the memory type is WT.
	1	x	UC	While the MTRR WB setting indicates that it's cacheable writeback memory, the PCD setting indicates the memory is not cacheable, so the memory type is UC.

Detailed Description of the MTRRs

A detailed description of the MTRRs can be found in the appendix entitled "The MTRR Registers" on page 567.

7 *The Processor Caches*

The Previous Chapter

In preparation for this chapter's discussion of the processor's caches, the previous chapter introduced the register set that tells the processor its rules of conduct within various areas of memory. The Memory Type and Range Registers, or MTRRs, must be programmed after startup to define the various regions of memory within the 64GB's of memory space and how the processor core and caches must behave when performing accesses within each region.

This Chapter

This chapter provides a detailed description of the processor's L1 data and code caches, as well as its unified L2 cache. This includes a discussion of self-modifying code and toggle mode transfer order during the transfer of a cache line on the bus.

The Next Chapter

This chapter concludes Section One of the hardware part of the book—the discussion of the processor's internal operation. The next chapter starts Section Two, the bus section, and introduces the electrical characteristics of the Pentium Pro processor's bus.

Cache Overview

It should be noted that the size and structure of the processor's L2 cache and L1 data and code caches are processor implementation-specific.

Figure 7-1 on page 150 provides an overview of the processor's caches. The L1 code cache services requests for instructions generated by the instruction prefetcher (the prefetcher is the only unit that accesses the code cache and it only reads from it, so the code cache is read-only), while the L1 data cache services memory data read and write requests generated by the processor's execution units when they are executing any instruction that requires a memory data access. The unified L2 cache resides on a dedicated bus referred to as the backside bus. It services misses on the L1 caches, and, in the event of an L2 miss, it issues a transaction request to the external bus unit to obtain the requested code or data line from external memory. The information is placed in the L2 cache and is also forwarded to the appropriate L1 cache for storage.

Figure 7-1: Processor Cache Overview

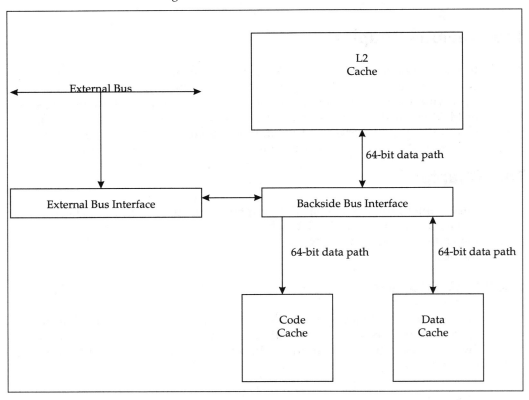

Introduction to Data Cache Features

The initial implementation of the data cache is **8KB, 2-way set-associative**, implementing all four of the MESI cache states. It services memory data read and write requests initiated by the processor execution units and has the following features:

- **ECC protected.** Each entry in the directories and the data storage ways are ECC (Error Correcting Code) protected. For more information, see "ECC Error Handling" on page 195.
- The L1 data cache handles memory write misses in areas of memory designated as WB (writeback) by performing an **allocate-on-write** operation. For more information, see "Write Miss On L1 Data Cache" on page 167.
- **Non-blocking**—a miss goes to the bus, but does not inhibit lookups for subsequent memory data accesses submitted by the execution units.
- Can **handle up to 4 misses** at once. When four L2 cache accesses are already in progress and additional misses occur on the L1 data cache, the data cache cannot forward any additional access requests that miss the data cache to the L2 until one of the outstanding requests completes.
- The data cache is **pipelined**—on back-to-back execution unit data accesses that hit on the data cache, it can produce one result per processor clock.
- It can handle **up to four pipelined lookups** simultaneously.
- Implements **two data ports** and can service one load request, or a **simultaneous load and store** (as long as they target different lines or different halves of the same line).
- Implements **a snoop port** to handle snooping of transactions generated by other initiators.
- When a miss has previously occurred for a line and the line is in the process of being fetched from either the L2 cache or from external memory, any subsequent misses for the same line do not generate additional memory reads (i.e., the additional reads are "squashed").

For detail on the data cache, refer to the section entitled "L1 Data Cache" on page 160.

Introduction to Code Cache Features

The initial implementation of the code cache is an 8KB, 4-way set-associative cache that only implements two of the MESI cache states: S and I (because the code cache is only read by the processor core, never written to). For detail on the code cache, refer to the section entitled "L1 Code Cache" on page 154.

Introduction to L2 Cache Features

The current processors implement a unified L2 cache that services misses on the L1 code and data caches. Later versions of the processor may or may not include the L2 cache (e.g., the Pentium II processor includes an external L2 cache; for more information, refer to "Dual-Independent Bus Architecture (DIBA)" on page 387). Unified refers to the fact that the L2 cache keeps copies of both code and data lines for the two L1 caches. The current implementations are 256KB, 512KB and 1MB in size and have a 4-way set-associative structure. The L2 cache has the following characterisitics:

- **ECC protected.** Each entry in the directories and the data storage ways are ECC (Error Correcting Code) protected. For more information, see "ECC Error Handling" on page 195.
- The L2 cache is **non-blocking**—a miss goes to the bus, but does not inhibit lookups for subsequent L1 cache misses.
- The L2 cache handles memory write misses in areas of memory designated as WB (writeback) by performing an **allocate-on-write** operation. For more information, see "Write Miss On L1 Data Cache" on page 167.
- When a miss has already occurred for a line and the line is in the process of being fetched from memory, any subsequent misses for the same line do not generate additional memory reads (i.e., the redundant reads are **squashed**.)
- **Can handle up to 4 misses** at once. When four external memory read line transactions caused by L2 misses are already in progress and additional misses occur on the L1 caches, L2 hits supply data to the L1 caches while L2 misses are stored in a queue that can hold up to 12 lookup requests. As each memory read completes on the external bus, the additional requests are popped off the queue one at a time and the lookup is performed.
- The L2 cache is **pipelined**—on back-to-back L1 cache misses that hit on the L2 cache, it can complete one lookup per processor clock.
- Implements **two snoop ports** to handle both internal (see "Self-Modifying Code and Self-Snooping" on page 191) and external snoops.
- It can handle **up to four pipelined lookups** simultaneously.

For details on the L2 cache, refer to the section entitled "Unified L2 Cache" on page 179.

Introduction to Snooping

In order to ensure that this processor's core and other processors that initiate memory bus transactions are always dealing with the freshest copy of the information, the processor always snoops memory bus transactions initiated by other processors (or bus masters other than processors). Snooping is performed as follows:

1. Latch all transaction requests generated by other initiators.
2. If it is a memory transaction, present the latched memory address to the three internal caches for a lookup.
3. If the targeted line isn't present in any of the caches, indicate a miss as the snoop result in the snoop phase of the transaction.
4. If the targeted line is present in one or more of the processor's caches but hasn't been modified since it was read from memory (in other words, the line is in the E or S state), indicate a snoop hit (unless the snooped transaction is a write or a read and invalidate; in that case, a cache miss is indicated and the line is invalidated) to the initiator of the transaction in the snoop phase of the transaction. Additional actions that may be necessary are defined later in this chapter.
5. If the targeted line is in the processor's data or L2 cache in the modified state (i.e., it has been modified by this processor since it was read from memory and the update hasn't yet been written to memory), indicate a snoop hit on a modified line to the initiator of the transaction in the snoop phase of the transaction. Additional actions that may be necessary are defined later in this chapter.

In addition, other processors snoop memory accesses that this processor generates on the bus and report back the snoop result to the initiating processor. Additional information can be found later in this chapter.

Determining Processor's Cache Sizes and Structures

The OS can tune its use of memory to yield optimal processor performance if it understands the geometry of the processor's caches and TLBs. The CPUID instruction may be executed with a request to return information regarding the size and organization of:

- L2 cache
- L1 data cache
- L1 code cache
- Code TLB
- Data TLBs

For detailed information on the CPUID instruction, refer to the chapter entitled "Instruction Set Enhancements" on page 409.

L1 Code Cache

As stated earlier, the size and structure of the L1 code cache (also referred to as the instruction cache or Icache) is processor implementation-specific. The initial versions of the processor implement an 8KB, 4-way, set-associative code cache (pictured in Figure 7-2 on page 155), but as future processor core speeds increase, the cache sizes may also be increased because the faster core can process code faster. Each entry in the directories and the data storage ways are ECC (Error Correcting Code) protected. For more information, see "ECC Error Handling" on page 195.

Code Cache Uses MESI Subset: S and I

The code cache exists for only one reason: to supply requested code to the instruction prefetcher. The prefetcher issues only read requests to the code cache, so it is a read-only cache. A line stored in the code cache can only be in one of two possible states, valid or invalid, implemented as the S and I states. In other words, the code cache implements a subset of the MESI cache protocol consisting of the S and I states.

Code Cache Contains Only Raw Code

When a line of code is fetched from memory and is stored in the code cache, it consists of raw code. The designers could have chosen to prescan the code stream as it is fetched from memory and store boundary markers in the code cache to demark the boundaries between instructions within the cache line. This would preclude the need to scan the code line as it enters the instruction pipeline for decode so each of the variable-length IA instructions can be aligned with the appropriate decoder. However, this would bloat the size of the code cache. Note that the Pentium's code cache stores boundary markers.

Rather, the Pentium Pro designers chose to store only raw code in the code cache. As each 16-byte block of code is forwarded to the IFU2 pipeline stage, instruction boundary markers are dynamically inserted in the block (in the IFU2 stage) before forwarding it to the IFU3 stage to align the instructions with the instruction decoders. For a detailed description of the pipeline stages, refer to the chapter entitled "The Fetch, Decode, Execute Engine" on page 75.

Figure 7-2: The L1 Code Cache

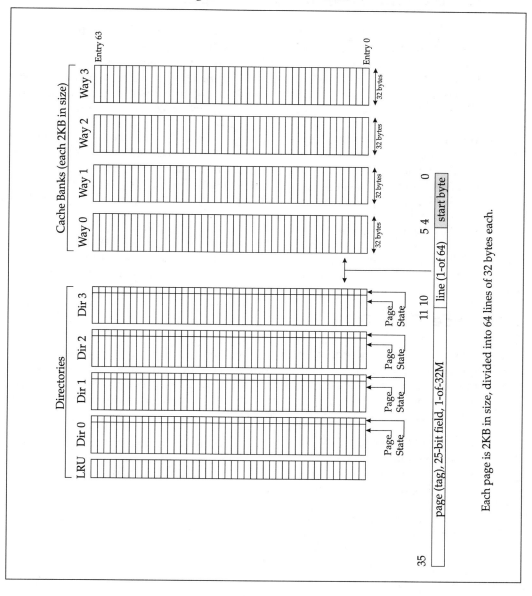

Code Cache View of Memory Space

When performing a lookup, the code cache views memory as divided into pages equal to the size of one of its cache banks (or ways). Each of its four cache ways is 2KB in size, so it views the 64GB of memory space as consisting of 32M pages, each 2KB in size. Furthermore, it views each memory page as having the same structure as one of its cache ways (i.e., a 2KB page of memory is subdivided into 64 lines, each of which is 32 bytes in size).

When a 32-bit linear memory address is submitted to the code cache by the instruction prefetcher, it is first presented to the code TLB which resides at the front end of the code cache. The TLB translates the 32-bit linear address to a 36-bit physical address (see "Paging Enhancements" on page 439). The 36-bit physical memory address is viewed as illustrated in Figure 7-2 on page 155:

- The upper 25 bits identifies the target page (1-of-32M).
- The middle 6 bits identifies the line within the page (1-of-64).
- The lower 5 bits identify the exact start address of the target instruction within the line and is not necessary to perform the lookup in the cache.

Code TLB (ITLB)

The code TLB is incorporated in the front end of the code cache, translating the 32-bit linear code address produced by the prefetcher into the 36-bit physical memory address before the lookup is performed. The size and organization of the code TLB is processor design-specific. The current versions of the processor have the following code TLB geometries:

- The TLB for page table entries related to 4KB code pages is 4-way set-associative with 64 entries.
- The TLB for page table entries related to 2MB and 4MB code pages is 4-way set-associative with 4 entries.

For a detailed description of the linear-to-physical address translation process, refer to "Paging Enhancements" on page 439.

Code Cache Lookup

Refer to Figure 7-2 on page 155. The target line number, contained in address bits [10:5], is used to index into the code cache directory and select a set of four entries to compare against. Each directory entry consists of a 25-bit tag field and a 1-bit state field. The cache compares the target page number to each of the selected set of four entries that are currently in the S state.

Code Cache Hit

If the target page number matches the tag field in one of the entries in the S state, it is a cache hit. The code cache has a copy of the desired line from the target page. The line is in the cache way associated with the directory entry, stored in the line identified by address bits [10:5]. The code cache supplies the requested 32-byte line to the instruction streaming buffer (i.e., the instruction prefetch queue). The prefetch queue in turn forwards a 16-byte code block to the next stage of the pipeline where:

*   Instruction boundary markers can be placed in it.
*   If the code block contains any branches, the dynamic branch prediction logic (i.e., the BTB) attempts to predict whether or not the branch will be taken when it arrives at the JEU execution stage.

A detailed description of the processor core may be found in the chapter entitled "The Fetch, Decode, Execute Engine" on page 75.

Code Cache Miss

On a code cache miss, the memory read request is forwarded to the L2 cache for a lookup. For a discussion of the code cache's relationship to the L2 cache, refer to "Relationship of L2 to L1 Code Cache" on page 164. For a detailed description of the L2 cache, refer to the section entitled "Unified L2 Cache" on page 179.

Code Cache LRU Algorithm: Make Room for the New Guy

When a miss occurs in the L1 code cache, the line is supplied either by the L2 cache or from external memory. In either case, the new line must be stored in the code cache. The discussion of the cache lookup described how the target line number is used as the index into the cache directory and selects a set of four entries to compare against.

Assume that all four of the selected set of entries are currently in use. In other words, the code cache has copies of the targeted line, but from four pages other than the desired page. A cache miss occurs. As stated earlier, the line will be supplied either from the L2 cache or from memory. When received, it should be obvious that the line must be stored in the code cache. It will be stored in the cache in the same relative position as it resided in within the memory page—in other words, within the same line number in one of the four cache ways. One of the four entries in the selected set must therefore be overwritten (i.e., cast out) with the new line and the new page number must be stored in the respective entry of the associated directory.

Figure 7-2 on page 155 illustrates that each set of four directory entries has an associated LRU (Least-Recently Used) bit field that is used to keep track of the least-recently used of the set of four entries. Intel does not document the LRU bit field width or usage, but it wouldn't be a big surprise if they used the same algorithm as was used for the 4-way, set-associative cache found in the 486 processor. In the 486, a 3-bit LRU field is associated with each set of four entries. LRU bit 0 indicates whether the pair of entries in directories 0 and 1 contains the LRU line, or the pair of entries in directories 2 and 3. Bit 1 indicates which of the pair consisting of entries 0 and 1 contains the LRU line, while bit 2 indicates the LRU line within the pair consisting of entries 3 and 4. If any of the entries in the set of four is currently invalid, the new line (and its tag, or page address) will be placed in the invalid entry. Intel did not define which empty entry would be used if there were more than one in the selected set. If all of the entries are currently in use, the processor consults the LRU bits to select the entry to overwrite. The newly-fetched line's source page number is then stored in the tag field in the selected directory entry and the line itself is stored in the same line of the respective cache way. The LRU bits are then updated to reflect the new ranking amongst the four entries (i.e., the new LRU). The bit that provides the ranking for the pair that was just updated would be flipped to its opposite state to indicate that, within the entry pair, the other entry is now the LRU. Bit 0 is flipped to its opposite state, indicating that the other pair is now the LRU pair.

Code Cache Castout

When a line that was in the code cache is overwritten with a newly read line from a different page of memory, this is referred to as a *castout* of a cache line. Since code cache lines are always the same as memory, the castout line can just be erased and needn't be cast back to the L2 and to memory. The line may still be in the L2 cache (if it also hasn't been cast out to make room for a new line) and will remain there until the L2's LRU algorithm determines that it must be cast out to make room for a new line being read from memory. Intel doesn't state whether, if the line is no longer in L2, the line in the code cache is cast back to the L2 rather than just being invalidated.

Code Cache Snoop Ports

The L1 code cache is triple-ported. It receives read requests from the prefetcher through one of its ports. In addition, it implements two snoop ports:

- **External snoop port**. When the processor latches a transaction request issued by another initiator, the address is forwarded to the internal caches for a lookup if it is a memory request. Refer to Table 7-1 on page 159 for the results of the snoop. Note that the table assumes that the line is not in the L1 data cache.
- **Internal snoop port**. Anytime a memory data write access is performed, the memory address is submitted to all three caches. If it results in a hit on the code cache, the code line is invalidated (S->I). For a detailed explanation, refer to the section entitled "Self-Modifying Code and Self-Snooping" on page 191.

Table 7-1: Results of External Snoop Presented to Code Cache

Type of External Transaction by Other Initiator	Initial State of Line in Code Cache	Snoop Result and Final State of Line in Code Cache
Memory read or write	I	• Indicate snoop miss to initiator. • Line stays in I state.
Memory read	S	• Indicate snoop hit to initiator. • Line stays in S state.
Memory write	S	• Indicate snoop miss to initiator (because the line is invalidated as a result of the write). • Invalidate line (S->I) because processor cannot snarf data being written to memory by another initiator.

Table 7-1: Results of External Snoop Presented to Code Cache (Continued)

Type of External Transaction by Other Initiator	Initial State of Line in Code Cache	Snoop Result and Final State of Line in Code Cache
Memory read and invalidate	I or S	• If line in I state, indicate snoop miss and line stays in I state. • If line in S state, indicate snoop miss (because the line is invalidated as a result of the read and invalidate) and line transitions from S->I state.

L1 Data Cache

As stated earlier, the size and structure of the L1 data cache is processor implementation-specific. The initial versions of the processor implement an 8KB, 2-way, set-associative data cache (pictured in Figure 7-3 on page 161), but as processor core speeds increase, the cache sizes may also be increased because the faster core can process code and data faster. Each of the data cache's cache banks, or ways, are further divided into two banks (more on this later).

Data Cache Uses MESI Cache Protocol

The L1 data cache exists for only one reason: to service memory data read and write requests originated as a result of code execution. Each line storage location within the data cache can currently be in one of four possible states:

- **Invalid state (I)**. There is no valid line in the entry.
- **Exclusive state (E)**. The line in the entry is valid, is still the same as memory (i.e., it is fresh, or clean), and no other processor has a copy of the line in its caches.
- **Shared state (S)**. The line in the entry is valid, still the same as memory, and one or more other processors may also have copies of the line (or may not because the processor cannot discriminate between reads by processors and reads performed by other, non-caching entities such as a host/PCI bridge).
- **Modified state (M)**. The line in the entry is valid, has been updated by this processor since it was read into the cache, and no other processor has a copy of the line in its caches. The line in memory is stale.

Figure 7-3: L1 Data Cache

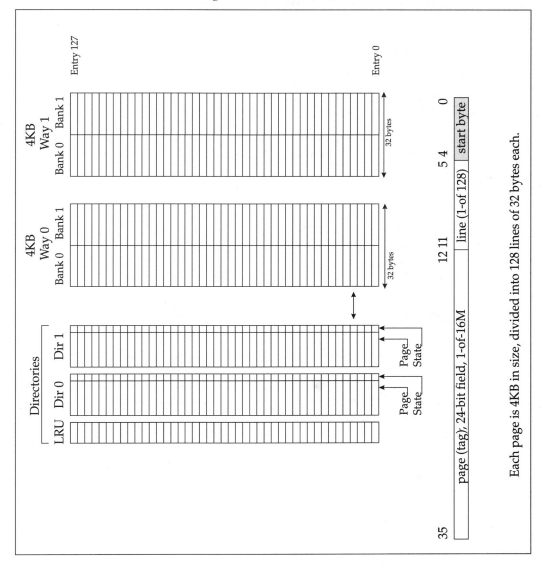

Each page is 4KB in size, divided into 128 lines of 32 bytes each.

Data Cache View of Memory Space

When performing a lookup, the data cache views memory as divided into pages equal to the size of one of its cache banks (or ways). Each of its cache ways is 4KB in size, so it views the 64GB of memory space as consisting of 16M pages, each 4KB in size. Furthermore, it views each memory page as having the same structure as one of its cache ways (i.e., a 4KB page of memory is subdivided into 128 lines, each of which is 32 bytes in size).

When a 32-bit linear memory address is submitted to the data cache by the processor core, it is first submitted to the data TLB (which resides at the front end of the data cache). The TLB translates the 32-bit linear address to a 36-bit physical memory address. The 36-bit physical memory address is viewed as illustrated in Figure 7-3 on page 161:

- The upper 24 bits identifies the target page (1-of-16M).
- The middle 7 bits identifies the line within the page (1-of-128).
- The lower 5 bits identify the exact start address of the target data within the line and is not necessary to perform the lookup in the cache.

Data TLB (DTLB)

The data TLB is incorporated in the front end of the data cache, translating the 32-bit linear address produced by the load and store units into the 36-bit physical memory address before the lookup is performed. The size and organization of the data TLB is processor design-specific. The current versions of the processor have the following geometry:

- the TLB for page table entries related to 4KB data pages is 4-way set-associative with 64 entries.
- The TLB for page table entries related to 2MB and 4MB data pages is 4-way set-associative with 8 entries.

For a detailed description of the linear-to-physical memory address translation process, refer to "Paging Enhancements" on page 439.

Data Cache Lookup

The target line number, contained in address bits [11:5], is used to index into the data cache directory and select a set of two entries to compare against. Each directory entry consists of a 24-bit tag field and a two-bit state field. The cache compares the target page number to each of the selected set of two entries that are currently in the valid state (E, S, or M).

Data Cache Hit

If the target page number matches the tag field in one of the entries in the E, S, or M state, it is a cache hit. The data cache has a copy of the target line from the target page. The line is in the cache way associated with the directory entry, residing in the entry selected by address bits [11:5]. The action taken by the data cache depends on:

* whether the data access is a read or a write
* the current state of the line
* the rules of conduct defined for this area of memory.

The sections that follow describe the actions taken by the data cache as a result of both cache hits and misses.

Relationship of L2 and L1 Caches

Refer to Figure 7-4 on page 164. The L2 cache acts as the backup for the L1 data and code caches. The sections that follow describe this relationship.

Figure 7-4: Relationship of L2 to L1 Caches

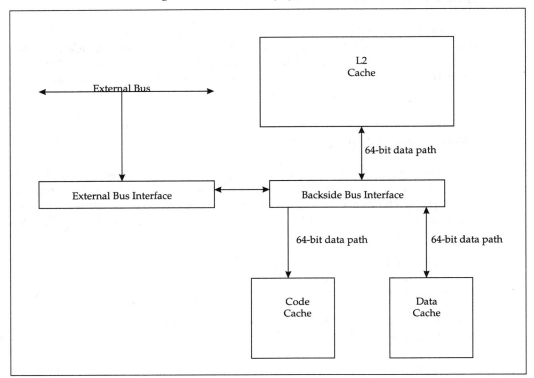

Relationship of L2 to L1 Code Cache

As stated earlier, the code cache only implements a subset of the MESI cache line states: S and I. The L2's relationship with the L1 code cache is therefore very simple. When the prefetcher request a line of code from the code cache, the request results in a hit or a miss.

In the event of a miss, the code cache issues a request to L2 cache. A lookup is performed in the L2 cache, resulting in a hit or a miss. If a hit, the requested line is supplied to the code cache one quadword at a time, critical quadword first. The line is placed in the code cache in the S state.

If the request results in an L2 cache miss, the L2 cache issues a request to the external bus interface and the line is read from external memory. During the transaction's snoop phase, caches in other processors report whether or not they have a copy of the line. If no other cache has a copy (snoop miss), the L2 cache places its copy in the E state upon completing the line read from memory. The code cache places its copy in the S state (the code cache only implements the S and I states). If any other processor's cache has a copy in the E or S state, the line is read from memory and is placed in the L2 and code caches in the S state. If any other processor's cache has a copy in the M state, the line is supplied from that processor's cache and is placed in the L2 and code caches in the S state. At the same time that the M line is supplied to this processor by the other processor, it is also written into memory. The line in the other processor's cache is therefore no longer different than memory. It transitions from the M to the S state.

Relationship of L2 and L1 Data Cache

Both the L2 and the L1 data caches are MESI caches. The relationship is therefore a little more complex than the L2's relationship with the code cache. The sections that follow provide a detailed description of the relationship. All of the cases described assume that the access is within a memory region defined as cacheable (i.e., the memory type is WT, WP, or WB). Furthermore, the discussion assumes that the L2 basically acts like a lookaside cache. As an example, assume that a line is read from memory and no one else has a copy (as indicated in the snoop phase of the transaction). If the area of memory is defined as WB, the line is placed in both caches (L2 and L1 data) in the E state, otherwise it's placed in the S state (lines from WT or WP memory are only stored in the S state). If any other processor indicates that it has a copy, the line is placed in both caches in the S state.

Intel does not document the interaction between the L2 and the data cache, however, so this discussion is based on hopefully intelligent speculation. It should be stressed that, even if this description is not the exact way that they have implemented it, it would work if designed this way. Furthermore, if they implemented it differently, it would be a variation on this discussion—not radically different.

Read Miss on L1 and L2

This discussion assumes:

*   caching has been enabled (in CR0)
*   the MTRRs have been initialized (defining some memory space as being cacheable)
*   the read is within an area defined as cacheable (i.e., the memory type is WT, WP, or WB).

In the event of a miss on both caches, the L2 cache issues a request to the external bus interface to perform a 32 byte read from memory. When this read transaction is performed, the system's other caches report the state of their copies of the line during the transaction's snoop phase. There are three possibilities:

1. Miss on all other caches.
2. Hit on one or more caches on a clean copy of the line (S or E state).
3. Hit on one other cache on a modified (M) copy of the line.

The sections that follow describe the actions taken in each of these cases.

Read Miss On All Other Caches. In this case, the line is read from memory. The state in which the line is stored depends on the rules of conduct defined within the memory area:

1. If defined as a WB area, the line is placed in the L2 and data caches in the E state.
2. If defined as a WT or WP area, the line is placed in the L2 and data caches in the S state.

Read Hit On E or S Line in One or More Other Caches. In this case, the line is read from memory. The line is placed in the L2 and data caches in the S state.

Read Hit On Modified Line in One Other Cache. In this case, the line is supplied by the cache that has the modified copy. At the same time that the line is being supplied to this processor's caches, it's accepted by the memory controller. Upon completion of the transfer, the line in the other processor's cache is therefore no longer different than memory, so the other processor transitions the state of its copy of the line from the M to the S state. In this processor's L2 and data caches, the line is placed in the S state.

Write Hit On L1 Data Cache

The following sections describe the actions taken when a data write is performed that hits on a line in the data cache. The actions taken depend on the state of the line and on the rules of conduct within the addressed memory region.

Write Hit on S Line in Data Cache. Unless, the area is designated as WP, the data cache line is updated. A write hit on an S line in a WP area has no effect on the data cache. Additional actions taken depend on the rules of conduct defined for the addressed memory area:

1. In a WT or WP area, the line stays in the S state and the write data is posted in the processor's posted write buffer to be written back to memory later. If the line is in both the L2 and the code cache, the line in both caches is invalidated (see "Self-Modifying Code and Self-Snooping" on page 191). If the line is only in the L2 cache, it is invalidated.

2. In a WB area, the data cache line changes to the M state. The line was in the data and L2 caches in the S state, indicating that at least one other processor has a copy of the line. A read and invalidate transaction for 0 bytes is sent to the external bus to kill copies of the line in all other caches. If the line is in both the L2 and the code cache, the line in both caches is invalidated (see "Self-Modifying Code and Self-Snooping" on page 191). If it's only in the L2 cache, it remains in the S state, but is stale (i.e., it has not been updated).

Write Hit On E Line in Data Cache. E copies of lines will only exists for regions of memory defined as WB. Lines from WT and WP areas are always stored in the S state. The write data is absorbed into the data cache line and the state of the line is changed from E to M. If the line is in both the L2 and the code cache, the line in both caches is invalidated (see "Self-Modifying Code and Self-Snooping" on page 191). If it's only in the L2 cache, it remains in the E state, but is stale (i.e., it has not been updated).

Write Hit On M Line in Data Cache. M copies of lines will only exist for regions of memory defined as WB. Lines from WT and WP areas are always stored in the S state. The write data is absorbed into the data cache line and the line stays in the M state.

Write Miss On L1 Data Cache

The actions taken by the processor depend on the rules of conduct defined for the memory area:

1. If defined as a WT or WP area, the write is posted in the processor's posted write buffer to be written back to memory later. If the line is in L2 and it's a WT memory region, the L2 copy is updated. If it's a WP memory region, the L2 copy is unaffected.

2. If defined as a WB area, the processor uses an "allocate-on-write" policy. It issues a read request to the L2 cache. This results either in a hit or a miss on the L2 cache.
   - If it results in a hit on L2, the line is supplied to the data cache from L2. The L2 copy of the line is invalidated. The data cache copy is immediately updated and marked modified (i.e., I->M).
   - If it results in an L2 miss, the line is read from memory using a 32-byte read and invalidate transaction to kill copies that may reside in

other caches. When the line is received, it isn't placed in the L2 cache, but is placed in the data cache, immediately updated, and placed in the M state (i.e., I->M).

L1 Data Cache Castout

When a data cache miss occurs, a read request is issued to the L2 cache. The line is then supplied to the data cache either from the L2 or from memory. In either case, the new line has to be stored in the data cache. If there aren't any empty entries in the selected set of cache entries, the data cache consults the LRU field (see "Data Cache LRU Algorithm: Make Room for the New Guy" on page 168) associated with the selected set of entries to determine which entry to castout to make room for the new line. The line being replaced (i.e., cast out), is in the E, S, or M state.:

- If the line is in the E or S state, it is still the same as the line in memory. When the line was read from memory, it was placed in both the L2 and the data caches. The line may or may not still be in the L2 cache (it may have been cast out to make room for a new line at some earlier point in time). If the line is still in L2, the line in the data cache is invalidated to make room for the new line. However, if the line is no longer in the L2 cache, the processor designers may have chosen to copy the line being cast out from the data cache to the L2 cache and invalidate it in the data cache, or may just invalidate it in the data cache. Intel doesn't define the action that is taken, but it's probably the former of the two (because keeping a copy of the line yields better performance if it's accessed again).
- If the line is in the M state, it is copied from the data cache to the L2 cache (still in the M state) and is invalidated in the data cache to make room for the new line.

Data Cache LRU Algorithm: Make Room for the New Guy

When a miss occurs in the L1 data cache, the line is supplied either by the L2 cache or from external memory. In either case, the new line must be stored in the data cache. The discussion of the data cache lookup described how the target line number is used as the index into the cache directory and selects a set of two entries to compare against.

Assume that both of the selected set of entries are currently in use. In other words, the data cache has copies of the targeted line, but from two pages other than the desired page. A cache miss occurs. As stated earlier, the line will be supplied either from the L2 cache or from memory. When received, it should be obvious that the line must be stored in the data cache. It will be stored in the cache in the same relative position as it resided in within the memory page—in other words, within the same line number in one of the two cache ways. One of the two entries in the selected set must therefore be overwritten (i.e., castout) with the new line and the new page number must be stored in the respective entry of the associated directory.

Figure 7-3 on page 161 illustrates that each set of two directory entries has an associated LRU (Least-Recently Used) bit that is used to keep track of the least-recently used of the set of two entries. When both entries are currently valid (E, S, or M) and the same line of a different page is read in, the processor consults the LRU bit to determine which of the two entries to overwrite. The LRU bit selects the one to be overwritten. After the new entry is made, the LRU bit for the pair is flipped to its opposite state to reflect the new ranking (i.e., the entry that wasn't updated is now the LRU of the two). As described earlier, if the cast out line is in the M state, it is copied to the L2 cache.

Figure 7-5: L1 Data Cache

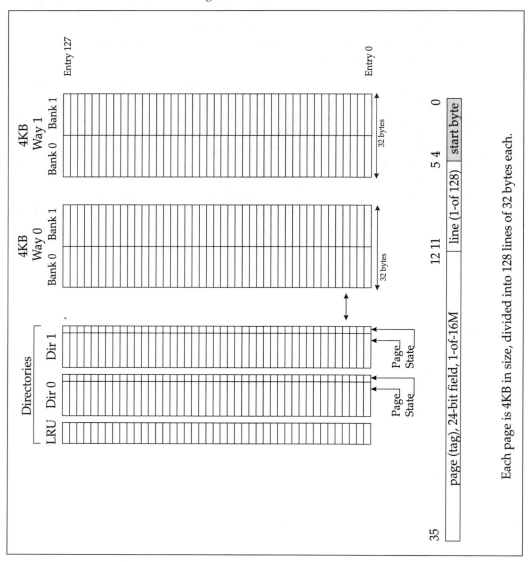

Chapter 7: The Processor Caches

Data Cache Pipeline

Figure 7-6 on page 172 illustrates the data and L2 cache pipeline stages.

1. When a load or a store is dispatched to the load or store execution units for execution, the memory address is submitted to the L1 data cache in the L1 pipeline stage.
2. During the next two clocks, the L2 and L3 stages, the lookup and, if a hit, the data transfer takes place.
3. If the access is a miss in the data cache and its a load, it enters the initial L2 cache pipeline stage, the L4 stage, where the address is submitted to the L2 cache for a lookup.
4. During the next two clocks, the L5 and L6 stages, the lookup and, if a hit, the data transfer of the critical quadword to the data cache takes place.

It should be obvious that a new memory request can be submitted in each clock cycle. Refer to the example pictured in Figure 7-7 on page 172. In the example, all of the accesses are hits on the L1 data cache. For a discussion of the L2 cache, refer to the section entitled "Unified L2 Cache" on page 179.

1. **Clock one**: The address for access one is latched in the L1 stage.
2. **Clock two**: Access one advances to the L2 stage and access two's address is latched (L1 stage of access two). Access one's access to the cache begins.
3. **Clock three**: access one advances to the L3 stage and the cache is read or written. Access two advances to the L2 stage and its access to the cache begins. Access three enters the L1 stage and it's address is latched.
4. **Clock four**: access two advances to the L3 stage and the cache is read or written. Access three advances to the L2 stage and its access to the cache begins. Access four enters the L1 stage and it's address is latched.
5. **Clock five**: access three advances to the L3 stage and the cache is read or written. Access four advances to the L2 stage and its access to the cache begins. Access five enter the L1 stage and it's address is latched.

The cache is completing a data access request in each clock.

Figure 7-6: Cache Pipeline Stages

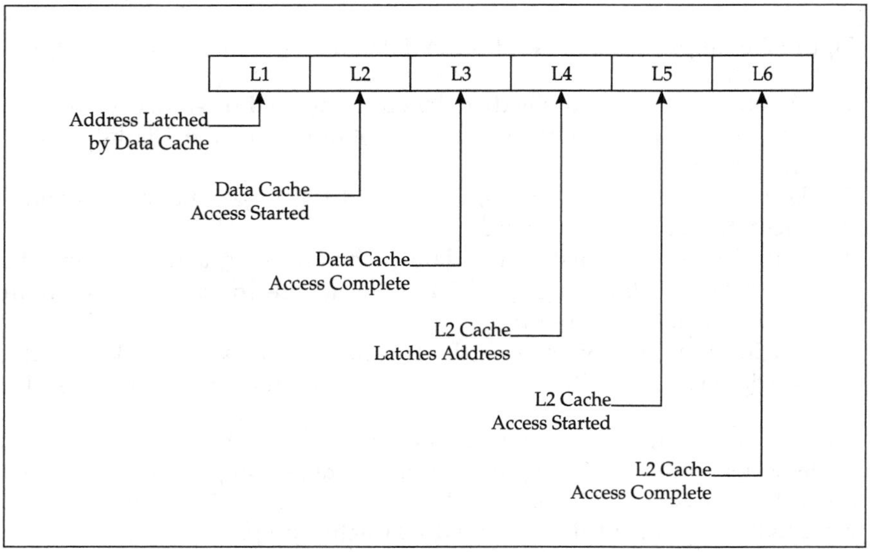

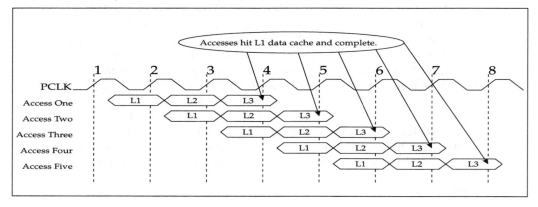

Figure 7-7: Example of Pipelined Data Cache Accesses

Data Cache is Non-Blocking

Earlier Processor Caches Blocked, but Who Cares?

In previous processors, a miss on the processor's cache resulted in a processor stall—no further memory requests could be submitted to the cache until the completion of the cache line fill from external memory. This means that data access requests generated by subsequent instructions that were executed could not be submitted for a lookup, thereby stalling the completion of those instructions. However, this was a moot point in the earlier Intel x86 processors because they always executed instructions in strict program order—if an instruction earlier in the program cannot complete due to a cache miss, the earlier processors would not proceed on to execute instructions that occur later in the program.

Pentium Pro Data Cache is Non-Blocking, and That's Important!

When a miss occurs on the Pentium Pro's data cache, however, the request is forwarded to the processor's L2 cache and the data cache is immediately available to service memory access requests (i.e., it does not block them) that might be generated by the execution of subsequent load or store instructions in the program. This is extremely important in a processor that performs out-of-order (OOO) execution—it couldn't work without it! When the data associated with the data cache miss is subsequently returned from the L2 cache or memory, it is placed into the data cache, the data access request initiated by the earlier, stalled instruction completes, and the instruction becomes ready for retirement. There are some rules regarding the order in which the data cache will accept requests generated as a result of out-of-order instruction execution:

- Loads generated by subsequent instructions can be serviced before a previously-stalled load completes.
- Loads generated by subsequent instructions can be serviced before a previously-stalled store completes, *as long as the load is from a different line.*
- Stores generated by subsequent instructions cannot be done before a previously-stalled store completes—*stores are always completed in order.*

Data Cache has Two Service Ports

Two Address and Two Data Buses

Refer to Figure 7-8 on page 175. The data cache has two, uni-directional data paths, each 64-bits wide, that connect it to the execution units:

- On a read that hits the data cache, the data cache output bus can deliver between one and eight bytes to the load execution unit per clock cycle.
- On a write that hits the data cache, the data cache input bus can deliver between one and eight bytes from the store data execution unit to the data cache.

The cache also has two address buses so that it can simultaneously receive two addresses generated by two execution units (load unit and store address unit) for data cache lookups.

The result is as follows:

- The data cache can deliver the data for one load request per clock.
- The data cache can accept write data for one store request per clock.
- The data cache can simultaneously (i.e., in the same clock) deliver data for a load request and accept the data for a store request (but see "Simultaneous Load/Store Constraint" on page 176).

Figure 7-8: Data and Address Bus Interconnect between Data Cache and Execution Units

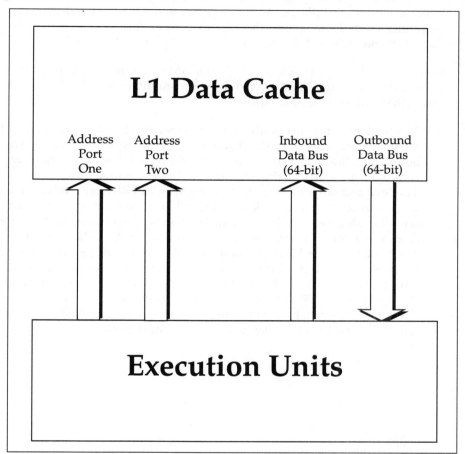

Simultaneous Load/Store Constraint

There is a constraint placed on the third scenario—the load and store can only be serviced simultaneously if they are in different cache ways or in the same cache way, but different line halves. Refer to Figure 7-9 on page 177.

Each of the data cache ways are divided into two, individually-addressable halves, or banks. If a load and store were simultaneously submitted to the cache, there are several possibilities:

- **The load and store hit in different cache ways**. The data cache can address the line in one way for the load and gate out the requested data onto its outbound data bus. It can simultaneously address the line in the other way and accept the write data arriving on the inbound data bus.
- **The load and store hit within the same way, but different halves**. The data cache can address the bank for the load and gate out the requested data onto its outbound data bus. It can simultaneously address the bank for the store and accept the write data arriving on the inbound data bus.
- **The load and store hit in the same half (i.e., bank) of the same way**. When the bank of SRAM is addressed, you can tell it that this is a read, or that it's a write, but you can't tell it that it's a read and write at the same time. The data pins on the SRAMs would have to simultaneously input and output data! It won't work. In this case, the data cache would service one request in one clock, and then the other request in the next clock.

Figure 7-9: Data Cache Structure

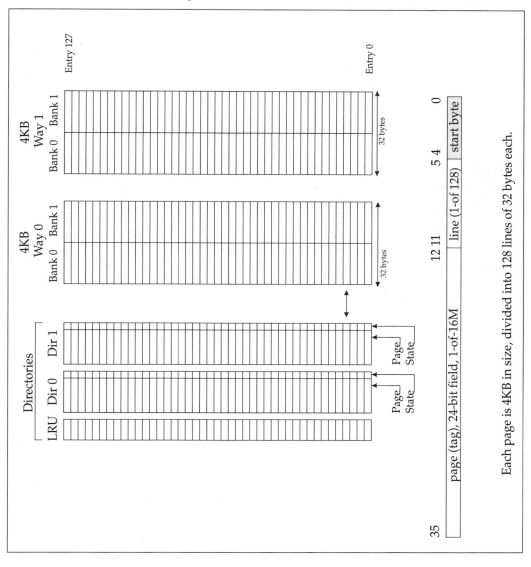

Each page is 4KB in size, divided into 128 lines of 32 bytes each.

Data Cache Snoop Ports

The L1 data cache is triple-ported. It can receive two simultaneous memory requests from the load and store address execution units. In addition, it implements a snoop port. When the processor latches a memory transaction request issued by another initiator, the address is forwarded to the internal caches for a lookup if it is a memory request. Refer to Table 7-2 on page 178 for the results of the snoop.

Table 7-2: Results of External Snoop Presented to Data Cache

Type of External Transaction by Other Initiator	Initial State of Line in Data Cache	Snoop Result and Final State of Line in Data Cache
Memory read or write	I	• Indicate snoop miss to initiator. • Line stays in I state.
Memory read	E	• Indicate snoop hit to initiator. • Change state E->S.
Memory read	S	• Indicate snoop hit to initiator. • No state change.
Memory read	M	• Indicate snoop hit on modified line to initiator. • Make copy of line in 32-byte processor writeback buffer and immediately write to memory (and initiator). The write to memory is referred to as an implicit writeback operation. • Change state of line from M->S.
Memory write	S or E	• Indicate snoop miss to initiator (because the line is invalidated as a result of the write). • Invalidate line (S->I or E->I).

Table 7-2: Results of External Snoop Presented to Data Cache (Continued)

Type of External Transaction by Other Initiator	Initial State of Line in Data Cache	Snoop Result and Final State of Line in Data Cache
Memory write	M	• Indicate snoop hit on modified line to initiator. • Unload line from cache to processor's 32-byte writeback buffer and invalidate line (M->I). • Immediately write line in writeback buffer to memory (implicit writeback).
Memory read and invalidate	S or E	• Indicate snoop miss to initiator (because the line is invalidated as a result of the read and invalidate). • Invalidate line (S->I or E->I).
Memory read and invalidate	M	• Indicate snoop hit on modified line to initiator. • Unload line from cache to processor's 32-byte writeback buffer and invalidate line (M->I). • Immediately write line in writeback buffer to memory (implicit writeback) and to the initiator.

Unified L2 Cache

The current processor versions implement a 4-way set-associative unified L2 cache. The size and presence of the L2 cache is implementation-specific. The initial implementations are 256KB and 512KB in size. A recently-released 200MHz version has a 1MB L2 cache.

L2 Cache Uses MESI Protocol

When the L1 code or data cache has a miss, it submits its request to the processor's L2 cache for a lookup. The L2 lookup results either in a hit or a miss. If it's a miss, the L2 cache issues a request to the external bus unit to fetch the line from memory. Meanwhile, the L2 cache continues to service requests issued by the L1 caches (like the data cache, it's non-blocking). Eventually, the line is fetched from external memory and is placed in the L2 and L1 caches. If the snoop result was a hit, the line is placed in the L2 cache in the S state. If the snoop resulted in a miss on all other caches, the line is placed in the L2 cache in the E state. Assuming that the data cache issued the request, the line is placed in the data cache in the E or the S state, depending on the snoop result. For more information on the relationship of the L2 and data caches, refer to "Relationship of L2 and L1 Caches" on page 163.

Figure 7-10: 256KB L2 Cache

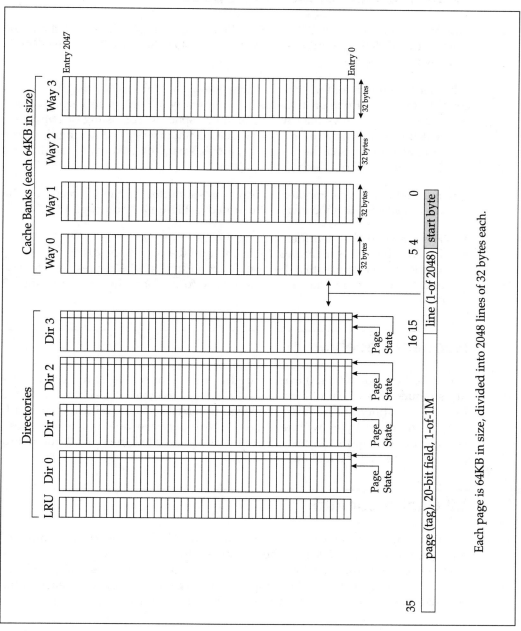

L2 Cache View of Memory Space

This explanation uses the 256KB L2 cache as the example. Note that the cache ways in the 512KB L2 would be twice as deep—4096 lines vs. 2048 lines—but is still 4-way set-associative.

When performing a lookup, the L2 cache views memory as divided into pages equal to the size of one of its cache banks (or ways). Each of its cache ways is 64KB in size, so it views the 64GB of memory space as consisting of 1M pages, each 64KB in size. Furthermore, it views each memory page as having the same structure as one of its cache ways (i.e., a 64KB page of memory is subdivided into 2048 lines, each of which is 32 bytes in size).

When a 36-bit physical memory address is submitted to the L2 cache by the code or data cache, it is viewed as illustrated in Figure 7-10 on page 181:

- The upper 20 bits identifies the target page (1-of-1M).
- The middle 11 bits identifies the line within the page (1-of-2048).
- The lower 5 bits identify the exact start address of the requested information within the line and is not necessary to perform the lookup in the L2 cache.

Request Received

An L1 cache (code or data) experienced a miss because one of the processor's units requested an item of information. The address that was submitted to the L1 cache identified the quadword needed (referred to as the critical quadword) and the required bytes within it (somewhere between one and eight bytes). Upon experiencing the L1 miss, the L1 cache forwarded the critical quadword address to the L2 for a lookup.

L2 Cache Lookup

The target line number, contained in address bits [15:5] of the critical quadword address, is used to index into the L2 cache directory and select a set of four entries to compare against. Each directory entry consists of a 20-bit tag field and a two bit state field. The cache compares the target page number to each of the selected set of four entries that are currently in the valid state (E, S, or M).

L2 Cache Hit

If the lookup results in a hit on the L2 cache and it's a read request, the requested line is sent back to the L1 cache that requested it. Because the data path between the L2 cache and the L1 caches is only 64-bits wide (see Figure 7-11 on page 183), the line is sent back to the L1 cache one quadword at a time. The critical quadword is always sent back first in order to satisfy and unstall the instruction that caused the miss. The other three quadwords that comprise the line are then sent back (Intel does not define the order in which they are transferred). As illustrated in Figure 7-11 on page 183, there is only data path to service both L1 caches. This means that only one of the L1 caches can be sent data at a time.

Figure 7-11: Data Path between L2 and L1 Caches

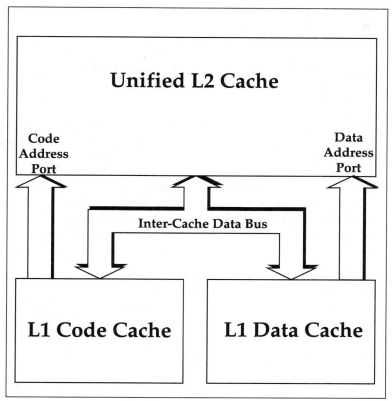

L2 Cache Miss

When an L2 cache miss occurs, the line must be fetched from memory. The backside bus unit issues a request to the external bus unit. The external bus unit arbitrates for the request signal group (see "Obtaining Bus Ownership" on page 221) and issues a request for the line, requesting the critical quadword first. The 32-byte line is supplied to the processor one quadword at a time, critical quadword first, in toggle mode transfer order (see "Toggle Mode Transfer Order" on page 189). The critical quadword is sent back to the requesting L1 cache immediately upon receipt (so that the execution unit that initiated the request can unstall). It is also placed in the entry selected in the L2 and L1 caches. The remaining three quadwords are transferred back to the processor and, when the entire line has been received, the L2 cache places it in the E or the S state, and the L1 cache places it in the appropriate state (if the code cache, it is placed in the S state; if the data cache, it is placed in the appropriate state—see "L1 Data Cache" on page 160.

L2 Cache LRU Algorithm: Make Room for the New Guy

When a cache miss occurs and a new line must be fetched from memory, it must then be stored somewhere in the L2 cache. When the cache lookup was performed, the target line number in bits [15:5] was used as the index into the cache directories, selecting a set of four directory entries to examine. If all four of the entries are currently valid but do not have a copy of the selected line from the targeted page, the cache uses the LRU bit field (see Figure 7-10 on page 181) associated with the selected set of four entries to determine which of the four to cast out to make room for the new line when it arrives from memory. The entry selected for castout is in the E, S, or M state.

If the castout line is in the E or S state, it can just be erased. If in the M state, however, it is the freshest copy of the line (the one in memory is stale). The processor unloads it from the cache (to make room for the new line) into a 32-byte writeback buffer and schedules it to be written back to memory. The writeback of the modified line is not considered to be a high-priority operation. If the processor has other writes that are considered more important, they will occur first.

Whenever another bus initiator starts a memory transaction, the processor must snoop the memory address in its caches. It should be obvious that it must also snoop it in its writeback buffers. If the initiator is addressing the modified line currently sitting in a writeback buffer waiting to be written back to memory, the processor will signal a hit on a modified line and immediately supply the data to memory from its writeback buffer. This is referred to as an implicit writeback of a modified line (see the chapter entitled "The Response and Data Phases" on page 297 for more information).

The L2 cache is a 4-way set-associative cache, as is the L1 code cache. As with the L1 code cache, Intel does not document how the LRU algorithm is implemented. For an explanation of the 486 method (which is also a 4-way set-associative cache), refer to "Code Cache LRU Algorithm: Make Room for the New Guy" on page 157.

L2 Cache Pipeline

Refer to Figure 7-12 on page 186. When a miss occurs in the L1 data or code caches, the critical quadword address is forwarded to the L2 cache for a lookup.

1. The address is latched by the L2 cache in the L4 stage.
2. The access to the L2 cache is started in the L5 stage.
3. The access to the L2 cache is completed in the L6 stage.

A load or store that hits the L1 data cache completes in 3 clocks, while one that misses L1 but hits the L2 completes in 6 clocks (if it results in a hit). If the load or store misses L2, it can't complete until the critical quadword arrives from memory.

It should be obvious that a new memory request can be submitted to the L2 cache in each clock cycle. Refer to the example pictured in Figure 7-13 on page 187. In the example, accesses one, three and four are data cache hits, while accesses two and five are misses on the L1 data cache and hits on the L2 cache. For a discussion of the L1 data cache, refer to the section entitled "L1 Data Cache" on page 160.

Figure 7-12: The L1 Data and L2 Cache Pipeline Stages

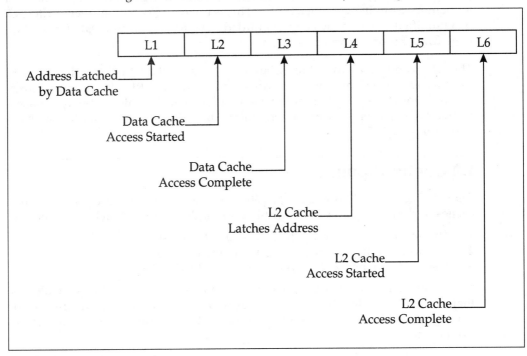

Figure 7-13: Example of Pipelined L2 Cache Accesses Resulting in Hits

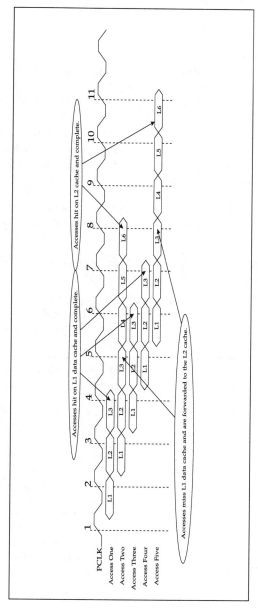

L2 Cache Snoop Ports

The L2 cache has two snoop ports:

- **Internal snoop port**. When a data write (i.e., a store) is performed that hits the L1 data cache, the address is also submitted to the L2 cache via its internal snoop port and, if valid, the appropriate action is taken. Refer to "Relationship of L2 and L1 Caches" on page 163 and "Self-Modifying Code and Self-Snooping" on page 191.
- **External snoop port**. When the processor latches a transaction request issued by another initiator, the address is forwarded to the three internal caches for a lookup if it is a memory request. Refer to Table 7-3 on page 188 for the results of the snoop.

Table 7-3: Results of External Snoop Presented to L2 Cache

Type of External Transaction by Other Initiator	Initial State of Line in L2 Cache	Snoop Result and Final State of Line in L2 Cache
Any type	I	No effect on line state. Snoop result = miss.
Memory read	E or S	Snoop result = hit. If the line is in the E state, E->S. If in S state, no change.
	M	Snoop result = hit on modified line. Line is supplied to request agent and memory from L2 cache and its state is changed from M->S.
Memory write	E or S	Line invalidated (S->I). Snoop result = miss.
	M	Snoop result = hit on modified line. Line is supplied to request agent and memory from L2 cache and its state is changed from M->I.

Table 7-3: Results of External Snoop Presented to L2 Cache (Continued)

Type of External Transaction by Other Initiator	Initial State of Line in L2 Cache	Snoop Result and Final State of Line in L2 Cache
Memory read and invalidate	E or S	Line invalidated (S->I). Snoop result = miss.
	M	Snoop result = hit on modified line. Line is supplied to request agent and memory from L2 cache and its state is changed from M->I.

Toggle Mode Transfer Order

The processor transfers a full 32-byte cache line to or from memory under the following circumstances:

1. When a **miss** occurs **on the L1 and L2** caches, the line is read from memory.
2. When a **write miss** occurs on the data cache **in** a memory **area designated as WB**, the L1 data cache first attempts to read the line from the L2 cache. If it misses L2, the line is read from memory using the memory read and invalidate transaction.
3. When a new line is being read into the L2 cache from memory, the L2 cache's LRU algorithm is used to select which of the selected set of four L2 entries it will be stored in. If the selected entry is currently occupied by a modified line from another area of memory, the L2 cache unloads (i.e., **casts out**) the modified line from the cache to make room for the new line. The modified line is placed in a writeback buffer and scheduled to be written back to memory. When the memory write is later performed on the bus, it will write the full line to memory.
4. When the processor snoops an external transaction request initiated by another bus agent, it may result in a **snoop hit on a modified line** in the data cache. The processor supplies the data line to the bus agent (and changes the state of its line based on the type of transaction).

Whenever a full line is transferred over the bus, it is transferred in toggle mode order, critical quadword first. Refer to Table 7-4 on page 190. The transfer order of the four quadwords that comprise the line is based on the position of the critical quadword within the line. As an example, assume that an instruction must read two bytes from memory starting at location 1012h. These two bytes reside in the quadword comprised of locations 1010h through 1017h. In turn, this quadword is the third quadword in the line that consists of locations 1000h through 101Fh—quadwords 1000h through 1007h, 1008h through 100Fh, *1010h through 1017h*, and 1018h through 101Fh. The transfer order will be:

- First quadword transferred is the critical quadword that contains the two bytes requested by the execution unit—1010h through 1017h.
- Second quadword transferred is 1018h through 101Fh.
- Third quadword transferred is 1000h through 1007h.
- Fourth quadword transferred is 1008h through 100F.

Table 7-4: Toggle Mode Quadword Transfer Order

In Critical Quadword	2nd quadword transferred	3rd quadword transferred is	4th quadword transferred is
If least-significant address 2 digits = 00h	one with least-significant 2 address digits = 08h	one with least-significant 2 address digits = 10h	one with least-significant 2 address digits = 18h
If least-significant 2 address digits = 08h	one with least-significant 2 address digits = 00h	one with least-significant 2 address digits = 18h	one with least-significant 2 address digits = 10h
If least-significant 2 address digits = 10h	one with least-significant 2 address digits = 18h	one with least-significant 2 address digits = 00h	one with least-significant 2 address digits = 08h
If least-significant 2 address digits = 18h	one with least-significant 2 address digits = 10h	one with least-significant 2 address digits = 08h	one with least-significant 2 address digits = 00h

The toggle mode transfer order is the one used by Intel since the advent of the 486 processor and is based on implementing main memory using an interleaved memory architecture (pictured in Figure 7-14 on page 191). Notice that the quadwords are woven, or interleaved, between the two banks. As each of the four accesses is performed, it is always the opposite DRAM memory bank that is being accessed. During each quadword access, the bank of memory that is not being accessed is charging back up after it was accessed. By the time the access to the current bank is completed, the other bank is all charged up and ready to accept another access. This bank-swapping results in good performance because the processor doesn't have to wait for the DRAM memory chips' precharge delay to elapse before accessing the next quadword in the series.

Figure 7-14: 2-Way Interleaved Memory Architecture

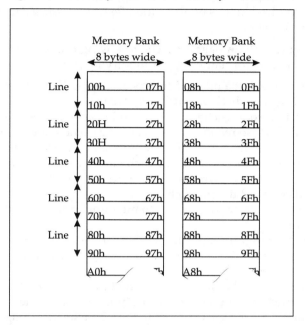

Self-Modifying Code and Self-Snooping

Description

Normally the instructions that comprise a program are always executed as they were originally written by the programmer. Sometimes, however, the programmer chooses to start off executing an instruction or series of instructions as originally composed, but then later modifies the instruction(s) on the fly so that when executed the next time, it will execute in its modified form and have a different effect. This is accomplished by reading the instruction(s) into the processor's register set, modifying it, and then writing it back to memory. The next time the prefetcher fetches the modified instruction(s), they execute in their modified form and have the desired (i.e., altered) effect.

Generally speaking, self-modifying code is considered evil. Processor designers have to support it because people write it, but they usually don't optimize its performance—quite the opposite—you usually take quite a performance hit when it's executed. As one example, read the section entitled "The Internal

Snoop" in MindShare's book entitled *Pentium Processor System Architecture* (published by Addison-Wesley). For another, refer to the section on self-modifying code in MindShare's book entitled *PowerPC System Architecture* (published by Addison-Wesley).

Refer to Figure 7-15 on page 194. The following numbered list defines the Pentium Pro's method for handling self-modifying code:

1. The first time that a piece of code is executed, the prefetcher issues a request for the line of code that contains the instructions.
2. If there is a code cache miss, the code cache issues the request to the L2 cache. If this also results in a miss, the L2 cache issues a request to the external bus unit to fetch the line from memory. When the line is returned from memory, it is placed in the L2 cache and is also placed in the code cache. The code cache, in turn, passes it on to the prefetch streaming buffer (what used to be called the prefetch queue).
3. The instructions are decoded into micro-ops and are executed in their original form.
4. When the programmer later wishes to modify one or more instructions in this program, he or she uses a `mov` instruction to read the instruction into a register.
5. The memory read request is submitted to the data cache, resulting in a miss (the instruction is in the code cache, not the data cache).
6. The data cache issues a request to the L2 cache, resulting in an L2 cache hit. The L2 supplies the data (it's really code being temporarily treated as data) to the L1 data cache and the data cache supplies it to the load execution unit which places the data in the target register.
7. The programmer then modifies the instruction in the register.
8. Using a `mov` instruction, the programmer writes the data (i.e., the altered instruction) back to memory.
9. The write request is submitted to the L1 data, L1 code, and L2 caches as well as to the prefetch streaming buffer.
10. The code cache and L2 cache both have hits and invalidate their copy of the code line.
11. As the code line may have already been read into the prefetch streaming buffer again (due to a branch prediction), the processor also performs a lookup in the streaming buffer. If it's a hit, the buffer is flushed. Note that whereas the lookup in the caches is based on the physical memory address, the streaming buffer lookup is based on the linear address (before the paging unit converts it to a physical address). This means that the programmer should always use the same linear address to fetch and to modify the instruction.
12. The data cache has a hit and updates its copy of the line. However, because it is also a hit on the code cache (the lookup is performed in all three caches

simultaneously), the updated line is unloaded from the data cache (i.e., it's placed in a 32-byte writeback buffer, invalidated in the data cache, and is scheduled to be written back to memory).

13. The next time that the prefetcher attempts to read the line (to execute the code again), it results in a miss on both the L1 code and L2 caches and the processor initiates a memory read transaction to read the line from memory.

14. The processor snoops its own read transaction (*self-snooping!*) in its caches (it always does this, I just didn't mention it before) and in its writeback buffers. There are two possible cases: the modified line that was unloaded from the data cache earlier has either already been written back to memory or it has not.

   • **Case A**: If the self-snoop doesn't result in a hit in its writeback buffers, the line has already been written back to memory and the processor reads the line from memory into its L2 and code caches.

   • **Case B**: If there is a hit on its writeback buffers, the line has not yet been written back to memory. The processor drives the modified line onto the bus during the data phase of the transaction and reads it back into the L2 and code caches *at the same time!* Main memory also receives the modified line.

15. The code cache passes the line to the prefetch streaming buffer and the instructions are decoded and executed in their modified form.

Figure 7-15: Processor Cache Overview

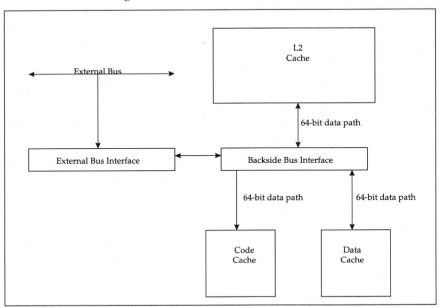

Don't Let Your Data and Code Get Too Friendly!

Even though you may not write self-modifying code, the scenario described in the previous section can still occur, resulting in terrible performance for your program. Consider the case where you place some data in memory immediately following a program. The instructions at the end of your program and the data may reside within the same line. When you read any of these data items into a register, the entire line, comprised of mixed code and data, is read into the data cache. If you change the data in the register and then write it back to memory, it results in a hit on the data, code and L2 caches. The procedure described in the preceding section is then performed (in other words, the processor thinks that you are modifying code in the data cache).

ECC Error Handling

When a cache entry is made, ECC information is stored with the tag and with the line. Whenever the entry is read (during a lookup) the tag and the line are checked against their ECC data. If an uncorrectable error is detected, the processor asserts its IERR# output. If the machine check exception is enabled (CR4[MCE] = 1), an error is reported in one of the machine check architecture register banks (see "Machine Check Architecture" on page 477). Alternately, the processor can be configured via its EBL_CR_POWERON MSR (see "Program-Accessible Startup Features" on page 45) to assert its IERR# and BERR# outputs when an internal error occurs. When the chipset detects BERR# asserted, it can assert NMI to one of the processors to invoke the NMI handler. ECC information is also stored with the line of information and is checked for correctness whenever the line is read.

Procedure to Disable All Caching

The correct procedure is as follows:

1. Disable caching by setting CR0[CD] to one and CR0[NW] to zero.
2. Execute the WBINVD instruction. This will cause the processor to write back all modified lines to memory and then invalidate both L1 caches and the L2 cache.
3. Disable the MTRRs (see "State of the MTRRs after Reset" on page 137) by setting the default memory type to UC, or set all MTRRs to the UC memory type.

To ensure memory consistency, the cache invalidation must be done with caching disabled (see step 1).

Hardware
Section 2:
Bus Intro
and Arbitration

The Previous Section

The chapters that comprise Part 2, Section 1 focused on the processor's internal operation.

This Section

The chapters that comprise Part 2, Section 2 step outside the processor and introduce the processor's bus and transaction protocol. It consists of the following chapters:

- "Bus Electrical Characteristics" on page 199.
- "Bus Basics" on page 207.
- "Obtaining Bus Ownership" on page 221.

The Next Section

Part 2 Section 3 provides a detailed description of each phase that a transaction passes through from inception to completion.

8 Bus Electrical Characteristics

The Previous Chapter

The previous chapter provided a detailed description of the processor's L1 data and code caches, as well as its unified L2 cache. This included a discussion of self-modifying code and toggle mode transfer order during transfer of a cache line on the bus.

This Chapter

This chapter introduces the electrical characteristics of the Pentium Pro processor's bus.

The Next Chapter

The next chapter provides an introduction to the features of the bus and also introduces concepts critical to understanding its operation.

Introduction

One of the keys to a high-speed signaling environment is to utilize a low-voltage swing (LVS) to change the state of a signal from one state to the other. The Pentium Pro bus falls into this category. It permits the operation of the bus at speeds of 60MHz or higher. The bus is implemented using a modified version of the industry standard GTL (Gunning Transceiver Logic) specification, referred to by Intel as GTL+. The spec has been modified to provide larger noise margins and reduce ringing. This was accomplished by using a higher termination voltage and controlling the edge rates. The net result is that the bus supports more electrical loads (currently up to eight devices) than it would if implemented using the standard GTL spec. The sections that follow introduce the basic concepts behind the bus's operation. A detailed GTL+ spec can be found in the Intel processor data book.

Pentium Pro and Pentium II System Architecture

Everything's Relative

Every device that resides on the bus implements a comparator (i.e., a differential receiver) at each of its inputs. When a device samples the state of one of its bus inputs (sampling occurs on the rising-edge of BCLK), the value sampled (i.e., the voltage level) is compared to a standard reference voltage supplied to the device by a voltage divider network on the motherboard (see Figure 8-1 on page 200, where Vtt is the pullup, or termination, voltage). *Vtt = 1.5Vdc +/- 10%*. If the sampled voltage is higher than the reference voltage by a sufficient margin, it represents an electrical high, while if it's sufficiently lower than the reference voltage, it represents an electrical low (the margins are pictured in Figure 8-2 on page 201 and are described in "How High is High and How Low is Low?" on page 204).

The great thing about this bus is that the differential receivers in bus devices determine highs and lows in a voltage-independent manner. The devices don't have to be redesigned if different voltage levels are used to indicate a high and a low— just supply a different reference voltage to the device!

Figure 8-1: Each GTL Input Uses a Comparator

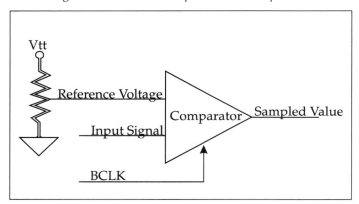

Figure 8-2: Logic Levels

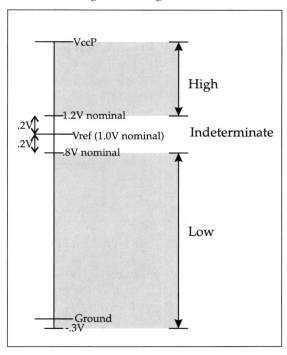

All Signals Active Low

All signals on the bus are open-drain, asserted low signals. This includes the data bus and the address bus! The address bus is designated as A[35:3]#, the # sign indicating asserted when low. A logical one on an address signal is represented by an electrical low, and a logical zero as an electrical high. The same is true for the data bus, D[63:0]#. *Just as a reminder (it was mentioned earlier in the book), Intel represents bus signal values in the data book's tables as logical values, not electrical values—so pay close attention to the fact that this is the reverse of their values when viewed on the bus.*

To place an electrical high on a signal, don't drive it. The pullup resistors (see Figure 8-3 on page 202) keep the line high. In other words, the only time that a device actually drives a GTL+ signal is when it asserts it to place an electrical low on the line. To deassert a signal, turn off the output driver. The pullups pull the line back high (very rapidly!).

Powerful Pullups Snap Lines High Fast

The values chosen for the termination pullups used on either end of a GTL+ trace (see Figure 8-3 on page 202) are such that they return the line back to the electrically-high state very rapidly. The signals therefore have very fast edge rates and tend to overshoot and ring for some time before settling. The resistor values for the pullups on the ends of a trace match either:

- the effective impedance of the trace or
- the average impedance of all of the GTL+ trace runs.

The Rt (pullup resistor value) is typically in the range from 25 to 65 ohms.

The Layout

Refer to Figure 8-3 on page 202. Each signal line is daisy-chained between bus agents and is pulled up to Vtt on both ends. No stubs are permitted when connecting each device to the trace run. In reality, however, it is impossible to have a completely stubless connection to each of the bus agents. The only stub permitted is the connection to each device's pin pad and each of these should not exceed 250ps (the maximum allowable flight time for the signal to traverse the stub) in length. Maintaining 3" +/- 30% inter-device spacing minimizes the variation in noise margins between networks (note that this is a recommendation, not a rule).

Figure 8-3: GTL Bus Layout Basics

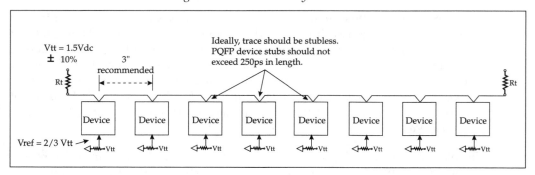

Chapter 8: Bus Electrical Characteristics

Synchronous Bus

A device starts to drive a signal on the bus on the rising-edge of BCLK and signals are only sampled on the rising-edge of the BCLK (Bus Clock) at the point where the BCLK rising-edge cross the Vtt level. BCLK is not a GTL+ signal. Rather, it is a 3.3V-tolerant signal and is supplied to all bus agents from a central source. This ensures that all of the bus devices are synchronized to the same clock.

Setup and Hold Specs

Refer to Figure 8-4 on page 204.

Setup Time

The minimum setup time is 2.2ns. Setup time is defined as: the minimum time from the input signal crossing the Vref threshold (i.e., the reference voltage) on its way from a low to a high or a high to a low to when the BCLK signal's rising-edge crosses the Vtt threshold(i.e., the pullup voltage value).

Hold Time

The minimum hold time is specified as:

- .45ns for the 150MHz processor with a 256KB L2 cache
- .7ns for other versions of the processor.

The hold time is defined as: the minimum time from BCLK crossing the Vtt threshold to when the input signal crosses the Vref threshold.

Figure 8-4: Setup and Hold Specs

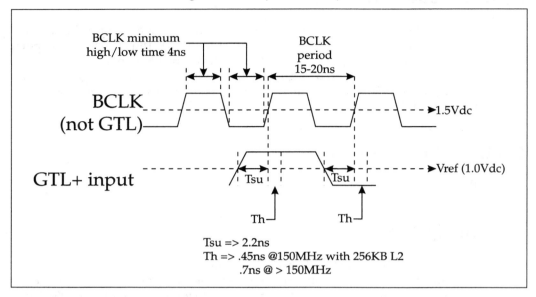

How High is High and How Low is Low?

When the value at an input is sampled (when the rising-edge of the BCLK crosses the Vtt level), it is determined to be a **low or high** as follows:

- -.3Vdc<=**LOW**<=Vref-.2Vdc
- Vref+.2Vdc<=**HIGH**<=VccP

where Vref = 2/3 of Vtt and VccP is the processor die's operating voltage. For the Pentium Pro processor, the **VccP** is specified as follows:

- For the 150Mhz processor with 256KB L2 cache: 2.945Vdc<=VccP<=3.255, typical = 3.1Vdc.
- For all other processor versions: 3.135Vdc<=VccP<=3.465Vdc, typical = 3.3Vdc.

Vtt = 1.5Vdc +/- 10%.
Vref = 2/3 of Vtt +/- 2%.
Vref therefore = 1.0Vdc.

Chapter 8: Bus Electrical Characteristics

After You See Something, You have One Clock to Do Something About It

The protocol is defined in a manner that always allows one clock after a condition is detected before an agent must present a reply. As an example, refer to Figure 8-5 on page 205. Assume that a processor detects that it has acquired bus ownership on the rising-edge of clock one. It takes action on this by assuming bus ownership starting on the rising-edge of clock two and driving out its transaction request onto the appropriate signals. It doesn't have to detect the condition on the rising-edge of clock one and present its reply in the same clock so that it will be seen by others on the rising-edge of clock two.

Figure 8-5: Example

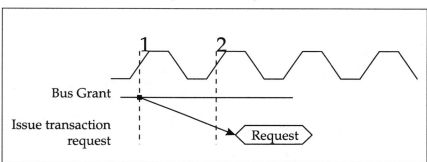

9 *Bus Basics*

The Previous Chapter

The previous chapter introduced the electrical characteristics of the Pentium Pro processor's bus.

This Chapter

This chapter provides an introduction to the features of the bus and introduces terminology and concepts critical to an understanding of its operation.

The Next Chapter

Before a request agent can issue a new transaction to the bus, it must arbitrate for and win ownership of the request signal group. The next chapter covers all of the issues related to obtaining ownership of the request signal group. This includes:

- bus arbitration among symmetric agents (i.e., the processors).
- bus arbitration by the priority agent(s) (e.g., the host/PCI bridge) and how this affects arbitration among the symmetric agents.
- How bus locking affects arbitration.
- How an agent or agents can block the issuance of new requests.

Agents

Agent Types

All devices that resides on the processor bus are referred to as *agents*. Basically, there are three type of agents:

- **Request agent** is the device that initiates a transaction (in other words, the initiator) by issuing a request (e.g., a memory read or write, or an IO read or write). It is commonly referred to as the transaction *initiator*.

- **Response agent** is the target of the transaction (e.g., an IO target or a memory target).
- **Snoop agents** are any devices on the bus that have memory caches (usually processors, but, as an example, in addition to the processors there could be an external, L3 cache that resides on the bus). Whenever any initiator starts a transaction, it is latched by all bus agents including the snoopers. If it is a memory transaction, the memory address is then submitted to the snoopers' caches for a lookup and the results of this "snoop" are reported back to the transaction initiator. The results will be one of the following:
  - **snoop miss**—doesn't have a copy of the addressed line at all.
  - **snoop hit**—one or more of the snoopers has a copy of the addressed line in the E or S state and it hasn't been changed since being read from memory.
  - **snoop hit on a modified line**—one of the snoopers has a copy of the line and one or more of the bytes in the line has been changed since the line was copied into the cache from memory. The line in memory is stale.

Multiple Personalities

Some agents are only capable of acting as response agents (i.e., the target of the transaction). As an example, the main memory controller typically acts as the target of memory reads and writes. It never initiates transactions, nor does it ever act as a snoop agent in a transaction.

Some agents are capable of acting as the response agent in some transactions and as the request agent for other transactions. As an example, in Figure 9-1 on page 210 one of the host/PCI bridges may:

- act as the response agent (i.e., the target) of a processor-initiated transaction to read data from an IO port in a PCI device beyond the bridge.
- act as the request initiator of a memory write transaction when a PCI master behind the bridge is writing data to main memory.

An agent may act as the request agent for transactions that it initiates and as the snoop agent for memory transactions initiators by others. An example would be a processor. It not only initiates transactions on an as-needed basis, but also snoops memory transactions that are initiated by the other processors or by the host/PCI bridges (for PCI masters).

Uniprocessor vs. Multiprocessor Bus

As noted in "Bus on Earlier Processors Inefficient for Multiprocessing" on page 26, the Pentium bus is ill-suited in a platform wherein multiple processors reside on the host bus (see Figure 9-1 on page 210) and must therefore compete for ownership of it when they need to perform a transaction.

The Pentium Pro bus has been specifically designed to support multiple processors on the same bus. The following major changes have been made:

- In a typical Pentium Pro bus environment, up to eight transactions can be currently outstanding at various stages of completion.
- If the target of a transaction cannot deal with a new transaction right now (e.g., due to a logic busy condition), rather than tie up the bus by inserting wait states, it will issue a *retry* to the initiator. This causes the initiator to wait a little while and try the transaction again at a later time. This frees up the bus for other initiators.
- If the target of a read or write transaction realizes that it will take a fairly long time to complete the data transfer (i.e., provide read data or accept write data), it can instruct the initiator to break the connection and the target will later initiate a transaction to complete the transfer. This is referred to as *transaction deferral*.

These mechanisms prevent any properly-designed bus agent from tying up the bus for extended periods of time. A detailed description of the processor's bus is presented later in the book.

Figure 9-1: Block Diagram of a Typical Server System

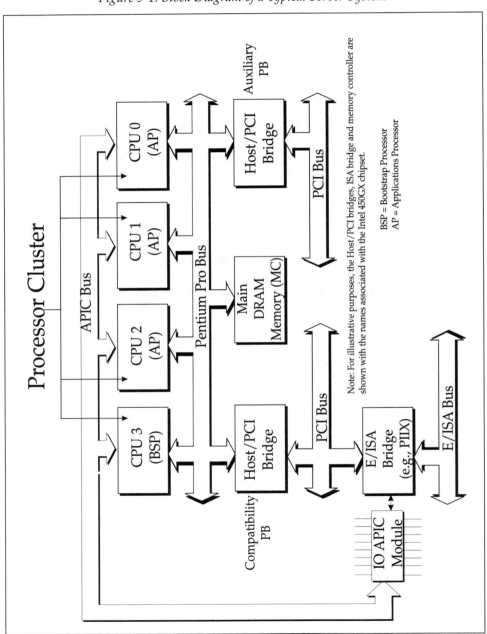

Request Agents

Request Agent Types

There are two type of request agents:

- **symmetric request agents**—most typically, these are the processors. With regard to bus arbitration, the symmetric request agents have equal importance with respect to each other and use a rotational priority scheme for bus arbitration. Note that a custom-designed request agent other than a processor could be designed to operate as a symmetric agent. The symmetric agent bus arbitration scheme supports up to but no more than four symmetric request agents in the rotation.
- **priority request agents**—the system designer may include one or more request agents that are considered more important than the symmetric request agents. If a priority agent is competing against the symmetric agents for bus ownership, it wins and they lose.

Agent ID

What Agent ID Used For

When a request agent issues a transaction request, two of the items of information that it provides to the addressed response agent are:

- its unique agent ID
- a unique transaction ID

This information is only used by the response agent if it chooses to memorize the transaction and break the connection with the request agent. It then processes the read or write request off-line and, when the data has been read or written, it arbitrates for the bus and issues a *deferred reply transaction*. Using the agent and transaction IDs delivered earlier, it addresses the request agent that initially issued the read or write request and completes the transaction. A detailed description of deferred transactions can be found in "Transaction Deferral" on page 327.

How Agent ID Assigned

Each agent that is capable of initiating transaction requests must be assigned a unique agent ID at startup time. The agent typically accomplishes this by sampling one or more of its inputs on the trailing-edge of reset or when the power supply output voltages stabilize (i.e., on the rising-edge of the POWERGOOD signal). The manner in which the processors obtain their agent IDs is covered in "Agent ID Assignment" on page 224.

Transaction Phases

Pentium Transaction Phases

Each transaction initiated on the Pentium bus passes through three phases (or stages) from its inception to its completion:

*   **Arbitration phase**—If the initiator doesn't currently own the bus, it requests ownership from the arbiter and awaits the granting of ownership.
*   **Address phase**—After acquiring bus ownership, the initiator drives out an address and transaction type and asserts ADS# for one clock to indicate that a transaction has been initiated and a valid address and transaction type are on the bus. All agents latch the information and begin the decode to determine which of them is the target of the transaction.
*   **Data phase**— The initiator waits for the target to provide the requested read data or to accept the write data.

Pentium Pro Transaction Phases

Each transaction initiated on the Pentium Pro bus proceeds through the following phases from its inception to its completion (note that some transaction types do not require a data transfer and therefore do not include the data phase):

*   Arbitration phase
*   Request phase
*   Error phase
*   Snoop phase
*   Response phase
*   Data phase

Transaction Pipelining

Bus Divided into Signal Groups

Refer to Figure 9-2 on page 213. The bus is divided into signal groups. Each signal group is only used during a particular phase of the transaction.

Figure 9-2: Bus Signal Groups

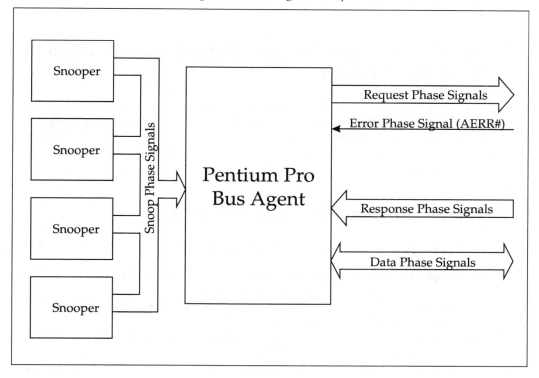

Step One: Gain Ownership of Request Signal Group

The bus is divided into groups of signals, each of which is only used during a particular phase of a transaction. When a request agent wishes to acquire bus ownership in order to issue a transaction request, it arbitrates for ownership of the portion of the bus referred to as the *request signal group*.

Step Two: Issue Transaction Request

The transaction request is driven onto the request signal group during the request phase of the transaction. All of the other bus agents are required to latch the new transaction request. Once the request agent has completed delivery of the transaction request to the other bus agents, it ceases to drive the signals that comprise the request signal group. One BCLK period after the current request bus owner begins to turn off its drivers, the same agent or another agent could take ownership of the request signal group and begin to drive out another transaction request.

Step Three: Yield Request Signal Group, Proceed to Next Signal Group

The request agent doesn't have to request ownership of the signal group used during the phase that follows the request phase. As the request agent finishes each phase, it relinquishes control of the signal group used in that phase and automatically takes ownership (or observes, as the case may be) of the signal group used in the next phase.

Phases Proceed in Predefined Order

The phases are passed through in a predefined order:

1. **Request phase**. Detailed description can be found in the chapter entitled "The Request and Error Phases" on page 261.
2. **Error Phase**. Detailed description can be found in the chapter entitled "The Request and Error Phases" on page 261.
3. **Snoop Phase**. Detailed description can be found in the chapter entitled "The Snoop Phase" on page 277.
4. **Response Phase**. Detailed description can be found in the chapter entitled "The Response and Data Phases" on page 297.
5. **Data Phase**. Detailed description can be found in the chapter entitled "The Response and Data Phases" on page 297.

The sections that follow provide a brief description of the phases.

Request Phase

The request agent uses the request signal group to issue the transaction request to the other bus agents. All of the other bus agents latch the request. The response agents (i.e., the targets) begin the decode to determine which of them is the target of the transaction. The snoop agents determine if it's a memory transaction. If it is, they must perform a cache lookup and deliver the snoop result during the snoop phase of this transaction. A detailed description of the request phase can be found in "Request Phase" on page 262.

Error Phase

The other bus agents check the parity of the request just latched. If the parity is correct, no action is taken. If one or more of them detect a parity error (in other words, the request was corrupted in flight), they each assert the AERR# signal for one BCLK at the end of the error phase (AERR# is a one of the few bus signals that is a multiple-owner, open-drain signal). The request agent checks the AERR# signal at the end of the error phase to see if they all received the request without error. If there was an error, the remaining phases of the transaction are cancelled (the request agent may choose to wait a few clocks and reattempt the transaction from scratch). If the request was received by all agents without error, the request agent proceeds to the snoop phase of the transaction. A detailed description of the error phase can be found in "Error Phase" on page 273.

Snoop Phase

After checking the state of the AERR# signal (and assuming that there wasn't an error), the request agent proceeds to the snoop phase and begins sampling the snoop result signal group. The snoop agents are responsible for delivering the result of their cache snoop during this phase. In addition, the currently-addressed response agent can assert the DEFER# signal if it intends to issue a retry or a deferred response during the response phase. Once the snoop result has been received, the request agent stops sampling the snoop result signals and the snoop agents cease driving them. A detailed description of the snoop phase can be found in "The Snoop Phase" on page 277.

Response Phase

Having completed the snoop phase, the request agent proceeds to the response phase and begins sampling the response signal group. The response agent (i.e., the target addressed by the request) is responsible for delivering its response (i.e., how it intends to handle the request) to the request agent during this phase. Once the response has been received, the request agent stops sampling the response signal group and the response agent ceases to drive the response. The response delivered indicates one of the following:

- tells the request agent to **retry** the transaction later.
- indicates a **hard failure** (don't retry and no data transfer; typically causes a machine check exception).
- if a write, it **will accept** the **data** in the data phase.
- if a read, it **will supply** the **data** during the data phase.
- if a snooper indicated a hit on a modified line, the entire line will be transferred from the snooper to memory (and, if it's a read, to the request agent as well)—referred to as an **implicit writeback** response.
- instructs the request agent to end the transaction with no data transferred. The response agent will obtain or deliver the data off-line and will later initiate a deferred reply transaction to indicate completion. This is referred to as the **deferred response**.

A detailed description of the response phase can be found in "The Response and Data Phases" on page 297.

Data Phase

Most transactions involve a data transfer, but some don't. If a transaction involves a data transfer, the request agent proceeds to the data phase of the transaction. If it's a write transaction, the request agent takes ownership of the data bus and delivers the data to the response agent during this phase. If it's a read transaction, the response agent takes ownership of the data bus and delivers the data to the request agent. Once the data phase completes, the transaction has completed and the request and response agents stop using the data bus. A detailed description of the data phase can be found in "The Response and Data Phases" on page 297.

Next Agent Can't Use Signal Group Until Current Agent Done With It

When a request agent has finished driving its transaction request onto the request signal group, another request agent can take ownership of the request signal group and issue another transaction—and additional requests can be issued by the same or different request agents as the previous agent completes delivery of its request. This is pictured in Figure 9-3 on page 218.

At a given instant in time, a number of transactions may be in progress at various stages of completion. As an example, at time 10 in Figure 9-3 on page 218 there are eight transactions active on the bus at various phases on their way to completion. The figure also highlights that some of the phases can take some time complete:

- the **snoop phase** (see times 9 and 10 in the figure) can be stretched by the snoopers if any of them needs more time in order to produce the results of the cache lookup.
- the **response phase** (see times 8, 9 and 10) can be stretched by the currently-addressed target if it requires extra time before it decides what its response to the transaction will be.
- the **data phase** (see times 6 through 10) of the transaction cannot be completed until the request and response agents are ready to transfer the data.

In those cases where the current owner(s) of a signal group is not yet done using it, the next owner(s) cannot start using it until the previous agent's done and the signal group has been completely released.

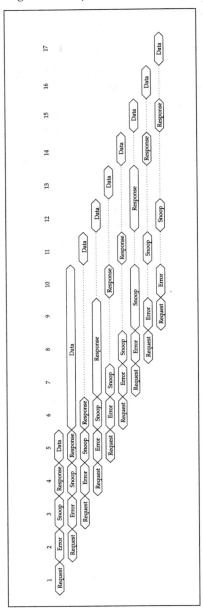

Figure 9-3: Pipelined Transactions

Transaction Tracking

Request Agent Transaction Tracking

It should be obvious that a request agent must keep track of each transaction that it has issued as each passes through the various phases on its way to completion. The request agent has distinct responsibilities during each phase:

- issues transaction request during **request phase**.
- checks for good request transmission during **error phase**.
- waits for and checks snoop result during **snoop phase**.
- waits for and checks response from response agent during **response phase**.
- during the **data phase** of a read or write transaction, accepts or sources data.
- if in the response phase the response agent indicates that it wishes to **defer** completion until a later time, the request agent must remember this transaction until the response agent initiates a deferred reply transaction at a later time.

In order to fulfill these responsibilities, the request agent must keep track of all outstanding transactions issued by itself as well as those issued by other request agents. As each of its outstanding transactions enters a new phase, it must interact with the appropriate signal group.

Snoop Agent Transaction Tracking

The group of snoop agents that reside on the bus must also keep track of each transaction currently outstanding on the bus.

- At the appropriate times, they must present the snoop result for each transaction. As illustrated in Figure 9-3 on page 218 (in time 11), sometimes the delivery of the snoop result for a particular transaction must be delayed until all of the snoopers have presented the snoop result for the previous transaction.
- When a snoop results in a hit on a modified line, the snooper must be prepared to writeback the modified to line to the currently-addressed memory response agent (and to the request agent if it's a read) during the data phase of the transaction.

Response Agent Transaction Tracking

A response agent must track the following:

- it must latch each new transaction request and determine if it is the target of the transaction.
- if it is the target and it intends to issue a retry or a deferred response during the response phase, it must assert DEFER# during the snoop phase.
- if it is the target, the response agent must indicate how it wants to handle the transaction during the response phase of the transaction.
- if it is the target and this is a read, the response agent will have to return data to the request agent when the data phase is entered.
- if it is the target and this is a write, the response agent must be prepared to accept the write data when the data phase is entered.
- if it is the target and the snoop result is a hit on a modified line, the response agent must be prepared to accept the line from the snooper during the data phase of the transaction.

The IOQ

In order to properly interact with the bus at each stage of the appropriate transactions, each bus agent must maintain a record of all transactions currently in progress, what phase each is currently in, and what responsibilities (if any) it has during each phase. This record is kept in a buffer referred to as the agent's in-order queue, or IOQ. When each transaction receives a response guaranteeing that the transaction will be completed now (in other words, it isn't being deferred), the transaction is deleted from the queue.

10 *Obtaining Bus Ownership*

The Previous Chapter

The previous chapter provided an introduction to the features of the bus and introduced terminology and concepts critical to an understanding of its operation.

This Chapter

Before a request agent can issue a new transaction to the bus, it must arbitrate for and win ownership of the request signal group. This chapter covers all of the issues related to obtaining ownership of the request signal group. This includes:

- bus arbitration among symmetric agents (i.e., the processors).
- bus arbitration by the priority agent(s) and how this affects arbitration among the symmetric agents.
- How bus locking affects arbitration.
- How (and why) an agent or agents can block the issuance of new requests.

The Next Chapter

This chapter described the acquisition of the request signal group. Once ownership has been acquired the request agent initiates the request phase of the transaction. The next chapter provides a detailed description of the request and error phases of any transaction.

Request Phase

There are a number of references to the request phase of the transaction in this chapter. After a request agent has arbitrated for and won ownership of the request signal group, it may then initiate a transaction by issuing a transaction request during the request phase of the transaction. This consists of the output of two packets of information and the assertion of ADS# (Address Strobe) during the output of the first packet. For a detailed description of the request phase, refer to the chapter entitled "The Request and Error Phases" on page 261.

Symmetric Agent Arbitration—Democracy at Work

A symmetric system is one is which any processor is capable of handling (i.e., executing) any task. The job of the SMP (symmetrical multiprocessing) OS is to attempt to keep all of the processors equally busy at all times (in other words, executing various tasks). At a given instant in time, one or more of the processors may require ownership of the request signal group in order to communicate with an external device. In a well-designed system, the bus arbitration scheme used to decide which of the processors gets ownership next is based on rotational priority—each of the processors has equal importance.

No External Arbiter Required

Refer to Figure 10-1 on page 223. The Pentium Pro processors that make up a cluster (i.e., the group of processors that reside on the processor bus) have a built-in rotational priority scheme. No external arbitration logic is necessary to decide which of them requires the request signal group and which gets it next. Each of the processors always keeps track of:

*   whether any of them currently owns the signal group
*   which of them owned the group last (or still owns it)
*   and which of them gets to use it next (assuming it is asking for ownership).

In order for them to track this information, each must know its own agent ID as well as the agent ID of the processor that last gained ownership of the request signal group. If you know who had ownership last (or still has it), then you know the agent ID whose turn it is next (because it's a rotational scheme).

Figure 10-1: System Block Diagram

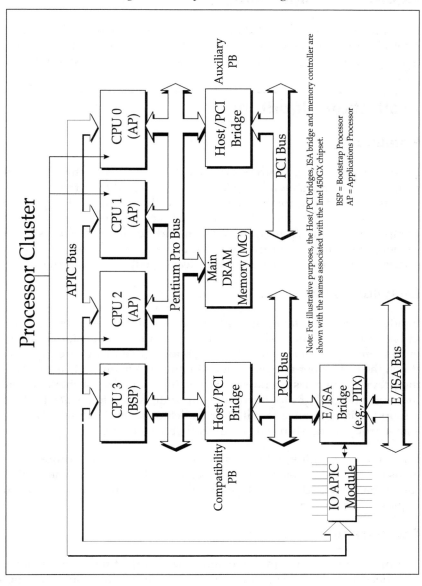

Agent ID Assignment

Each processor is assigned its agent ID automatically at the trailing-edge of reset when it samples the state of its BR[3:1]# inputs (see the detailed description in "Processor's Agent and APIC ID Assignment" on page 42).

Arbitration Algorithm

Rotating ID

As stated earlier, each processor must keep track of which of them gained request signal group ownership last. This is referred to as the *rotating ID*. When reset is asserted, the rotating ID is reset to three in all of the processors. This means that they all think that processor (i.e., agent) three owned the signal group last and therefore agent zero should get it next (if it asks for it). The sequence in which the processors gain ownership (if all of the processors were asking for ownership when reset was deasserted) is 0, 1, 2, 3, 0, 1, etc.

Busy/Idle State

In addition to the rotating ID, each processor must also keep track of whether the last processor that gained ownership of the request signal group retained ownership or has released it (and therefore none of them currently owns it). When the last owner retains ownership, the ownership state is said to be *busy*. If the previous owner surrendered ownership and none of them currently owns the request signal group, the ownership state is said to be *idle*. Each of the processors maintains an internal state indicator to indicate whether the request signal group ownership state is currently busy or idle.

It is incorrect to think of busy as meaning that one of the processors currently owns the request signal group and is using it. Rather, it only means that the processor has retained ownership—it may or may not currently be using the request signal group.

Bus Parking

The processor may retain ownership after completing a transaction in case it may need the request signal group again in the future (note that the Pentium Pro processor does this). This is referred to as parking ownership on yourself. If a processor is successful at retaining ownership until such time as it may require the signal group again, parking provides faster access to the request signal group (because you don't have to issue a request for the current symmetric owner to surrender ownership). More information on parking can be found in "Bus Parking Revisited" on page 230.

Be Fair!

When a processor parks ownership on itself, it may retain ownership until another processor requests ownership (i.e., until it detects the assertion of another processor's BREQ signal). In other words, be fair to the other processors—don't hog the bus.

What Signal Group are You Arbitrating For?

When an agent wins the arbitration, it takes ownership of the request signal group and uses it to issue a transaction request to the other agents that reside on the processor bus. A detailed account of the request phase of the transaction can be found in the chapter entitled "The Request and Error Phases" on page 261.

Requesting Ownership

Refer to Figure 10-2 on page 226. The temptation is great to think that agent 0 uses its BR0# output to request ownership, agent 1 uses its BR1# output, etc., but it's not true. When any processor wants to issue a new transaction request, it uses its bus request signal, BR0#, to request ownership. BR[3:1]# are inputs that are sampled to see if any of the other processors is also requesting ownership at the same time. If agent 0 is issuing a request, the BREQ0# signal line is asserted. If agent 1 is issuing a request, the BREQ1# signal line is asserted, etc. Each of the processors knows which of the BREQn# signal lines belongs to it and which belongs to each of the other processors.

Figure 10-2: Symmetric Agent Arbitration Signals

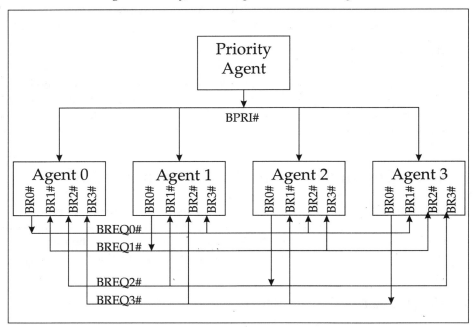

Example of One Symmetric Agent Requesting Ownership

Figure 10-3 on page 227 illustrates processor 0 requesting ownership. The following list describes the figure.

1. Prior to the rising-edge of clock one, none of the processors was requesting ownership (e.g., immediately after reset removal). The bus ownership state within each of them is "idle" and the last one that had ownership was agent 3 (note that this is the condition immediately after reset is removed).
2. During the clock immediately prior to clock 1, agent 0 needs to perform a transaction and asserts BREQ0# to indicate this.
3. On the rising-edge of clock one, agents 1, 2, and 3 detect that agent 0 is requesting ownership. *A change in the state of the BREQn# signals from none asserted in one clock to one or more asserted in the next is an arbitration event.*
4. One clock later, during clock two, all of the processors change the state of their rotating ID indicator to indicate that agent 0 is now the owner. They also change their ownership state indicators to indicate that the ownership state is now busy—in other words, one of them now owns the portion of bus required to issue a new transaction. Note that the rotating ID

and ownership state indicators are strictly internal to the processors. They are not presented on any output pins.

5. In clock two, agent 0 takes ownership of the signals required to issue a new transaction and drives out its request and asserts ADS# (Address Strobe) to indicate that a new transaction is being issued to the bus. It leaves BREQ0# asserted either because it wants to issue another transaction request immediately after this one, or in case it needs the bus again in the future (see "Bus Parking Revisited" on page 230).

Figure 10-3: Example of One Processor Requesting Ownership

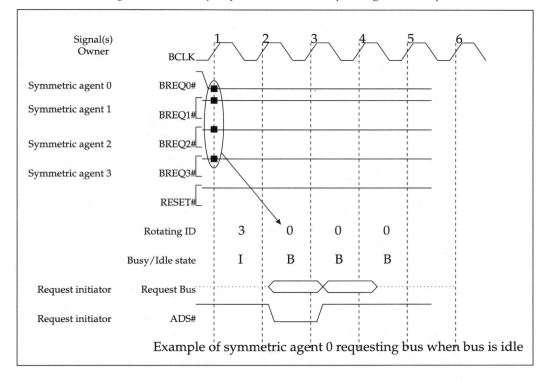

Example of symmetric agent 0 requesting bus when bus is idle

Example of Two Symmetric Agents Requesting Ownership

Figure 10-4 on page 229 illustrates a case where symmetric agents 0 and 3 are both requesting ownership. Arbitration events (where the symmetric agents must decide which of them ownership will pass to) occur on the rising-edge of clocks 1, 3, and 6. The following list describes the figure.

1. Prior to clock 1, none of the symmetric agents were requesting ownership. The previous owner was agent 2 and the ownership state is currently idle (i.e., none of the symmetric agents has ownership). *Please note that the Pentium Pro processor always leaves its BREQ asserted (in case it may need to issue another request in the future) when it initiates a transaction request. In other words, it uses parking.*

2. On clock 1, requests from agents 0 and 3 are both seen. *This is an arbitration event.*

3. In clock 2, all symmetric agents change the rotating ID from 2 to 3 and the ownership state from idle to busy. Agent 3 takes ownership of the request signal group, issues a request and asserts ADS# (Address Strobe) to indicate that a new transaction request is being issued. As it's issuing the request, agent 3, recognizing that one (or more) other symmetric agents are also requesting ownership, does the polite thing—it deasserts BREQ3# to relinquish ownership.

4. On clock 3, an *arbitration event* is detected (agent 3 has relinquished ownership). All symmetric agents see that only agent 0 is requesting ownership. Having been polite to agent 0, agent 3 reasserts BREQ3# to request ownership again (because it has another transaction to issue).

5. One clock later (in clock 4), all symmetric agents change their rotating ID to 0 and the ownership state stays busy (there was a hand off of ownership from one to the other). Before taking ownership, however, agent 0 must wait for agent 3 to completely cease driving the request signal group.

6. In clock 5, agent 0 begins to drive its request onto the request signal group and asserts ADS#. Having detected BREQ3# asserted, it also deasserts BREQ0# to hand ownership back to agent 3.

7. In clock 6, an *arbitration event* is detected (agent 0 has relinquished ownership). All symmetric agents see that only agent 3 is requesting ownership.

8. In clock 7, all symmetric agents change their rotating ID to 3 and the ownership state stays busy. Before taking ownership, however, agent 3 must wait for agent 0 to completely cease driving the request signal group.

9. In clock 8, agent 3 begins to drive its request onto the request signal group and asserts ADS#. It keeps BREQ3# asserted either because it has another transaction request to issue or to park ownership on itself in case it needs in the future.

Figure 10-4: Example of Two Symmetric Agents Requesting Ownership

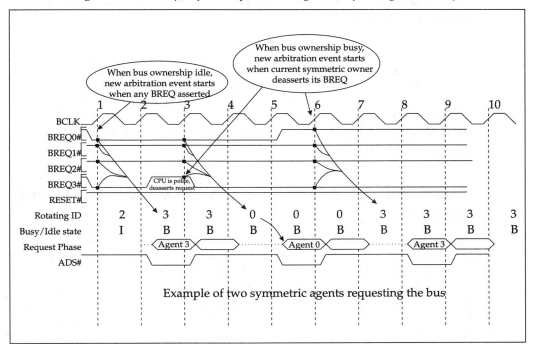

Example of two symmetric agents requesting the bus

Definition of an Arbitration Event

An arbitration event is defined as the passing of ownership (of the request signal group) from one symmetric agent to another. This occurs under the following circumstances:

- When none of the BREQ*n*# lines are asserted during one clock and then one or more are seen asserted in the next clock. An example of this can be seen in Figure 10-3 on page 227 during the clock that precedes clock one.
- When the current symmetric owner of the request signal group relinquishes ownership by deasserting its BREQ*n*# signal and one or more of the other BREQ*n*# lines have previously been asserted.

In either case, the symmetric agents must collectively decide (based on who owned it last and therefore who's next in the rotation) which of them will assume ownership of the request signal group in the next clock.

Once BREQn# Asserted, Keep Asserted Until Ownership Attained

Once a symmetric agent asserts its BREQn# signal, it must keep it asserted until it attains ownership (see "Other Guys are Very Polite" on page 276 for a description of the only exception). Once ownership is attained, the agent may or may not generate a transaction request (usually it will). If the agent no longer needs to generate the transaction request for which it originally asserted its BREQn#, it can deassert its BREQn# (without generating a transaction request) once it has attained ownership.

Example Case Where Transaction Cancelled Before Started

An example would be the case where the processor has a modified line sitting in one of its writeback buffers waiting to be cast back to memory (to make room for a new line being read into the L2 cache). The processor had asserted its BREQn# to request ownership to do the cast out. Before it acquired ownership, however, another agent attained ownership and issued a read for the same line. The processor waiting to writeback the line snoops its writeback buffers, asserts HITM# (hit on modified line) and supplies the modified line directly to the agent that issued the read request. There is no longer a need to perform the writeback transaction, but the processor must keep its BREQn# asserted until it attains ownership. It then deasserts its BREQn# without starting a transaction. The other symmetric agents will see that it is yielding ownership on the next clock and, if any other symmetric agents have their BREQs asserted, ownership passes to the next in the rotation.

Bus Parking Revisited

A symmetric agent can park ownership of the request signal group on itself if it so desires (in other words, parking is optional). It does this by not deasserting its BREQn# signal when its issues a transaction request. This occurs under two circumstances:

1. Symmetric agent issues a transaction request and has another to issue immediately after the first. It can retain ownership of the request signal group by keeping its BREQn# asserted when issuing the first transaction request. Note that if any other symmetric agents are requesting ownership, this isn't very polite to them.

2. Symmetric agent issues a transaction request and keeps its BREQn# asserted in case it needs to issue a request in the future. It can retain ownership until another processor requests ownership (i.e., until it detects the assertion of another processor's BREQ signal).

Most of the time, *the Pentium Pro processor uses method 2*. There are some cases where the processor must prevent any other agent from gaining bus ownership in between two of its transactions, however, and then it uses method 1 (for more information see "Locking—Shared Resource Acquisition" on page 241).

Examples of symmetric ownership parking are illustrated in clock 2 of Figure 10-3 on page 227 and clock 8 of Figure 10-4 on page 229.

Priority Agent Arbitration—Despotism

Example Priority Agents

While the symmetric agents are very polite to each other, the system may include one or more agents that play by different rules. They are referred to as priority agents. Refer to Figure 10-5 on page 232. As an example, in the 450GX chipset, both of the PBs (i.e., the host/PCI bridges) are priority agents. They use the BPRI# signal (note that there is only one BPRI# signal) to request ownership when they need to issue a transaction request on the processor bus. The PBs act as the surrogate processor bus request agent when a PCI master (or an ISA or EISA master) requires access to main memory.

Only one device is permitted to assert BPRI# at a time. In the case where there are multiple priority agents, there must therefore be some method for the priority agents to arbitrate amongst themselves to determine which of them gets to use BPRI# to request ownership (if more than one of them needs to issue a transaction request at the same time). In the case of the 450GX's two PBs, they use two signals, IOREQ# and IOGNT#, to decide which of them gets to use BPRI#. In the case where both of them need to issue a transaction request, the compatibility PB wins.

Figure 10-5: System Block Diagram

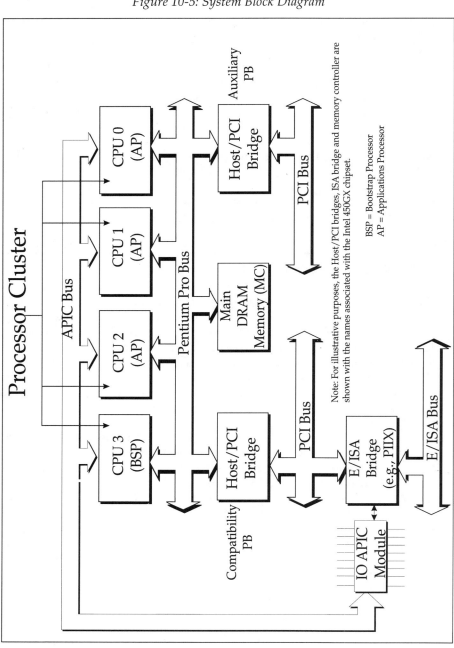

Priority Agent Beats Symmetric Agents, Unless...

When a priority agent is requesting ownership at the same time that one or more of the symmetric agents are also requesting ownership, the priority agent wins.

The only case where the priority agent will be unsuccessful in winning ownership of the bus is the case where a symmetric agent has already acquired ownership and has asserted the LOCK# signal. This prevents the priority agent from acquiring ownership until the symmetric agent deasserts the LOCK# signal. The reasons why a symmetric agent might assert LOCK# are covered in the section entitled "Locking—Shared Resource Acquisition" on page 241. The priority agent must deal with the cases described in Table 10-1 on page 233.

Table 10-1: Possible Cases Involving Priority Agent Arbitration

Case	Resulting Actions
A symmetric agent initiates a transaction request in the same clock that the priority agent asserts BPRI#, but does not assert LOCK#.	In this case, the priority agent assumes ownership after the symmetric agent finishes delivery of its transaction request. This will be **3 clocks after BPRI# assertion**.
A symmetric agent initiates a transaction request and asserts LOCK# in the same clock that the priority agent is asserting BPRI#.	The priority agent cannot assume ownership until the symmetric agent deasserts LOCK#.
A symmetric agent has acquired ownership on the same rising-edge of the clock that BPRI# is sampled asserted. In this case, the symmetric agent proceeds with its transaction request and may or may not assert LOCK#.	• If **LOCK#** is **asserted**, the priority agent doesn't acquire ownership until LOCK# is deasserted by the symmetric agent. • If **LOCK# isn't asserted**, the priority agent acquires ownership as soon as the symmetric agent completes issuing its transaction request. This will be **2 clocks after BPRI# is asserted**.

Using Simple Approach, Priority Agent Suffers Penalty

Refer to Figure 10-6 on page 236. A priority agent may be designed in such a manner that it doesn't check to see if a symmetric agent has started a transaction request (in other words, it doesn't check the state of the ADS# signal) in order to determine when (and if) it can take ownership of the request signal group. Rather, it checks in the two clocks immediately following its assertion of BPRI# to see if LOCK# is asserted. If LOCK# is sampled asserted on the rising-edge of either of the two clocks immediately after BPRI# is asserted, then a symmetric agent had already asserted LOCK# and the priority agent can't take ownership until LOCK# is deasserted. If LOCK# is sampled deasserted during both of these two clocks, however, one of three conditions is true (but the priority agent doesn't know which):

1. No symmetric agent has initiated a transaction request during these two clocks and LOCK# is not being held asserted by a symmetric agent that issued an earlier transaction request.
2. A symmetric agent started a transaction request on the same clock that BPRI# was driven asserted, but did not assert LOCK#.
3. A symmetric agent started a transaction request on the clock after BPRI# was asserted, but did not assert LOCK#.

In any of these cases, the priority agent has gained ownership. However, because it doesn't check ADS# to determine which of the three cases is true, it must assume the worst case—case number 3. In this case, the symmetric agent has sampled BPRI# asserted on the same rising-edge of the clock that the symmetric agent initiated its transaction request, it does not assert LOCK#, and it will therefore honor the BPRI# assertion. The priority agent cannot assume ownership, however, until 3 clocks after the symmetric agent starts its transaction request. This is *a **total of 4 clocks after BPRI# is asserted**.*

1. An arbitration event occurs on clock 2 in Figure 10-6 on page 236 and agent 0 acquires ownership in clock 3 (BPRI# is not yet asserted, so agent 0 is not prevented from taking ownership). Also on clock 2, the priority agent asserts BPRI# to request ownership, but this isn't detected by agent 0 until clock 3, the clock in which it starts to drive out a transaction request. This means that agent 0 has successfully acquired ownership and will proceed with the issuance of its transaction request.
2. When agent 0 starts its request in clock 3, it keeps BREQ0# asserted in case it has another transaction to issue later. Also in clock 3, agent 1 asserts

BREQ1# to request ownership, but it won't gain symmetric ownership until agent 0 relinquishes ownership.

3. The priority agent uses the simple approach to test for ownership acquisition. It samples LOCK# on clocks 3 and 4 to see if any symmetric agent has asserted it. In this case, it is sampled deasserted both times, indicating either that no symmetric agent is issuing a request, or one is, but has not asserted LOCK#. In either case, it means the priority agent will be the next owner of the request signal group.

4. Agent 0 samples BREQ1# asserted on clock 4 and relinquishes symmetric ownership in clock 5.

5. An arbitration event occurs on clock 6 when BREQ0# is sampled deasserted indicating that agent 0 has relinquished ownership to agent 1. In clock 7, ownership passes to agent 1.

6. On clock 6, 4 clocks after it asserted BPRI#, the priority agent takes ownership of the request signal group, initiates a transaction request, and deasserts BPRI# to let the next symmetric agent use the request signal group after it is done. Note that if none of the symmetric agents had their BREQn# lines asserted, the priority agent could have left BPRI# asserted to park ownership on itself in case it needed to issue another transaction request in the future. Since both agents 0 and 1 have asserted their respective BREQs, however, the priority agent is a gentleman and releases BPRI#.

7. On clock 7, symmetric ownership passes to agent 1. In addition, BPRI# is sampled deasserted by the symmetric agents, indicating that the next symmetric owner can start issuing a request 2 clocks later (on clock 9).

8. When agent 1 issues its transaction request on clock 9, it keeps BREQ1# asserted to park symmetric ownership on itself in case it needs to issue another transaction request later.

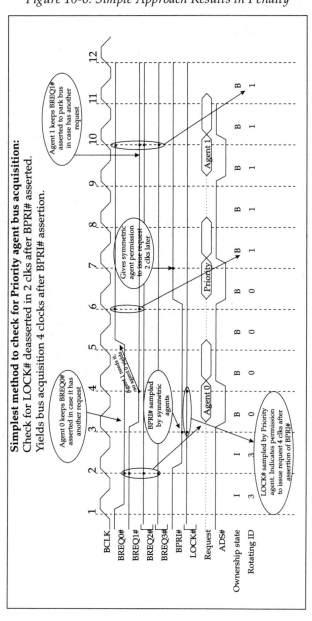

Figure 10-6: Simple Approach Results in Penalty

Smarter Priority Agent Gets Ownership Faster

The previous section demonstrated that a priority agent that only checks the state of the LOCK# signal to determine if and when it has attained ownership takes at least four clocks to attain ownership (longer if LOCK# is sampled asserted). This section describes how a priority agent that checks both ADS# and LOCK# can *attain ownership in 2 or 3, rather than 4 clocks*.

Table 10-1 on page 233 detailed the possibilities when a priority agent asserts BPRI# to request ownership. If the priority agent checks to see (by sampling ADS#) if a symmetric agent has actually started a transaction request in the same clock that it asserts BPRI# or the clock immediately following its assertion, it can decrease the latency in gaining ownership from 4 to 3 clocks (Figure 10-8 on page 240) or 2 (Figure 10-7 on page 238).

Ownership Attained in 2 BCLKs

If the priority agent samples ADS# asserted (indicating that a symmetric agent has initiated a transaction request) and LOCK# deasserted (but it isn't locking the request signal group) in the same clock that it asserts BPRI#, the priority agent can assume ownership in 2 clocks. Refer to Figure 10-7 on page 238.

1. On clock 2, the priority agent begins to assert BPRI#. At the same time, agent 0 initiates a transaction request and asserts ADS#. The priority agent samples ADS# asserted and LOCK# deasserted, indicating that a symmetric agent has initiated a transaction request but has not locked the request signal group.
2. All of the symmetric agents sample BPRI# asserted on clock 3, indicating that the priority agent will be the next owner of the request signal group.
3. On clock 4, after agent 0 has completed issuance of its transaction request, the priority agent initiates its transaction request. BREQ1# is also sampled asserted (by the other symmetric agents as well as the priority agent), indicating that symmetric agent 1 wishes to issue a transaction request. Being a good bus citizen, the priority agent deasserts BPRI# to yield the bus to the symmetric agent.
4. On clock 5, agent 0 deasserts BREQ0# to yield symmetric ownership to agent 1.
5. On clock 6, the symmetric agents detect BREQ0# deasserted and select the next symmetric owner, agent 1.
6. On clock 7, symmetric ownership passes to agent 1 and it initiates its transaction.

Figure 10-7: Example Where Priority Agent Attains Ownership in 2 Clocks

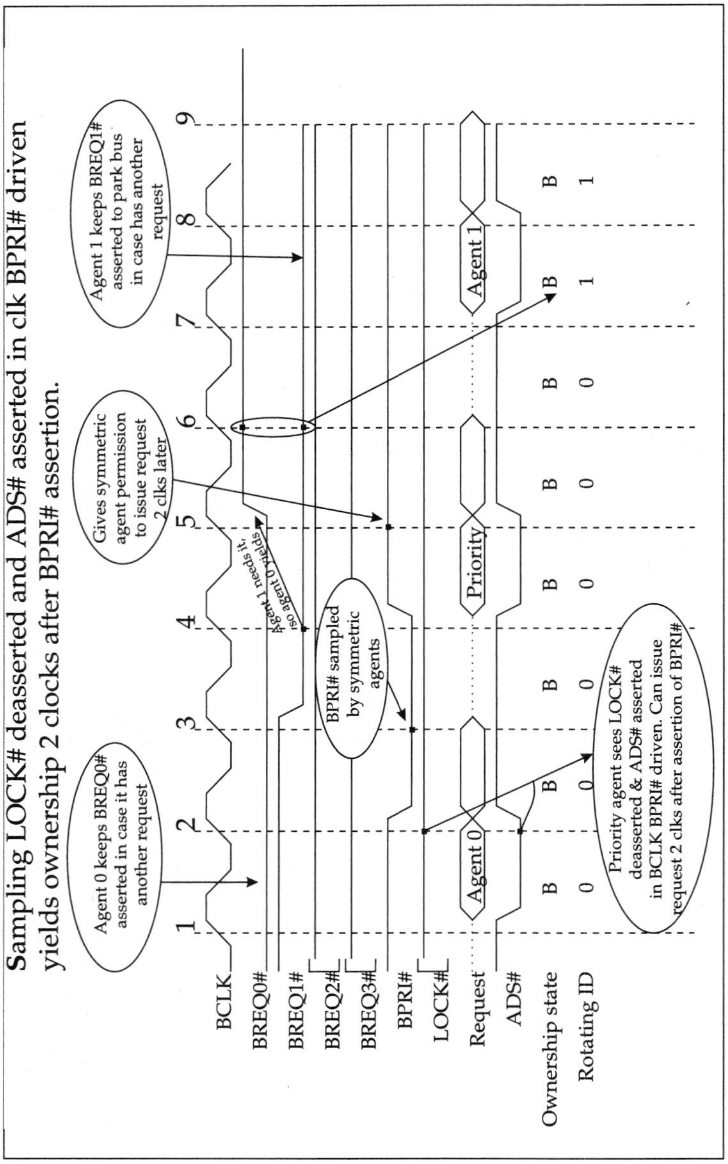
Sampling LOCK# deasserted and ADS# asserted in clk BPRI# driven yields ownership 2 clocks after BPRI# assertion.
BCLK
BREQ0#
BREQ1#
BREQ2#
BREQ3#
BPRI#
LOCK#
Request
ADS#
Ownership state
Rotating ID
1 2 3 4 5 6 7 8 9
Agent 0 keeps BREQ0# asserted in case it has another request
BPRI# sampled by symmetric agents
Agent 1 needs it, so agent 0 yields
Gives symmetric agent permission to issue request 2 clks later
Agent 1 keeps BREQ1# asserted to park bus in case has another request
Priority agent sees LOCK# deasserted & ADS# asserted in BCLK BPRI# driven. Can issue request 2 clks after assertion of BPRI#
Agent 0
Priority
Agent 1
B B B B B B B B
0 0 0 0 0 0 1 1

Chapter 10: Obtaining Bus Ownership

Ownership Attained in 3 BCLKs

If the priority agent samples ADS# asserted (indicating that a symmetric agent has initiated a transaction request) and LOCK# deasserted (but it isn't locking the request signal group) in the clock after it asserts BPRI#, the priority agent can assume ownership in 3 clocks. Refer to Figure 10-8 on page 240.

1. On clock 1, agent 0 initiates a transaction request and the priority agent asserts BPRI# to request ownership. ADS# is sampled deasserted, indicating that a symmetric agent didn't start a transaction request in the previous BCLK. Check ADS# and LOCK# again on next clock.
2. On clock 2, ADS# sampled asserted, indicating that a symmetric agent has just initiated a transaction request. LOCK# is sampled deasserted, indicating that the symmetric agent didn't lock the request signal group.
3. The priority agent can assume ownership after the symmetric agent completes issuing its transaction request. This occurs on clock 4.

Figure 10-8: Example Where Priority Agent Attains Ownership in 3 Clocks

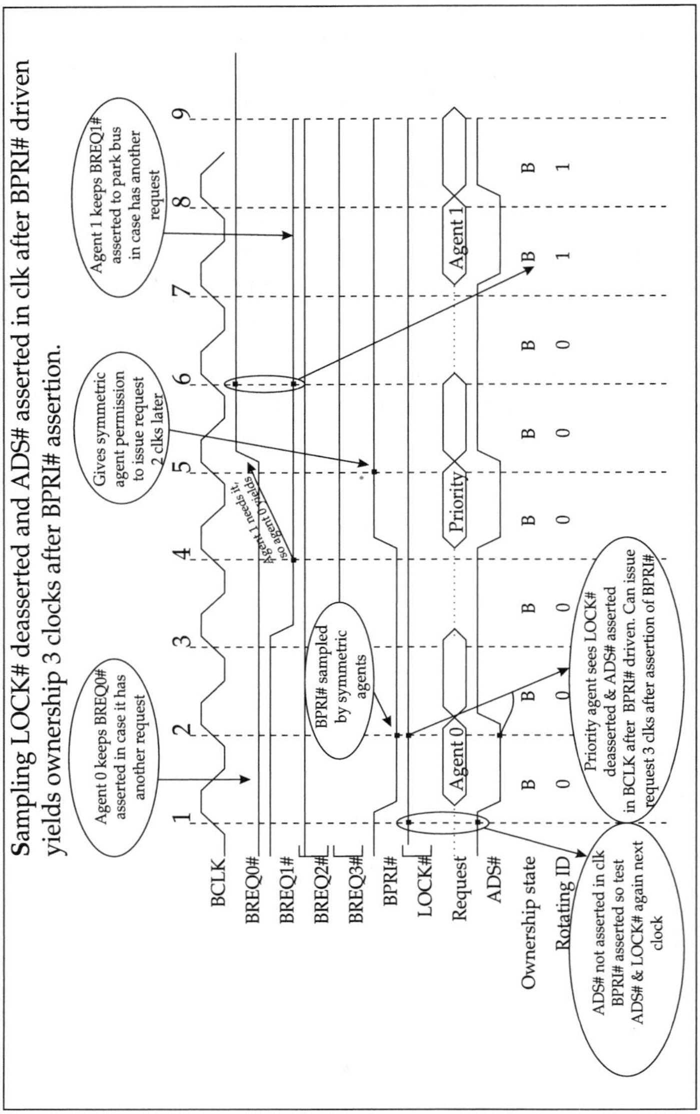

Be Fair to the Common People

The spec dictates that the priority agent must keep BPRI# deasserted for at least two clocks after its last deassertion of BPRI#. This opens a window that permits the symmetric agents to get ownership of the request signal group if any of them need to issue a transaction request.

Priority Agent Parking

The specification says that the priority agent can keep BPRI# asserted when it asserts ADS# and initiates its final (or only) transaction request. The exact wording is "provided it can guarantee forward progress of the symmetric agents." In other words, **be fair to the common people**. If the priority agent has parked ownership on itself by keeping it BPRI# asserted, it can retain ownership until:

- it has to initiate another transaction request, or
- it samples any of the BREQn# lines asserted, indicating that one or more of the symmetric agents require access to the request signal group,

whichever comes first.

Locking—Shared Resource Acquisition

The previous section,"Priority Agent Arbitration—Despotism," illustrated how the assertion of LOCK# by a symmetric agent prevents the priority agent from getting ownership. This section describes the reasons why a symmetric agent might need to perform a series of transactions without fear of any other agent performing an access in between its own transctions.

Shared Resource Concept

Assume that the OS sets aside an area of memory to be used by tasks executing on multiple processors (or even by different tasks executed by the same processor) as a shared memory buffer. It is intended to be used as follows:

1. Before using the buffer (i.e., reading from or writing to it), a task must first test a flag to ensure that the buffer isn't currently owned by another task. If the buffer is currently unavailable, the task wishing to gain ownership should periodically check back to see when it becomes available.
2. When the flag indicates that the buffer is available, the task sets the flag, indicating that it has exclusive ownership of the buffer. The buffer is then unavailable if any other task should attempt to gain ownership of it.

3. Having gained exclusive ownership of the buffer, the task can now read and write the buffer.

4. If the buffer is in an area of memory designated as WT, WC, or UC memory (refer to "Rules of Conduct" on page 133), writes are absorbed into the processor's posted write buffers. *These buffers are not snooped* when other agents access memory. In this case, when the task is done using the buffer, it should ensure that all of its updates (i.e., memory writes) have been flushed all the way to memory.

5. After ensuring that the buffer has received all updates, the task should release ownership of the buffer so it can be used by other tasks.

Testing Availability and Gaining Ownership of Shared Resources

The OS typically uses a memory location (or series of memory locations) as the flag indicating the availability or unavailability of a particular shared resource. This is referred to as a *memory semaphore*. It is used as follows:

1. Before using the buffer (i.e., reading from or writing to it), a task reads the buffer's semaphore (via a memory read) to ensure that the buffer isn't currently owned by another task. If the buffer is currently unavailable (usually indicated by a non-zero semaphore value), the task wishing to gain ownership should periodically check back to see when it becomes available.

2. When the flag indicates that the buffer is available (semaphore contains a zero value), the task writes a non-zero value into the semaphore to indicate that it now has exclusive ownership of the buffer. The buffer will then be unavailable if any other task should test the semaphore.

3. Having gained exclusive ownership of the buffer, the task can now read and write the buffer.

4. If the memory buffer area is designated as WC, WT, or UC memory, when the task is done using the buffer, it should ensure that any buffer updates (i.e., memory writes) have been flushed all the way to memory.

5. After ensuring that the buffer has received all updates, the task releases ownership of the buffer (by clearing the semaphore to zero) so it can be used by other tasks.

Race Condition Can Present Problem

Consider the following possibility:

1. The task executing on processor 0 reads the semaphore to determine the buffer's availability.

2. The task tests the semaphore's value and determines that the buffer is available (semaphore value is zero).

3. After the task on processor 0 has completed the memory read to obtain and test the semaphore value, a task executing on processor 1 has initiated a memory read request to test the state of the same semaphore. It completes the read and begins testing the value.

4. The processor 0 task initiates a memory write request to update the semaphore to a non-zero value to mark the shared buffer as unavailable. After it completes the write, it considers itself the sole owner of the buffer.

5. The processor 1 task also determined the buffer is available and it now performs a memory write request to update the semaphore to a non-zero value to mark the shared buffer as unavailable. It completes the write and it also now considers itself the sole owner of the buffer.

Two tasks executing on two separate processors now each believe that it has exclusive ownership of the buffer.

Guaranteeing Atomicity of Read/Modify/Write

This problem came about because processor 1 was able to read the semaphore immediately after processor 0 read it. The two processors were in a race condition. Processor 0 then wrote to it immediately, followed by processor 1 writing to it. The tasks on the two processors each ended up believing it had sole ownership of the buffer.

The problem can be prevented if processor 0 could prevent other initiator's from using the bus from the time it initiates its read until the time it updates the semaphore to a non-zero value. In other words, it should lock the bus while it performs the read/modify/write (frequently referred to as a RMW) of the semaphore.

To do this, the programmer uses special instructions to perform the RMW operation. When using these instructions, the processor (refer to Figure 10-9 on page 244):

1. asserts the LOCK# signal when it initiates the memory read, keeps LOCK# asserted while it performs the internal semaphore test, and performs the memory write to update the semaphore before releasing the LOCK# signal. The assertion of LOCK# prevents the priority agent from obtaining bus ownership during this period.

2. also keeps its BREQn# output asserted throughout this period to keep any of the other processors from obtaining ownership of the request signal group.

Figure 10-9: Example of Symmetric Agent Performing Locked Transaction Series

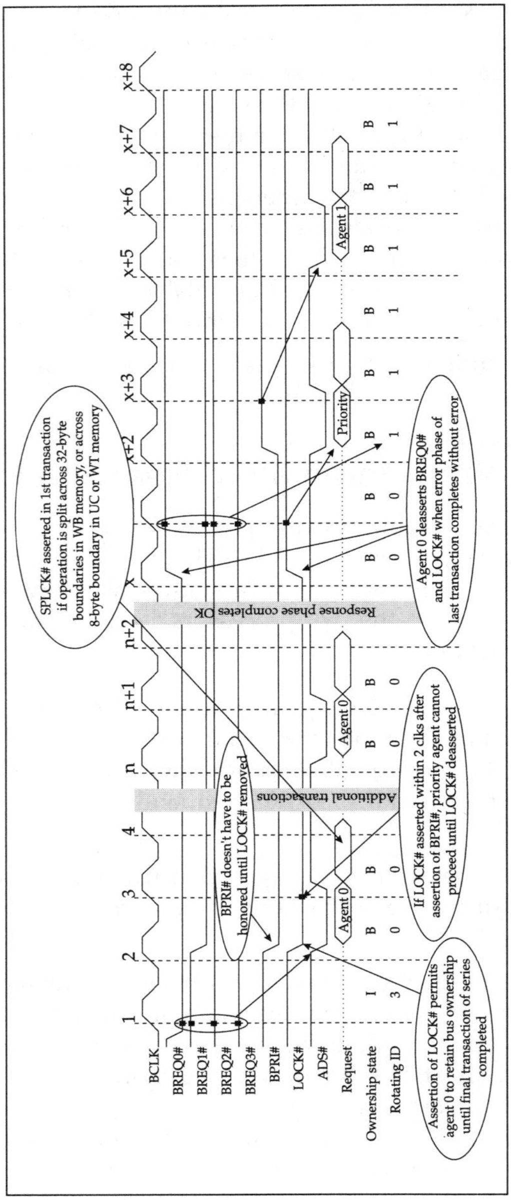

Chapter 10: Obtaining Bus Ownership

LOCK Instruction Prefix

The following instructions may be prefixed with the lock prefix to force the assertion of LOCK# for the duration of the read and write:

- bit test and modify instructions: BTS, BTR, and BTC.
- exchange instructions: XADD, CMPXCHG, and CMPXCG8B.
- XCHG instruction doesn't require the lock prefix to assert LOCK#.
- the following single-operand arithmetic and logical operations: INC, DEC, NOT, and NEG.
- the following two-operand arithmetic and logical operations: ADD, ADC, SUB, SBB, AND, OR, and XOR.

Processor Automatically Asserts LOCK# for Some Operations

The processor automatically asserts LOCK# under the following circumstances:

- execution of the XCHG instruction when it accesses memory.
- during a task switch, setting the Busy flag of a TSS (task state segment). For information on the TSS and Busy flag, refer to the MindShare book entitled *Protected Mode Software Architecture* (published by Addison-Wesley).
- when the processor reads a segment descriptor from memory, it asserts LOCK# during the read, tests the state of the descriptor's Accessed bit and, if clear, performs the memory write to set the bit in the descriptor in memory before releasing LOCK#.
- when updating the Accessed and/or Dirty bits in page directory and page table entries.

Use Locked RMW to Obtain and Give Up Semaphore Ownership

The programmer should always:

- use a locked RMW instruction to obtain ownership of the semaphore, and
- use a locked instruction to release ownership (in other words, perform a locked RMW to change the semaphore back to zero).

Locked instructions are *serializing, synchronizing* operations. Remember that the Pentium Pro processor performs out-of-order execution. This means that if the programmer used an unlocked RMW to release the semaphore, it could be executed before all of the code that precedes it has been executed. Using a locked

RMW instruction ensures that the processor will execute all instructions before the locked instruction prior to executing it (i.e., it is serializing). In addition, the locked instruction is synchronizing—it forces all posted writes within the processor to be flushed to external memory before executing the next instruction. This ensures that the buffer has received all updates before it is released.

Duration of Locked Transaction Series

The number of transactions necessary to perform the RMW on a semaphore depends on the placement in memory (i.e., its alignment) and the size of the semaphore. The Pentium Pro processor has a 64-bit data bus (eight data paths) and addresses memory on quadword boundaries. Using the address bus, it can therefore identify a block of eight memory locations aligned on a quadword boundary and use its byte enables to identify which bytes are to be read or written within the addressed quadword. This being the case, it **can read or write** a **semaphore using one transaction** under the following circumstances:

- semaphore is one byte wide.
- semaphore is one word wide (16-bits) and is aligned on a word address boundary.
- semaphore is one dword wide (32-bits) and is aligned on a dword address boundary.
- semaphore is one quadword wide (64-bits) and is aligned on a quadword address boundary.

Earlier x86 processors had 32- rather than 64-bit data buses, so software written to be executed on any x86 processor can only guarantee a single access read or write under the following circumstances:

- semaphore is one byte wide.
- semaphore is one word wide (16-bits) and is wholly-contained with in dword.
- semaphore is one dword wide (32-bits) and is aligned on a dword address boundary.

When performing a RMW operation on a semaphore that falls completely within one quadword, the Pentium Pro processor only has to perform one read and one write transaction (a **total of two transactions**) to accomplish the RMW.

However, if a semaphore value is set up in memory starting on a misaligned address boundary (for example, a dword semaphore that straddles two quadwords), the processor must perform two reads to get the semaphore and two writes to update it (a **total of four transactions**). This is inefficient from the processor's standpoint and also from a system perspective (because the bus is locked for a longer period). When a semaphore is split across boundaries, the processor will assert LOCK# when it initiates the first memory read and keep it asserted for the four resulting transactions. In addition, it will **also assert SPLCK#** (Split Lock) to inform the addressed memory (or an L3 cache) that the currently-addressed quadword and the next should be locked. Refer to Table 11-11 on page 273.

The **worst-case alignment scenarios** occur when a semaphore **straddles cache line or page boundaries**. In the case of a semaphore that straddles cache line boundaries where neither line is currently in the processor's caches, the processor must fetch both 32-byte lines from memory to obtain the semaphore and must lock the bus for this entire period (for additional information, refer to"Disable Cache Line Boundary Lock" on page 426). In the case of a semaphore that straddles 4KB page boundaries where neither page is currently in memory, two complete pages, 8KB of information, must be read into memory from mass storage before the processor can read the semaphore.

Back-to-Back RMW Operations

The LOCK# signal is always deasserted between two sequences of locked transactions (i.e., two RMW operations) on the processor bus.

Locking a Cache Line

When the processor begins the locked RMW operation, there are several possible cases:

- the semaphore value isn't in the cache.
- the semaphore value is in the cache in the E state.
- the semaphore value is in the cache in the S state.
- the semaphore value is in the cache in the M state.

Intel states that the Pentium Pro processor implements *cache line locking in* areas of memory designated as *WB memory*. It should be noted that Intel provides almost no information on how this works, but the author is as certain as can be that the following descriptions are accurate. Some important points to keep in mind are covered in the sections that follow.

Advantage of Cache Line Locking

Bus locking is inefficient—for the duration of a processor's RMW operation, no other bus agent can initiate a new transaction. If there are a lot of RMW operations being performed by the processors and/or priority agents, this can severely degrade system performance. If a semaphore is cached by the Pentium Pro processor, the RMW operation can be performed without locking the bus.

New Directory Bit—Cache Line Locked

Intel states that a cache line can be locked. This implies that there is a lock bit in each L1 data cache and L2 cache directory entry that is used for this purpose.

Read and Invalidate Transaction (RWITM, or Kill)

In the event of a race condition, you don't want multiple processors that have a cached copy of the line (in the S state) to be testing the same cached semaphore simultaneously. Therefore, before performing a locked RMW operation in the cache, a processor must first gain exclusive ownership of the line. This implies that you have to kill everyone else's copy of the line. Intel has included a special transaction type, read and invalidate, specifically for this purpose. The PowerPC 60x bus has two transaction types that perform a similar role: kill and RWITM (read with intent to modify).

Line in E or M State

A processor that has a copy of the line in the E or M state has the only copy of the line and therefore doesn't have to worry about another processor testing a copy of the semaphore in its cache at the same time that it is doing so. However, it is possible that another processor attempting to read the semaphore will experience a cache miss and initiate a read and invalidate transaction to obtain an exclusive copy of the line on which to perform its RMW. The processor with the E or M copy must prevent the other processor from obtaining the line that contains the semaphore until it has finished its own RMW operation on the semaphore within the line. This is accomplished by marking the line locked in the cache when the read of the internal RMW is initiated. When the snoop of the other processor's read and invalidate transaction results in a hit on a locked line, the processor delays presentation of the snoop result to the other processor until it's RMW has been completed. It then indicates the state of the line after the RMW. This could be either I or M:

1. It would be I if, when read from the line, the semaphore had been set to a non-zero value by another task at an earlier time. In this case, the processor doesn't update the line. Rather, it invalidates the line and indicates a snoop miss.

2. It would be M (snoop hit on M copy) in two cases:
   - The programmer didn't update the semaphore because it was already set, but some other item in the line had previously been updated (in other words, the line was in the M state before the RMW was initiated).
   - When read from the M line, the semaphore was zero, so the programmer wrote to the semaphore to update it and the line stayed in the M state.

Semaphore Not in Processor's L1 or L2 Cache

If the semaphore is not in the L1 data or the L2 cache when the attempt is made to read it, it results in a cache miss. The read request is submitted to the external bus unit and the processor initiates a read and invalidate transaction (has the effect of killing copies of the line in other processors' caches) to obtain the 32 byte line from memory. The read and invalidate transaction is used by the processor in cases when it is reading data from memory with the intent to modify it when the data has been obtained. This implies that any other processor that has a copy of the line in the E or S state should kill its copy of the line. If another processor has a copy of the line in the M state, it should source the line directly to the requesting processor and then kill its copy. When the line has been read from memory or from another processor's cache (in the case of a hit on an M line), the processor marks it locked in the data cache. It then performs the RMW operation. The line is unlocked when the RMW operation has been completed.

During this processor's RMW operation, another processor may initiate a read or a RMW that misses its cache, resulting in a read or a read and invalidate transaction for the same line. A snoop is performed in this processor's cache and hits on the locked line. The snoop result to the other processor is delayed (stretching the other processor's snoop phase) until the processor's RMW has been completed. The snoop result is then delivered to the other processor. Either the semaphore wasn't updated (and the line therefore wasn't modified), or it was (and the line was marked modified). If the line was modified, the line is provided directly to the other processor from this processor's cache (and is invalidated if the other processor's transaction type is the read and invalidate). Otherwise, the other processor obtains the line from memory. If the other processor's transaction is a read (rather than a read and invalidate), the line is marked S in this processor's cache. If the other processor's transaction was a read and invalidate, the line is invalidated in this processor's cache.

In the case where two processors are in a race condition where they are both initiating RMW operations that miss their caches, they both initiate read and invalidate transactions on the bus. Since they can't both initiate a transaction simultaneously, however, one wins bus ownership first and initiates its read and invalidate. The second processor then initiates its read and invalidate transaction. The first processor obtains the line from memory and marks it locked while it performs the RMW. When the second processor's read and invalidate transaction reaches its snoop phase, the first processor snoops its cache and hits on the locked line. It delays the delivery of the snoop result until it completes its RMW operation and then delivers the snoop result to the second processor. If the line is not modified, it indicates a miss to the second processor and invalidates its copy. On the other hand, if the RMW operation modified the line, it indicates a hit on a modified line, sources the line directly to the second processor, and invalidates its copy of the line. The second processor now has a copy of the line and can perform its RMW operation.

Semaphore in Cache in E State

If the read of the RMW hits on an E copy of the line in the data or L2 cache, no other processor has a copy of the line in its cache. The line is marked locked in the cache (in case another processor tries to read the line during the RMW operation) and the RMW operation is then performed on the semaphore within line. The lock is then removed.

Semaphore in Cache in S State

If the read of the RMW hits on an S copy of the line in the data or L2 cache, at least one other processor has a copy of the line. Before this processor can perform the RMW, it must first gain exclusive ownership of the line by killing copies in the caches of other processors. It does this by issuing a read and invalidate transaction for 0 bytes of data (this is a kill). Any other processor that has a copy of the line must kill its copy. The line is then marked locked in the cache while the RMW operation is performed, after which it is unlocked.

Semaphore in Cache in M State

If the read of the RMW hits on an M copy of the line in the data or L2 cache, no other processor has a copy of the line in its cache. The line is marked locked in the cache (in case another processor tries to read the line during the RMW operation) and the RMW operation is then performed on the semaphore within the line. The lock is then removed.

Blocking New Requests—Stop! I'm Full!

The section entitled "Transaction Tracking" on page 219 introduced the concept of transaction tracking and the IOQ (in-order queue). Each agent has an IOQ that it uses to keep track of each transaction that is currently outstanding on the bus. The depth of an agent's IOQ is device-specific. The Pentium Pro processor has a selectable queue depth of either one or eight. The queue depths of the 450GX chipset agents is also selectable as one or eight. The queue depth of the 440FX chipset is four.

When the maximum number of transactions (minus one) that a device can track are currently outstanding on the bus at various stages of completion, the agent cannot permit any agent to initiate a new transaction. If a new transaction were initiated, the agent would be incapable of tracking it and consequently would lose track of all activity on the bus.

For this reason, agents must have the ability to throttle the ability of other agents to initiate new transactions. That is the purpose of the BNR# (Block Next Request) signal. An agent must assert BNR# when its In Order Queue (IOQ) has one entry remaining empty. This is necessary because a new transaction request could be issued by another agent at the same time that an agent begins to assert BNR#. The one entry that is remaining can then be used to latch and track the newly-issued transaction. There is no danger that another transaction will be issued to the bus because all agents have detected BNR# by this time.

BNR# could also be used by a debug tool to create a controlled situation where no additional transactions can be issued to the bus until the current transaction has been completed. In other words, transactions could be single-stepped onto the bus to simplify the debug process.

BNR# is Shared Signal

BNR# is a shared, open-drain signal because multiple bus agents may assert it simultaneously to indicate that they are not ready to deal with a new transaction.

Stalled/Throttled/Free Indicator

Each agent capable of initiating transactions must maintain an internal indicator referred to as the stalled/throttled/free indicator. Refer to Figure 10-10 on page 252. At powerup or when reset is asserted, all initiators (i.e., request agents) reset this indicator to the stalled state. All request agents are required to start sampling BNR# on a periodic basis starting soon after reset is removed (see "BNR# Behavior at Powerup" on page 253) and must remain in the stalled state until BNR# is sampled deasserted. This prevents any agent from issuing a transaction until BNR# is sampled deasserted, indicating that all agents are prepared to deal with a new transaction.

Figure 10-10: Stalled/Throttled/Free Indicator States

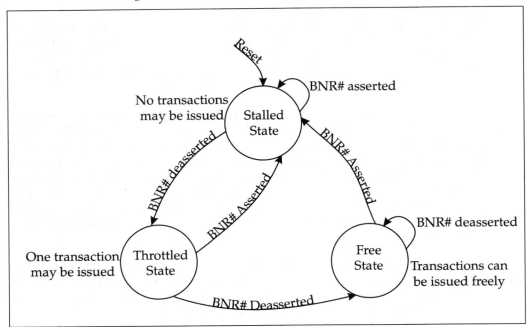

Open Gate, Let One Out, Close Gate

When BNR# is sampled deasserted the first time, all request agents transition their indicators from the stalled to the throttled state. This gives permission to the current request signal group owner to initiate a transaction request. If BNR# is sampled asserted on the next sample point, all request agents transition the indicator from throttled back to the stalled state. This one time deassertion and then immediate reassertion of BNR# is analogous to opening the gate to let one transaction out and then closing the gate again. This mechanism can be used to permit a new transaction to be issued by the next owner only when everyone is ready to deal with it. A debug tool could use BNR# in this manner to permit issuance and tracking of just one transaction from inception to completion.

Open Gate, Leave It Open, Let Them All Out

When everyone is stalled and BNR# is then sampled deasserted one time, they all transition to the throttled state and one transaction may be issued by the current request signal group owner. If BNR# is then again sampled deasserted a second time, all request agents transition the indicator from the throttled to the free state. All request agents are then free to issue new transactions as they acquire ownership of the request signal group. This would permit a new transaction request to be issued to the bus once every three clocks.

Gate Wide Open and then Slammed Shut

When the request agents are operating in the free state and BNR# is then sampled asserted, they all transition from the free to the stalled state and are prevented from issuing any new transactions until the next time BNR# is sampled deasserted. As described earlier, they all then transition from stalled to throttled and one new transaction can be issued. Depending on whether BNR# is sampled deasserted or asserted at the next sample point, they all then transition from throttled to free, or from throttled back to stalled, respectively.

BNR# Behavior at Powerup

Figure 10-11 on page 255 illustrates the behavior of BNR# during and immediately after the assertion of reset.

1. If BNR# was asserted before the assertion of reset, it must be deasserted within one clock after reset is sampled asserted. In addition, all request agents must reset their stalled/throttled/free indicators to the stalled state.
2. The first BNR# sample point is two clocks after reset is sampled deasserted. If it is sampled asserted, all request agents must remain in the stalled state.
3. When asserted, BNR# should remain asserted for only one clock.
4. When request agents are in the stalled state, they sample BNR# every two clocks.
5. On clock 14, BNR# is sampled deasserted and all request agents change to the throttled state one clock later (clock 15). This permits the request agent that is the winner of the first arbitration to issue one transaction request (in clocks 15 and 16).
6. BNR# is sampled every two clocks when in the throttled state. It is sampled

deasserted for a second time on clock 16, causing all request agents to transition to the free state one clock later (in clock 17).

7. As the agents transition to the free state, they begin sampling BNR# three clocks after ADS# is asserted by any agent.

BNR# and the Built-In Self-Test (BIST)

Any processor that has been instructed to perform its BIST at the trailing-edge of reset will assert BNR# until it has completed its BIST. This is done because the processor's local APIC is incapable of taking part in the automatic selection of the bootstrap processor while its BIST is still in progress. In other words, it cannot receive BIPI messages issued by the local APICs in other processors until its BIST completes. None of the processors will issue BIPI messages until BNR# is sampled deasserted. For information on initiation of a processor's BIST, see "Run BIST Option" on page 39. For information on the selection of the bootstrap processor, see "Selection of Bootstrap Processor (BSP)" on page 56.

Figure 10-11: BNR# at Powerup or After Reset

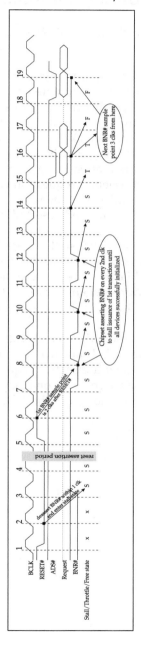

BNR# Behavior During Runtime

Figure 10-12 on page 257 illustrates BNR# behavior after reset (i.e., during runtime).

1. The priority agent had acquired ownership of the request signal group in the clock prior to clock 1 and initiated a transaction request. It deasserted BPRI# as it did so to yield ownership to symmetric agent 0 (BREQ0# was asserted). The indicator is in the free state and BNR# is being sampled by all request agents every three clocks.
2. On clock one, agent 0 samples BPRI# deasserted, indicating that it will be the next owner of the request signal group.
3. Agent 0 initiates a transaction request on clock three (its indicator is in the free state, giving it permission to do so).
4. On clock four, BNR# is sampled asserted, indicating that one or more bus agents cannot handle the issuance of any more transactions. The indicator transitions from the free to the stalled state in clock five and the BNR# sample rate changes to every two clocks. No new transactions can be issued by any request agent while they are in the stalled state.
5. In clock five, the priority agent reasserts BPRI# because it wants to issue another transaction. It cannot do so, however, until BNR# is sampled deasserted.
6. BNR# is sampled deasserted on clock eight and all request agents change the indicator to the throttled state in clock nine. This gives the priority agent permission to issue a new transaction request in clock nine.
7. BNR# is sampled deasserted again on clock 10 and all request agents transition to the free state in clock 11. The BNR# sample rate changes back to every three clocks.

Figure 10-12: BNR# During Runtime

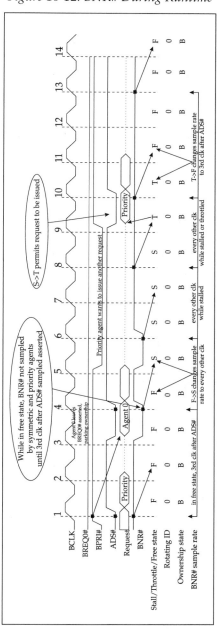

Hardware Section 3:
The Transaction Phases

The Previous Section

The chapters that comprised Part 2, Section 2 introduced the processor's bus and transaction protocol.

This Section

The chapters that comprise Part 2, Section 3 provide a detailed description of each phase that a transaction passes through from inception to completion. It consists of the following chapters:

- "The Request and Error Phases" on page 261.
- "The Snoop Phase" on page 277.
- "The Response and Data Phases" on page 297.

The Next Section

Part 2, Section 4 covers additional transaction and bus topics not covered in the previous sections.

11 *The Request and Error Phases*

The Previous Chapter

Before a request agent can issue a new transaction to the bus, it must arbitrate for and win ownership of the request signal group.The previous chapter covered all of the issues related to obtaining request signal group ownership.

This Chapter

This chapter provides a detailed description of the request and error phases of any transaction.

The Next Chapter

The error phase of a transaction is always immediately followed by the snoop phase. The next chapter provides a detailed description of the snoop phase of a transaction.

Caution

As stated earlier in the book, unless noted otherwise the representation of all signal states in tables is in logical, not electrical values. As an example, the first row in Table 11-4 on page 267 shows a 00000b on REQ[4:0]# indicates a deferred reply transaction type. This means that REQ[4:0]# are deasserted (electrical ones) when driven onto REQ[4:0]#.

Request Phase

Introduction to the Request Phase

Once ownership of the request signal group has been acquired (see "Obtaining Bus Ownership" on page 221), the request agent uses the request signal group to broadcast the transaction request. This includes the address and transaction type, as well as additional information about the transaction. The **request signal group** consists of the following signals:

- **A[35:3]#.** Address bus.
- **AP[1:0]#.** Address bus parity bits.
- **REQ[4:0]#.** Request bus.
- **RP#.** Parity bit for REQ[4:0]# and ADS#.
- **ADS#.** Address Strobe.

The request phase is always two clocks in duration. The information about the transaction is output in two packets (see Figure 11-1 on page 262), one during each clock. ADS# is asserted during the first clock and deasserted during the second. Its assertion indicates that a new transaction request is being broadcast. All bus agents, not only response agents (i.e., targets), latch both packets. As discussed earlier, all agents must track the transaction as it passes through each phase from inception to completion. In addition, if it is a memory transaction, snoop agents (i.e., processors with internal caches) must submit the memory address to their caches for a lookup and must deliver the snoop result during the transaction's snoop phase. The response agents must decode the address and transaction type to determine which of them is the target of the transaction.

Figure 11-1: Two Information Packets Broadcast during Request Phase

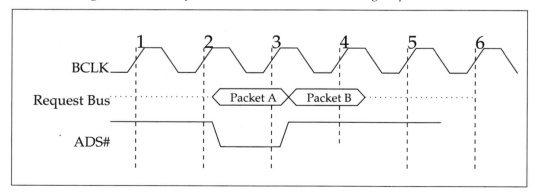

Chapter 11: The Request and Error Phases

Request Signal Group is Multiplexed

There is more transaction-related information to be output during the request phase than there are pins on the processor. To address this problem, the same signal group is used during each of the two clocks that comprise the request phase, but different information is output on these pins during each clock. Intel refers to the two information packets as packets A and B.

In the Intel data book, the information output in the two packets is referred in the following manner:

- the information output on the address (A[35:3]#) and request (REQ[4:0]#) signal groups during Packet A is referred to as Aa[35:3]# and REQa[4:0]#.
- the information output on the address (A[35:3]#) and request (REQ[4:0]#) signal groups during Packet B is referred to as Ab[35:3]# and REQb[4:0]#.

The information output during Packet B are actually internal signals that are gated onto the address and request pins during the second clock. Table 11-1 on page 263 indicates the names of the internal signals driven onto A[35:3]# during the second clock.

Table 11-1: Packet B Signal Names

Output Pin(s)	Signal Names
A[31:24]#	**ATTR[7:0]#**. Attribute signals. See Table 11-8 on page 271.
A[23:16]#	**DID[7:0]#**. Deferred ID. See Table 11-9 on page 271.
A[15:8]#	**BE[7:0]#**. The eight byte enable signals indicate which of the bytes in the currently-addressed quadword are to be transferred (i.e., read or written).
A[7:3]#	**EXF[4:0]#**. Extended function signals. See Table 11-11 on page 273.

Introduction to the Transaction Types

The transaction types currently defined for the bus are listed in Table 11-2 on page 264. The table provides a brief description of each transaction type.

Table 11-2: Currently-Defined Transaction Types

Transaction Type	Brief Description
Deferred Reply	Initiated by a response agent that had deferred the completion of an earlier transaction (because it was going to take a long time). This transaction addresses the request agent that had initiated the previously-deferred transaction and is used to deliver the transaction completion status (and, if a read, the read data) to the initiator. For more information, refer to "Transaction Deferral" on page 327.
Interrupt Acknowledge	Generated by a processor in response to an interrupt from an 8259 interrupt controller to read the interrupt vector. For more information, refer to "Interrupt Acknowledge Transaction" on page 354.
Special Transaction	Generated by the processor to broadcast a message regarding an internal event (e.g., shutdown, halt, etc.). For more information on the Special Transaction, refer to "Central Agent Transactions" on page 353.
Branch Trace Message	Generated by the processor when a branch is taken. Writes out the address of the branch instruction as well as the branch target address. For more information on the Branch Trace Message transaction, refer to "Central Agent Transactions" on page 353.
IO Read	Generated by the processor when executing an IN or INS instruction to read data or status from an IO device. Can also be generated by an agent other than a processor (e.g., a host/PCI bridge).

Table 11-2: Currently-Defined Transaction Types (Continued)

Transaction Type	Brief Description
IO Write	Generated by the processor when executing an OUT or OUTS instruction to write data or a command to an IO device. Can also be generated by an agent other than a processor (e.g., a host/PCI bridge).
Memory Read and Invalidate	Generated by the processor to gain exclusive ownership of a cache line. Caused by a cache read miss when performing a read/modify/write (RMW) operation, or before performing a RMW on a line in the cache in the shared state.Also generated when a write miss occurs in a WB memory area. For more information, refer to "Locking—Shared Resource Acquisition" on page 241.
Memory Code Read	Generated by the processor when fetching instructions from memory.
Memory Data Read	Generated by the processor when executing an instruction that requires the reading of data from memory (i.e., a load).
Memory Write (may not be retried)	Generated by the processor when writing back a modified line to memory (a cast out) to make room for a new line in the L1 data cache.
Memory Write (may be retried)	Generated by the processor when executing an instruction that requires the writing of data to memory (i.e., a store).

Contents of Request Packet A

Table 11-3 on page 266 defines the information driven onto the request signal group during the first clock of the request phase. It consists of the address and transaction type. This is sufficient information for response agents to begin the decode to determine which of them is the target device. Table 11-4 on page 267 details the encoding of the transaction types.

Table 11-3: Request Packet A

Signal(s)	Description
ADS#	**Address Strobe** is asserted by the agent issuing the request, indicating that the agent is providing all of the request information during this clock and the one that follows. This information represents the address, the request type, and additional information about the transaction.
A[35:3]#	The quadword-aligned IO or memory **address** is presented to the other agents. If this is a deferred reply transaction, the address of the request agent that initiated the previously-deferred transaction is presented.
REQ[4:0]#	**Request**. The request (i.e., transaction type) is presented on these signal lines. Table 11-4 on page 267 defines the request codes currently defined for the Pentium Pro processor.
AP[1:0]#	**Address Parity** bits 1 and 0. AP1# is an even parity bit that covers A[35:24]#, while AP0# is an even parity bit that covers A[23:3]#. Each bit must either be a low or a high to force an even number of electrically low signals on the set of covered signals plus the respective parity signal.
RP#	**Request Parity**. RP# is an even parity bit that covers REQ[4:0]# and ADS#. RP# must either be a low or a high to force an even number of electrically low signals on the set of covered signals plus the parity signal.

Table 11-4: Request Types (**note**: 0 = signal deasserted, 1 = signal asserted)

Packet A (Request)					Packet B (Extended Request)					Request Type
REQ4#	REQ3#	REQ2#	REQ1#	REQ0#	REQ4#	REQ3#	REQ2#	REQ1#	REQ0#	
0	0	0	0	0	x	x	x	x	x	**Deferred Reply**. Initiated by response agent to complete a request that was received earlier. For more information, see "Transaction Deferral" on page 327.
0	0	0	0	1						Reserved (ignore).
0	1	0	0	0	DSZ field. Always 00b (= 64-bit data bus width) for Pentium Pro. Ignored by responder.		x	0	0	**Interrupt Acknowledge**. Generated by a processor when an interrupt request is received from an 8259A interrupt controller.
									1	**Special Transaction**. For more information, see "Central Agent Transactions" on page 353.
								1	x	Reserved (Central Agent Response).
0	1	0	0	1				0	0	**Branch Trace Message**. For more information, see "Central Agent Transactions" on page 353.
									1	Reserved (Central Agent Response).
								1	x	Reserved (Central Agent Response).
1	0	0	0	0				LEN		**IO Read**. For more information, see "IO Transactions" on page 349.
				1						**IO Write**. For more information, see "IO Transactions" on page 349.
1	1	0	0	x				x	x	Reserved (ignore)
ASZ (Table 11-6 on page 268)		0	1	0				LEN		**Memory Read and Invalidate**. For more information, see "Locking—Shared Resource Acquisition" on page 241.
				1						Reserved (memory write).
		1	0	0						**Memory Code Read** (REQ1# in Packet A = 0).
				1						**Memory Data Read** (REQ1# in Packet A = 1).
			0	1						**Memory Write (don't retry)**. REQ1# in Packet A = 0. Only used when casting modified line to memory to make room for new line in L1 data cache.
				1						**Memory Write (may be retried)**. REQ1# in Packet A = 1.

Table 11-5: Data Transfer Length Field (see Table 11-4 on page 267)

LEN[1:0]#	State of Byte Enables	Size of Transfer
00b	Specify bytes to be transferred within addressed quadword.	Quadword or subset of quadword.
01b	All asserted.	16 bytes (two quadwords). Pentium Pro doesn't use, but other agents, such as a host/PCI bridge, may.
10b	All asserted.	32 bytes (four quadwords).
11b	Not defined.	Reserved

Table 11-6: Address Space Size Field (see Table 11-4 on page 267)

ASIZ[1:0]#	Description
00b	The memory address is within the range from 0 through 4GB - 1. It should be decoded by any memory targets (i.e., response agents) that reside (at least partially) below the 4GB boundary.
01b	The memory address is within the range from 4GB through 64GB - 1. It should be decoded by any memory targets (i.e., response agents) that reside (at least partially) above the 4GB boundary, but below the 64GB boundary.
10b	Reserved.
11b	Reserved.

32-bit vs. 36-bit Addresses

All of the memory transaction types contain an address size field (see ASZ in Table 11-4 on page 267 and Table 11-6 on page 268). Please note that although the spec only currently defines two ASZ bit patterns, there are two more available for future assignment. In other words, Intel may design future processors with address buses wider (or, although unlikely, more narrow) than the current 36 bits. It is currently permissible to design:

1. **32-bit address request agent**. Request agents that are only capable of generating 32-bit memory addresses and only use up to A[31]# (they don't drive A[35:32]#). They are therefore only capable of addressing memory that resides in the lower 4GB. Whenever a request agent of this type generates a memory transaction, it must indicate (on the ASZ lines) that it is only generating a 32-bit address on the lower part of the bus to address a memory target that resides below the 4GB boundary.

2. **32-bit address memory response agent**. Memory response agents that only latch and decode up to A[31]#. By definition, then, these memory response agents reside in the lower 4GB of memory space. A memory agent of this type must check the state of the ASZ lines received in request packet A and only decode the address if ASZ indicates that it is below the 4GB boundary. If it ignored ASZ, it may decode the lower 32 bits of a 36-bit (or wider) address destined for a memory target that resides above the 4GB - 1 boundary. This could result in two memory response agents driving bus signals simultaneously.

3. **36-bit address request agent**. Request agents that are capable of generating 36-bit memory addresses and use up to A[35]#. They are therefore capable of addressing memory that resides in the lower 64GB. Whenever a request agent of this type generates a memory transaction, it must indicate (on the ASZ lines) whether it is generating an address above or below the 4GB boundary.

4. **36-bit address memory response agent**. Memory response agents that latch and decode up to A[35]#. By definition, then, these memory response agents can reside anywhere in the lower 64GB of memory space. A memory agent of this type must check the state of the ASZ lines received in request packet A and only decode the address if ASZ indicates that it is below the 4GB boundary or below the 64GB boundary. If it ignored ASZ, it may decode the lower 36 bits of an address destined for a memory target that resides above the 64GB boundary (this wouldn't happen now, but it could happen in the future). This could result in two memory response agents driving bus signals simultaneously.

Contents of Request Packet B

Table 11-7 on page 270 defines the information driven onto the request signal group during the second clock of the request phase. It contains additional information about the transaction request.

Table 11-7: Request Packet B

Signal(s)	Description
REQ[4:0]#	**Extended Request** field (see Table 11-4 on page 267).
A[35:32]#	**Optional debug information**. Not defined in publicly-released Intel documents.
A[31:24]#	**Attribute field**. Also referred to as **ATTR[7:0]#**. Just as it is important for the processor's internal logic to know the **rules of conduct** within a memory area being accessed, external logic (e.g., an L3 cache) must also behave correctly when a memory access within a particular memory region is being accessed. This value is supplied by the MTRR registers and the page table entry for the page being accessed. See Table 11-8 on page 271.
A[23:16]#	**Deferred ID field**. A response agent may choose to defer completion of a transaction request until a later time. When it is ready to complete the transaction, the response agent becomes a request agent and initiates a deferred reply transaction to address the request agent (using the DID field) that originally initiated the transaction. It must also identify which transaction is being completed. Also referred to as **DID[7:0]#**. See Table 11-9 on page 271.
A[15:8]#	**Byte Enables**. Also referred to as **BE[7:0]#**. Specifies the bytes to be transferred within the currently-addressed quadword (see Table 11-5 on page 268). In the case of the special transaction type, the message being broadcast is encoded on the byte enables as indicated in Table 11-10 on page 272.
A[7:3]#	**Extended Functions field**. Contains additional signals related to SMM, locking, and whether or not the response agent is permitted to defer transaction completion until a later time. Also referred to as **EXF[4:0]#**. See Table 11-11 on page 273.
AP[1:0]#	**Address Parity** bits 1 and 0. AP1# is an even parity bit that covers A[35:24]#, while AP0# is an even parity bit that covers A[23:3]#. Each bit must either be a low or a high to force an even number of electrically low signals on the set of covered signals plus the respective parity signal.

Chapter 11: The Request and Error Phases

Table 11-7: Request Packet B (Continued)

Signal(s)	Description
RP#	**Request Parity**. RP# is an even parity bit that covers REQ[4:0]# and ADS#. RP# must either be a low or a high to force an even number of electrically low signals on the set of covered signals plus the parity signal.

Table 11-8: Attribute Field—Rules of Conduct (see Table 11-7 on page 270)

ATTRIB[7:0]# (A[31:24]#)	Memory Type	Description
00000000b	UC	Address is within memory range designated as **uncacheable** by MTRRs and/or page table entry.
0000100b	WC	Address is within memory range designated as **write-combining** by MTRRs and/or page table entry.
00000101b	WT	Address is within memory range designated as **write-through** by MTRRs and/or page table entry.
00000110b	WP	Address is within memory range designated as **write protected** by MTRRs and/or page table entry.
00000111b	WB	Address is within memory range designated as **write-back** by MTRRs and/or page table entry.
all other values	Reserved	

Table 11-9: Deferred ID Composition (see Table 11-7 on page 270)

Bit Field	Description
DID7#	**Agent Type**. Type 0 = Symmetric agent, while type 1 = priority agent. Delivered by request initiator on A23# during transmission of request Packet B.

Table 11-9: Deferred ID Composition (see Table 11-7 on page 270) (Continued)

Bit Field	Description
DID[6:4]#	**Agent ID** of request initiator. Delivered by request initiator on A[22:20]# during transmission of request Packet B.
DID[3:0]#	**Transaction ID**. Delivered by request initiator on A[19:16]# during transmission of request packet B. Each deferrable transaction (DEN# asserted in packet B on A4#) initiated by a processor will have a unique transaction ID. When one of these transactions has passed its snoop phase without being deferred, its deferred ID may be reused by the request agent. When a response agent initiates the deferred reply transaction, it uses the deferred ID as the address of the reply.

Table 11-10: Messages Broadcast Using Special Transaction (see Table 11-7 on page 270)

Message Type	Byte Enable Settings
Shutdown. For more information about any of the messages, see "Central Agent Transactions" on page 353.	00000001b
Flush	00000010b
Halt	00000011b
Sync	00000100b
Flush Acknowledge	00000101b
Stop Grant Acknowledge	00000110b
SMI Acknowledge	00000111b
Reserved	all other encodings

Chapter 11: The Request and Error Phases

Table 11-11: Extended Function Field (see Table 11-7 on page 270)

Bit	Description
EXF4#	**SMMEM#, System Management Memory.** When asserted, System Management memory is being accessed (rather than regular memory).
EXF3#	**SPLCK#. Split Lock.** When asserted, processor is accessing a memory semaphore that splits across cache lines in WB memory or across quadwords in UC or WT memory. Results in locked transaction series consisting of 2 reads to read semaphore from memory followed later by 2 writes to update semaphore. For more information, refer to "Locking— Shared Resource Acquisition" on page 241.
EXF2#	Reserved.
EXF1#	**DEN#. Defer Enable.** When asserted by the request agent, response agent is permitted to defer completion until a later time. For more information, see "Transaction Deferral" on page 327.
EXF0#	Reserved.

Error Phase

In-Flight Corruption

Refer to Figure 11-2 on page 274. All agents latch request packets A and B of the transaction request on clocks two and three, respectively. The request phase consists of clocks one and two, while the error phase consists of clocks three and four (it is always two clocks in duration). When packet A is latched on clock two, all agents check the parity on AP[1:0]# and RP# during clock two. When packet B is latched on clock three, all agents check the parity for the packet during clock three. If an error is detected in either packet, all agents that received a corrupted packet assert AERR# for one clock during clock four (do not assert AERR# during clock three if packet A is corrupted). Note that AERR# is one of the six GTL+ signals that is a shared, open-drain signal that can be driven by multiple devices simultaneously.

Figure 11-2: Error Phase

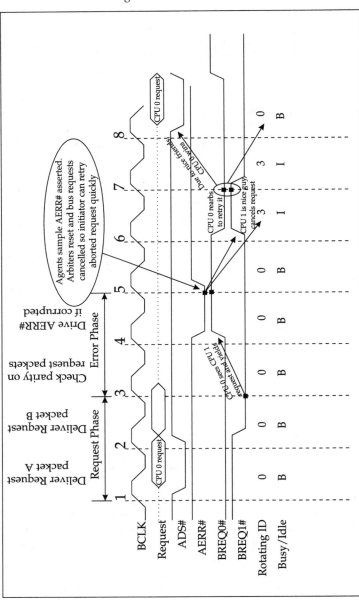

Chapter 11: The Request and Error Phases

Who Samples AERR#?

Request Agent

If it was enabled to do so at powerup time (see "Error Observation Options" on page 39), the request agent that initiated the transaction request samples AERR# on clock five. If AERR# is sampled deasserted, the transaction request was received correctly by all other bus agents and the transaction may proceed. If AERR# is sampled asserted, however, the transaction is cancelled (i.e., it is deleted from the request agent's IOQ).

Other Bus Agents

All other bus agents latch packets A and B of the transaction request. If they were enabled to do so at powerup time (see "Error Observation Options" on page 39), they sample AERR# on clock five. If AERR# is sampled deasserted, the transaction remains in their IOQs and will be tracked until its completion. If AERR# is sampled asserted, however, the transaction is cancelled (i.e., it is deleted from the agents' IOQs).

Who Drives AERR#?

Any bus agent that was enabled to drive AERR# at powerup time (see "Program-Accessible Startup Features" on page 45), will assert AERR# in clock four if it detects that either of the transaction request packets were corrupted in flight.

Request Agent's Response to AERR# Assertion

If the request agent samples AERR# asserted on clock five, it cancels (i.e., aborts) the transaction. Optionally, it may reattempt the transaction. Whether it retries and the number of retry attempts is device-specific. *The Pentium Pro processor has a retry count of one for all transactions that result in AERR#.* If AERR# is sampled asserted and the transaction will be retried, the request agent asks for request signal group ownership again in clock six. If it's a symmetric agent and it had deasserted its BREQn# when it initiated the transaction, it reasserts its BREQn# signal. If it's a priority agent and it had deasserted BPRI# when it initiated the transaction, it reasserts BPRI#.

If the retry also fails, the Pentium Pro processor generates a machine check exception (if CR4[MCE] = 1) and latches the address and transaction type into the machine check architecture registers (see "Machine Check Architecture" on page 477).

Other Guys are Very Polite

Refer to Figure 11-2 on page 274. When they sample AERR# asserted, any other request agents that might have been requesting ownership of the request signal group deassert their requests for one clock. This opens a window for the request agent that experienced the bad request phase to win ownership to reattempt the transaction (on clock eight). However, all of the other symmetric agents had already sampled the BREQn# signals and registered which of them wanted the bus next (normally, a symmetric agent is not permitted to deassert an already asserted BREQn# line until it has gained ownership; however, this is a special case to help out a friend who has fallen on hard times). To avoid confusing their arbitration mechanisms, all of the symmetric agents reset their rotating ID to three and the ownership state to idle.

12 *The Snoop Phase*

The Previous Chapter

The previous chapter provided a detailed description of the request and error phases of a transaction.

This Chapter

Unless the transaction is cancelled by an error in its error phase, the error phase of a transaction is always immediately followed by the snoop phase. This chapter provides a detailed description of the snoop phase.

The Next Chapter

The snoop phase of the transaction is always immediately followed by the response and possibly the data phase. The next chapter provides a detailed description of the response and data phases.

Agents Involved in Snoop Phase

Refer to Figure 12-1 on page 279. The following agents are involved in the snoop phase of the transaction:

- The **request agent** issues the transaction request. This can be one of the processors, or one of the host/PCI bridges. If the transaction is a memory transaction, it also checks the snoop result presented in the snoop phase.
- The **snoop agents** are the processors. They latch the transaction and, if it's a memory transaction, submit the memory address to their internal caches for a lookup. They present the snoop result to the request agent. If the snoop resulted in a hit on a modified line in a processor's cache, that snoop agent (i.e., processor) supplies the modified line in the data phase (see next bullet). If it's a non-memory transaction, the processors do not snoop the transaction.

- The **response agent** is the currently-addressed target. This could be main memory, the configuration registers or IO ports within the memory controller or within one of the host/PCI bridges, a target residing on one of the PCI buses, or a target residing on the ISA or EISA bus. If the response agent is main memory, it must observe the snoop response presented by the snoop agents. If the access results in a miss on all the caches, or in a hit on a clean line, the memory controller supplies the read data or, if a write, accepts the write data presented by the request agent. However, if the transaction is a read that hits on a modified line, the snoop agent supplies the modified line directly to the request agent and also writes it to memory (in other words, the transaction started out a read from main memory's perspective and turned into a write, but it remained a read from the request agent's perspective). If the transaction is a write that hits on a modified line, the memory controller accepts the write data from the request agent, then accepts the modified line from the snoop agent, and finally merges the write data into the modified line and writes the resulting line into memory.

Figure 12-1: System Block Diagram

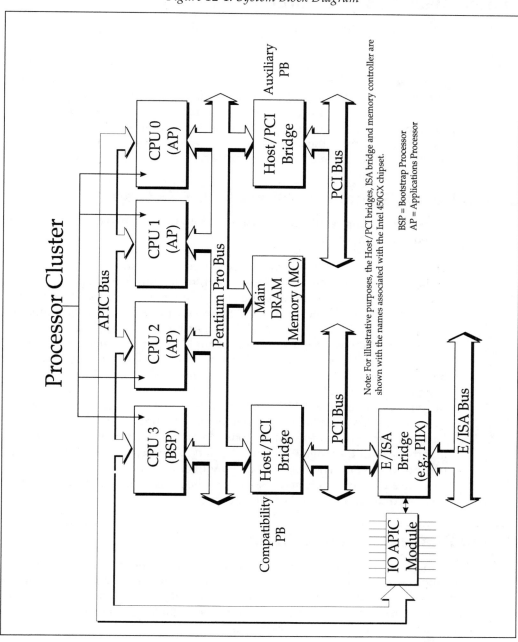

Snoop Phase Has Two Purposes

In the snoop phase, the request agent samples the snoop result signals to determine:

1. if the currently-addressed response agent (i.e., the target) intends to complete the transaction now or it will be retried or its completion deferred until a later time (because it will take a while to complete).
2. if the transaction is a memory read or write that the response agent will complete now (i.e., it doesn't intend to defer its completion), does any other cache have a copy of the line and, if so, in what state (clean or modified) will its line be at the completion of the transaction?

Snoop Result Signals are Shared, DEFER# Isn't

There are three snoop result signals (divided into two groups) that are sampled by the request agent during the snoop phase:

1. The **HIT# and HITM#** are the signals used by the snoop agents (i.e., the caches) to deliver the cache snoop result, or to stall the completion of the snoop phase if one or more of the snoop agents isn't ready to deliver the snoop result (see "Line in E or M State" on page 248 for an example of snoop stall). Both HIT# and HITM# might be driven by multiple snoopers if any of them need to stall the completion of the snoop phase until the snoop resultis available. At that time, each of the snoopers that have been stalling would stop driving both lines and either drive neither (if it's a miss), just HIT# (if it's a hit on an E or S line), or just HITM# (if it's a hit on a modified line). HIT# and HITM# are shared, open-drain signals that may be driven by more than one device at a time.
2. Only the currently-addressed response agent (i.e., the target) is permitted to assert the **DEFER#** signal during the snoop phase, so it is not a shared, open-drain signal. The response agent will only assert DEFER# if it intends to issue a retry or a deferred response to the request agent. These topics are discussed towards the end of this chapter.

Snoop Phase Duration Is Variable

Refer to Figure 12-2 on page 281. The snoop phase begins immediately after the error phase completes (clocks 5, 8, and 11) and completes when a valid snoop result (something other than both HIT# and HITM# asserted) is presented to the request and response agents by the snoop agents. Table 12-1 on page 282 defines the meaning of the various snoop results.

Figure 12-2: Snoop Phase

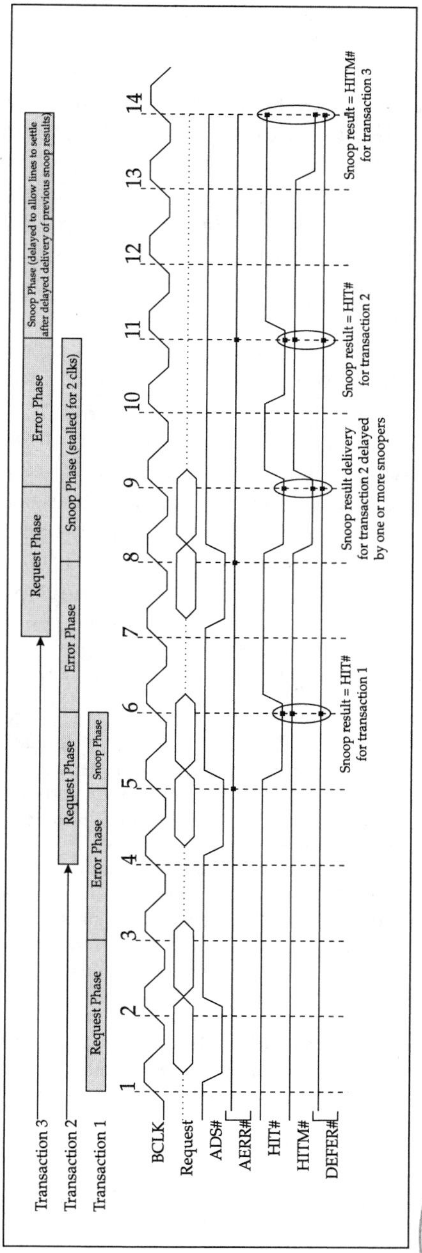

1. In Figure 12-2 on page 281, transaction one's snoop phase completes one clock after it starts (on clock six) when HIT# is sampled asserted with HITM# and DEFER# deasserted. This indicates a hit on a line in the E state in one cache, or a hit on lines in the S state in two or more processors.

2. Transaction two's snoop phase starts on clock eight and the snoop result is first sampled one clock later on clock nine. However, in this case both HIT# and HITM# are sampled asserted indicating a snoop stall (one or more of the snoop agents aren't ready to deliver the actual snoop result). As a result, the request agent stretches the duration of the snoop phase by two clocks and then samples the snoop result again on clock 11. This time a good result is sampled—HIT# is asserted alone, indicating a hit on a line in the E state in one cache, or a hit on lines in the S state in two or more processors.

3. Transaction three's snoop phase starts on clock 11 when its error phase ends. Because the snoop result for the previous transaction was delayed (i.e., stalled), transaction three's request agent delays its first sampling of the current transaction's snoop result until three clocks after the previous transaction's snoop result was sampled. This allows two clocks for the lines to settle and one for the current transaction's snoop result to be driven. After the snoop agents deliver the previous transaction's snoop result, they turn off their drivers to allow HIT# or HITM# to return high. In order to let these shared lines settle, they must delay driving the next snoop result until two clocks after they turn their drivers off.

Table 12-1: Snoop Result Table (0 = deasserted, 1 = asserted)

HIT#	HITM#	DEFER#	Interpretation
0	0	0	**Clean snoop** (HIT# and HITM# both deasserted indicates a miss in all caches) and transaction completion not deferred by response agent.
0	0	1	Transaction **completion deferred** by response agent. Ignore the snoop result. In the response phase, the response agent will issue **either** a **retry** or a **deferred response**. If it issues a deferred response, the real snoop result will be delivered later in the deferred reply transaction initiated by the response agent. If the response agent issues a retry response, the request agent must retry the transaction from scratch later.
0	1	0	**Hit on a modified line**. Snoop agent with modified line will supply the line to the response agent in the data phase (and to the request agent if it's a read).

Table 12-1: Snoop Result Table (0 = deasserted, 1 = asserted) (Continued)

HIT#	HITM#	DEFER#	Interpretation
0	1	1	**Hit on a modified line**. Assertion of **HITM#** in an **unlocked transaction overrides** the assertion of **DEFER#** (in other words, transaction completion will not be deferred). Snoop agent with modified line will supply the line to the response agent in the data phase (and to the request agent if it's a read).
1	0	0	**Hit on** a **clean line** (E or S state) in one or more caches.
1	0	1	At least one cache has a copy of the line in the clean state (E or S state) and the response agent's assertion of **DEFER#** indicates that it will defer completion of the transaction until a later time. The **request agent ignores** assertion of **HIT#**. In the response phase, the response agent will either issue a **retry or a deferred response**. If it issues a retry, the request agent must retry the transaction from scratch again later. If the response agent issues a deferred response, the response agent initiates a deferred reply transaction at a later time and delivers the snoop result to the request agent. The request agent uses this deferred snoop result to choose the state of its copy of the line.
1	1	0	HIT# and HITM# both asserted indicates that at least one snoop agent cannot deliver the snoop result yet. This results in a **snoop stall**. The request agent waits two clocks before sampling the snoop result again. The stall continues until a good snoop result is delivered. Note that the state of **DEFER#** is **ignored** by the request agent **until** a good **snoop result** is **delivered** (something other than 11b on HIT# and HITM#).
1	1	1	Same as previous entry.

Is There a Snoop Stall Duration Limit?

No. The spec doesn't define a limit on how long the snoop phase may be stretched. However, to avoid hanging the system in the event of a failure, it is advisable for the chipset to monitor for excessive wait states inserted into the snoop phase and signal an error (e.g., via BERR#) if this condition occurs.

Memory Transaction Snooping

Snoop's Effects on Caches

When a memory transaction is snooped, the snoop result affects both the request agent and the snoop agents. There are a number of possible cases. The type of memory transaction, whether or not other caches have a copy of the line, and the state of the line(s) in other caches all have an effect. In addition, sometimes the length of the data transfer has an effect. Table 12-2 on page 284 defines the scenarios and the results.

Table 12-2: Effects of Snoop

Transaction Snooped	Snoop Result	Effects of Snoop Result
Memory read	Miss on all caches	Data read from memory. If a code cache line fill, the line is placed in the code cache in the S state (the code cache is SI, not MESI) and in the E state in the L2 cache. If a data cache line fill, the line is placed in the L2 and data caches in the E state.
	Hit on E or S line in one or more caches	Data read from memory. If a code cache line fill, the line is placed in the code and L2 caches in the S state. If a data cache line fill, the line is placed in the L2 and data caches in the S state. If a snoop agent had a copy of the line in the E state, it changes it to the S state.
	Hit on M line in one cache	The operation started as a read from memory, but this changes it to a read of the M line from the snoop agent's cache. From the memory controller's standpoint, the read has turned into an implicit writeback of the M line to memory. The memory controller issues an **implicit writeback** response to the request agent in the response phase and accepts the line from the snoop agent during the data phase. The snoop agent changes its copy from the M to the S state. The request agent may have requested less than a line, but a full line is returned in toggle mode order, critical quadword first. The request agent takes the data it requested and ignores the rest. If it requested the whole line, the line is placed in the L2 and code or data caches in the S state.

Table 12-2: Effects of Snoop (Continued)

Transaction Snooped	Snoop Result	Effects of Snoop Result
Memory write	Miss on all caches	Data written to memory. No effect on caches.
	Hit on E or S line in one or more caches	Snoopers indicate a miss. Invalidates lines in other caches (because the processors don't have the ability to snarf data being written to memory by other agents).
	Hit on M line in one cache	**Case 1: writing less than a line.** Memory controller accepts write data from request agent, then accepts implicit writeback of full line from snoop agent's cache. Memory controller than merges write data into writeback line and writes resultant line into memory. Snoop agent invalidates its copy of the line.
		Case 2: writing a full line. Memory controller accepts write data from request agent, then asserts TRDY# to snoop agent to indicate its readiness to accept the implicit writeback of full line from snoop agent's cache. The snoop agent can respond in one of two ways: • If it doesn't check the length of the write data, it asserts DBSY# and uses the data bus to supply the modified line to the memory controller. The memory controller than merges write data into writeback line and writes resultant line into memory. Alternately, the memory controller could discard the modified line. • Alternatively, it could note that the request agent is writing a full line and decide that it won't send the modified line to the response agent (i.e., the memory controller). This is indicated by not asserting DBSY# in response to the assertion of TRDY#. The memory controller writes the line received from the request agent into memory. In either case, the snoop agent invalidates its copy of the line.

Table 12-2: Effects of Snoop (Continued)

Transaction Snooped	Snoop Result	Effects of Snoop Result
Memory read and invalidate for 32 bytes	Miss on all caches	Data is read from memory and is placed in the data and L2 caches. The transaction is basically a read with intent to modify. If the programmer immediately modified one or more locations within the line (e.g., update of a semaphore), the line is now in the M state. If the programmer chooses not to update any locations in the line (e.g., the semaphore tested is already set), the line is placed in the E state.
	Hit on E or S line in one or more caches	Snoopers indicate a miss. Data is read from memory and is placed in the data cache. The line(s) in the other caches are invalidated. The transaction is basically a read with intent to modify. If the programmer immediately modified one or more locations within the line (e.g., update of a semaphore), the line is now in the M state. If the programmer chooses not to update any locations in the line (e.g., the semaphore tested is already set), the line is placed in the E state.
	Hit on M line in one cache	Data is supplied to the request agent and the response agent (i.e., the memory controller) from the modified line in the snoop agent's cache. Snoop agent invalidates its copy of the line. Response agent (i.e., the memory controller) may or may not write the line into memory. Since the line was read with the intent to modify it once it is placed in the data cache, the memory controller designer may choose not to waste memory bandwidth. If the programmer immediately modified one or more locations within the line (e.g., update of a semaphore), the line is now in the M state. If the programmer chooses not to update any locations in the line (e.g., the semaphore tested is already set), the line is placed in the E state.

Table 12-2: Effects of Snoop (Continued)

Transaction Snooped	Snoop Result	Effects of Snoop Result
Memory read and invalidate for 0 bytes	Miss on all caches	**Processor would not perform this transaction** because it already had a copy of the line in its data cache (why else would it be reading 0 bytes?) in the E state (E because no one else had a copy). If it didn't have a copy itself, it would be performing a read and invalidate for a full line, not 0 bytes.
	Hit on E or S line in one or more caches	• In the case where another processor has a copy in the E state, the processor performing the transaction would have had a miss on its cache and would be performing a read and invalidate for a full line, not 0 bytes. • In the case where the processor performing the transaction has a copy in the S state, the transaction kills the line in the other caches that have it in the S state. The snoopers indicate a miss. If the programmer immediately modified one or more locations within the line (e.g., update of a semaphore), the line is now in the M state. If the programmer chooses not to update any locations in the line (e.g., the semaphore tested is already set), the line is placed in the E state.
	Hit on M line in one cache **(doesn't happen)**	If another processor has a copy of the line in the M state, then the processor performing the transaction doesn't have a copy. It would therefore have a miss on its data cache and would perform a read and invalidate for a full line, not 0 bytes.

After Snoop Stall, How Soon Can Next Snoop Result be Presented?

Because the snoop result for the previous transaction was delayed, the next transaction's request agent delays its first sampling of the current transaction's snoop result until three clocks after the previous transaction's snoop result was sampled. This allows two clocks for the lines to settle and then one for the current transaction's snoop result to be driven. After the snoop agents deliver the previous transaction's snoop result, they turn off their drivers to allow HIT# or HITM# to return high. In order to let these shared lines settle, they must delay driving the next snoop result until two clocks after they turn their drivers off.

Self-Snooping

A Pentium Pro processor snoops all memory transactions that occur on the external bus, including those initiated by itself. This is true even in a single-processor system. For an example of self-snooping, refer to "Self-Modifying Code and Self-Snooping" on page 191.

Non-Memory Transactions Have a Snoop Phase

All transactions, including non-memory transactions, have a snoop phase. For non-memory transactions, however, there are only three valid snoop responses:

1. A snoop miss (HIT# and HITM# both deasserted).
2. Defer (DEFER# asserted), indicating that the currently-addressed target will issue a retry or a deferred response in the transaction's response phase.
3. Snoop stall (HIT# and HITM# both asserted), indicating that the snoop phase is to be extended by two clocks. A non-memory response agent is permitted to stall the snoop response to give itself more time for internal operations to complete before presenting a miss or defer as the snoop result.

The non-memory transaction types are the deferred reply, interrupt acknowledge, special, branch trace message, IO read, and IO write transactions. For more information on these transaction types, refer to "Central Agent Transactions" on page 353, "IO Transactions" on page 349, and "Transaction Deferral" on page 327.

Transaction Retry and Deferral

Permission to Defer Transaction Completion

The request agent uses the state of its DEN# output (Defer Enable) in packet B of the request phase (see "Contents of Request Packet B" on page 269) to grant or deny the response agent permission to defer the transaction's completion until a later time. Note that this does not deny the response agent permission to retry the transaction.

- When DEN# is deasserted, permission to defer is denied. Permission is denied under the following circumstances:
    - when a processor is performing a memory write to cast a modified line back to memory to make room for a new line being read into the data cache.
    - when an agent is performing a locked transaction series.
    - when an agent is performing a deferred reply transaction.
    - An agent that requires fast completion of its transaction may deassert DEN#, denying the response agent permission to defer the transaction for later completion.
- When DEN# is asserted, permission is granted to assert DEFER# and issue a deferred response.

DEFER# Assertion Delays Transaction Completion

When the currently-addressed response agent does not assert DEFER# in the snoop phase, the agent is promising to complete the transaction now (with something other than a retry or a deferral for later completion).

If DEFER# is asserted in the snoop phase, the response agent will either issue a retry or a deferred response to the request agent in the response phase. In both of these cases, the response agent is saying that it cannot complete the transaction now. There are two possible cases:

1. If the request agent must complete this transaction before it can proceed with subsequent transactions (in other words, it's important for proper device driver operation that its transactions complete in program-initiated order), then the request agent must not issue any new transactions until it successfully completes the current transaction at a later time (by reattempting the retried transaction or receiving the deferred reply transaction from the response agent).
2. If the request agent doesn't have to complete this transaction before issuing subsequent transactions, it can choose to issue different transactions before reattempting the retried transaction or receiving the deferred reply transaction from the response agent.

Transaction Retry

If a target cannot deal with the current transaction right now (e.g., due to a temporary logic busy condition), it may choose to assert DEFER# in the snoop phase and issue a retry response even if DEN# was deasserted in packet B of the request phase.

When the request agent samples DEFER# asserted in the snoop phase followed by a retry response in the response phase, it is obligated to retry the transaction from scratch on a periodic basis until it completes the transaction. All agents, including the request agent, delete the transaction from their IOQ buffers when the retry response is seen in the response phase. If the transaction involves a data transfer, the data phase is cancelled.

Transaction Deferral

Mail Delivery Analogy

A good analogy for a deferred transaction is sending a letter with a request for delivery notification. The read or write transaction is delivered. At a later time, the response agent sends a delivery notice back to the transaction originator (and, if it's a read, delivers the requested data). Note that the response agent may have had a problem when delivering the transaction to the addressed target and must then report the problem faithfully in the response phase of the deferred reply transaction.

Example System Operation Overview

Refer to the system model pictured in Figure 12-3 on page 291 during the following discussion. The illustration shows a cluster of four processors. The processors share access to memory.

Any processor may issue a transaction request targeting a device residing beyond either one of the host/PCI bridges. During the startup process, the host/PCI bridges are configured to recognize the IO and memory ranges assigned to the devices that reside beyond the bridge.

When any of the processors attempts to perform a read or write with a target residing beyond a host/PCI bridge, it can result in very long latency during the data phase of the transaction.

The Wrong Way. When the transaction is initiated, all of the agents on the processor bus latch the transaction and each of the response agents examines the address and transaction type to determine which of them is the targeted response agent. Assuming that the processor is targeting a device that resides beyond one of the host/PCI bridges, that bridge must act as the response agent for the transaction. Essentially, it is the surrogate for the addressed target which resides somewhere on the other side of the bridge. If the transaction is a read, the bridge takes ownership of the processor data bus (by asserting DBSY#), but keeps DRDY# deasserted until it has the requested read data. When it finally receives the data from the target beyond the bridge, it then presents the data to the processor and asserts DRDY# to indicate its presence.

Figure 12-3: System with Four Processors and Two Host/PCI Bridges

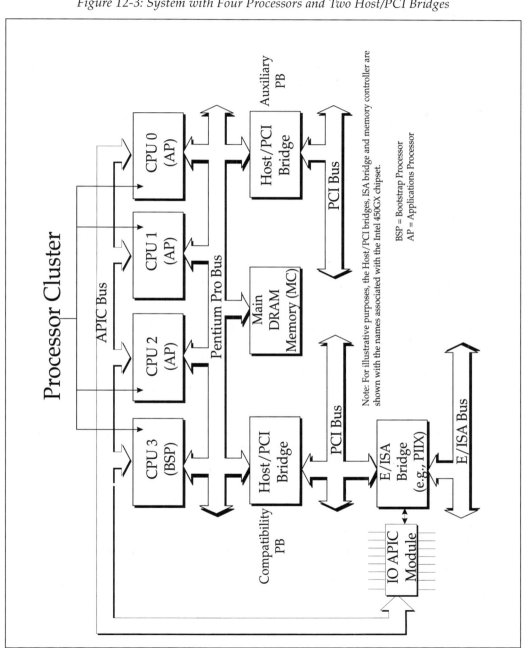

Before the bridge can provide the requested read data from the target or can deliver the write data to the target, it must first arbitrate for ownership of the PCI bus. When it asserts its REQ# to the PCI bus arbiter, the following conditions may be true:

- the PCI bus is currently in use by a PCI master performing a burst read or write transaction with another device on the PCI bus.
- one or more other bus masters that reside on the PCI bus may also be asserting their REQ# to the PCI bus arbiter.
- the host/PCI bridge may have been the last owner of the PCI bus and the arbiter may use a rotational priority scheme.

If all of the above conditions are true, the host/PCI bridge will not attain ownership of the PCI bus until each of the other PCI masters has each received ownership of the PCI bus. Upon attaining ownership, each master may then retain ownership of the bus until it has exhausted its assigned timeslice (i.e., master latency timer, or MLT). When the host/PCI bridge finally attains ownership (that could be quite a while) and initiates the read or write PCI transaction, it must then wait up to five PCI clocks for the PCI target to claim the transaction (i.e., assert DEVSEL#). Once the target has claimed the transaction, it will issue a retry to the bridge if the transaction will take more than 16 clocks from its start (the assertion of FRAME#) to transfer (read or write) the first dword. This 16 clock rule was added in the 2.1 PCI specification. The target has memorized the transaction and is processing it off-line. The host bridge must then periodically retry the transaction until the target finally hands over the read data or indicates that it has accepted the write data. The absolute worst-case scenario occurs if the targeted device resides on the ISA bus (an extremely slow, 8MHz bus populated by horrendously slow devices).

If the host/bridge had kept DRDY# deasserted on the processor bus during this entire period of time, the data bus would remain busy (DBSY# asserted). This means that all transaction requests (that require a data transfer) subsequently issued by any bus agents (including the same one) will stall.

The result—gridlock!

The Right Way. Rather than tie up the processor bus, the bridge asserts DEFER# to the processor in the snoop phase and issues the **deferred** response in its response phase. This informs the processor that the transaction will be completed at a later time. The processor moves the transaction from its IOQ to its deferred transaction queue. All other processor bus agents delete the transaction from their IOQs. The bridge has "memorized" the following information:

- Whether or not the response agent is permitted to defer the transaction (refer to "Permission to Defer Transaction Completion" on page 288).
- The address and transaction type (refer to "Contents of Request Packet A" on page 266).
- The DID field delivered in packet B of the request phase (refer to "Contents of Request Packet B" on page 269). This will permit the bridge to "address" the processor later when it initiates its deferred reply transaction to complete the original transaction.
- If the transaction is a read, the amount of data to be read ("Contents of Request Packet B" on page 269).
- If the transaction is a write, the data to be written.

When the read or write transaction eventually completes on the PCI bus, the bridge must deliver completion notification to the processor that initiated the read or write. To do this, it arbitrates for processor request signal group ownership (by asserting BPRI#). When it has acquired ownership of the request signal group, it initiates a deferred reply transaction. The DID that was originally received from the processor is used as the address in request packet A. All bus agents latch the transaction request and detect that it is a completion notice for a previously-issued transaction that is still awaiting completion. The processor that originally initiated the transaction has a match on its agent and transaction IDs, identifying this as the completion notice for the previously-deferred transaction.

Bridge Should be a Faithful Messenger

During the snoop phase of the deferred reply transaction, the bridge and the processor change roles—the processor becomes the request agent and the bridge becomes the snoop agent. *The deferred reply transaction is never snooped by snoop agents*. Rather, the bridge now supplies the snoop result that it received on the PCI bus (since there aren't any caches on PCI buses, the result is a miss—HIT# and HITM# are deasserted).

In the response phase, the bridge acts as the response agent and delivers the response it received from the PCI target:

- If the transaction was a write and the data was delivered to the PCI target successfully, the response is the No Data response.
- If the transaction was a write and the data wasn't delivered to the PCI target successfully (due to master abort, target abort, or a parity error), the response is the Hard Failure response and the transaction failed.
- If the transaction was a read and the data was read from the PCI target successfully, the response is the Normal Data response and the read data is supplied in the data phase.

- If the transaction was a read and the data wasn't read successfully, the response is the Hard Failure response and the transaction failed.

Detailed Deferred Transaction Description

For a more detailed description of deferred transactions, refer to "Transaction Deferral" on page 327.

What if HITM# and DEFER# both Asserted?

For all unlocked transactions (i.e., LOCK# not asserted), assertion of HITM# overrides the assertion of DEFER#. In other words, if HITM# is asserted, the response agent provides the implicit writeback response in the response phase and the snoop agent writes the modified line to memory (and, if it's a read transaction, the line is also received by the request agent).

Consider a system with two processor clusters linked by a cluster bridge (see Figure 12-4 on page 295). A bus 0 processor initiates a memory read from the bus 1 memory controller that hits on a modified line in the cache of one of the bus 0 processors. In other words, the bus 0 processor with the modified copy of the line had read the line from the bus 1 memory controller earlier in time and had subsequently made one or more changes to the line in its data cache. In this case, the most up-to-date copy of the line is the modified one in the cache. Rather than passing the read to the bus 1 memory controller, the bus 0 cache therefore supplies the read data to the request agent and to the cluster bridge. The cluster bridge arbitrates for ownership of bus 1 and writes the fresh copy of the line to the bus 1 memory controller.

Figure 12-4: Two Processor Clusters Linked by Cluster Bridge

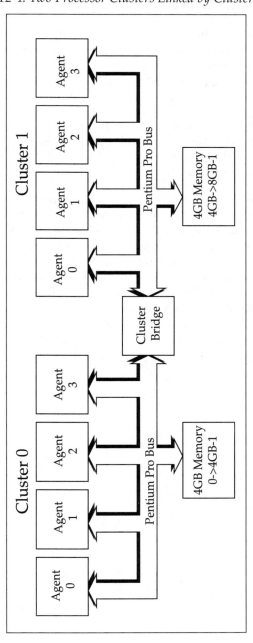

How Does Locking Change Things?

If DEFER# and HITM# are both asserted in the snoop phase of the first of a locked transaction series (typically a memory read to read a semaphore, segment descriptor, page table entry, etc.), the transaction is not deferred. Rather, the snoop agent supplies the modified line to memory (and to the request agent) as an implicit writeback operation.

When the transaction completes, the request agent is required to re-arbitrate and must repeat the transaction and assert LOCK# again. The Intel data book does not explain the rationale for this and as of this writing, the author has been unable to come up with it on his own (very frustrating).

It is forbidden for the response agent to respond to the second and any subsequent transactions of the locked series with DEFER# without HITM# also asserted. The data book says that this is considered to be a protocol violation and goes on to say that the response agent must issue a retry response in the response phase, forcing the request agent to retry the entire locked transaction series from the beginning. The author finds this confusing. The data book makes it sound like the response agent, which violated the spec by issuing DEFER# in the snoop phase of something other than the first transaction of the locked series, is then responsible for punishing itself and the request initiator by issuing a retry response in the response phase. Why would the response agent assert DEFER# knowing full-well that it was violating the spec?

13 *The Response and Data Phases*

The Previous Chapter

The previous chapter provided a detailed description of the snoop phase.

This Chapter

The response phase immediately follows the snoop phase. The snoop result helps the response agent determine what its response to the transaction will be. It should be noted that the response and data phases of a transaction may overlap and that the data phase may also overlap other phases of a transaction. This chapter provides a detailed description of the response and data phases.

The Next Chapter

A response agent may defer completion of a transaction. The next chapter provides a detailed description of deferred transaction handling.

Note on Deferred Transactions

Please note that a detailed description of deferred transactions can be found in the chapter entitled "Transaction Deferral" on page 327.

Purpose of Response Phase

In the response phase of the transaction, the response agent must indicate to the request agent whether:

- it will service the request immediately.
- it can't service it now, but will be able to later.

- it will service it off-line and get back to the request agent with the completion later.
- it is broken and can't service the request at all.
- a snoop agent has a copy of the targeted line in the modified state and will supply the line to the memory controller (and to the request agent if it's a read).

The possible responses are:

1. the response agent may command the request agent to **retry** the transaction repeatedly until it succeeds (or fails). In other words, it can't service the request now, but will be able to later.
2. the response agent may inform the request agent that it will **defer** completion of the transaction until a later time. In other words, it will service the request (read or write) off-line and get back to the request agent with the completion later.
3. the response agent may indicate a **hard failure** to the request agent. In other words, it is broken and can't service the request at all.
4. If the transaction is one that doesn't require the response agent to send data to the request agent (i.e., it is a write transaction, a special transaction, or a memory read or memory read and invalidate transaction for 0 bytes), the response agent indicates that, as requested, **no data** will be returned to the request agent. The request will be service immediately.
5. If the transaction is a memory read or write that results in a hit on a modified line in the snoop phase, the response agent indicates that the snoop agent will transfer the entire modified line to memory (referred to as an **implicit writeback** operation) in the data phase of the transaction (and, if it's a read transaction, to the request agent at the same time).
6. If the transaction is any form of a read transaction (memory read, memory read and invalidate for 32 bytes, IO read, or interrupt acknowledge), the response agent indicates whether or not (it may choose to defer delivery of the read data until a later time) it will return the requested data in the data phase. This is referred to as the **normal data** response.

Response Phase Signal Group

The following signals are used in the response phase:

- **RS[2:0]#. Response bus.** Used to deliver the response to the request agent.
- **RSP#. Response bus parity bit**. The parity signal that covers RS[2:0]#. It is an even parity signal that is driven low or high to force an even number of electrical lows in the overall 4-bit pattern that includes RSP#.
- **TRDY# (Target Ready)**. Only asserted by the response agent if data is to be

Chapter 13: The Response and Data Phases

written to the response agent by either the request agent, a snoop agent (implicit writeback of a modified line), or both. The assertion of TRDY# indicates the response agent's readiness to accept the write data.

Response Phase Start Point

The response phase starts immediately after the snoop phase completes.

Response Phase End Point

The response phase ends when the response agent delivers a valid response to the request agent. This implies that the response agent can stall the response phase (i.e., insert wait states) until it is ready to present its response.

The specification doesn't place a limit on the number of wait states that may be inserted into the snoop phase of a transaction. However, the system designer may choose to monitor the behavior of agents to ensure that none of them inserts excessive wait states. This would adversely affect all subsequently-issued transactions that are awaiting delivery of their respective snoop results.

List of Responses

Table 13-1 on page 299 lists the possible responses that can be presented on RS[2:0]#.

Table 13-1: Response List (0 = deasserted, 1 asserted)

RS[2:0]#	Description
000b	Idle. This is referred to as the idle state. None of the response signals are asserted. This is the state of RS[2:0]# before and after the response has been delivered to the request agent. In other words, immediately upon entry into the response phase, RS[2:0]# are in this state and will remain in this state until a valid response is presented. When any of the valid responses are driven (for one clock), one or more of the RS[2:0]# signals are driven low. A look at the other table entries shows that all of the valid response patterns have at least one of the RS signals asserted (remember that a 1 = asserted, or electrical low). After one clock, the response is removed. The RS signals then all return to the deasserted state (in other words, back to the idle state).

Table 13-1: Response List (0 = deasserted, 1 asserted) (Continued)

RS[2:0]#	Description
001b	**Retry.** The response agent may command the request agent to retry the transaction repeatedly until the transaction succeeds (or fails). In other words, it can't service the request now, but will be able to later.
010b	**Deferred.** The response agent may inform the request agent that it will defer completion of the transaction until a later time. In other words, it will service the request off-line and get back to the request agent with the completion later.
011b	Reserved.
100b	**Hard Failure.** The response agent may indicate a hard failure to the request agent. In other words, it is broken and can't service the request at all.
101b	**No Data.** This response indicates that no data was requested by the request agent and no data will therefore be delivered. This is the proper response to a write (although data is written to the device, none is requested from it). It is also the proper response to a transaction that doesn't require any data to be transferred—the special transaction, the memory read and invalidate for 0 bytes, the memory read for 0 bytes, or the IO read for 0 bytes.

Table 13-1: Response List (0 = deasserted, 1 asserted) (Continued)

RS[2:0]#	Description
110b	**Implicit Writeback.** This is the response given if the memory transaction resulted in a hit on a modified line (i.e., HITM# was asserted in the snoop phase). This means that the snoop agent that has the modified line will supply the modified line to the response agent (i.e., the memory controller) as well as to the request agent (if it's a read transaction). The author thinks of this as the "don't be startled" response. The request agent may be attempting to read less than a line of information and, if the snoop agent supplies the data, it always sends the full line. The **implicit writeback** response tells the request agent that four quadwords (32 bytes) will be transferred rather than the smaller data packet actually requested. The four quadwords are transferred in toggle mode order, critical quadword first. This means that the first quadword sent back by the snoop agent will be the first one requested by the request agent and, if a second quadword was also requested (i.e., a 16 byte read request), the second quadword sent back is the first quadword's toggle mode partner. The request agent should just take the quadword(s) requested and ignore the rest. The memory controller (i.e., the response agent), on the other hand, will accept the full line.
111b	**Normal Data.** This is the proper response to any read request (that doesn't hit on a modified line and is not deferred)—a memory read, a memory read and invalidate for 32 bytes, an IO read, an interrupt acknowledge, or a deferred reply that is returning previously-requested read data.

Response Phase May Complete Transaction

In all transactions that do not involve a data transfer, the delivery of the response ends the transaction. This would include the following transactions:

- the special transaction broadcasts a processor message encoded on the byte enables, but does not read or write data.
- a memory read, a memory read and invalidate for 0 bytes, or an IO read for 0 bytes transfers no data.
- a read transaction that receives a **deferred** response from the response agent. In other words, the response agent will initiate a deferred reply transaction at a later time and transfer the read data to the request agent at that time.

Any transaction that performs a read or write that does not receive a **deferred, retry,** or **hard fail** response will have both a response and a data phase.

Pentium Pro and Pentium II System Architecture

Data Phase Signal Group

Table 13-2 on page 302 defines the signals used during the data phase of a transaction.

Table 13-2: Data Phase-related Signals

Signal(s)	Description
DBSY#	**Data Bus Busy**. Asserted by agent that will drive data on the data bus (response agent on read; request agent on a write; snoop agent on a snoop hit on modified line) when it takes ownership of the data bus. Stays asserted at least until 1 clk before final transfer completes.
DRDY#	**Data Ready**. Asserted by agent driving data on data bus to indicate that the data is valid. Can be deasserted during the data phase to insert wait states into the data phase.
D[63:0]#	**Data bus**. 8 data paths used to transfer up to a quadword at a time.
DEP[7:0]#	**Data bus ECC protection** bits. When used as ECC bits, permits correction of single-bit failures and detection of double-bit failures. Each of these bits is related to one of the eight data paths.

Five Example Scenarios

Transaction that Doesn't Transfer Data

Figure 13-1 on page 304 illustrates a transaction that doesn't require a data transfer at all. This would include:

1. Special transaction.
2. Transaction that receives a retry response.
3. Transactions that receive a hard failure response.
4. Read transaction that receives a deferred response (data will be transferred at a later time in another transaction). and doesn't hit on a modified line (the case where it hits a modified line is described in "Read that Hits a Modified Line" on page 311).
5. Memory read or memory read and invalidate for 0 bytes.

Chapter 13: The Response and Data Phases

In these cases, the data bus is not used by the request agent (because it's not a write), the response agent (because no data is being read), or any of the snoopers (because it doesn't hit a modified line).

The response phase is entered immediately upon delivery of the transaction's snoop result (see clock 6). However, the target of this transaction must ensure that it **doesn't drive** its **response until both of the following conditions** have been **met**:

1. The **snoop phase for this transaction must have completed**. A response agent must detect the final snoop result (see clock 6) before it can determine what it's response will be.
2. The response agent **observed** the **target of** the **previous transaction deliver its response and then idle the response signals**. In order to allow signal settling time, it must not drive its response until at least two clocks after the response from the previous response agent is seen. This allows one clock for the previous target to backoff its drivers from RS[2:0]# and one clock for the lines to settle before the target of the current transaction starts to turn on its RS drivers. Remember that it is permissible for the target of a transaction to delay the delivery of its response (by keeping RS[2:0]# deasserted) until is ready to deliver it. It then drives its response (see Table 13-1 on page 299) for one clock and releases the RS[2:0]# signals (which return to the idle state). Assume that the target of the current transaction isn't paying attention (i.e., it's not properly tracking all currently outstanding transactions) and drives its response to its request agent before the target of the previously-issued transaction drives its response to the request agent that addressed it. The request agent that issued the earlier transaction would receive the response from the wrong target for a transaction that it didn't issue. This would absolutely confuse everyone involved. Another possibility is that both targets would simultaneously drive the RS signals, resulting in a wire-ORed (i.e., bogus) result.

The appropriate response for a transaction that doesn't require a data transfer is the no data response (see clock 8).

Figure 13-1: Transaction That Doesn't Require Data Transfer

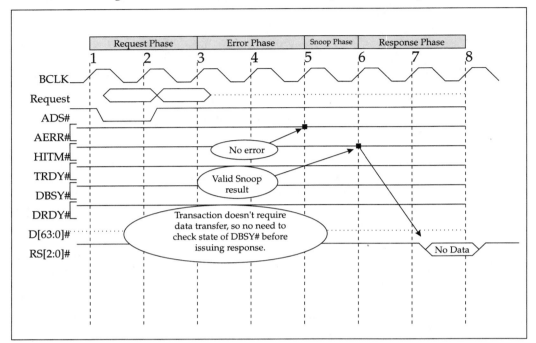

Read that Doesn't Hit a Modified Line and is Not Deferred

Basics

Figure 13-2 on page 305 illustrates a read for two quadwords (16 bytes) that doesn't hit a modified line and isn't deferred. In other words:

1. the response agent will take ownership of the data bus and transfer the requested data to the request agent.
2. the response agent will supply the Normal Data response at the same time that it takes ownership of the data bus.
3. none of the snoop agents has a copy of the line in the modified state and therefore a snooper will not be writing data to memory.

Figure 13-2: Read that Doesn't Hit a Modified Line and Isn't Deferred

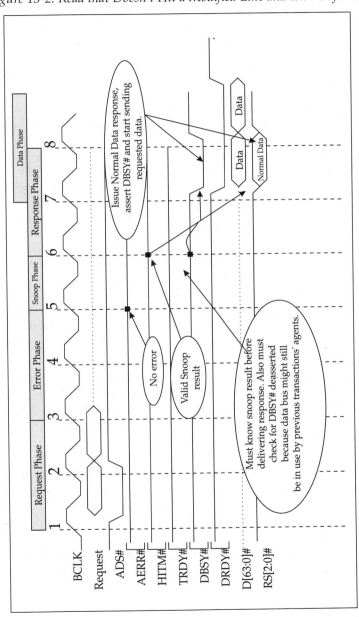

Detailed Description

On a read transaction, the response agent delivers the Normal Data response (see clock 8) if it intends to transfer the requested data. At the same time that it drives the response, it takes ownership of the data bus in preparation for driving the requested read data back to the request agent. **Before delivering** its **response**, the response agent **must be sure that all of the following conditions are met**:

1. The response agent doesn't deliver its response until it has received its snoop result (see clock 6—it **needs** the **snoop result** to determine what its response will be).

2. The response agent doesn't deliver its response until the **previously-issued transaction's response agent has issued its response** and the RS lines have settled (you don't want to confuse the previous transaction's request agent by giving it the response to the next transaction and you don't want to start driving the RS lines until they have quit ringing). At the earliest, the response for the current transaction can be driven three clocks after the previous response was driven—this allows one clock for the previous response to be driven, one clock for the response agent to backoff its drivers, and one clock for the RS lines to settle.

3. If the **previously-issued transaction** requires a data transfer, the response agent doesn't deliver its response until the request or response agent (whichever is using the data bus) has **completed** its **data transfer** and given up ownership of the data bus (i.e., it has deasserted DBSY#; see clock 6).

In Figure 13-2 on page 305, the response agent takes ownership of the data bus by asserting DBSY# in clock 7. When it's ready to drive the first data item (up to eight bytes of data), it asserts DRDY# and drives the data. If it's not ready to drive the data, it asserts DBSY#, but holds off on the assertion of DRDY# until the clock where it begins driving the data.

In the figure, the response agent asserts DBSY# and DRDY# and drives the first quadword onto the data bus in clock 7. On clock 8, the request agent samples the data and the state of the DRDY# signal. DRDY# is asserted, qualifying the data as valid. In clock 8, the response agent leaves DRDY# asserted and drives the second quadword onto the data bus. In addition, it deasserts DBSY#, relinquishing ownership of the data bus. On clock 9, the request agent samples the second quadword from the data bus and the state of DRDY#. DRDY# is asserted, qualifying the second quadword as valid.

Chapter 13: The Response and Data Phases

How Does Response Agent Know Transfer Length?

The request agent delivers the transfer length in the LEN field of packet B during the request phase (refer to "Contents of Request Packet B" on page 269). The possible lengths are:

- One quadword or a subset thereof (the byte enables in packet B indicate which bytes within the addressed quadword).
- Two full quadwords (16 bytes) in toggle mode order.
- Four full quadwords (32 bytes) in toggle mode order.

What's the Earliest that DBSY# Can be Deasserted?

The earliest point at which DBSY# can be deasserted is in the clock that the data bus owner is ready to transfer the final data item (clock 8 in Figure 13-2 on page 305). There's no danger of the next data bus user taking ownership too soon because the next owner won't sample DBSY# deasserted until the next clock and cannot take ownership until one clock after that. This provides the current data bus owner with one clock to drive the final data item and one clock to backoff from the data bus before the next owner can assert DBSY# and take ownership of the data bus.

Relaxed DBSY# Deassertion

The specification permits what is referred to as relaxed DBSY# deassertion. In clock 8 of Figure 13-2 on page 305, DBSY# is deasserted in the clock in which the data bus owner is ready to transfer the final data item. It is permissible to keep DBSY# asserted until the final data item is transferred (on clock 9), and then deassert both DRDY# and DBSY# at the same time. It is also permissible to keep DBSY# asserted for any number of clocks after the final data item is transferred. Be aware, however, that this will adversely affect the performance of the next device awaiting the release of DBSY# so that it may take ownership of the data bus.

Write that Doesn't Hit a Modified Line and Isn't Deferred

Figure 13-3 on page 308 illustrates two transactions:

- 2-quadword (16 byte) write, doesn't hit modified line and isn't deferred.
- 4-quadword (32-byte) write, doesn't hit modified line and isn't deferred.

In both cases, the request agent writes data to the response agent in the data phase of the transaction. The following discussion focuses on the second of these two transactions.

Figure 13-3: Write that Doesn't Hit a Modified Line and Isn't Deferred

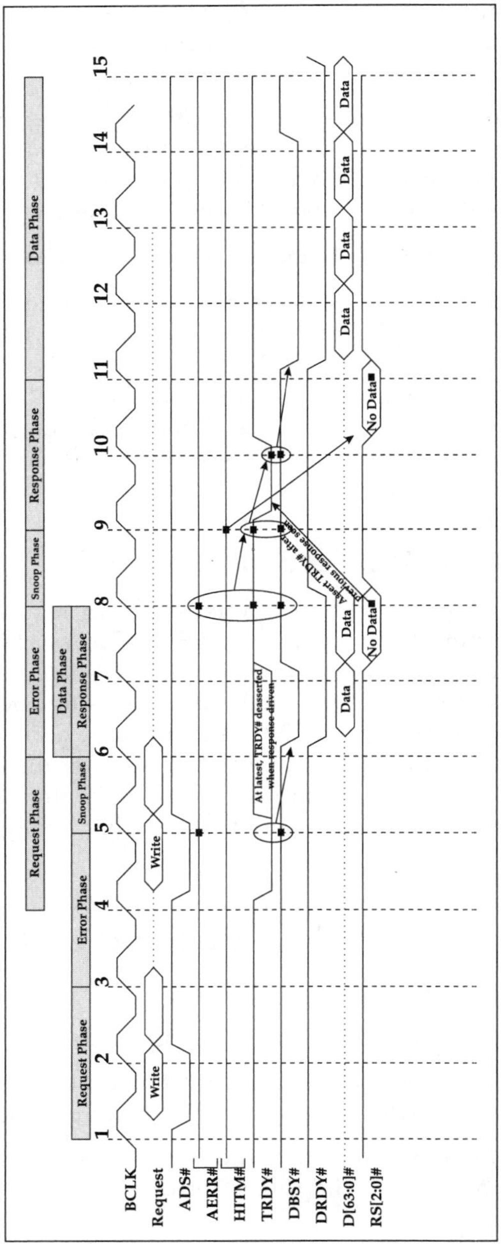

Chapter 13: The Response and Data Phases

Basics

1. When it is ready to receive the write data from the request agent, the response agent asserts TRDY#.
2. When the request agent samples TRDY# asserted (the response agent is ready to receive the write data) and, if the previous transaction required a data transfer, DBSY# has been deasserted (the data bus is free for it to use), it asserts DBSY# in preparation for driving the write data to the response agent.
3. The response agent supplies the No Data response in the response phase.
4. None of the snoop agents has a copy of the line in the modified state and therefore a snooper will not be writing data to memory.

Previous Transaction May Involve a Write

On a write transaction, the response agent asserts TRDY# when it is ready to receive the write data from the request agent. It must make sure that it doesn't start driving TRDY# too early, however. As shown in Figure 13-3 on page 308, the previous transaction may involve a write as well (either because it's a write transaction or because it hits on a modified line and the snoop agent writes the modified line to memory). In this case, the response agent of the previous transaction asserts TRDY# when it's ready to accept the write data. After being asserted, TRDY# is deasserted, at the latest, when a transaction's response is driven (see clock 7).

Earliest TRDY# Assertion is 1 Clock After Previous Response Issued

In the current transaction, it's therefore definitely safe to assert TRDY# (if the response agent is ready to accept write data) one clock after the previous response agent provides its response (see clock 9). By then, if TRDY# had been asserted by the previous transaction's response agent, it has been deasserted and has quit ringing.

When Does Request Agent First Sample TRDY#?

On a write transaction, the request agent first samples TRDY# at the end of the error phase (see clock 8) at the same time that it samples AERR#. If the transaction isn't cancelled by the assertion of AERR#, it will proceed. The earliest at which TRDY# should therefore be asserted (assuming that the response for the previous transaction has been seen—see previous two sections) is three clocks after ADS# is asserted (in other words, during the second clock of the transaction's error phase, clock 7).

When Does Request Agent Start Using Data Bus?

When the request agent samples AERR# deasserted (see clock 8), the transaction proceeds. The request agent **starts sampling TRDY# and DBSY# at the end of the error phase** at the same time that it samples AERR#. **There are three cases**:

1. Request agent samples **TRDY# asserted and DBSY# deasserted**—This is not the case in the figure. AERR# and DBSY# are deasserted when first sampled on clock 8, but TRDY# isn't asserted until clock 10. The request agent will therefore continue to sample TRDY# and DBSY# on each clock until TRDY# is asserted and DBSY# is deasserted. This indicates that the response agent is ready to receive the data (TRDY# asserted) and the data bus is not in use (DBSY# deasserted). When these conditions are met, the request agent can take ownership of the data bus (assert DBSY#) one clock later to start driving the write data to the response agent.
2. Request agent samples **TRDY# asserted and DBSY# asserted**—Although the response agent is ready to accept the data (TRDY# asserted), the agents involved in the previous transaction are still using the data bus (DBSY# still asserted). In this case, the request agent must not take ownership of the data bus until it samples TRDY# asserted and DBSY# deasserted. It then takes ownership of the data bus (assert DBSY#) one clock later.
3. Request agent samples **DBSY# deasserted and TRDY# deasserted** (see clocks 8 and 9)—Although the data bus is free, the response agent is not yet ready to accept the data. The request agent must not take ownership of the data bus until it samples TRDY# asserted and DBSY# deasserted (see clock 10).

When Can TRDY# Be Deasserted?

Once asserted, the earliest at which TRDY# can be deasserted is when the response agent is sure that the request agent has seen TRDY# asserted and DBSY# deasserted (so it can take ownership of the data bus).

If the target samples DBSY# deasserted on the same clock that it starts asserting TRDY# (see clock 9), it knows that the request agent will see TRDY# asserted and DBSY# deasserted on the next clock (see clock 10). The response agent can therefore turn off TRDY# one clock after it asserts it (see clock 10). This one clock assertion of TRDY# may be done as long as it's not sooner than three clocks from the previous deassertion of TRDY#.

If the response agent doesn't sample DBSY# deasserted when it starts asserting TRDY# (this is not the case in clock 9 of the figure), it must keep TRDY# asserted until it samples DBSY# deasserted. When the response agent sees this, it can

Chapter 13: The Response and Data Phases

deassert TRDY#. It knows that the request agent has seen it as well and that it will take ownership of the data bus one clock later (see clock 11). At the latest, the target must deassert TRDY# when it delivers the No Data response (see clock 10).

When Does Request Agent Take Ownership of Data Bus?

The request agent takes ownership of the data bus one clock after seeing TRDY# asserted (response agent is ready to take the data) and DBSY# deasserted (previous data bus user has relinquished ownership). This occurs in clocks 10 and 11 of the figure.

Deliver the Data

As the request agent drives each quadword onto the bus, it asserts DRDY# to indicate its presence. In the figure, this occurs on clocks 11 through 14. The response agent latches the data from the bus on clocks 12 through 15 along with the state of the DRDY# signal. DRDY# asserted indicates that the data latched is valid. In clock 14, the request agent deasserts DBSY# to relinquish data bus ownership. In clock 15, it deasserts DRDY# as well (the final data item has been transferred).

On AERR# or Hard Failure Response

If the request agent receives an AERR# in the error phase or a hard failure response in the response phase, it may have already accepted some write data from the request agent. If it has, the response agent discards the data. In other words, it is important that data written to a response agent should initially be accepted into a buffer and only written to the target memory or IO location(s) if there's no AERR# and no hard failure response.

Snoop Agents Change State of Line from E->I or S->I

If any snoop agent had a hit on a line in the E or S state, it changes it to the I state (because it cannot snarf data being written to memory by another request agent).

Read that Hits a Modified Line

Figure 13-4 on page 313 illustrates a read that hits on a modified line. Refer to this figure during the following discussion. The read could be for any amount of data up to a full line.

Basics

1. The request agent starts a read transaction to read data from memory.
2. The snoop results in the assertion of HITM#, indicating that a snoop agent has a copy of the requested line in the modified state.
3. The HITM# indication informs the response agent (i.e., the memory controller) that it does not have a fresh copy of the requested line. Rather the snoop agent has it and will supply the line to memory and to the request agent.
4. The transaction is still a read from the request agent's standpoint, but from the memory controller standpoint has changed from a read by the request agent into a write to memory by the snoop agent.
5. The memory controller must provide the Implicit Writeback response in the response phase.
6. When the memory controller is ready to accept the modified line (in other words, it has a 32-byte buffer available), it asserts TRDY# to the snoop agent.
7. The snoop agent is waiting to see TRDY# asserted (memory is ready to accept the write data) and DBSY# deasserted (the data bus isn't busy). It keeps sampling both signals until this state is seen. It then asserts DBSY# to take ownership of the data bus in preparation for writing the data to memory.
8. The modified line is then provided to memory and to the request agent. The four quadwords are provided in toggle mode order, critical quadword first. If the request agent has only requested a subset of the quadword, it just takes what it asked for and ignores the remaining quadwords. The memory must accept the entire line.
9. The snoop agent has freshened up memory, so it changes the state of the line in its cache from modified to shared (because it has just watched someone else read the line).

Figure 13-4: Read that Hits a Modified Line

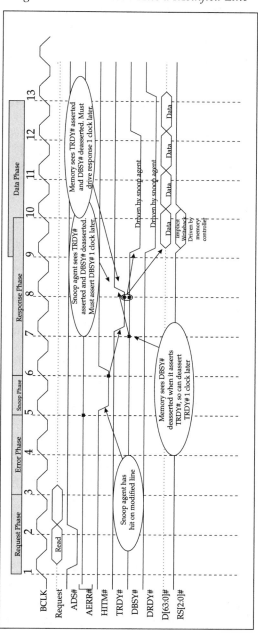

Transaction Starts as a Read from Memory

The request agent issues a memory read request in the request phase (starting on clock 1). Assuming that the transaction isn't cancelled by the assertion of AERR# in the error phase (see clock 5), the snoop phase is entered and the snoop agent that has a copy of the requested line in the modified state asserts HITM# (see clock 5).

From Memory Standpoint, Changes from Read to Write

The assertion of HITM# (see clock 6) informs the memory controller that its copy of the requested line is stale and that the snoop agent will supply the modified line to memory and to the request agent in the data phase of the transaction. The transaction remains a read from the request agent's standpoint.

Memory Asserts TRDY# to Accept Data

Assuming that the previous transaction's response has already been seen (TRDY#, if it had been asserted, has therefore been deasserted) and that memory is ready to accept the data, the memory controller asserts TRDY# to the snoop agent (see clock 7). If DBSY# is in the deasserted state (indicating that the previous data bus owner has relinquished ownership) on the clock that TRDY# is driven asserted, the memory controller can deassert TRDY# one clock after it asserts it (because it is assured that the snoop agent sees TRDY# asserted and DBSY# deasserted one clock after TRDY# is asserted). Otherwise, it must keep TRDY# asserted until it samples DBSY# deasserted.

After indicating the HITM#, the snoop agent starts sampling TRDY# and DBSY# two clocks after the snoop phase ends (see clock 8) to determine when it can take ownership of the data bus. The response agent must be ready to accept the data (TRDY# asserted) and the previous data bus owner must have relinquished ownership (DBSY# deasserted).

Memory Must Drive Response At Right Time

The memory controller must drive the Implicit Writeback response (on clock 9) one clock after sampling TRDY# asserted and DBSY# deasserted (see clock 8). This is necessary because:

- On a read, DBSY# must be asserted at the same time that the response is driven.
- When the snoop agent samples TRDY# asserted and DBSY# deasserted, it will assert DBSY# one clock later in preparation for driving the write data.

Chapter 13: The Response and Data Phases

Snoop Agent Asserts DBSY# and Memory Drives Response

As stated earlier, when the snoop agent sees TRDY# asserted and DBSY# deasserted (see clock 8), it takes ownership of the data bus one clock later by asserting DBSY# (see clock 9). At the same time, the memory controller drives the Implicit Writeback response to the request agent.

Snoop Agent Supplies Line to Memory and to Request Agent

After asserting DBSY#, the snoop agent writes the line to memory and to the request agent. As it provides each of the four quadwords, it asserts DRDY# to indicate the presence of the quadword. On a read, the request agent starts sampling DRDY# on the clock that the response is received (clock 10) and latches a quadword each time that DRDY# is sampled asserted. Note that if the read is only for one or two quadwords and it hits a modified line (implicit writeback response), the request agent will only take the quadwords that it requested and will ignore the remaining quadwords.

Snoop Agent Changes State of Line from M->S

When memory has received the fresh line, the line is no longer modified in the snoop agent's cache, so it changes it from the M to the S state (because it knows the request agent read it and, if it has a cache, has placed the line in the S state).

Write that Hits a Modified Line

Figure 13-5 on page 317 illustrates a two-quadword memory write that hits a modified line in the cache of one of the snoop agents' caches. Refer to this figure during the following discussion.

1. Transaction starts as a write from the request agent to the response agent (i.e., the memory controller).
2. The response agent asserts TRDY# in clock 4 and samples DBSY# deasserted as it starts asserting TRDY#. This means that the request agent will see TRDY# asserted and DBSY# deasserted on the next clock (clock 5), giving it permission to take ownership of the data bus in clock 6. The response agent can therefore deassert TRDY# one clock after it asserts it.
3. AERR# isn't asserted in the error phase (see clock 5), so the transaction proceeds.
4. At the end of the error phase, AERR# is sampled deasserted and the request agent samples TRDY# for the first time to see if the memory controller is ready to accept the write data. In addition, DBSY# is sampled to see if the data bus is still in use by the previous transaction's agents. The request

agent doesn't acquire data bus ownership until the clock where it samples TRDY# asserted and DBSY# deasserted (see clock 5).

5. In the snoop phase, a snoop agent that has a copy of the target line in the modified state asserts HITM# (see clock 6). This informs the memory controller that it will receive write data from two sources—first the write data from the request agent and then the modified line from the snoop agent.

6. When TRDY# has been sampled asserted and DBSY# is sampled deasserted (see clock 5), the request agent asserts DBSY# (see clock 6), taking ownership of the data bus in preparation for writing its data to the memory controller.

7. The request agent drives out the first of the two quadwords in clock 6 and asserts DRDY# to indicate its presence on the data bus. The response agent samples the data and DRDY# on clock 7. DRDY# is sampled asserted, qualifying the data just latched as valid. In clock 7, the request agent drives the second quadword onto the data bus and keeps DRDY# asserted to indicate its presence. It also deasserts DBSY#, relinquishing ownership of the data bus. The response agent samples the data and DRDY# on clock 8. DRDY# is sampled asserted, qualifying the data just latched as valid. All of the data has been written to the response agent.

8. When the memory controller samples TRDY# asserted and DBSY# deasserted (see clock 5), the memory controller deasserts TRDY# for at least one clock and then reasserts it (in clock 7). The second assertion of TRDY# informs the snoop agent that the memory controller is ready to accept the modified line (in other words, it has a 32-byte buffer available to receive the line).

9. When the snoop agent samples TRDY# asserted for the second time (in clock 8), it also samples DBSY# to see if the request agent has surrendered ownership of the data bus yet. When it samples DBSY# deasserted (see clock 8), it asserts DBSY# (see clock 9) to take ownership of the data bus.

10. When the memory controller has asserted TRDY# for the second time and then samples DBSY# (see clock 8) deasserted (indicating that the request agent is through with its write), it deasserts TRDY# (see clock 9) and drives the Implicit Writeback response to the request agent.

11. Starting in clock 9, the snoop agent uses the data bus to write the line to memory. As it drives each of the four quadwords onto the data bus, it asserts DRDY# to indicate its presence. As it drives the final quadword onto the bus (in clock 12), it deasserts DBSY# to relinquish data bus ownership. When it has transferred the final quadword (on clock 13), it deasserts DRDY#.

12. In addition, the snoop agent invalidates its copy of the line (because it cannot snarf the data written to memory by the request agent to update its copy).

Figure 13-5: Write that Hits a Modified Line

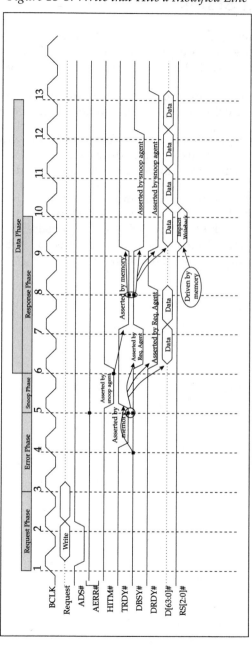

Data Phase Wait States

The agent sourcing the data can delay delivery of each quadword by keeping DRDY# deasserted until it presents each quadword. As it drives a quadword onto the bus, it asserts DRDY# to indicate its presence on the bus.

Figure 13-6 on page 319 illustrates a two-quadword read where the response agent takes two clocks (one wait state) to deliver each quadword.

Figure 13-7 on page 320 illustrates a four-quadword write wherein the request agent delivers the first quadword in 0-wait states, and inserts one wait state into the delivery of each of the subsequent three quadwords.

The specification doesn't place a limit on the number of wait states that may be inserted into the transfer of a quadword. However, the system designer may choose to monitor the behavior of agents to ensure that none of them inserts excessive wait states. This would adversely affect all subsequently-issued transactions that require the use of the data bus.

Figure 13-6: Example of Two-Quadword Read with Wait States

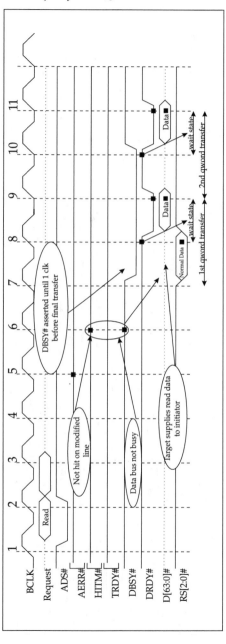

Figure 13-7: Example of Four Quadword Write with Wait States

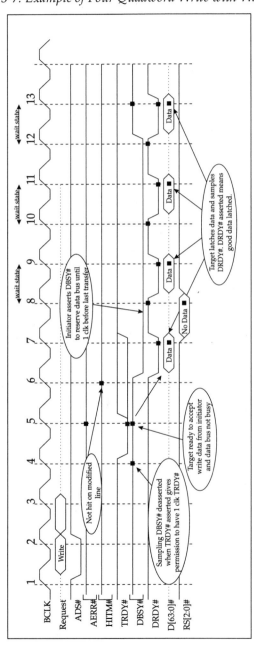

Chapter 13: The Response and Data Phases

Special Case—Single Quadword, 0-Wait State Transfer

Figure 13-8 on page 322 illustrates a single-quadword, 0-wait state write. When a transaction only transfers one quadword (or a subset thereof), and the agent sourcing the data can immediately supply the data when it gains data bus ownership, the agent does not have to assert DBSY#. It just asserts DRDY# immediately upon acquiring data bus ownership and drives out the quadword. In Figure 13-8 on page 322:

1. The request agent samples TRDY# asserted and DBSY# deasserted on clock 5 and takes ownership of the data bus on clock 6.
2. The request agent asserts DRDY# immediately upon acquiring data bus ownership (on clock 6) and drives out the quadword.
3. The response agent samples the data and the state of DRDY# on clock 7. DRDY# is sampled asserted, qualifying the data as valid.

There is no danger of an ownership collision on the data bus. Whether the next transaction is a read or a write, the agent that will source data cannot take ownership of the data bus until the response for this transaction has been seen.

Figure 13-8: Example of Single-Quadword, 0-Wait State Write

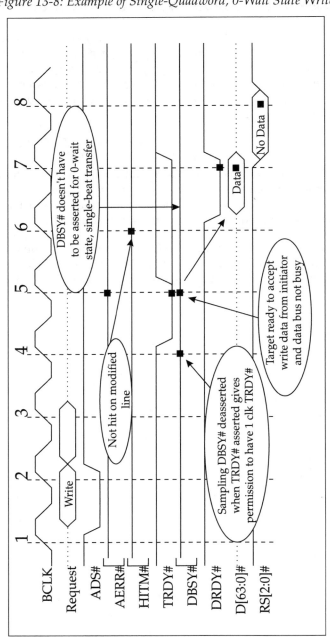

Chapter 13: The Response and Data Phases

Response Phase Parity

The RS[2:0]# signals are protected by the RSP# parity bit. During the response phase, it must be left high or driven low to force an even number of electrical lows in the overall 4-bit pattern. Note that if the response agent stalls the response phase (because it doesn't have the response ready to be delivered yet), proper parity must be provided for each of idle periods until the actual response is driven.

Hardware Section 4:
Other Bus Topics

The Previous Section

The chapters that comprise Part 2, Section 3 focused on the phases that a transaction passes through from inception to completion.

This Section

The chapters that comprise Part 2, Section 4 cover additional transaction and bus topics not covered in the previous sections. This is the final section of Part 2 and concludes the discussion of the processor's hardware characteristics. It consists of the following chapters:

- "Transaction Deferral" on page 327.
- "IO Transactions" on page 349.
- "Central Agent Transactions" on page 353.
- "Other Signals" on page 365.

The Next Part

This section completes the Part 2 discussion of the Pentium Pro processor's hardware characteristics. Part 3 focuses on the Pentium II processor.

14 *Transaction Deferral*

The Previous Chapter

The previous chapter concluded "Hardware Section 3: The Transaction Phases." It provided a detailed description of the response and data phases of a transaction.

This Chapter

This chapter is the first chapter of "Hardware Section 4: Other Bus Topics" and provides a detailed description of transaction deferral and the deferred reply transaction.

The Next Chapter

The next chapter provides detailed information regarding IO read and write transactions.

Introduction to Transaction Deferral

For an introduction to the topic of transaction deferral, refer to the discussion that starts with "Transaction Retry and Deferral" on page 288. After reading that discussion, then proceed with the remainder of this chapter.

Example System Model

The sections in this chapter describe deferred transactions and deferred reply transactions using the example system model pictured in Figure 14-1 on page 328.

Figure 14-1: Example System with one Pentium Pro Bus and Two Host/PCI Bridges

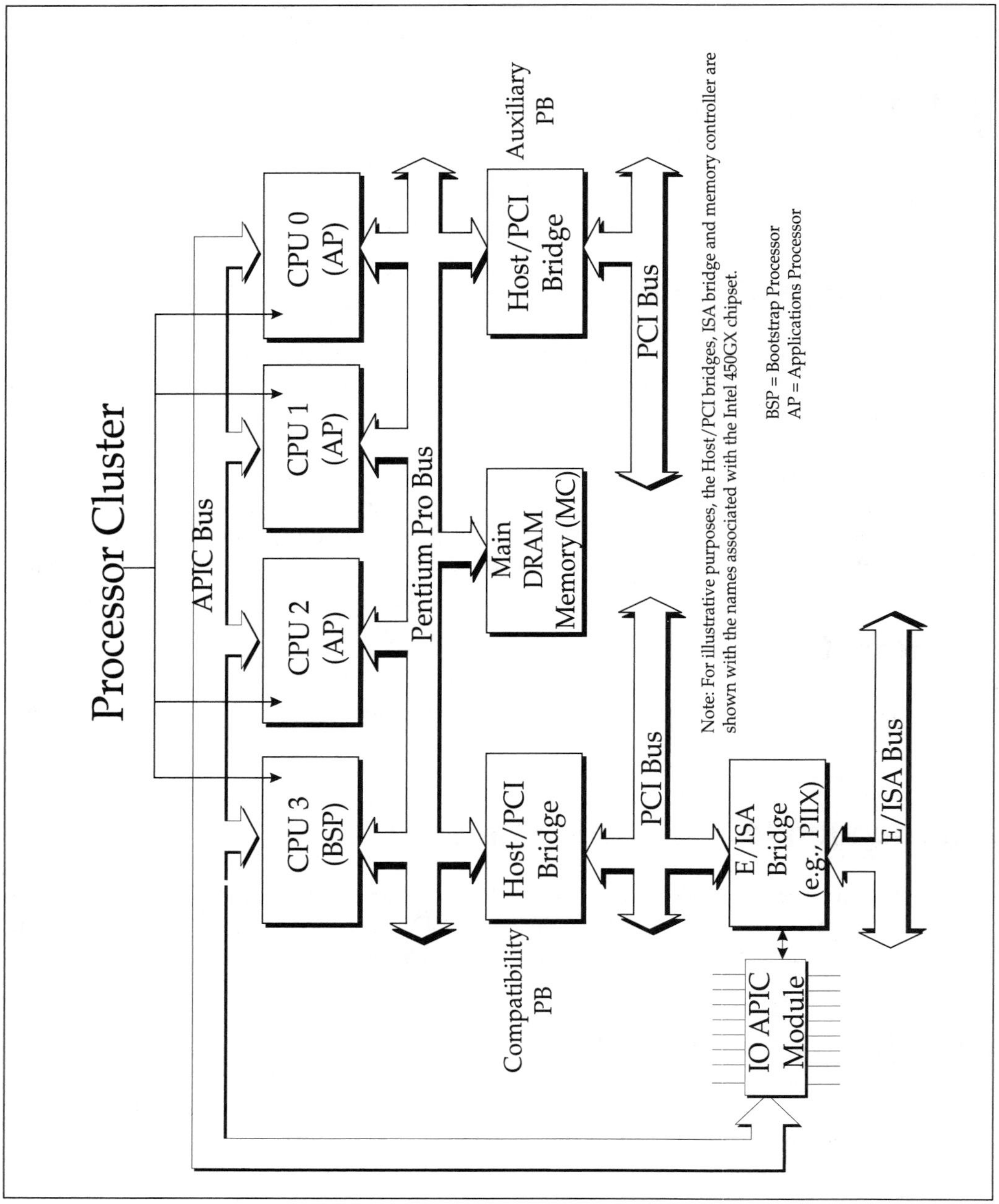

Typical PC Server Model

This discussion focuses on the use of transaction deferral and deferred reply transactions to increase the overall performance of the system pictured in Figure 14-1 on page 328. Please note that there are some references to PCI bus operation. For a detailed description of the PCI bus protocol, refer to the MindShare book entitled *PCI System Architecture* (published by Addison-Wesley).

The Problem

When any of the processors attempts to perform a read or write with a target residing on either of the PCI buses or on the EISA or ISA bus, it can result in very long latency during the data phase of the transaction.

When the transaction is initiated, all of the agents on the processor bus latch the transaction and each of the response agents examines the address and transaction type to determine which of them is the targeted response agent. Assuming that the processor is targeting a device that resides beyond one of the host/PCI bridges, that bridge must act as the response agent for the transaction. Essentially, it is the surrogate for the addressed target which resides somewhere on the other side of the bridge. If the transaction is a read, the bridge takes ownership of the processor data bus (by asserting DBSY#), but keeps DRDY# deasserted until it can present the requested read data. It then presents the data to the processor and asserts DRDY# to indicate its presence.

Before the bridge can provide the requested read data from the target or can deliver the write data to the target, it must first arbitrate for ownership of the PCI bus. When it asserts its REQ# to the PCI bus arbiter, the following conditions may be true:

- the PCI bus is currently in use by a PCI master performing a burst read or write transaction with another device on the PCI bus.
- one or more other bus masters that reside on the PCI bus may also be asserting their REQ# to the PCI bus arbiter.
- the host/PCI bridge may have been the last owner of the PCI bus and the arbiter may use a rotational priority scheme.

If all of the above conditions are true, the host/PCI bridge will not attain ownership of the PCI bus until each of the other PCI masters has each received ownership of the PCI bus. Upon attaining ownership, each master may then retain ownership of the bus until it has exhausted its assigned timeslice (i.e., master latency timer, or MLT). When the host/PCI bridge finally attains ownership (that could be quite a while) and initiates the PCI read or write transaction, it must then wait up to five PCI clocks for the PCI target to claim the transaction (i.e., assert DEVSEL#). Once the target has claimed the transaction, it will issue a retry to the bridge if the transaction will take more than 16 clocks from its start (the assertion of FRAME#) to transfer (read or write) the first dword. This 16 clock rule was added in the 2.1 PCI specification. The target has memorized the transaction and is processing it off-line. The host bridge must then periodically retry the transaction until the target finally presents the read data or indicates that it has accepted the write data. The absolute worst-case scenario occurs if the targeted device resides on the ISA bus (an extremely slow, 8MHz bus populated by horrendously slow devices).

If the host/bridge had kept DRDY# deasserted on the processor bus during this entire period of time, the data bus would remain busy (DBSY# asserted). This means that all transaction requests (that require a data transfer) subsequently issued by any bus agents (including the same one) will stall.

The result—gridlock!

Possible Solutions

The designers of the host/PCI bridge can take one of three possible approaches:

1. **Hang the bus** for extensive periods of time (as described in the previous section). This is certainly the least-desirable approach.
2. The host/PCI bridge can **memorize the transaction and issue a retry response** to the processor. This obligates the processor to re-request the processor bus and retry the transaction on a periodic basis until it gets a good response and the read or write completes. The bridge then arbitrates for the PCI bus and proceeds as described in the previous section. When the bridge has finally completed the requested transaction on the PCI side, it waits for the processor's next retry. When it latches a transaction issued on the processor side, it compares the agent and transaction IDs to see if it matches the transaction that was issued a retry response earlier. When it has a match, it permits the transaction to complete—if it's a read, it supplies the read data that it obtained from the PCI side and a Normal Data response; if it's a write, it accepts the data and issues a No Data response. Although better than option one, the retried processor's repeated intrusions into the symmetric arbitration and its usage of the request, AERR#, snoop, and response signal groups will significantly diminish the performance of the other processors. *This is the approach used by the Intel 450GX and 450KX host/PCI bridges.*

3. The **optimal approach is** for the host/PCI bridge to memorize the transaction and issued the **deferred response** to the processor. The processor will not retry the transaction. Rather, it will wait for the response agent to initiate a **deferred reply** transaction to provide the completion notice and, if a read, the read data. The processor therefore doesn't waste valuable bus time with fruitless re-issues of the transaction and the bus remains available for the processors to use (including this processor if MTRRs permit out-of-order execution in the area addressed by the transaction). *This is the approach used by the Intel 440FX bridge. Subsequent bridges will almost certainly use this method as well.*

An Example Read

Read Transaction Memorized and Deferred Response Issued

Refer to Figure 14-1 on page 328 and Figure 14-2 on page 332 during this example. Assume that a processor initiates a read transaction that targets a device residing beyond one of the host/PCI bridges:

1. The bridge memorizes the transaction, including the Deferred ID, or DID, delivered in request packet B.
2. This example assumes that the request initiator permits the response agent to defer the transaction (DEN# is asserted in request packet B).
3. The bridge asserts DEFER# to the request agent in the snoop phase, indicating that it intends to issue a retry or a deferred response in the response phase.
4. In the response phase of the transaction, the bridge acts as the response agent and issues the deferred response. This causes the request agent to mark the transaction request as deferred and to move it from its IOQ to its deferred transaction queue. All other agents remove it from their IOQs and cease tracking it. Effectively, the read transaction is now in a state of suspension until, at a later time, the response agent (i.e., the bridge) addresses the request agent using a deferred reply transaction.
5. The data phase of the transaction has been deferred and will occur later during the deferred reply transaction that will be initiated by the bridge (when it has obtained the read data).

Figure 14-2: Read Transaction Receives a Deferred Response

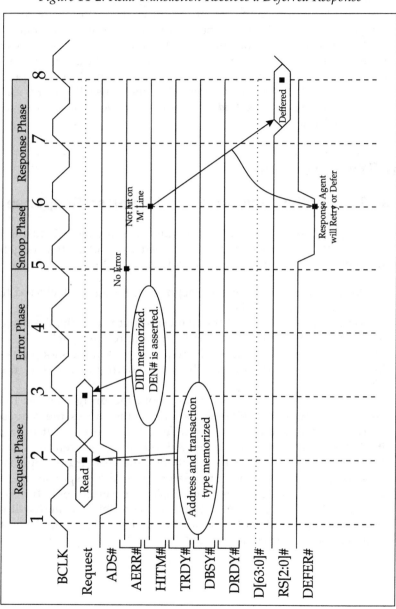

Bridge Performs PCI Read Transaction

As discussed earlier, the bridge performs the equivalent PCI read transaction to obtain the requested data from the target device. The **PCI transaction completes in one of the following ways**:

1. the transaction **completes successfully** and the requested data is read from the target and stored in a temporary buffer in the bridge. In this case, the bridge must indicate the normal data response in the response phase of the deferred reply transaction.
2. the transaction results in a **target abort** from the target, indicating that it is broken. In this case, the bridge must indicate the hard failure response in the response phase of the deferred reply transaction.
3. the transaction ends in a **master abort** because no target responded to the transaction (i.e., DEVSEL# was not sampled asserted within the four PCI clocks after the transaction's address phase completed). In this case, the bridge must indicate the hard failure response in the response phase of the deferred reply transaction.
4. **Read parity error** detected. In this case, the bridge may re-attempt the PCI transaction to see if the data can be read successfully on a second attempt (if the bridge has specific knowledge that the addressed device will not suffer side effects from a re-attempt of the transaction). If it still fails or if no re-attempt is made, the bridge must indicate one of the following responses in the response phase of the deferred reply transaction:
    *   the hard failure response, or
    *   the normal data response, but pass the bad data and parity to the request agent as is.

Deferred Reply Transaction Issued

Refer to Figure 14-3 on page 335 during the following discussion. When the PCI transaction has completed, the bridge uses BPRI# to arbitrate for ownership of the processor bus. Be aware that, in Figure 14-1 on page 328, the two host/PCI bridges both use the BPRI# signal to request ownership of the processor bus, but only one is permitted to drive BPRI# at a time. Before asserting BPRI#, therefore, if both of the bridges require ownership of the processor bus, they must use sideband signals to arbitrate between themselves for ownership of the BPRI# signal. The winner then asserts BPRI# to request ownership of the request signal group.

Having acquired ownership of the request signal group, the bridge then issues a deferred reply transaction. During the request and error phases, the bridge acts as the request agent and the processor addressed by the deferred ID (see

Table 14-1 on page 336) acts as the target of the transaction. The information indicated in Table 14-1 on page 336 is driven out during the transmission of packets A and B. All agents on the bus latch the two packets during the request phase, check parity, and issue AERR# in the error phase if there's a problem. If there isn't a problem, the transaction proceeds to the snoop phase.

Figure 14-3: Deferred Reply Transaction for Read

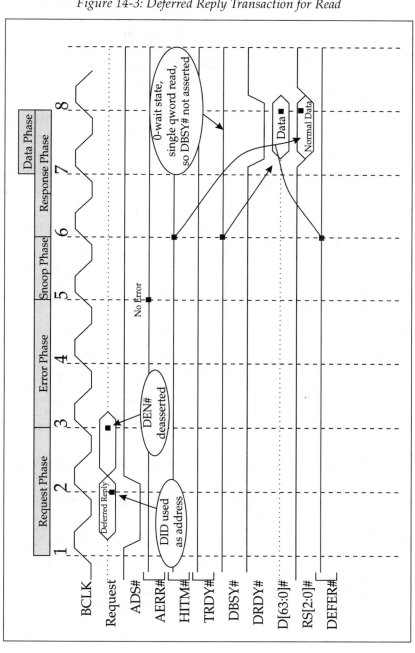

Table 14-1: Request Packet A and B Content in Deferred Reply Transaction

Signals	Description
Request Packet A Content	
REQ[4:0]#	00000b = Deferred reply transaction type.
A[35:24]#	Don't care, but must be in a stable state because the address parity, AP[1:0]#, must be correct.
A[23]#	DID[7]#. Request agent type.
A[22:20]#	DID[6:4]#. Agent ID.
A[19:16]#	DID[3:0]#. Transaction ID.
A[15:3]#	Don't care, but must be in a stable state because the address parity, AP[1:0]#, must be correct.
AP[1:0]#	Address parity bits must be correct (see Table 11-3 on page 266).
RP#	REQ[4:0]#/ADS# parity bit, RP#, must be correct (see Table 11-3 on page 266).
ADS#	ADS# (Address Strobe) is asserted to signal the start of a new transaction.
Request Packet B Content	
SPLCK#	Split Lock is output on the A[6]# pin and must be deasserted.
DEN#	**Defer Enable** is output on the A[4]# pin and must be **deasserted** (the deferred reply transaction may not be deferred).
A[35:3]#	Don't care, but must be in a stable state because the address parity, AP[1:0]#, must be correct.
REQ[4:0]#	Don't care, but must be in a stable state because the REQ[4:0]# parity bit, RP#, must be correct.
AP[1:0]#	Address parity bits must be correct (see Table 11-7 on page 270).
RP#	REQ[4:0]#/ADS# parity bit, RP#, must be correct (see Table 11-7 on page 270).
ADS#	ADS# is deasserted during the packet B transmission.

Original Request Agent Selected

All of the agents match the DID field latched in packet A (from A[23:16]#) to identify a previously-deferred transaction that may have been in a state of suspension in their deferred transaction queues. The request agent that originated the read has a match on its agent type, agent ID, and transaction ID.

Bridge Provides Snoop Result

Until the snoop phase, the bridge is the request agent of the deferred reply transaction, but an interesting thing happens in the snoop phase. The deferred reply transaction is never snooped by the processor bus snoop agents. Rather, the snoop result is supplied by the bridge (i.e., the agent that deferred the transaction earlier) with the snoop result obtained from caches that may exist on the PCI bus when it performed the read. Since typical system designs do not permit PCI agents to cache memory information, the snoop result delivered on HIT# and HITM# indicates a cache miss (both are deasserted). In addition, the DEFER# signal is not asserted (DEN# is always deasserted in request packet B during a deferred reply transaction).

Response Phase—Role Reversal

Once the snoop result is delivered to the processor by the bridge, the response phase of the transaction is entered. The role reversal is now complete—the bridge initiated the deferred reply transaction, but now acts as its response agent; and the processor started out as the target and now serves as the request agent. In other words, the processor and the bridge have returned to the roles they originally played when the transaction was first initiated by the processor. Depending on how the transaction completed on the PCI side, the bridge delivers one of the following responses:

1. If the transaction completed successfully and the requested data was read from the target and stored in a temporary buffer in the bridge, the bridge must indicate the normal data response in the response phase of the deferred reply transaction.
2. If the transaction resulted in a target abort from the target, indicating that it is broken, the bridge must indicate the hard failure response in the response phase of the deferred reply transaction.
3. If the transaction ended in a master abort because no target responded to the transaction (i.e., DEVSEL# was not sampled asserted within the four PCI clocks after the transaction's address phase completed), the bridge must indicate the hard failure response in the response phase of the deferred reply transaction.

4. If a read parity error was detected, the bridge may re-attempt the PCI transaction to see if the data can be read successfully on a second attempt (if the bridge has specific knowledge that the addressed device will not suffer side effects from a re-attempt of the transaction). If it still fails or if no re-attempt is made, the bridge must indicate one of the following responses in the response phase of the deferred reply transaction:
   - the hard failure response, or
   - the normal data response, but pass the bad data and parity to the request agent as is.

Data Phase

Assuming that the read completed successfully on the PCI bus, the normal data response is issued by the bridge. The data phase of a read transaction starts when the normal data response is issued. The bridge asserts DBSY# to take ownership of the data bus. When it presents the data, it asserts DRDY#. In this case, it should be able to present the data quite rapidly because the data is being delivered from a temporary buffer within the bridge. When the last data item is being delivered, the bridge deasserts DBSY#, but keeps DRDY# asserted until the next clock. The processor samples the final data item and DRDY# asserted, indicating that it has latched valid data. The transaction has been completed.

Trackers Retire Transaction

The normal data response indicates that the data will be supplied to the request agent. Once the processor that initiated the original transaction as well as the other bus agents see the normal data response, the IOQs (i.e., the transaction trackers) in all bus agents retire the transaction from their deferred transaction queues.

Other Possible Responses

As indicated earlier, the PCI transaction may not have completed successfully. Table 14-2 on page 339 describes the relationship between the completion status of the PCI transaction and how the deferred reply transaction is completed.

Table 14-2: PCI Read Transaction Completion and Deferred Reply Completion

Completion Status of PCI Transaction	Completion Status of Deferred Reply Transaction
The **transaction completed successfully** and the requested data was read from the target and stored in a temporary buffer in the bridge.	The bridge must indicate the normal data response in the response phase of the deferred reply transaction and pass the read data back during the data phase.
The transaction resulted in a **target abort** from the target, indicating that it is broken.	The bridge must indicate the hard failure response in the response phase of the deferred reply transaction. There will be no data phase in the deferred reply transaction. When the processor receives the hard failure response, it generates a machine check exception.
The transaction ended in a **master abort** because no target responded to the transaction (i.e., DEVSEL# was not sampled asserted within the four PCI clocks after the transaction's address phase completed)	The bridge must indicate the hard failure response in the response phase of the deferred reply transaction. There will be no data phase in the deferred reply transaction. When the processor receives the hard failure response, it generates a machine check exception.
PCI transaction received a retry.	In this case, the PCI specification requires the host/PCI bridge to continually retry the PCI transaction until it completes successfully or is terminated by a target or master abort.

Table 14-2: PCI Read Transaction Completion and Deferred Reply Completion (Continued)

Completion Status of PCI Transaction	Completion Status of Deferred Reply Transaction
A **read parity error** was detected. The bridge may re-attempt the PCI transaction to see if the data can be read successfully on a second attempt (if the bridge has specific knowledge that the addressed device will not suffer side effects from a re-attempt of the transaction).	If it still fails or if no re-attempt is made, the bridge must indicate one of the following responses in the response phase of the deferred reply transaction: • the hard failure response (when the processor receives the hard failure response, it generates a machine check exception), or • the normal data response, but pass the bad data and parity to the request agent as is. In this case, it would be left up to the processor to detect the corrupted data.

An Example Write

The previous section, "An Example Read" on page 331, described the actions of the bridge upon receipt of a read transaction that targeted a device residing on the PCI bus. This section describes the same scenario, but replaces the read with a write transaction.

Transaction and Write Data Memorized, Deferred Response Issued

Refer to Figure 14-1 on page 328 and Figure 14-4 on page 342 during this example. Assume that a processor initiates a write transaction that targets a device residing beyond one of the host/PCI bridges:

1. The bridge memorizes the transaction, including the Deferred ID, or DID, delivered in request packet B.
2. This example assumes that the request initiator permits the response agent to defer the transaction (DEN# is asserted in request packet B).
3. The bridge asserts TRDY#, indicating its willingness to accept the write data into a buffer within the bridge.
4. When the request agent samples TRDY# asserted and DBSY# deasserted (the data bus is no longer in use by the previous owner), it takes ownership of the data bus one clock later (by asserting DBSY#). It then drives the data

(one or more quadwords) to the bridge, asserting DRDY# as each is made available. The bridge latches the data.

5. In the snoop phase, the bridge asserts DEFER# to the request agent, indicating that it intends to issue a retry or a deferred response in the response phase.

6. In the response phase of the transaction, the bridge acts as the response agent and issues the deferred response. This causes the request agent to move the transaction from its IOQ into its deferred transaction queue. All other agents delete it from their IOQs. Effectively, the write transaction is now in a state of suspension until, at a later time, the response agent (i.e., the bridge) addresses the request agent using a deferred reply transaction.

7. During the deferred reply transaction that will be initiated by the bridge at a later time (when it has delivered the write data), the bridge will indicate the delivery status of the write data.

Figure 14-4: Write Transaction Receives Deferred Response

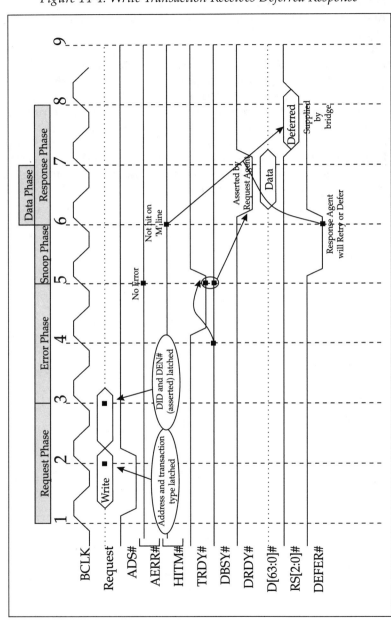

PCI Transaction Performed and Data Delivered to Target

As discussed earlier, the bridge performs the equivalent PCI write transaction to deliver the write data to the target device. The **PCI transaction completes in one of the following ways**:

1. the transaction **completes successfully**. The bridge notes the successful delivery of the data. In this case, the bridge must indicate the no data response in the response phase of the deferred reply transaction.
2. the transaction results in a **target abort** from the target, indicating that it is broken. In this case, the bridge must indicate the hard failure response in the response phase of the deferred reply transaction.
3. the transaction ends in a **master abort** because no target responded to the transaction (i.e., DEVSEL# was not sampled asserted within the four PCI clocks after the transaction's address phase completed). In this case, the bridge must indicate the hard failure response in the response phase of the deferred reply transaction.
4. **Write parity error** detected. In this case, the bridge may re-attempt the PCI transaction to see if the data can be written successfully on a second attempt (if the bridge has specific knowledge that the addressed device will not suffer side effects from a re-attempt of the transaction). If it still fails or if no re-attempt is made, the bridge must indicate the hard failure response in the response phase of the deferred reply transaction.

Deferred Reply Transaction Issued

Refer to Figure 14-5 on page 344 during the following discussion. When the PCI transaction has completed, the bridge uses BPRI# to arbitrate for ownership of the request signal group. Be aware that, in Figure 14-1 on page 328, the two host/PCI bridges both use the BPRI# signal to request ownership of the request signal group, but only one is permitted to drive it at a time. Before asserting BPRI#, therefore, if both of the bridges require ownership, they must use side-band signals to arbitrate between themselves for ownership of the BPRI# signal. The winner then asserts BPRI# to request ownership of the request signal group.

Having acquired ownership of the request signal group, the bridge then issues a deferred reply transaction. During the request and error phases, the bridge acts as the request agent and the processor addressed by the deferred ID (see Table 14-1 on page 336) acts as the target of the transaction. The information indicated in Table 14-1 on page 336 is driven out during the transmission of packets A and B. All agents on the bus latch the two packets during the request phase, check parity, and issue AERR# in the error phase if there's a problem. If there isn't a problem, the transaction proceeds to the snoop phase.

Figure 14-5: Deferred Reply Transaction for Write

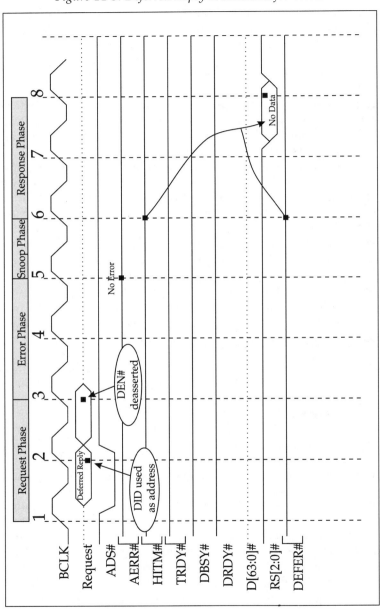

Original Request Agent Selected

All of the agents with outstanding deferred transactions compare the DID field latched in packet A (from A[23:16]#) to identify the previously-deferred transaction that may be in a state of suspension in their deferred transaction queues. The request agent that originated the write has a match on its agent type, agent ID, and transaction ID.

Bridge Provides Snoop Result

Until the snoop phase, the bridge is the request agent of the deferred reply transaction, but an interesting thing happens in the snoop phase. The deferred reply transaction is never snooped by the processor bus snoop agents. Rather, the snoop result is supplied by the bridge (i.e., the agent that deferred the transaction earlier) with the snoop result obtained from caches on the PCI bus (if there are any) when it performed the write. Since typical system designs do not permit PCI agents to cache memory information, the snoop result delivered on HIT# and HITM# indicates a cache miss (both are deasserted). In addition, the DEFER# signal is not asserted (DEN# must always be deasserted in request packet B during a deferred reply transaction).

Response Phase—Role Reversal

Once the snoop result is delivered to the processor by the bridge, the response phase of the transaction is entered. The role reversal is now complete—the bridge initiated the deferred reply transaction, but now acts as its response agent; and the processor started out as the target and now serves as the request agent. In other words, the processor and the bridge have returned to the roles they originally played when the transaction was first initiated by the processor. Depending on how the transaction completed on the PCI side, the bridge delivers one of the following responses:

1. If the transaction completed successfully and the data was written to the target, the bridge must indicate the no data response in the response phase of the deferred reply transaction.
2. If the transaction resulted in a target abort from the target, indicating that it is broken, the bridge must indicate the hard failure response in the response phase of the deferred reply transaction.
3. If the transaction ended in a master abort because no target responded to the transaction (i.e., DEVSEL# was not sampled asserted within the four PCI clocks after the transaction's address phase completed), the bridge must indicate the hard failure response in the response phase of the deferred reply transaction.

4. If a write parity error was detected, the bridge may re-attempt the PCI transaction to see if the data can be written successfully on a second attempt (if the bridge has specific knowledge that the addressed device will not suffer side effects from a re-attempt of the transaction). If it still fails or if no re-attempt is made, the bridge must indicate the hard failure response in the response phase of the deferred reply transaction.

There is No Data Phase

The write data was transferred to the bridge in the data phase of the original write transaction that was deferred. The deferred reply transaction therefore completes with the response phase.

Trackers Retire Transaction

The no data response indicates that the data was accepted by the PCI target. Once the processor that initiated the original transaction as well as the other bus agents see the no data response, they retire the transaction from their deferred transaction queue.

Other Possible Responses

As indicated earlier, the PCI transaction may not have completed successfully. Table 14-3 on page 346 describes the relationship between the completion status of the PCI transaction and how the deferred reply transaction is completed.

Table 14-3: PCI Write Transaction Completion and Deferred Reply Completion

Completion Status of PCI Transaction	Completion Status of Deferred Reply Transaction
The **transaction completed successfully** and the write data was written to the target.	The bridge must indicate the no data response in the response phase of the deferred reply transaction.
The transaction resulted in a **target abort** from the target, indicating that it is broken.	The bridge must indicate the hard failure response in the response phase of the deferred reply transaction. When the processor receives the hard failure response, it generates a machine check exception.

Table 14-3: PCI Write Transaction Completion and Deferred Reply Completion (Continued)

Completion Status of PCI Transaction	Completion Status of Deferred Reply Transaction
The transaction ended in a **master abort** because no target responded to the transaction (i.e., DEVSEL# was not sampled asserted within the four PCI clocks after the transaction's address phase completed)	The bridge must indicate the hard failure response in the response phase of the deferred reply transaction. When the processor receives the hard failure response, it generates a machine check exception.
PCI transaction received a **retry**.	In this case, the PCI specification requires the host/PCI bridge to continually retry the PCI transaction until it completes successfully or is terminated by a target or master abort. *It should be noted, however, that if the other bus were another Pentium Pro bus rather than a PCI bus and a retry response were received, the bridge is required to assert DEFER# in the snoop phase of the deferred reply transaction and must issue a retry response in the response phase. All bus agents then delete the transaction from their IOQs and the processor is then required to retry the transaction from scratch.*
A **write parity error** was detected. The bridge may re-attempt the PCI transaction to see if the data can be written successfully on a second attempt (if the bridge has specific knowledge that the addressed device will not suffer side effects from a re-attempt of the transaction).	If it still fails or if no re-attempt is made, the bridge must indicate the hard failure response in the response phase of the deferred reply transaction.

Pentium Pro Support for Transaction Deferral

The Pentium Pro processor can have up to four of its transactions in the deferred (i.e., suspended) state at a given moment in time.

15 *IO Transactions*

The Previous Chapter

The previous chapter provided a detailed description of transaction deferral and the deferred reply transaction.

This Chapter

This chapter describes the specifics of IO read and write transactions from two perspectives:

- IO transactions as performed by the Pentium Pro processor.
- IO transactions that can be performed by agents other than the processor (or as they may be performed by future processors).

The Next Chapter

The next chapter provides a detailed description of the following transaction types:

- Interrupt acknowledge transaction.
- Special transaction.
- Branch trace message transaction.

Introduction

There is nothing exotic about IO transactions. Like any other transaction type, an IO transaction consists of a request, error, snoop, response and data phase. The following is a summary of general IO transaction characteristics:

- Since the processors never cache information from IO space, there will never be a hit on a cache line.
- The only appropriate snoop results are a miss (HIT# and HITM# both deasserted), or snoop stall (both asserted).

- DEFER# may be asserted by the response agent if it intends to issue a retry or a deferred response in the response phase.
- In the response phase, the only response that may not be issued is the implicit writeback response (because there will never be a hit on a modified IO cache line).

IO Address Range

The IO address range supported by the Pentium Pro processor is from 000000000h through 000010002h (range is **64KB+3** in size). This is backward-compatible with previous x86 processors. Consider the following:

- a 2-byte IO access starting at IO address FFFFh. In this case, the 2-bytes of data straddles the 64KB address boundary. Since these two bytes reside in different quadwords, the processor would perform this as two, separate, single-quadword transactions.
- a 4-byte IO access starting at IO address FFFFh, FFFEh, or FFFDh. As before, the target dword straddles the 64KB address boundary, and the processor would perform this as two, separate, single-quadword transactions.

In both cases, when accessing above the 64KB boundary, the processor would be asserting A[16]#.

Data Transfer Length

Behavior Permitted by Specification

When an IO read or write transaction is initiated, the data transfer length is output by the request agent in request packet B (see Table 11-4 on page 267). The specification permits IO data transfer lengths of:

- a **quadword or less**. Any combination of byte enables are valid, including none.
- **two full quadwords**. All byte enables must be asserted in request packet B.
- **four full quadwords**. All byte enables must be asserted in request packet B.

On a 0-byte read, the response must be the no data response, unless DEFER# is asserted by the response agent (indicating that it intends to retry or defer the transaction).

On a 0-byte write, the response agent must assert TRDY#, but the request agent must not assert DBSY# or DRDY# in response. Note that the author doesn't know why an agent would initiate a 0-byte IO transaction. The x86 processors are incapable of doing this.

How Pentium Pro Processor Operates

The Pentium Pro processor is only capable of initiating IO read and write transactions due to the execution of IO read (IN or INS) or write (OUT or OUTS) instructions. The programmer may only specify the AL, AX, or EAX register as the target or source register for the read or write. This restricts the transfers to:

- a single byte.
- two contiguous bytes.
- four contiguous bytes.

This means that, at most, the transfer length will always be less than a quadword and, at a maximum, four contiguous byte enables will be asserted. If the accessed data crosses a dword address boundary, the processor will behave as follows:

- if the transaction is an IO read and the access crosses the dword boundary within a quadword, one access is performed with the appropriate byte enables asserted.
- if the transaction is an IO read and the access crosses a quadword boundary, two separate single-quadword accesses are performed with the appropriate byte enables asserted.
- if the transaction is an IO write and the access crosses the dword boundary within a quadword, two accesses are performed with the appropriate byte enables asserted.
- if the transaction is an IO write and the access crosses a quadword boundary, two separate single-quadword accesses are performed with the appropriate byte enables asserted.

16 Central Agent Transactions

The Previous Chapter

The previous chapter described the specifics of IO read and write transactions from two perspectives:

- IO transactions as performed by the Pentium Pro processor.
- IO transactions that can be performed by agents other than the processor (or as they may be performed by future processors).

This Chapter

This chapter provides a detailed description of the following transaction types:

- Interrupt acknowledge transaction.
- Special transaction.
- Branch trace message transaction.

The Next Chapter

The next chapter focuses on the processor's remaining signals and concludes the description of the processor's hardware operation.

Point-to-Point vs. Broadcast

Most transactions are point-to-point transactions—the request agent addresses a specific area of memory or IO space for a read or a write and the addressed target acts as the transaction's response agent.

Some transactions generated by the processor don't target any specific memory or IO device, however. Rather, the processor is performing one of the following operations:

1. performing an **interrupt acknowledge** transaction to request the interrupt vector from the interrupt controller. In this case, the host/PCI bridge would act as the response agent (because the interrupt controller typically resides beyond the bridge).
2. performing a **special transaction** to broadcast a message to everyone. No one is targeted by the transaction, but someone has to act as the response agent. It is typically the host/PCI bridge.
3. performing a **branch trace message transaction** to inform a debug tool that, when executed, a branch was taken. Once again, no one in particular is being addressed and yet someone has to act as the response agent. It is typically the host/PCI bridge.

Intel refers to these as *central agent transactions* because one device typically acts as the default response agent for these transaction types. In a typical system (see Figure 16-1 on page 356), that device is typically the one Intel refers to as the compatibility bridge.

Interrupt Acknowledge Transaction

Background

An x86-based system frequently incorporates an interrupt controller that receives interrupt requests from IO devices and passes them onto the processor (or processor cluster). The interrupt controller will either consist of a pair of cascaded 8259As in a single processor system, or an IO APIC module in a multi-processor system. Refer to Figure 16-1 on page 356. In Intel chipsets, the interrupt controller is incorporated in the PCI-to-ISA or PCI-to-EISA bridge. This is a strategically convenient place for it because the interrupt requests from PCI and EISA or ISA targets can easily be connected to it. As an example, the Intel ISA bridge (i.e., the SIO.A or the PIIX) incorporates the 8259A interrupt controllers (systems with ISA are typically single-processor systems), while the EISA bridge incorporates an IO APIC module (EISA systems are typically multi-processor systems targeting the server or workstation market).

Assuming that the system uses the 8259A interrupt controller, the interrupt controller asserts its INTR (interrupt request) output when it detects any interrupt requests from IO devices. This is connected to the INTR pin (also referred to as the LINT0 pin) on one of the processors (typically the only processor). In response to its assertion, the processor takes the following actions:

1. Assuming that recognition of external interrupts is enabled (in other words, the programmer has not executed a CLI instruction), the processor will recognize the request when it completes the execution of the current instruction.
2. The processor ceases to execute the interrupted program.
3. The processor generates an Interrupt Acknowledge transaction to read the interrupt vector of the highest priority request from the interrupt controller.
4. The processor uses the 8-bit vector as an index into the interrupt table in memory and reads the new CS:IP value from the selected entry.
5. The processor pushes the contents of its CS, IP and EFLAGS registers into stack memory (to mark its place in the interrupted program).
6. The processor then disables recognition of additional external interrupts (i.e., it clears the IF bit in the EFLAGS register).
7. Using the new CS:IP value, the processor jumps to the target interrupt service routine and executes it.

Pentium Pro and Pentium II System Architecture

Figure 16-1: Typical System Block Diagram

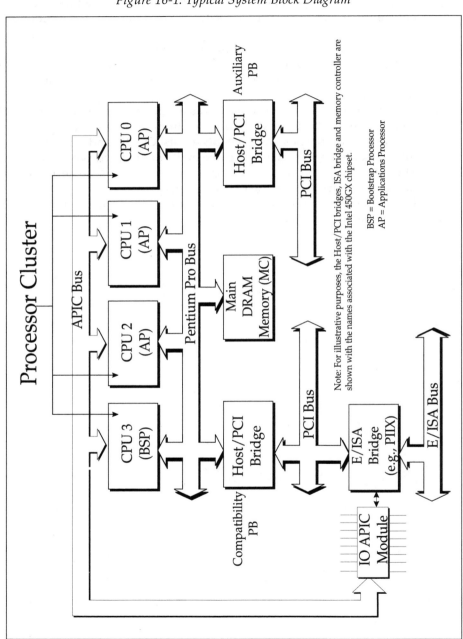

Chapter 16: Central Agent Transactions

How Pentium Pro is Different

This is where the Pentium Pro processor is different than the previous x86 processors. The earlier processors generated two, back-to-back interrupt acknowledge transactions—one to command the interrupt controller to prioritize its pending requests, the second to request the interrupt vector for the most important one. However, the Pentium Pro processor only generates one interrupt acknowledge transaction. This transaction has the following characteristics:

- In packet A, the request type issued on REQ[4:0]# is 01000b (this is the logical, not electrical, value). For more information, refer to Table 11-4 on page 267.
- Although the content of the address bus in packet A is "don't care," it must be stable and is factored into the address parity on AP[1:0]#.
- In packet B, REQ[4:0]# is 00x00b, where x is "don't care."
- In packet B, with the exception of A[15:8]# (the byte enables) and A[4]# (DEN#, defer enable), the content of the address bus is "don't care."
- In packet B, **DEN# is asserted**, granting the response agent permission to defer or retry the transaction if it so chooses.
- In packet B, only **BE[0]# is asserted**, indicating that it's a single byte read to obtain the interrupt vector over data path 0 (D[7:0]#).

Host/PCI Bridge is Response Agent

In Figure 16-1 on page 356, the compatibility bridge acts as the response agent because the interrupt controller resides beyond the bridge (within the PCI/ISA bridge). Since it will take some time to obtain the vector from the other bridge, the host/PCI bridge may choose to issue a deferred response to the processor. The compatibility bridge arbitrates for ownership of the PCI bus and generates a PCI interrupt acknowledge transaction (see the chapter on commands in MindShare's *PCI System Architecture* book, published by Addison-Wesley). When the PCI/ISA bridge latches the interrupt acknowledge transaction, it acts as the target of the transaction and provides the interrupt vector over PCI data path 0. The host/PCI bridge latches the vector and supplies it to the processor over data path 0. If the transaction had been deferred, a deferred reply transaction is used to provide the vector to the processor.

Special Transaction

General

Under special circumstances, an x86 processor generates a special transaction to broadcast a message to everyone. In other words, this is not a point-to-point transaction that targets a particular agent. As indicated earlier, every transaction requires that a response agent respond, and the compatibility bridge (see Figure 16-1 on page 356) is typically the response agent (i.e., the central agent) for the special transaction. This transaction has the following characteristics:

- Although the content of the address bus in packet A is "don't care," it is factored into the address parity on AP[1:0]#. For more information, refer to Table 11-4 on page 267.
- In packet A, the request type issued on REQ[4:0]# is 01000b (this is the logical, not electrical, value).
- In packet B, REQ[4:0]# is 00x01b, where x is "don't care."
- Although the content of A[35:16]# and A[7:3]# in packet B are "don't care," it is factored into the address parity on AP[1:0]#.
- In packet B, the byte enables indicate the type of message being broadcast (see next section).

Message Types

As stated in the previous section, the message type is driven out on BE[7:0]# (A[15:8]#) in packet B. Table 16-1 on page 359 indicates the types of messages that are currently defined.

Chapter 16: Central Agent Transactions

Table 16-1: Message Types

BE[7:0]#	Message Type
00h	**Nop**. Intel does not define what type of internal event causes the processor to generate this message.
01h	**Shutdown**. Indicates that the processor has incurred a severe software error. As with previous x86 processors, the Pentium Pro generates this message when it encounters a triple-fault condition. In other words, it has received another exception while attempting to call the double-fault exception handler. In response to the triple-fault, the processor ceases program execution and generates this message. Whether or not a system pays any attention to this message and, if so, the action taken by the system, is system design-specific. In a PC system, the host/PCI bridge generates a PCI special cycle transaction and broadcasts the shutdown message in the data phase of the PCI transaction. When detected by the PCI/ISA or PCI/EISA bridge, the bridge asserts reset to the system and then removes it. This causes the system to start over with the POST.
02h	**Flush**. Generated by the processor when it executes an **INVD** (invalidate caches) **instruction**. This instruction causes the processor to invalidate all of its internal caches without writing modified lines back to memory. The processor also broadcasts this message to inform any external caches that they should also invalidate their contents. It should be noted that this message does not cause other processors to invalidate their internal caches. If this is the programmer's intent, the processor's local APIC should be instructed to send an IPI (inter-processor interrupt message packet) to the other processors over the APIC bus that instructs them to do the same.
03h	**Halt**. Generated by the processor when it executes a HALT instruction. Whether or not a system pays any attention to this message and, if so, the action taken by the system, is system design-specific. In a PC system, the host/PCI bridge generates a PCI special cycle transaction and broadcasts the halt message in the data phase of the PCI transaction (in case any of the PCI agents care that a processor has halted).
04h	**Sync**. Generated by the processor when it executes an **WBINVD** (write back and invalidate caches) **instruction**. This instruction causes the processor to first write back all modified lines to memory, after which it invalidates all of its internal caches. The processor also broadcasts this message to inform any external caches that they should do the same. It should be noted that this message does not cause other processors to take this action in their internal caches. If this is the programmer's intent, the processor's local APIC should be instructed to send an IPI (inter-processor interrupt message packet) to the other processors over the APIC bus that instructs them to do the same.
05h	**Flush Acknowledge**. When external logic asserts the processor's FLUSH# input, this causes the processor to first write back all modified lines to memory, after which it invalidates all of its internal caches. The processor then broadcasts this message to inform system logic that it has completed the operation.

Table 16-1: Message Types (Continued)

BE[7:0]#	Message Type
06h	**Stop Grant Acknowledge**. When external logic asserts the processor's STPCLK# (Stop Clock) input, the processor turns off the clock to all of its internal units with the exception of its external bus interface, the Time Stamp Counter (TSC), and the local APIC. This is referred to as the stop grant state and greatly diminishes the processor's power consumption. In addition, this message is broadcast to inform the system that the Stop Clock request has been honored.
07h	**SMI Acknowledge**. In response to a System Management interrupt received on SMI# (or via the APIC bus), the processor takes the following steps: • ceases to execute the currently-executing program. • using the special transaction, broadcasts the SMI Acknowledge message. Note that the SMMEM# signal is asserted in packet B of this transaction. This informs the central agent that until it indicates otherwise, system management memory is being addressed. In response, Intel chipsets generate SMIACT# (SMI Active) to the DRAM controller to enable its SMM memory decoder. • processor performs a series of memory writes to SMM to dump the contents of its register set to SMM. The processor is taking a "snapshot" of its context (i.e., register set contents) at the point of interruption. • processor then fetches and executes the SMM handler routine. • the final instruction in the SMM handler is always the RSM (Resume) instruction. When executed, the processor performs a series of memory reads to reload its register set from the register dump area. • after reloading its register set, the processor generates a second SMI Acknowledge message, this time with SMMEM# deasserted, informing the central agent that it will no longer be addressing SMM. In an Intel chipset, this causes the compatibility bridge to deassert the SMIACT# signal to the DRAM controller thereby disabling the SMM memory decoder. • the processor then resumes execution of the interrupted program.
08h-FFh	Reserved.

Branch Trace Message Transaction Used for Program Debug

What's the Problem?

Before processors had internal caches, every memory read and write was performed on the bus. With a bus analyzer, you could therefore see every instruction that was fetched from memory for decode and execution. You could see when a branch instruction was fetched and, when it was subsequently decoded and executed, you would see the processor alter its program flow when the processor begins to issue memory read requests from the branch target address. In other words, you had full visibility to watch your program being executed.

When a processor incorporates an internal cache, however, program execution tracing becomes a real problem. After it reads a program into the internal code cache, you lose that visibility. You don't know what's going on. Specifically, you can't tell when the processor executes a branch instruction and, as a result, alters its program flow to a different part of the program that may already be in the code cache.

What's the Solution?

The Pentium and Pentium Pro processors can be forced to generate a message each time that it executes a branch and changes its program flow. The transaction type is the branch trace message transaction. This capability must be enabled by software, however.

Enabling Branch Trace Message Capability

The programmer enables or disables branch trace message transaction capability using a bit in an MSR (model-specific registers) called the DEBUGCTL (debug control) register (see Figure 16-2 on page 362). Once enabled, the processor generates a branch trace message transaction each time that a branch executes and causes a change in program flow (in other words, the branch to the new address is taken). This is the only central agent transaction that writes data. It writes information during the data phase to inform a debug tool which branch has been taken as well as the address that is being branched to.

Figure 16-2: DEBUGCTL MSR

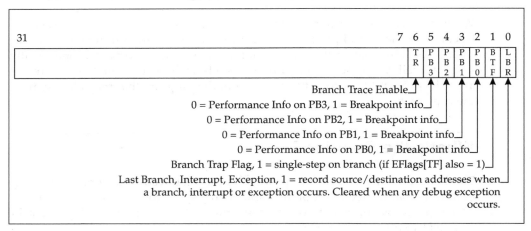

Branch Trace Message Transaction

As stated earlier, interrupt acknowledge and branch trace message are the only central agent transactions that transfer data. Interrupt acknowledge reads the vector from the 8259A interrupt controller, and the branch trace message transaction writes data to an external debug tool.

Packet A Composition

A[35:3]# is reserved and can be any value. REQ[4:0]# contains 01001b. ADS# is asserted to indicate the transaction start. All three parity bits must be correct.

Packet B Composition

All three parity bits must be correct. REQ[4:0]# contains 00X00b, where the most-significant two bits are the DSZ field (see Table 11-4 on page 267) and must always be 00b as currently defined. 'X' means "don't care." A[35:16]# are reserved. A[15:8]#, the byte enables, are all asserted, indicating that eight bytes of data will be written in the data phase. A[7:3]#, the EXF signals, are set as follows:

- EXF4#, or A[7]#, is the SMMEM# (system management memory) signal and is deasserted.
- EXF3#, or A[6]#, is the SPLCK# (split lock) signal and is deasserted.

Chapter 16: Central Agent Transactions

- EXF2#, or A[5]#, is reserved and can be any value.
- EXF1#, or A[4]#, is the DEN# (defer enable) signal and is asserted. Intel doesn't overtly say this, but they do say that DEN# is only deasserted for locked transactions, deferred reply transactions, and 32 byte writes performed by the processor to cast a modified line back to memory to make room in the cache for a new line.
- EXF0#, or A[3]#, is reserved and can be any value.

Proper Response

The proper response is the no data response (because it's a write). Intel does not say that other responses are not permitted, so the author interprets this to mean that, although unlikely, the retry, deferred, and hard failure responses would also be permitted.

Data Composition

The central agent is responsible for asserting TRDY# to tell the processor to take ownership of the data bus and drive the data. The processor then drives out the eight bytes of data and asserts DRDY#. The author is assuming that it can do this with no wait states and therefore doesn't have to assert DBSY# (see "Special Case—Single Quadword, 0-Wait State Transfer" on page 321). When the data is driven, either the central agent or, more likely, a third party (the debug tool) snarfs the data. The data has the following composition:

- D[31:0]# contains the linear branch target address (i.e., the address branched to).
- D[63:32]# contains one of the following:
  - the linear start address of the branch instruction if its execution caused an exception (Intel uses the phrase "if the instruction does not complete normally").
  - the linear start address of the instruction immediately following the branch if the branch did not cause an exception.

17 *Other Signals*

The Previous Chapter

The previous chapter provided a detailed description of the following transaction types:

- Interrupt acknowledge transaction.
- Special transaction.
- Branch trace message transaction.

This Chapter

The previous chapters discussed all of the signals directly involved in performing bus transactions. This chapter focuses on the processor's remaining signals.

The Next Chapter

The next chapter describes the differences between the Pentium Pro and Pentium II processors. It introduces the Slot 1 connector and the processor cartridge design that the Pentium II and future processors will utilize.

Error Reporting Signals

In addition to the AERR# signal that is used in the error phase of the transaction, there are other error signals utilized by bus agents to signal various types of error conditions. The sections that follow describe these signals.

Bus Initialize (BINIT#)

Description

BINIT# is asserted by an agent when the bus cannot be reliably used for future transactions. As an example, if an agent's IOQ is corrupted, it can no longer reliably track transactions and therefore cannot reliably interact with the bus at the appropriate times. How a processor uses BINIT# is set up as follows:

- The ability of a processor to assert BINIT# can be configured at power-up time (in EBL_CR_POWERON MSR; see "Program-Accessible Startup Features" on page 45).
- A10# is sampled on the trailing-edge of reset to determine whether to observe BINIT# (see "Error Observation Options" on page 39).

When BINIT# is detected, all agents clear their IOQs, their deferred transactions queues, and also reset their bus interface state machines to the idle ownership state and a rotating ID to 3.

The processor can be enabled to generate a machine check exception when BINIT# is detected or asserted. The machine check architecture registers can log an error indicating that either the processor observed someone else assert BINIT# or that it asserted BINIT#. The Intel documentation doesn't say, however, which processor will execute its machine check exception handler. The author assumes it would be the processor that asserted BINIT#. Multiple processors could observe it asserted by another agent and you typically wouldn't want all of them simultaneously executing the machine check exception handler.

There is the possibility that an agent other than a processor asserted BINIT#. In this event, the central agent (e.g., the compatibility bridge), could be configured to send an NMI to the processors over the APIC bus.

Assertion/Deassertion Protocol

See "BERR#/BINIT# Assertion/Deassertion Protocol" on page 367.

Bus Error (BERR#)

Description

BERR# is asserted by a bus agent to indicate that an error has been detected in the current transaction. An example would be an uncorrectable memory data error. Unlike BINIT#, however, BERR# assertion only applies to the current transaction, not to future transactions that may be generated on the bus. How a processor uses BERR# is set up as follows:

- A9# is sampled on the trailing-edge of reset to determine whether to observe BERR# (see "Error Observation Options" on page 39). *Be advised that the Pentium Pro processor does not support this option.*
- Ability of a processor to assert BERR# is configured at power-up time (in EBL_CR_POWERON MSR (see "Program-Accessible Startup Features" on page 45).

Using the machine check architecture MSRs, the processor can be enabled to generate a machine check exception on this event. Using the EBL_CR_POWERON MSR (see "Program-Accessible Startup Features" on page 45), the Pentium Pro processor can be configured to assert BERR#:

- to report an unrecoverable error (that is not handled by the machine check architecture) detected during a bus transaction when the processor is acting as the request agent.
- to report an internal error. In this case, BERR# is asserted once and then deasserted. In addition, IERR# is also asserted and remains asserted until NMI is recognized, or until RESET# or INIT# is asserted to the processor.

BERR#/BINIT# Assertion/Deassertion Protocol

BERR# and BINIT# are two of the six signals that may be driven by multiple agents simultaneously. The protocol demands that, when BERR# or BINIT# is asserted, it remain asserted for exactly three clocks.

- If an agent samples BERR# or BINIT# deasserted in the clock that it asserts it, it asserts BERR# or BINIT# for exactly three clocks and then releases it.
- If BERR# or BINIT# was already asserted by one or more other agents prior to an agent's assertion of BERR# or BINIT#, it must only assert BERR# or BINIT# for two clocks or one clock, depending on how long it has already been observed asserted. This results in BERR# or BINIT# only being asserted for exactly three clocks.

Internal Error (IERR#)

IERR# is generated by a processor when an unrecoverable internal error is detected that is not handled by the machine check architecture logic (because it is disabled). The processor can also be configured to assert BERR# once along with IERR# (see the preceding section).

Functional Redundancy Check Error (FRCERR)

At startup time, a pair of processors can be set up as master and checker (see "FRC Mode Enable/Disable" on page 40). The checker watches the master and, if the master does something that the checker wouldn't have, the checker asserts FRCERR. The master can be configured (via its MSRs) to observe FRCERR and generate a machine check exception (if enabled via CR4[MCE]=1) on its assertion.

PC-Compatibility Signals

The processor's PC Compatibility signal group consists of FERR#, IGNNE#, and A20M#.

A20 Mask (A20M#)

A20M# allows the processor to emulate the address wrap-around at the 1MB address boundary that occurs on the 8086/8088 processors. This pin should only be asserted to the processor when the processor is operating in real mode. When A20M# is asserted to the processor, the processor masks physical address bit 20 (forces it to zero) before performing a snoop in the internal caches or driving a memory address onto the bus. A complete description and historical background can be found in the MindShare book entitled *ISA System Architecture* (published by Addison-Wesley).

FERR# and IGNNE#

For a detailed historical background on floating-point operation in the ISA environment, refer to the MindShare book entitled *ISA System Architecture* (published by Addison-Wesley).

The programmer can select the processor's floating-point error handling methodology using the CR0[NE] bit. In an MS-DOS environment, the FP error handler is implemented as the IRQ13 handler and is incorporated within MS-DOS. This means that, when a FP error is encountered, the processor must somehow generate IRQ13 to the slave 8259A interrupt controller. The processor's FPU is embedded within the processor itself, so it must be configured to assert the processor's FERR# output when it encounters an error while attempting to execute a FP instruction. This is done by clearing CR0[NE] to zero. The processor then handles FP errors as follows:

- If external logic keeps the IGNNE# asserted, any FPU errors are ignored.
- If the IGNNE# input is deasserted and an unmasked FPU error is encountered while executing a FP instruction, the processor ceases program execution immediately before executing the next waiting FP instruction or WAIT/FWAIT instruction. The processor's FERR# output is asserted. Externally, FERR# is connected to the PC's IRQ13 interrupt request line. This causes the slave interrupt controller to generate a request to the master

interrupt controller, which, in turn, generates INTR to the processor. The processor interrupts the currently-executing program and requests the interrupt vector from the interrupt controllers. The vector associated with IRQ13, 75h, is supplied to the processor and the processor jumps to the interrupt service routine pointed to by entry 75h in the interrupt table in memory. This is the MS-DOS FP error handler routine. The handler reads the FPU's status to determine the error condition. If the error is one that can be fixed by the handler, the handler then performs an IO write of all zeros to IO port F0h to clear the FPU's error condition. When the chipset detects this write, it asserts IGNNE# to the processor, permitting the FPU to proceed to the next instruction.

If CR0[NE] is set to one by the OS, the PC-compatible FPU error reporting method is not used. Instead, the processor generates an exception 16d when a FP error is encountered and the processor jumps directly to the FP error handler within the OS.

Diagnostic Support Signals

The Pentium Pro implements some pins specifically to aid in system and program debug. Those signals are described in Table 17-1 on page 369 and Table 17-2 on page 370.

Table 17-1: Diagnostic-Support Signals

Signal(s)	Description
BP[3:2]#	**Breakpoint 3 and 2 output pins**. Asserted by processor if a match is detected on either breakpoint 2 or 3. Starting with the 386, all x86 processors incorporates a set of debug registers that can be used to set up and enable up to four program breakpoints (breakpoints 0 through 3). If an internal access matches the breakpoint conditions defined for one of these breakpoints, the processor asserts the respective BP output. For a detailed description of the debug registers, refer to the MindShare book entitled *Pentium Processor System Architecture* (published by Addison-Wesley). Also see the next entry.

Table 17-1: Diagnostic-Support Signals

Signal(s)	Description
BPM[1:0]#	**Breakpoint/Performance Monitoring outputs** 0 and 1. These pins can be configured either as breakpoint indicators (as described in the preceding entry), or to alert a debug tool that either performance monitoring counter 0 or 1 has either overflowed or has been incremented. For more information refer to the chapter entitled "Performance Monitoring and Timestamp" on page 499.
TCK, TDI, TDO, TMS, TRST	**Boundary Scan** interface signals. Used for boundary scan testing and for connection to an external test tool (i.e., an ITP, or In-Target Probe).

Table 17-2: Probe Port Signals

Signal(s)	Description
PREQ#	**Probe Request.** Asserted by an ITP (in-target probe) tool to command the processor to enter probe mode (so the tool can access the processor's internal registers through the probe port (i.e., the boundary scan interface).
PRDY#	**Probe Ready.** Asserted by the processor in response to assertion of PREQ#. Indicates processor is in probe mode and ready to receive commands/requests via the boundary scan interface.

Interrupt-Related Signals

The processor's interrupt-related signals are described in Table 17-3 on page 370.

Table 17-3: Interrupt-Related Signals

Signal(s)	Description
RESET#	**Hard reset.** Clears all caches, returns processor to startup state. For a description of the startup state, refer to the chapter entitled "Processor Startup" on page 51.

Table 17-3: Interrupt-Related Signals (Continued)

Signal(s)	Description
INIT#	**Soft reset**. Resets processor to startup state, but does not clear caches or affect floating-point or MCA registers. Also sampled on trailing-edge of reset to determine whether or not BIST should be run. This pin was first implemented on the 486 processor to avoid the massive performance dip when a 286 DOS extender program issues a reset to the processor to return the processor to real mode. For historical background, refer to the chapter entitled *The Reset Logic* in the MindShare book entitled *ISA System Architecture* (published by Addison-Wesley).
LINT0/INTR	**Local Interrupt input 0** (in APIC mode), or INTR (**Maskable External Interrupt**) input (in 8259 mode). The local APIC can be configured to treat this pin either as a local interrupt pin or as the external interrupt line from the 8259A interrupt controller. For more information on LINT0, refer to the chapter entitled *The APIC* in the MindShare book entitled *Pentium Processor System Architecture* (published by Addison-Wesley). For more information on INTR, refer to the chapter entitled *The Interrupt Subsystem* in the MindShare book entitled *ISA System Architecture* (published by Addison-Wesley).
LINT1/NMI	**Local Interrupt input 1** (in APIC mode), or **Non-Maskable Interrupt** input (in 8259 mode). The local APIC can be configured to treat this pin either as a local interrupt pin or as the NMI line from the PC chipset. For more information on LINT1, refer to the chapter entitled *The APIC* in the MindShare book entitled *Pentium Processor System Architecture* (published by Addison-Wesley). For more information on NMI, refer to the chapter entitled *The Interrupt Subsystem* in the MindShare book entitled *ISA System Architecture* (published by Addison-Wesley).
PICCLK	**APIC clock line**. Used to clock data between local APICs and IO APIC over PICD[1:0]. For more information, refer to the chapter entitled *The APIC* in the MindShare book entitled *Pentium Processor System Architecture* (published by Addison-Wesley).
PICD[1:0]	**APIC data lines** (see preceding entry).

Table 17-3: Interrupt-Related Signals (Continued)

Signal(s)	Description
SMI#	**System Management Interrupt**. Typically asserted by chipset when a power management event occurs. Causes processor to suspend normal operation and start execution of SMM handler. SMI can also be delivered over the APIC bus. For more information, refer to the chapter entitled *System Management Mode* in the MindShare book entitled *Pentium Processor System Architecture* (published by Addison-Wesley). Also refer to the description of the SMI Acknowledge message in Table 16-1 on page 359.

Processor Present Signals

The signals described in Table 17-4 on page 372 are used to indicate the presence of the processor and/or the upgrade processor.

Table 17-4: Processor Presence Signals

Signal	Description
UP#	**Upgrade Present** signal. Output from processor. In Pentium Pro, it's an open. In upgrade (Overdrive) processor, it's grounded. System board has pullup. Installing an Overdrive processor in lieu of the Pentium Pro asserts this signal. Used to disable voltage regulators that may be harmful to Overdrive processor.
CPUPRES#	**CPU Present**. Asserted by processor when installed.

Power Supply Pins

Table 17-5 on page 373 describes the processor's power supply-related pins.

Chapter 17: Other Signals

Table 17-5: Processor Power-related Pins

Signal	Description
POWERGOOD	3.3V-tolerant input. When asserted, indicates that clocks and the 3.3V, 5V, and VccP supplies are stable and within spec. When asserted, must be immediately followed by a minimum 1ms assertion of RESET#. Used to protect internal circuits from voltage sequencing issues.
Vcc5	5Vdc for processor cooling fan.
VccP	CPU die operating voltage.
VccS	L2 cache die operating voltage. Intel has subsequently removed all reference to these pins. These pins are now defined as *Reserved*.
VID[3:0]	Voltage ID. Identifies CPU die's power supply requirements (see Table 17-6 on page 373).
VREF[7:0]	Reference voltage inputs for GTL+ receivers (see "Everything's Relative" on page 200). Nominally = 1.0Vdc.
Vss	Ground.

Table 17-6: Voltage ID Encoding

VID[3:0] Value	Operating Voltage Required by CPU Die
0000b	3.5
0001b	3.4
0010b	3.3
0011b	3.2
0100b	3.1
0101b	3.0
0110b	2.9
0111b	2.8

Table 17-6: Voltage ID Encoding (Continued)

VID[3:0] Value	Operating Voltage Required by CPU Die
1000b	2.7
1001b	2.6
1010b	2.5
1011b	2.4
1100b	2.3 (support not expected)
1101b	2.2 (support not expected)
1110b	2.1 (support not expected)
1111b	CPU not present

Miscellaneous Signals

Table 17-7 on page 374 describes the processor's remaining signals.

Table 17-7: Miscellaneous Signals

Signal(s)	Description
BCLK	**Bus Clock** input. 3.3V signal. Used directly as bus clock. Also multiplied internally to yield processor core's internal PCLK (see "Processor Core Speed Selection" on page 41).
FLUSH#	When asserted, causes processor to write back all modified lines to memory and invalidate all cache entries. Processor then performs a Flush Acknowledge special transaction (see "Special Transaction" on page 358) to indicate that flush is complete. Also sampled at trailing-edge of reset to determine if processor should tri-state all of its outputs (see "Selecting Tri-State Mode" on page 41)
PLL[2:1]	**Phase-Locked Loop decoupling pins**. Should be connected to an external decoupling capacitor.

Table 17-7: Miscellaneous Signals (Continued)

Signal(s)	Description
STPCLK#	**Stop Clock**. When asserted to processor, causes processor to disable internal clock to all units except the bus interface, Timestamp Counter and APIC. Processor enters the Stop Grant state and generates a Stop Grant Acknowledge special transaction (see "Message Types" on page 358) to indicate that it has stopped the internal clock. Processor will still snoop external memory accesses by other agents.
TESTHI	**Test High** (3 pins). Must all be pulled up (preferred) or may be tied directly to VccP.
TESTLO	**Test Low** (13 pins). Must all be pulled low (preferred) or may be connected directly to Vss.
THERMTRIP#	**Thermal Trip**. When junction temperature exceeds ~ 135C, the processor stops execution and asserts this output. A reset will restart program execution if the junction temperature has fallen below the trip point. Otherwise, the processor remains stopped.

Part 3:
Pentium II
Processor

The Previous Part

Part 2 of the book provided a detailed description the hardware environment.

This Part

Part 3 of the book provides a description of the Pentium II processor and how it differs from the Pentium Pro processor.

The Next Part

Part 4 of the book provides a description of the processor's software characteristics.

18 *Pentium II Processor*

The Previous Chapter

The previous chapter focused on signals that aren't directly involved in performing bus transactions and concluded the description of the Pentium Pro processor's hardware operation.

This Chapter

This chapter describes the differences between the Pentium Pro and Pentium II processors. It introduces the Slot 1 connector and the processor cartridge design that the Pentium II and future processors will utilize.

The Next Chapter

The next chapter begins the description of the processor's software characteristics.

Introduction

The Pentium II processor is a derivative of the Pentium Pro processor, differing in the following respects:

- change in packaging
- support for the MMX instruction set and registers
- optimized for 16-bit code execution
- implements support for the Fast System Call instructions: SYSENTER and SYSEXIT.
- speed of L2 cache backside bus
- processor external bus speed
- L2 cache implemented using off-the-shelf synchronous burst SRAMs
- size of L1 caches
- supports power-conservation modes

- changed number of processors supported
- L2 cache ECC support
- Voltage ID bus expanded from four to five bits

The sections that follow describe the differences between the Pentium II and Pentium Pro processors. *Other than these areas of difference, the Pentium II and Pentium Pro processors are functionally identical.*

Single-Edge Cartridge

Pentium and Pentium Pro Sockets

The Pentium and Pentium Pro processors utilize PGA (i.e., pin grid array) packages and motherboard sockets. The Pentium sockets are referred to as sockets 1 through 7, with socket 7 being the de facto standard on today's Pentium motherboards. The Pentium Pro processor uses the socket 8 PGA configuration. Motherboard designers can license Socket 8 from Intel, but processor designers cannot.

Pentium II Processor Cartridge

With the advent of the Pentium II processor, Intel has switched to a Single-Edge Cartridge (i.e., SEC) processor package. The motherboard incorporates a single, in-line connector into which the processor card is installed. This is referred to as the Slot 1 connector (implying that additional slot connector variants will be introduced in the future). Motherboard designers can license Slot 1 from Intel, but processor designers cannot.

The processor core and L2 cache are contained on a card, referred to as the substrate, that installs into the Slot 1 connector. The substrate is completely enshrouded within a cover that provides EMI shielding and a metal thermal plate used to dissipate processor heat through a heat sink attached to the thermal plate. Figure 18-1 on page 381 illustrates a front view of the SEC cartridge with the cover in place, while Figure 18-2 on page 382 illustrates a side view. Note that the cover is located over the rear (non-processor) side of the substrate, while the thermal plate covers the processor side of the substrate. When Intel originally presented the cartridge to its customer base for comments, neither the processor core nor any of its support logic was visible. From a marketing perspective, the end-customer has grown accustomed to seeing the processor chip. To address this perception, Intel includes a label with a picture of the processor core die on the cover (see Figure 18-1 on page 381).

Figure 18-1: The SEC Cartridge Cover

Figure 18-2: SEC Cartridge Side-View

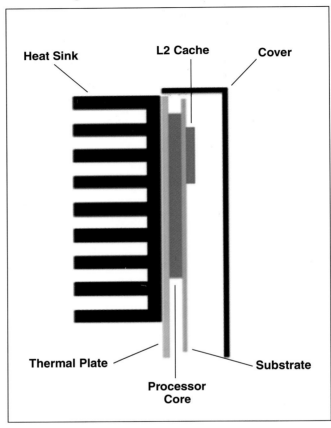

Processor Side of SEC Substrate

General

Figure 18-3 on page 384 illustrates the front side of the substrate. It contains the processor core and two of the L2 cache's four data SRAMs that are used for storing lines of memory information. It also contains a number of passive components not pictured in Figure 18-3 on page 384.

Processor Core

The processor core is implemented in a plastic LGA (Land Grid Array) package with a metal heat spreader attached to it. The LGA package is similar to a Ball Grid Array, or BGA, package utilizing small pads but no solder balls.

The LGA package is mounted on a small circuit board (see Figure 18-3 on page 384) which is attached to the substrate. When the cartridge is assembled, thermal grease is applied to the processor core's heat spreader and the thermal plate is placed in contact with the heat spreader (see Figure 18-2 on page 382). The heat sink, in turn, is attached to the thermal plate.

Non-Processor Side of SEC Substrate

The other side of the substrate (pictured in Figure 18-4 on page 385) contains the L2 cache's tag SRAM and two of the four data SRAMs. It also contains a numbered of passive components not pictured in Figure 18-4 on page 385.

Figure 18-3: Processor Core Side of SEC Substrate

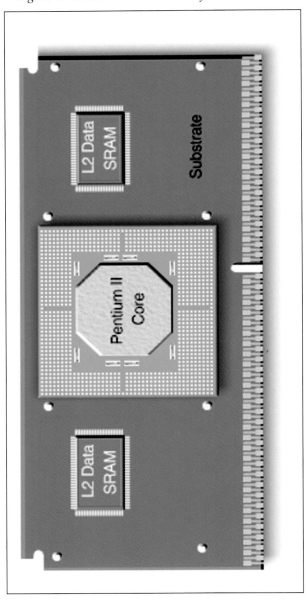

Figure 18-4: Non-Processor Side of SEC Substrate

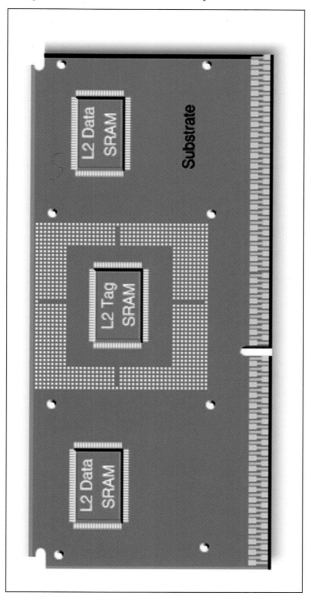

Pentium Pro and Pentium II System Architecture

Cartridge Block Diagram

Figure 18-5 on page 387 illustrates the basic relationship of the device's located on the substrate. As with the Pentium Pro processor, the processor core is linked to the outside world via two buses:

- the backside bus provides a dedicated path between the core and the L2 cache.
- the cartridge is installed into the Slot 1 motherboard connector, giving it access to the external, or frontside, bus.

Like the Pentium Pro, the Pentium II processor core can simultaneously transfer data on both the backside and frontside buses. However, the physical length of the traces between the Pentium Pro processor core and its L2 cache is extremely short, permitting the backside bus to operate at the full processor core speed. The Pentium II processor's backside bus, on the other hand, is physically much longer, necessitating a slower backside bus speed. In the currently-released versions of the Pentium II processor, the backside bus operates at one-half the processor core speed. As an example, the 266MHz Pentium II has a backside bus speed of 133MHz. Because the slower backside bus speed adversely affects processor core performance when accessing the L2 cache, the L1 cache sizes are double those found in the Pentium Pro processor. The increased L1 cache size permits the processor core to keep more memory-based information close to its heart, decreasing the number of accesses that need to be made to the L2 cache. For additional information regarding the caches, see "Dual-Independent Bus Architecture (DIBA)" on page 387. For additional information regarding bus speeds, see "Frequency of the Processor Core and Buses" on page 390.

Figure 18-5: Simplified Block Diagram of the Pentium II Processor Cartridge

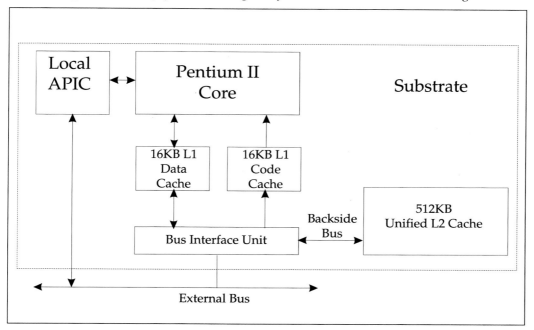

Dual-Independent Bus Architecture (DIBA)

Like the Pentium Pro processor, the Pentium II has a dedicated backside bus used to transfer data between the processor core and the L2 cache and an external, or frontside, bus used to communicate with other system devices. Intel has started referring to this as DIBA.

Caches

L1 Code and Data Caches

In order to compensate for the slower L2 cache bus (i.e., the backside bus), the size of the L1 data and code caches have been doubled in size (when compared to the Pentium Pro processor) from 8KB each to 16KB each. This can be verified by executing the CPUID instruction (see "Request for Cache and TLB Information" on page 414).

L2 Cache

On the currently-released versions of the Pentium II processor (as of 8/2/97), the L2 cache is only available in a 512KB size. It uses a proprietary Intel-designed tag SRAM designated as the 82459AB. This part can only support up to 512KB of L2 cache and would have to be redesigned to support larger caches. Intel does not define the architecture of the L2 cache (i.e., the set-associativity), but that can be easily determine using the CPUID instruction (see "Request for Cache and TLB Information" on page 414).

Currently, the L2 cache bus (i.e., the backside bus) operates at one-half the core frequency. It has been unofficially reported that the Pentium II also supports a full-speed and one-third speed backside bus. For more information on clock speeds, refer to "Frequency of the Processor Core and Buses" on page 390.

Cache Error Protection

In the Pentium Pro processor, the L1 and L2 caches are ECC protected. The versions of the Pentium II processor designed for desktop applications, have ECC protected L1 caches, but the L2 cache is not ECC protected. As of July 97, Intel also offers versions of the Pentium II processor that provide ECC protection on the L2 as well as the L1 caches. This feature is important for servers, but not for the desktop. The addition of ECC to the L2 cache adds a cycle to each L2 cache access, thereby degrading performance (in life, there's no such thing as a free ride). The L2 cache is still 512KB in size.

Processor Signature

The processor signature (i.e., type, family, model, stepping) returned by the Pentium II processor in the EDX register immediately after reset is removed (see"EDX Contains Processor Identification Info" on page 55) and upon execution of the CPUID instruction (see "CPUID Instruction Enhanced" on page 409) is:

- **Type**: 00 (original OEM processor).
- **Family**: 0110b (6d).
- **Model**: 0011b.
- **Stepping**: processor silicon revision-dependent.

CPUID Cache Geometry Information

The cache geometry information returned by a typical desktop-oriented Pentium II processor is listed in Table 18-1 on page 389, and has the following characteristics:

- the data TLB for 4KB pages is 4-way set-associative with 64 entries.
- the code TLB for 4MB and 2MB pages is 4-way set-associative with 4 entries.
- the code TLB for 4KB pages is 4-way set-associative with 32 entries.
- the L1 data cache is 16KB, 4-way set-associative with a 32-byte line size.
- the data TLB for 4MB and 2MB pages is 4-way set-associative with 8 entries.
- the L1 code cache is 16KB, 4-way set-associative with a 32-byte line size.
- the unified, L2 cache is 512KB, 4-way set-associative with a 32-byte line size.

Table 18-1: CPUID Cache Geometry Information Returned by Pentium II

Register	Byte 3	Byte 2	Byte 1	Byte 0
EAX	03h	02h	01h	01h
EBX	0	0	0	0
ECX	0	0	0	0
EDX	0Ch	04h	08h	43h

Fast System Call Instructions

The Pentium II processor is the first to implement the fast system call instructions, SYSENTER and SYSEXIT. To ascertain whether or not a processor supports these instructions, BOTH of the following must be true:

- The SEP (System Enter Present) feature bit returned by the CPUID instruction must be set to one.
- The processor family must be 6, the model must be 3 and the stepping must be 3 or greater (i.e., it must be at least a stepping 3 Pentium II processor or later).

These instructions are not documented in the currently-released (as of 8/7/97) Intel manuals.

Frequency of the Processor Core and Buses

The Pentium II processor is currently-available with core speeds of 233, 266 and 300MHz. The motherboard logic provides the BCLK to the cartridge. On the cartridge, the BCLK is used by the processor core's PLL and is multiplied to develop the core's internal clock as well as the clock for the L2 cache bus (i.e., the backside bus).

As with the Pentium Pro processor (see "Processor Core Speed Selection" on page 41), the Pentium II processor samples LINT[1:0], A20M#, and IGNNE# during RESET#'s assertion period to determine the processor core clock speed to be produced by the PLL from the BCLK. At the trailing-edge (i.e., the deassertion) of RESET#, the value on these four pins is latched and is used throughout the entire power-up session by the PLL to maintain the selected core clock speed. Table 18-2 on page 390 defines the relationship between the BCLK and the processor core's clock.

On the currently-released Pentium II processors, the L2 cache bus runs at one half of the core speed. As an example, a 266MHz Pentium II processor's PLL multiplies the 66MHz BCLK by four to yield the core speed. The core speed, in turn, is divided by two, yielding a backside bus (i.e., L2 cache bus) speed of 133MHz. The Deschutes version of the processor (see "Deschutes Version of the Pentium II Processor" on page 405) will support up to a 100MHz BCLK and processor core speeds of up to 400MHz (or greater).

It has been reported that the Pentium II processor can support a backside bus speed the same as the core's speed, but the author has no confirmation of this from Intel. Obviously, this would require very fast (and therefore very expensive) SRAMs to be used in implementing the L2 cache. It has also been reported that the Pentium II can support a one-third speed backside bus (likewise, the author has no confirmation of this from Intel).

Table 18-2: Ratio of Core Frequency to Bus Clock (BCLK) Frequency

Ratio of Bus Clock to Core Clock	LINT[1]	LINT[0}	A20M#	IGNNE#
1/2	L	L	L	L
1/4	L	L	H	L
2/7	L	H	L	H
2/9	L	H	H	L

Table 18-2: Ratio of Core Frequency to Bus Clock (BCLK) Frequency (Continued)

Ratio of Bus Clock to Core Clock	LINT[1]	LINT[0}	A20M#	IGNNE#
1/2	H	H	H	H

Signal Differences Between Pentium II and Pentium Pro

The external bus signals associated with the Pentium Pro and Pentium II processors differ as described in Table 18-3 on page 391.

Table 18-3: Pentium II/Pentium Pro Signal Differences

Signal(s)	Description
BR[3:0]#	While the Pentium Pro processor implements BR[3:0]#, the Pentium II processor only implements BR[1:0]#. For additional information, refer to "Multiprocessor Capability" on page 393.
BSEL#	The Pentium II processor and the Slot 1 connector define the BSEL# signal. This signal is not present on the Pentium Pro processor. This pin is included for future processors and motherboards and must be connected to ground on Pentium II motherboards. Intel does not document its purpose, but it may be the Bus Select pin, indicating whether the cartridge is installed into a Slot 1 or Slot 2 (used by future processors with bus enhancements) bus on the system board.
EMI	**Electromagnetic Interference.** The Slot 1 connector includes 5 pins that are used for to control EMI. They must be connected to motherboard and/or chassis ground via zero ohm resistors. The resistors must be placed in close proximity to the Slot 1 connector. The path to chassis ground must be short in length and have a low impedance.
SLOTOCC#	**Slot Occupied.** In conjunction with the voltage ID bus, VID[4:0], can be used to identify whether the second Slot 1 connector (in a dual processor system) is occupied by a processor cartridge, occupied by a terminator card, or not occupied. See Table 18-4 on page 392. For additional information, refer to "Test Access Port (TAP)" on page 404.

Table 18-3: Pentium II/Pentium Pro Signal Differences (Continued)

Signal(s)	Description
SLP#	**Sleep**. Power conservation pin. For additional information, refer to "Power-Conservation Modes" on page 395.

Table 18-4: Occupation Truth Table for Second Slot 1

SLOTOCC#	VID[4:0] Value	Description
0	anything other than 11111b	Cartridge with a processor core is in the second Slot 1 connector.
0	11111b	Terminator cartridge is in the second Slot 1 connector (i.e., no core present). For additional information, refer to "Test Access Port (TAP)" on page 404.
1	any value	Second Slot 1 connector is not occupied.

MMX

The Pentium Pro processor does not implement the MMX execution units or the MMX register set and therefore does not support the MMX instruction set. The Pentium II processor, on the other hand, implements MMX support. A description of the Pentium II processor's MMX support can be found in the chapter entitled "MMX: Matrix Math Extensions" on page 507.

With the exception of the MMX multiplier execution unit which is pipelined and has a latency of three processor clock cycles, the other MMX execution units have a latency of one processor clock cycle. The Pentium II's context switching times between floating-point and MMX modes has been improved over that demonstrated by the Pentium P55C MMX processor.

16-bit Code Optimization

The Pentium Pro processor design is optimized for 32-bit code execution. One of the characteristics of 32-bit code is that the data segment registers are almost never loaded with new values. 16-bit code, however, writes new values into the data segment registers (DS, ES, FS, and GS) quite frequently.

Pentium Pro Not Optimized

Unlike the processor's general-purpose registers, the Pentium Pro processor's data segment registers are not aliased. A write to a data segment register immediately changes the value in the real, IA data segment register. Micro-ops that reside downstream from the micro-op that changes the register may perform accesses (loads or stores) within the affected data segment. If the processor were permitted to speculatively execute instructions beyond the one that changes the data segment register before that micro-op had completed execution, they would be using the old, stale contents of the segment register and would address the wrong location.

For this reason, the processor will not execute any instructions beyond the segment register load instruction until the load has completed execution. The processor's performance degrades because it is restrained from out-of-order execution. *Since 16-bit code changes the contents of the data segment registers a lot, the processor suffers poor performance when executing 16-bit code.* Since Windows 95 implements quite a bit of 16-bit code, its performance suffers when executed on a Pentium Pro based system.

Pentium II Shadows the Data Segment Registers

Intel has fixed this problem in the Pentium II processor by aliasing (or shadowing) the data segment registers to micro-op entries in the ROB (as is already done for the general-purpose registers). This is accomplished in the RAT stage of the instruction pipeline. Intel estimates that the Pentium II processor's shadowing of the segment registers can increase performance when executing 16-bit code by as much as 8 to 10%.

Multiprocessor Capability

Pentium Pro Processor Bus Arbitration

The Pentium Pro bus supports up to four processors. Each processor has four processor bus request pins designated as BR[3:0]#. These four pins are connected to the bus request traces (BREQ[3:0]#) on the m6therboard as illustrated in Figure 18-6 on page 394. A complete description of the processor bus arbitration can be found in the section entitled "Symmetric Agent Arbitration—

Pentium Pro and Pentium II System Architecture

Democracy at Work" on page 222.

Figure 18-6: Pentium Pro Processor Bus Arbitration Interconnect

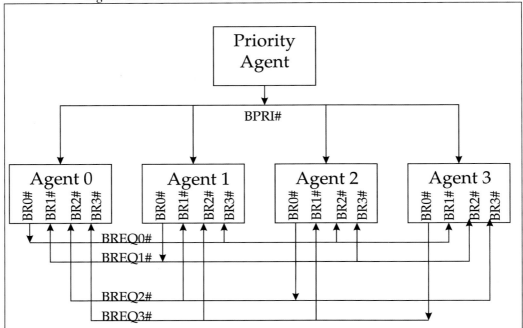

Pentium II Processor Bus Arbitration

The Pentium II processor's bus arbitration scheme is identical to that of the Pentium Pro processor, but it only supports up to two processors. This is because the processor only has two processor bus request pins, BR[1:0]# interconnected as illustrated in Figure 18-7 on page 395.

A future version of the processor (could be Pentium III, IV, or who knows) destined for four processor Pentium II servers and workstations will implement two additional bus request pins, BR[3:2]#.

Figure 18-7: Pentium II Processor Bus Arbitration Interconnect

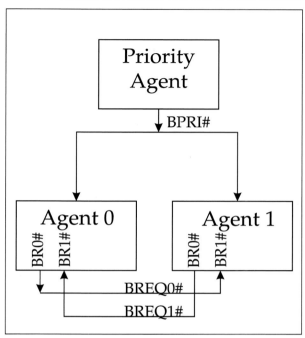

Power-Conservation Modes

Introduction

The Pentium Pro processor only implements the STPCLK# pin and the following power conservation states:

- Normal state.
- AutoHalt Power Down state.
- Stop Grant state.
- Halt/Grant Snoop state.

The Pentium II processor implements two additional states and another pin related to power conservation. The pin is the SLP# (Sleep) input pin. The additional power conservation states are:

- Sleep state.
- Deep Sleep state.

The following sections describe each of the six power conservation states. Refer to Figure 18-8 on page 397 during the discussion of the power conservation states.

Figure 18-8: Power Conservation States Flowchart

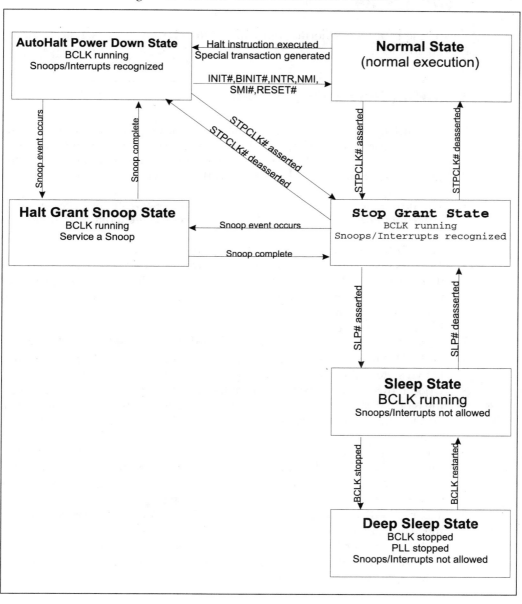

Normal State

This is the processor's normal operating state. No power conservation strategies are in effect.

AutoHalt Power Down State

When a HLT instruction is executed, the processor generates a special transaction to broadcast a Halt message on the external, GTL+ processor bus (see "Special Transaction" on page 358). It then leaves the Normal state and enters the AutoHalt Power Down state. This state has the following characteristics:

- The processor powers down all logic not necessary for the recognition of interrupts and the snooping of memory accesses generated by other bus masters.
- The BCLK signal on the external bus continues to run.
- The processor services any snoop events that occur on the external bus and then returns to the AutoHalt Power Down state. To do this, the processor transitions from the AutoHalt Power Down state to the Halt/Grant Snoop state. After the snoop is complete, the processor returns to the AutoHalt Power Down state.
- Upon the occurrence of an interrupt event (RESET#, SMI#, BINIT#, INIT#, or LINT[1:0] (NMI and INTR)), the processor exits the AutoHalt Power Down state and returns to the Normal state to service the interrupt.
- Upon return from the SMI interrupt handler, the processor will either enter the Normal state (if the instruction returned to is an instruction other than a HLT) or the AutoHalt Power Down state (if the instruction returned to is a HLT instruction).
- If FLUSH# is asserted while in the AutoHalt Power Down state, the flush is serviced (i.e., all modified lines are written back to main memory and the caches are invalidated). Upon completion of the writeback operation, the processor re-enters the AutoHalt Power Down state.
- The motherboard logic can generate a STPCLK# while the processor is in the AutoHalt Power Down state. This causes the processor to leave the AutoHalt Power Down state and enter the Stop Grant state. The processor remains in the Stop Grant state until STPCLK# is removed and then re-enters the AutoHalt Power Down state.

Stop Grant State

Entered from the following states:

- Entered from the Normal state when STPCLK# is asserted.
- Entered from the AutoHalt Power Down state when STPCLK# is asserted while in the AutoHalt Power Down state.

The Stop Grant state has the following characteristics:

- Upon entering the Stop Grant state from the Normal state, the processor generates a special transaction to broadcast a Stop Grant Acknowledge message on the external, GTL+ processor bus (see "Special Transaction" on page 358).
- The processor powers down all logic not necessary for the recognition of interrupts and the snooping of memory accesses generated by other bus masters.
- To ensure minimum power consumption, the motherboard logic should ensure that the GTL+ signals are not driven low during the Stop Grant period. In addition, all other input signals on the bus should be deasserted.
- The BCLK signal on the external bus continues to run.
- The processor services any snoop events that occur on the external bus and then returns to the Stop Grant state. To do this, the processor transitions from the Stop Grant state to the Halt/Grant Snoop state. After the snoop is complete, the processor returns to the Stop Grant state.
- Upon the occurrence of some interrupt events (SMI#, INIT#, or LINT[1:0] (NMI and INTR)), the processor latches the event. It will not be serviced until the processor returns to the Normal state (when STPCLK# is deasserted), however. Note that the processor can only latch one of each of these events while in the Stop Grant state.
- If FLUSH# is asserted while in the Stop Grant state, the flush is serviced (i.e., all modified lines are written back to main memory and the caches are invalidated). Upon completion of the writeback operation, the processor re-enters the Stop Grant state.
- RESET# causes the processor to return to initialized state (see "Processor's State After Reset" on page 52.
- A transition to the Sleep state occurs if the SLP# signal is asserted while in the Stop Grant state.

Halt/Grant Snoop State

The processor snoops all memory transactions generated on the Slot 1 bus during both the AutoHalt Power Down and the Stop Grant states. When the snoop phase of a memory transaction is detected, the processor temporarily transitions to the Halt/Grant Snoop state, snoops the transaction, and then returns to the state that it entered from.

Sleep State

The processor enters the Sleep state only from the Stop Grant state. This occurs when the SLP# (Sleep) pin is asserted while in the Stop Grant state. Upon entering the Sleep state, the processor powers off much of its logic, including that necessary for:

- snooping external memory accesses
- latching interrupt events

The Sleep state has the following characteristics:

- The processor maintains the contents of its registers and caches.
- The processor's PLL (phase-locked loop) continues to run.
- All internal clocks are stopped. This stops CMOS input receivers from switching, thereby diminishing power consumption.
- The SLP# pin is not recognized during the Normal or AutoHalt states.
- Snoop events that occur on the external bus while the processor is in the Sleep state or while the processor is transitioning in or out of the Sleep state will result in unpredictable behavior.
- No transitions or assertions of signals (with the exception of SLP# or RESET#) are allowed on the external, Slot 1 bus while the processor is in the Sleep state. Any transitions on any input signal before the processor has returned to the Stop Grant state will result in unpredictable behavior.
- If RESET# is asserted while in the Sleep state, the processor is initialized and immediately transitions to the Normal state (without passing through the Stop Grant state). The SLP# and STPCLK# signals must be deasserted immediately after RESET# is asserted.
- The SLP# pin has a minimum assertion period of one BCLK.

Deep Sleep State

This is the lowest power conservation state that the processor can be in and still maintain the contents of its registers and caches. The Deep Sleep state has the following characteristics:

- It can only be entered after the processor has entered the Sleep state.
- The processor enters the Deep Sleep state immediately when the motherboard logic stops the BCLK input to the processor's PLL. Intel recommends that the BCLK be stopped in the low state, lowering current consumption to leakage levels.
- To exit the Deep Sleep state and return to the Sleep state, the BCLK must be restarted and continue to run for a period of 1ms.
- Snoop events that occur on the external bus while the processor is in the Deep Sleep state will result in unpredictable behavior.
- No transitions or assertions of signals are allowed on the external, Slot 1 bus while the processor is in the Deep Sleep state. Any transitions on any input signal before the processor has returned to the Stop Grant state will result in unpredictable behavior.

Voltage Identification

While the Pentium Pro processor has four voltage ID pins, the Pentium II (and the slot 1 connector) has five pins, designated VID[4:0]. Table 18-5 on page 402 defines the encoding of the voltage ID bus. The voltage ID bus is used to support automatic selection of the power supply voltages for the processor core. On the substrate, each of these pins is either an open or is shorted to ground (Vss). A "1" in the table refers to an open, while a "0" refers to a short to ground. Table 18-5 on page 402 is a superset of the respective Pentium Pro table, Table 17-6 on page 373. The power supply must either supply the requested processor core voltage (VccCore) or disable itself. In order for the system to support all future variations of the Pentium II processor, it must support the VccCore voltages that are bolded in the table. Note that, in conjunction with the SLOTOCC# (slot occupied) signal, the VID bus can be used to detect the presence or absence of a processor core or a cartridge installed in the other slot 1 connector (if it's a dual processor system). For more information, refer to "Signal Differences Between Pentium II and Pentium Pro" on page 391.

Table 18-5: Voltage ID Definition

Processor Pins					
VID4	VID3	VID2	VID1	VID0	VccCore
0	1	1	1	1	Reserved
0	1	1	1	0	Reserved
0	1	1	0	1	Reserved
0	1	1	0	0	Reserved
0	1	0	1	1	Reserved
0	1	0	1	0	Reserved
0	1	0	0	1	Reserved
0	1	0	0	0	Reserved
0	0	1	1	1	Reserved
0	0	1	1	0	Reserved
0	0	1	0	1	1.80
0	0	1	0	0	1.85
0	0	0	1	1	1.90
0	0	0	1	0	1.95
0	0	0	0	1	2.00
0	0	0	0	0	2.05
1	1	1	1	1	No Core
1	1	1	1	0	2.1
1	1	1	0	1	2.2
1	1	1	0	0	2.3
1	1	0	1	1	2.4

Table 18-5: Voltage ID Definition (Continued)

Processor Pins					
VID4	**VID3**	**VID2**	**VID1**	**VID0**	**VccCore**
1	1	0	1	0	**2.5**
1	1	0	0	1	**2.6**
1	1	0	0	0	**2.7**
1	0	1	1	1	**2.8**
1	0	1	1	0	2.9
1	0	1	0	1	3.0
1	0	1	0	0	3.1
1	0	0	1	1	3.2
1	0	0	1	0	3.3
1	0	0	0	1	3.4
1	0	0	0	0	3.5

Treatment of Unused Bus Pins

Unused Reserved Pins

These pins must be left unconnected.

TESTHI Pins

These pins must be connected to 2.5V via a pullup resistor of between 1 and 10K ohm value.

When APIC Signals Are Unused

When the local APIC is not used, the PICCLK input must be driven with a valid clock input. The PICD[1:0] signals must be pulled up to 2.5V via a 150 ohm pullup resistor.

Unused GTL+ Inputs

These pins must be left unconnected. The processor cartridge provides the Vtt pullup on these signals.

Unused Active Low CMOS Inputs

These inputs must be connected to 2.5V via a pullup resistor within the range of 150 to 330 ohms.

Unused Active High Inputs

These pins must be connected to ground (Vss).

Unused Outputs

These pins should be left unconnected.

Test Access Port (TAP)

Like the Pentium Pro processor, the Pentium II implements a TAP connected to the boundary scan interface. In order for boundary scan to work, the scan chain must be continuous (i.e., no breaks in the chain). The TDO (test data out) pin from one device must be connected to the TDI (test data in) pin of the next device in the chain. To use a test tool on a dual-Pentium II system that only has one of the Slot 1 connectors occupied, it is necessary to install either a processor cartridge or a dummy terminator cartridge (that ties the TDI Slot 1 pin to the TDO Slot 1 pin) into the second Slot 1 connector.

In a dual-Pentium II system, a test tool (e.g., a probe tool such as the HP Run Control tool) can determine the tenant (i.e., the occupant) of the second Slot 1 connector by observing the SLOTOCC# pin and the VID (voltage ID) pins. For more information, refer to "Signal Differences Between Pentium II and Pentium Pro" on page 391.

Deschutes Version of the Pentium II Processor

The following information is based on information garnered from various public domain sources such as industry newsletters, information revealed by Intel in various industry forums, etc. The information may be second hand or based on media speculation. Also keep in mind that until a product is officially released by Intel, Intel reserves the right to make changes to the product without prior notice.

Sometime in the first half of 1998, Intel will release a version of the Pentium II processor code-named Deschutes. This processor may have the following characteristics:

- The processor will be based on Intel's P856, .25 micron, five-layer metal CMOS process. This will shrink the processor die, decrease the processor's power supply voltage (to 1.8V, rather than the current VccCore of 2.8V), and therefore its power consumption (permitting inclusion in laptop designs), and increase its operating frequency.
- Will debut at a core speed of at least 333MHz, eventually reaching a processor core frequency of 400MHz (or greater).
- In some versions, the speed of the GTL+ bus will be raised from 66MHz to 100MHz.
- Support for four processors, rather than two.
- Larger L2 cache on some variants (possibly 1MB or greater in size).
- Will be available in Intel's Mobile Module format for notebooks.
- For very slim notebooks, available in the form of a very small cartridge, enabling notebook designs as thin as 1.25 inches.
- In late 1998, will be available in a Mobile Module format with a separate connector to connect to an AGP graphics adapter.
- Will be available in both Slot 1 and Slot 2 (see "Slot 2" on page 405) configurations.

Slot 2

Although Intel will continue to use the Slot 1 connector for desktops, low-end workstations and one or two processor servers, in mid-1998 it will move to a Slot 2 connector for high-end four processor systems. Slot 2 will be a superset of

Slot 1 and the new SEC cartridge will be physically larger to accomodate the larger L2 caches required in high-end servers. While the Slot 1 connector has 240 pins, the Slot 2 connector will have 330 pins. The additional pins will probably accomodate additional, power, ground and EMI-related pins, as well as the BR[2:3]# pins to support four-processor bus arbitration. The backside bus will run at the same speed as the processor core (rather than half-speed).

Pentium II Chip Sets

As of this writing (8/2/97), Pentium II-based motherboards are typically built around the Intel 440FX chipset (for more information, refer to the chapter entitled "440FX Chipset" on page 559). This chipset does not support AGP and only supports a processor bus speed of up to 66MHz. The 440LX chipset, to be released in the second half of 1997, will add AGP support and system management functions such as InstantOn capability. The top processor bus speed, however, will still be 66MHz. Intel has announced a new chipset to be released in 1998. The 440BX chipset, to be released in the first half of 1998, will support AGP and a 100MHz GTL+ processor bus, a feature that is necessary to take advantage of the Deschutes processor's speed.

Boxed Processor

The purpose of this section is to provide a brief definition of the term *Boxed Processor*. For a detailed description of the boxed processor, refer to the Intel documentation.

The boxed processor is intended for system integrators who build systems from motherboards and standard components. The boxed processor cartridge is shipped with an attached heat sink and fan. It is necessary that the motherboard designer include a heat sink support mechanism on the motherboard to provide support for the heat sink/fan portion of the boxed processor. In addition, sufficient clearance must be provided in both the motherboard and the overall system design.

Part 4:
Processor's Software
Characteristics

The Previous Part

Part 3 of the book provided a description of the Pentium II processor and how it differs from the Pentium Pro processor.

This Part

Part 4 of the book provides a detailed description of the enhancements to the software enviroment that have been introduced in the Pentium Pro processor. This part is divided into the following chapters:

- "Instruction Set Enhancements" on page 409.
- "Register Set Enhancements" on page 423.
- "Paging Enhancements" on page 439.
- "Interrupt Enhancements" on page 463.
- "Machine Check Architecture" on page 477.
- "Performance Monitoring and Timestamp" on page 499.
- "MMX: Matrix Math Extensions" on page 507.

The Next Part

Part 5 of the book provides an overview of the Intel 450KX, 450GX, and 440FX chipsets.

19 *Instruction Set Enhancements*

This Chapter

This chapter describes new instructions as well as enhancement of previously-implemented instructions.

The Next Chapter

The next chapter describes new registers, the bits within them, and the new features that they are associated with.

Introduction

The purpose of this chapter is to introduce the new instructions that have been added to the Pentium Pro processor. For a complete description of each of these instructions, refer to the Intel *Pentium Pro Programmer's Reference Guide*.

CPUID Instruction Enhanced

Before Executing CPUID, Determine if Supported

Before executing the CPUID instruction, the programmer must first ascertain if the processor implements it. This is accomplished by attempting to write a one into the EFLAGS[ID] bit (see Figure 19-1 on page 410). If the bit can be changed to a one, then the processor supports it.

It would seem that the attempted execution of the CPUID instruction on a processor that does not support it would result in an invalid opcode exception. However, Intel specifically says (in AP Note AP-485) "Do not depend on the absence of an invalid opcode trap on the CPUID opcode to detect the CPUID instruction." This implies that at least one of the earlier processors that doesn't support the CPUID instruction does not generate an invalid opcode exception when an attempt is made to execute the CPUID instruction.

Figure 19-1: EFLAGS Register

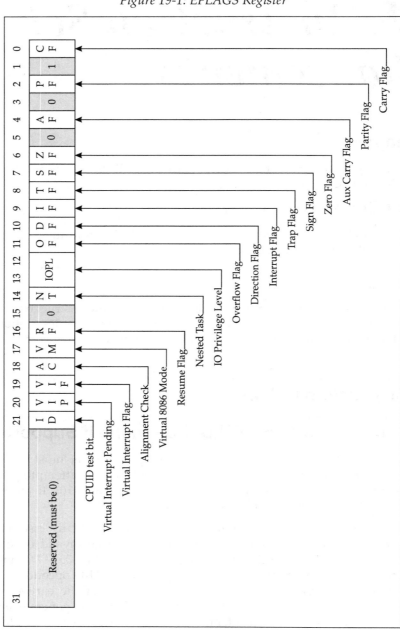

Chapter 19: Instruction Set Enhancements

Basic Description

When executed, the CPUID instruction returns information about the processor in the processor's registers. The CPUID instruction was first implemented in the first version of the Pentium processor. All subsequently-introduced versions of the Pentium and the 486 processors implemented CPUID. However, prior to the Pentium Pro processor, the amount of information returned by the CPUID instruction was minimal. It consisted of the vendor ID string and the processor family, model and stepping (i.e., the revision level of the processor silicon).

When executed by the Pentium Pro processor, the CPUID instruction can return a wealth of information about the processor. This includes:

- processor family, model and stepping (i.e., revision).
- features supported by the processor.
- the size and structure of all of the processor's internal caches. This includes the L1 and L2 caches, as well as the data and code TLBs (Translation Lookaside Buffers).

Before executing the CPUID instruction, the programmer first loads a request type indicator into the EAX register. When the CPUID instruction is executed, the processor examines the value in EAX to determine what information is being requested. The requested information is then supplied in the processor's registers. Different processor implementations may support different request types. The request type values defined for the current implementation of the processor are:

- EAX = 0 indicates a request for the **vendor ID string and** the **maximum EAX input value** (i.e., request type) supported by the processor.
- EAX = 1 indicates a request for the **processor version information and** the **features supported** by the processor.
- EAX = 2 indicates a request for information about the processor's **caches and TLBs.**

Vendor ID and Max Input Value Request

Before issuing other request types to the processor, the EAX input value of 0 should be used first to ascertain the request types supported by this processor implementation. As indicated earlier, in response to the type 0 request, the processor provides the maximum EAX value (i.e., request type) supported by the processor. Armed with this information, requests for additional information may be issued.

Request for Vendor ID String and Max EAX Value

Request type 0 returns the processor's vendor ID string and the max-allowable EAX request type value. The vendor ID string is returned as packed ASCII data in the EBX, ECX and EDX registers. The maximum-allowable EAX input value (currently = 2) is returned in EAX.

Request for Version and Supported Features

Refer to Figure 19-2 on page 413. Request type 1 returns the processor version (in EAX) and the features it supports (in EDX). The processor types currently defined are listed in Table 19-1 on page 414. The Pentium Pro belongs to the sixth generation, or family, of x86 processors. Table 19-2 on page 414 lists the currently-defined type, family, and model numbers. The information in this table was extracted directly from Intel AP Note AP-485.

The contents of the EDX register indicate the features supported by the processor. The current versions of the Pentium Pro processor return all ones in the currently-defined bits. Refer to the indicated sections for an explanation of each of these features:

- **MMX-capable.** Returns 0 in Pentium Pro and 1 in Pentium II. For more information on MMX, refer to "MMX: Matrix Math Extensions" on page 507.
- **CMOV.** Refer to "Conditional Move (CMOV) Eliminates Branches" on page 417.
- **Machine check architecture**. "Machine Check Architecture" on page 477.
- **Global page feature**. "Paging Enhancements" on page 439.
- **MTRRs**. "Rules of Conduct" on page 133.
- **APIC**. A detailed description the APIC can be found in the MindShare book entitled *Pentium Processor System Architecture* (published by Addison-Wesley).
- **SEP (System Enter Present—SEP). Fast System Call**
- **CXS**. A description of the Compare and Exchange 8 Bytes instruction can be found in the MindShare book entitled *Pentium Processor System Architecture* (published by Addison-Wesley).
- **Machine check exception**. "Machine Check Architecture" on page 477.
- **Physical address extension (PAE)**. "Paging Enhancements" on page 439.
- **RDMSR and WRMSR**. "Accessing MSRs" on page 421.
- **Time stamp counter (TSC)**. "Time Stamp Counter Facility" on page 500.

- **Page size extensions (PSE)**. "Paging Enhancements" on page 439.
- **Debug extensions**. A detailed description the debug extensions can be found in the MindShare book entitled *Pentium Processor System Architecture* (published by Addison-Wesley).
- **VM86 mode extensions**. "Interrupt Enhancements" on page 463.
- **FPU present**. The meaning of this bit speaks for itself.

Figure 19-2: Processor Version and Features Supported Information

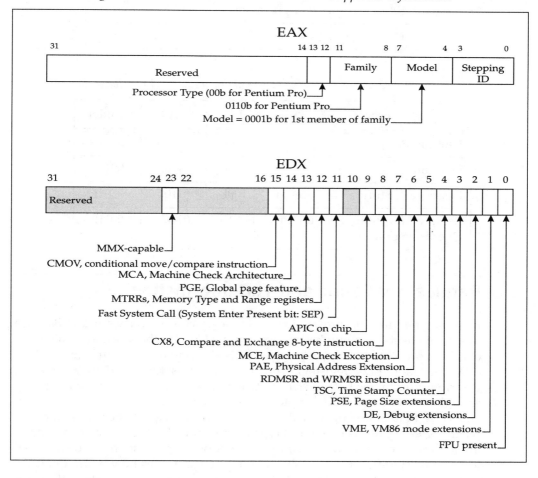

Table 19-1: Processor Type Field

Processor Type	Description
00b	Original OEM processor.
01b	Overdrive processor.
10b	Dual-processor.
11b	Reserved.

Table 19-2: Currently-Defined Type, Family, and Model Numbers

Processor	Type	Family	Model
Pentium Pro	00b	0110b	0001b
Pentium II	00b	0110b	0011b
Reserved for future P6 processor	00b	0110b	0101b
Reserved for future Pentium Pro Overdrive processor	01b	0110b	0011b

Request for Cache and TLB Information

Request type 2 returns information about the processor's caches and TLBs. Each processor has its own number of caches and TLBs and the size and architecture of each is processor design-dependent. This information is returned in the EAX, EBX, ECX and EDX registers. The information is formatted as a series of descriptors, each one byte in size. Note that these four registers may not be big enough to hold all of the descriptors necessary to describe a processor's caches and TLBs. In this case, the CPUID instruction would have to be executed multiple times, each time using request type 2, to obtain all of the descriptors pertaining to the processor. Upon executing the first type 2 request, the value returned in the least-significant byte of the EAX register indicates how many times the CPUID instruction must be executed with request type 2 to obtain all of the descriptors. Table 19-3 on page 415 indicates the descriptor types currently defined. Table 19-4 on page 416 defines the values returned for one implementation of the Pentium Pro processor.

Table 19-3: Currently-Defined Cache/TLB Descriptors

Hex Value	Description
00h	Null descriptor.
01h	The TLB for page table entries related to 4KB code pages is 4-way set-associative with 64 entries.
02h	The TLB for page table entries related to 2MB and 4MB code pages is 4-way set-associative with 4 entries.
03h	The TLB for page table entries related to 4KB data pages is 4-way set-associative with 64 entries.
04h	The TLB for page table entries related to 2MB and 4MB data pages is 4-way set-associative with 8 entries.
06h	The L1 code cache is 8KB in size, organized as a 4-way set-associative with 32 bytes per line.
0Ah	The L1 data cache is 8KB in size, organized as a 2-way set-associative with 32 bytes per line.
41h	The unified L2 cache is 128KB in size, organized as a 4-way set-associative cache with 32 bytes per line.
42h	The unified L2 cache is 256KB in size, organized as a 4-way set-associative cache with 32 bytes per line.
43h	The unified L2 cache is 512KB in size, organized as a 4-way set-associative cache with 32 bytes per line.
44h	Intel's currently-available documentation doesn't list the descriptor for the 1MB L2 cache, but is more than likely 44h.

Table 19-4: Descriptors Returned by One of the Current Processor Implementations

Register	Byte	Value	Description
EAX	0	01h	One execution of CPUID with request type 2 returns all descriptors.
	1	01h	The TLB for page table entries related to 4KB code pages is 4-way set-associative with 32 entries.
	2	02h	The TLB for page table entries related to 2MB and 4MB code pages is 4-way·set-associative with 4 entries.
	3	03h	The TLB for page table entries related to 4KB data pages is 4-way set-associative with 64 entries.
EBX	0-3	00h	Null descriptors.
ECX	0-3	00h	Null descriptors.
EDX	0	42h	The unified L2 cache is 256KB in size, organized as a 4-way set-associative cache with 32 bytes per line.
	1	0Ah	The L1 data cache is 8KB in size, organized as a 2-way set-associative with 32 bytes per line.
	2	04h	The TLB for page table entries related to 2Mb and 4MB data pages is 4-way set-associative with 8 entries.
	3	06h	The L1 code cache is 8KB in size, organized as a 4-way set-associative with 32 bytes per line.

CPUID is a Serializing Instruction

As described in the chapter entitled "The Fetch, Decode, Execute Engine" on page 75, the processor executes instructions in the ROB out-of-order. This means that an instruction found later in a program's flow may be executed before instructions found earlier in that program's flow. Sometimes it is important that all instructions up to a certain point in program execution have completed execution before executing any instructions beyond that point. The following is an example where this would be true.

Assume that the programmer wishes to time how long a particular portion of a program takes to execute. Before executing the code to be timed, the programmer takes a snapshot of the current time by reading the current contents of the Time Stamp Counter, or TSC. The portion of code in question is then executed, after which the TSC is read again. In a processor that doesn't execute instructions out-of-order, you are guaranteed that the second read of the TSC will not be executed until all of the instructions in the code sequence have completed execution. However, if the same program is executed by a processor that performs out-of-order execution (such as the Pentium Pro), the second TSC read may be performed before all of the instructions that precede it in the program have actually been executed. The elapsed time reading is therefore invalid. In addition, instructions that follow the second TSC read may already have been executed.

This problem can be fixed by preceding the second read of the TSC with a serializing instruction (such as CPUID). When the processor detects a serializing instruction in the ROB, it will not execute any of the instructions that follows the serializing instruction until all of the instructions that precede it have completed execution and all changes to flags registers and memory (the processor's posted write buffers are flushed) have been accomplished. This insures that all work has been completed up to the serializing instruction before it completes its execution.

Only when these conditions have been met are any of the instructions that follow the serializing instruction executed. The CPUID instruction can be executed at any privilege level and in both real and protected mode.

Serializing Instructions Impact Performance

Because serializing instructions prevent the processor from performing speculative execution from micro-ops that reside downstream within the ROB, they have a negative effect on performance. Liberal use of serializing instructions can noticeably impact performance, so they should only be used when absolutely necessary.

Conditional Move (CMOV) Eliminates Branches

As was stressed in "The Fetch, Decode, Execute Engine" on page 75, the processor has a deep instruction pipeline and also executes instructions out-of-order. For these reasons, mispredicted branch instructions can cause a fairly substantial decrease in performance. When a branch is executed and it is determined that its branch path was predicted incorrectly, all of the instructions currently in the prefetch streaming buffer and the earlier instruction pipeline stages must be flushed. In addition, any instructions that had been speculatively executed that occur after the branch in the program must also be deleted from the ROB.

The ideal program would have no branches, or only unconditional branches. Since this isn't realistic, however, a better plan would be to limit, as much as possible, the number of conditional branches found in a program. The conditional move instruction (CMOV) permits the elimination of a conditional branch by testing a condition and only performing the indicated move if the condition tests true.

Conditional FP Move (FCMOV) Eliminates Branches

The floating-point conditional move (FCMOV) is the floating-point equivalent of the CMOV instruction. It conditionally moves values between floating-point stack registers and permits the elimination of a conditional branch. Prior to executing the FCMOV instruction, the programmer would execute an FCOMI, FCOMIP, FUCOMI, or FCOMIP instruction (see next section) to set the appropriate condition bits in the integer EFLAGS register to be tested by the FCMOV instruction.

FCOMI, FCOMIP, FUCOMI, and FUCOMIP

The following instructions have been added to the floating-point instructions set and are intended for use with the FCMOV instruction:

- **FCOMI**. FP compare real and set integer flags (in the EFLAGS register, rather than the FPU flags) instruction.
- **FCOMIP**. FP compare real and set integer flags instruction. Also pops the FP register stack.
- **FUCOMI**. FP unordered compare real and set integer flags instruction
- **FUCOMIP**. FP unordered compare real and set integer flags instruction. Also pops the FP register stack.

Read Performance Monitoring Counter (RDPMC)

Technically, the RDPMC instruction was introduced in the Pentium processor. However, its definition and usage weren't documented in the public-domain documentation. Rather, it was described in the infamous appendix H. Intel has chosen to reveal most of the appendix H information in the Pentium Pro documentation, so it is being described here.

What's RDPMC Used For?

The Pentium and Pentium Pro processors incorporate performance monitoring logic that can be set up to record the duration of or number of occurrences of a particular event. Both processors implement two counters, each of which can be set up to monitor for different types of events. A detailed description of the performance monitoring facility can be found in "Performance Monitoring and Timestamp" on page 499.

This instruction is used to obtain (i.e., read) the current contents of one of the performance monitoring counters.

Who Can Execute RDPMC?

The CR4[PCE] bit governs the privilege level that the RDPMC instruction can be successfully executed at. When CR4[PCE] = 1 (see Figure 19-3 on page 419), programs executing at any privilege level can execute this instruction successfully. When CR4[PCE] = 0, only kernel OS code executing at privilege level 0 can successfully execute this instruction.

Figure 19-3: CR4

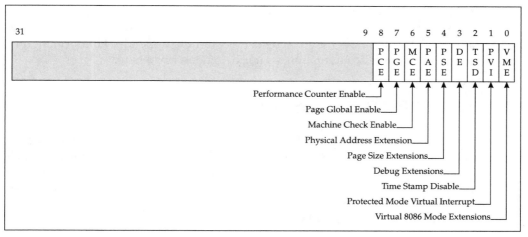

RDPMC Not Serializing Instruction

The RDPMC instruction is not a serializing instruction, so it may not obtain an accurate event count or duration (see "CPUID is a Serializing Instruction" on page 416 for more information on the need for serializing instructions). To ensure that all instructions prior to the RDPMC have completed execution and their results have been committed to registers and memory, precede the RDPMC with a serializing instruction (such as CPUID).

RDPMC Description

Prior to executing the RDPMC instruction, the programmer first specifies which of the performance monitoring counters is to be read (the current versions of the Pentium and Pentium Pro processors only implement counters 0 and 1; future processors could implement more). The ECX register is loaded with the target counter number (e.g., 0 or 1). Upon execution, the contents of the target counter are placed in the EDX:EAX register pair, with the upper 8 bits being placed in the lower 8 bits of EDX (the current implementations of the counters are 40 bits each) and upper 24 bits of EDX are zeroed.

Read Time Stamp Counter (RDTSC)

Like the RDPMC instruction, the RDPMC instruction was introduced in the Pentium processor. However, its definition and usage weren't documented in the public-domain documentation. Rather, it was described in the infamous appendix H. Intel has chosen to reveal most of the appendix H information in the Pentium Pro documentation, so it is being described here.

What's RDTSC Used For

The Pentium and Pentium Pro processors incorporate a 64-bit time stamp counter (TSC) that is cleared to 0 at reset and then is incremented once for each processor clock cycle. A detailed description of the time stamp facility can be found in "Time Stamp Counter Facility" on page 500 and in "Performance Monitoring and Timestamp" on page 499. This instruction is used to obtain (i.e., read) the current contents of the TSC.

Chapter 19: Instruction Set Enhancements

Who Can Execute RDTSC?

The CR4[TSD] bit (see Figure 19-3 on page 419) governs the privilege level that the RDTSC instruction can be successfully executed at. When CR4[TSD] = 0, programs executing at any privilege level can execute this instruction successfully. When CR4[TSD] = 1, only kernel OS code executing at privilege level 0 can successfully execute this instruction.

RDTSC Doesn't Serialize

The RDTSC instruction is not a serializing instruction, so it may not obtain an accurate count of the number of processor clock cycles that have elapsed while the previous instructions have executed (see "CPUID is a Serializing Instruction" on page 416 for more information on the need for serializing instructions). To ensure that all instructions prior to the RDTSC have completed execution and their results have been committed to registers and memory, precede the RDTSC with a serializing instruction (such as CPUID).

RDTSC Description

Upon execution, the **contents** of the 64-bit TSC is **placed in** the **EDX:EAX** register pair, with the upper 32 bits placed in EDX. The TSC may also be read using the RDMSR instruction (see "Accessing MSRs" on page 421).

My Favorite—UD2

UD2 is my favorite instruction: it is *by definition an architecturally defined undefined instruction* that, when executed, is guaranteed to generate an undefined opcode exception in any of the processor's operating modes. It was included in the instruction set for testing purposes, permitting the deliberate generation of an undefined opcode exception on any processor.

Accessing MSRs

The Pentium processor was the first x86 processor to include model-specific registers, or MSRs. The RDMSR and WRMSR instructions permit the MSRs to be read and written. Although these two instructions were not introduced in the Pentium Pro processor, there are many more MSRs implemented than in the Pentium and, consequently, these two instructions now accept many more input parameters than in the Pentium.

Testing for Processor MSR Support

Before executing either of these instructions, use the CPUID instruction with request type one to get the processor version and features information. The features supported information is returned in the EDX register and EDX[5] will be set to one if the instructions are supported (see Figure 19-2 on page 413).

Causes GP Exception If...

These instructions can only be executed in real mode or when executing at privilege level 0 in protected mode. If these conditions are violated, the processor generates a GP exception.

Input Parameters

Before executing either instruction, the programmer first loads the MSR address into the ECX register (the MSR addresses are listed in appendix C of the Intel *Operating System Writer's Guide*). When executing the WRMSR instruction, the 64-bit data value to be written to the selected MSR must be loaded into the EDX:EAX register pair. When executing the RDMSR instruction, the contents of the selected MSR is returned in the EDX:EAX register pair.

20 *Register Set Enhancements*

The Previous Chapter

The previous chapter provided a description of new instructions as well as enhancement of previously-implemented instructions.

This Chapter

This chapter describes new registers, the bits within them, and the new features that they are associated with. It also describes new bits added to pre-existent registers and the features that they are associated with.

The Next Chapter

The next chapter describes what Intel refers to as the BIOS update feature. A better name, however, might be the Microcode update feature.

New Registers

Introduction

The following new registers were introduced in the Pentium Pro processor:

- **New local APIC LVT entry**. A description of this enhancement can be found in "Interrupt Enhancements" on page 463 and in "Performance Monitoring and Timestamp" on page 499. Please note that the performance monitoring features were added in the Pentium processor, but were only documented with the release of the Pentium Pro processor.
- **DebugCTL, LastBranch and LastException MSRs**. A description of this enhancement can be found in "DebugCTL, LastBranch and LastException MSRs" on page 424.

- **Time Stamp Counter (TSC) MSR**. A description of this enhancement can be found in "Time Stamp Counter Facility" on page 500. Please note that the Time Stamp Counter feature was added in the Pentium processor, but was only documented with the release of the Pentium Pro processor.
- **MTRRs**. A description of this enhancement can be found in "Rules of Conduct" on page 133 and in "The MTRR Registers" on page 567.
- **Performance Monitoring Registers**. A description of this enhancement can be found in "Performance Monitoring and Timestamp" on page 499. Please note that the performance monitoring features were added in the Pentium processor, but were only documented with the release of the Pentium Pro processor.
- **Machine Check Architecture MSRs**. A description of this enhancement can be found in "Machine Check Architecture" on page 477.

DebugCTL, LastBranch and LastException MSRs

Introduction

The DebugCTL MSR (see Figure 20-1 on page 425) controls the following processor features related to program debugging:

- Enable/disable recording of source and target addresses related to the last branch, interrupt or exception (see "Last Branch, Interrupt or Exception Recording" on page 425).
- Enable/disable single-step exception on branches, interrupts or exceptions (see "Single-Step Exception on Branch, Exception or Interrupt" on page 426).
- Configure the processor's PMB (Performance Monitoring or Breakpoint) output pins as either breakpoint or performance monitoring event outputs (see "Performance Monitoring and Timestamp" on page 499).
- Enable/disable the processor's ability to generate the branch trace message transaction when a branch is taken (see "Branch Trace Message Transaction Used for Program Debug" on page 360).

Please note that, at the time of this writing, the Intel documentation has discrepancies related to the bit assignment of the DebugCTL MSR. Figure 10-2 on page 10-11 of the Operating System Writer's Manual and the layout of the DebugCTL register as defined in appendix C of the same book do not agree with each other.

Chapter 20: Register Set Enhancements

Figure 20-1: DebugCTL MSR

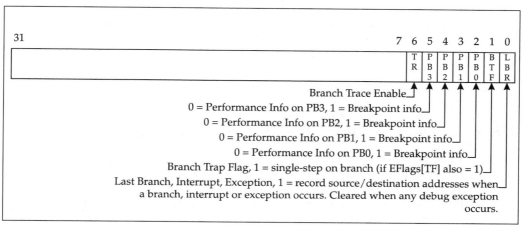

Last Branch, Interrupt or Exception Recording

When set to one, the LBR (Last Branch Recording; see Figure 20-1 on page 425) bit in the DebugCTL MSR causes the processor to record the source and target addresses of the last branch and the last exception or interrupt taken by the processor prior to a debug exception being generated. These addresses are recorded in four MSRs provided solely for this purpose:

- **LastBranchToIP** MSR. Records the last address branched to by a branch, exception, or interrupt.
- **LastBranchFromIP** MSR. Records the last address branched from by a branch, exception, or interrupt.
- **LastExceptionToIP** and **LastExceptionFromIP** MSRs. When an exception or interrupt occurs, the processor first copies the LastBranchToIP and LastBranchFromIP registers into these registers before recording the to and from addresses for the exception or interrupt in the LastBranchToIP and LastBranchFromIP registers. They can be thought of as the save registers for the last branch information.

When the processor generates a debug exception, the DebugCTL[LBR] bit is cleared before execution of the debug exception handler, but the contents of the last branch and last exception MSRs is untouched.

Single-Step Exception on Branch, Exception or Interrupt

See Figure 20-1 on page 425. When the DebugCTL[BTF] (Branch Trap Flag) and the EFLAGS[TF] bits are both set to one, the processor generates a single-step debug exception the next time it takes a branch, exception, or interrupt.

Before entering the debug single-step handler, both the DebugCTL[BTF] and EFLAGS[TF] are cleared, disabling the single-step exception.

MSR not Defined in Earlier Pentium Pro Documentation

An MSR has been added (as of the sB1 processor stepping) at MSR address 33h. The Intel documentation does not indicate the register's name nor its width. The author is assuming that it is a 32-bit MSR (because the two bits that are defined as used are bits 31:30. Figure 20-2 on page 427 illustrates the bits currently-defined by public domain documentation.

Disable Instruction Streaming Buffer

This bit was added as a workaround for problems associated with code that is different in the L1 code cache and in the instruction streaming buffers. The default state is 0, thereby enabling the instruction streaming buffers. For additional information, refer to errata 58 and 59 in the Intel document entitled *Pentium Pro Processor Specification Update*, order number 242689-019. As of this writing (8/2/97), this document is available at the Intel Developers' web site.

Disable Cache Line Boundary Lock

In the default state (0 = enable cache line boundary lock), RMW (read-modify-write) operations within a cache line and those that cross a cache line boundary will result in the assertion of the LOCK# signal for the duration of the data read and the data write, inclusive. When this feature bit is set to one, any RMW operation that crosses a cache line boundary will not result in the assertion of the LOCK# signal for the duration of the data read and the data write, inclusive. In other words, there is no gaurantee of atomicity (i.e., exclusive ownership) between the memory read and the memory write operations. For more information about RMW operation and locking, refer to "Locking—Shared Resource Acquisition" on page 241.

Figure 20-2: New MSR at MSR Address 33h

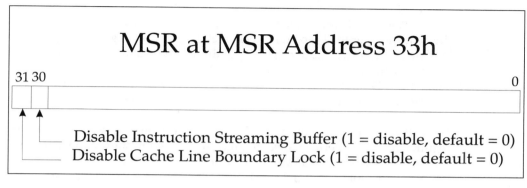

New Bits in Pre-Existent Registers

CR4 Enhancements

Refer to Figure 20-3 on page 428. The following feature control bits have been added to CR4:

- **VME. Virtual 8086 Mode Extensions**. For a detailed description of this feature, refer to "VM86 Mode Extensions" on page 465. Please note that this feature was added in the Pentium processor, but was only documented with the release of the Pentium Pro processor.
- **PVI. Protected Mode Virtual Interrupts**. For a detailed description of this feature, refer to "Interrupt Enhancements" on page 463. Please note that this feature was added in the Pentium processor, but was only documented with the release of the Pentium Pro processor.
- **TSD. Time Stamp Disable**. For a detailed description of this feature, refer to "Time Stamp Counter Facility" on page 500. Please note that this feature was added in the Pentium processor, but was only documented with the release of the Pentium Pro processor.
- **DE. Debug Extensions**. Please note that this feature was added in the Pentium processor. For a detailed description, refer to the MindShare book entitled *Pentium Processor System Architecture* (published by Addison-Wesley).
- **PSE. Page Size Extension**. For a detailed description of this feature, refer to "Paging Enhancements" on page 439. Please note that this feature was added in the Pentium processor, but was only documented with the release of the Pentium Pro processor.

- **PAE. Physical Address Extension.** For a detailed description of this feature, refer to "Paging Enhancements" on page 439. *This feature is new in the Pentium Pro processor.*
- **MCE. Machine Check Exception Enable.** For a detailed description of this feature, refer to "Machine Check Architecture" on page 477. Please note that this feature was added in the Pentium processor, but was only documented with the release of the Pentium Pro processor.
- **PGE. Page Global Enable.** For a detailed description of this feature, refer to "Paging Enhancements" on page 439. *This feature is new in the Pentium Pro processor.*
- **PCE. Performance Counter Enable.** For a detailed description of this feature, refer to "Performance Monitoring and Timestamp" on page 499. Please note that this feature was added in the Pentium processor, but was only documented with the release of the Pentium Pro processor.

Figure 20-3: CR4 Feature Bits

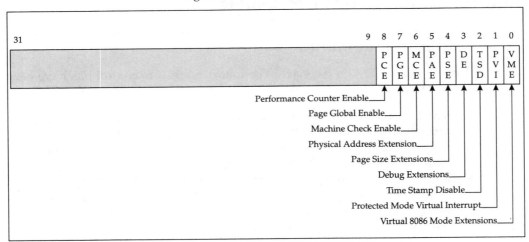

CR3 Enhancements

When the CR4 Physical Address Extension (PAE) bit is set to one, CR3 is no longer the Page Directory Base Address register. Rather, it is the Page Directory Pointer Table (PDPT) Base Address register. For a detailed description of the PAE feature, refer to "Paging Enhancements" on page 439.

Local APIC Base Address Relocation

Unlike the Pentium processor's local APIC, the base memory address of the Pentium Pro processor's local APIC register set is relocatable. The base address can be set within the first MB of memory space and the APIC can then be programmed in real mode. Code that is meant to be portable among both Pentium and Pentium Pro processors, however, should program the local APIC in extended memory (above the first MB) with the processor in protected mode.

21 *BIOS Update Feature*

The Previous Chapter

The previous chapter described new registers, the bits within them, and the new features that they are associated with. It also described new bits added to pre-existent registers and the features that they are associated with.

This Chapter

This chapter describes what Intel refers to as the BIOS Update Feature. A better name, however, might be the Microcode Update Feature.

The Next Chapter

The next chapter describes the following paging-related processor features:

- The **Page Size Extension (PSE) feature** introduced in the Pentium processor. Please note that this feature was added in the Pentium processor, but was only documented with the release of the Pentium Pro processor.
- **Physical Address Extension (PAE) feature** introduced in the Pentium Pro processor. This feature permits programs to access code or data within a 64GB rather than a 4GB range. In future processors, the PAE could permit access to up to 2^{64} memory space.
- The **Global Page (PGE) feature** introduced in the Pentium Pro processor.

The Problem

Today's processors are extremely complex—they may be the most complex machines ever designed by man. When dealing with such a level of complexity, it's impossible to avoid errors. In other words, every complex processor is shipped with bugs—some known, some not.

When the first version of a processor is shipped, that is referred to as the first stepping, or revision, of the silicon. As time goes on and bugs are uncovered, the manufacturer redesigns the silicon to eliminate the problems recognized at the time. This comprises the next stepping of the silicon. During the life of a processor, it typically passes through a number of steppings as improvements/fixes are included in the design.

If I purchase a machine with an earlier stepping of the processor and later decide that I want a later stepping (to eliminate problems or, possibly, to improve performance), I would have to purchase a new processor—an expensive proposition.

The Solution

At the heart of the Pentium Pro processor, microcode instructions are executed to accomplish many of the processor's internal operations. The processor's microcode is contained in ROM memory that resides within the processor core. In earlier processors, this ROM was truly read-only—the microcode burned into the ROM at the time of manufacture could not be changed.

Using a special procedure, revised microcode can be automatically loaded into the Pentium Pro processor each time that the system is powered up. The new microcode changes the manner in which the processor accomplishes internal operations and can eliminate bugs (what Intel refers to as *errata*). When a new revision of microcode is loaded into the processor after the machine is powered up, this effectively raises the silicon level, or stepping, to match a new stepping of the silicon that is currently being shipped from Intel's manufacturing plants. This is a very powerful and extremely cost-effective solution for Intel and motherboard manufacturers, as well as the end-user.

The BIOS Update Image

Introduction

When a microcode update must be applied to processors in the field, Intel supplies motherboard manufacturers with a binary image referred to as a BIOS Update. Refer to Figure 21-1 on page 433. A BIOS Update image is exactly 2048d bytes in length with the following composition:

- the first 48d bytes comprises the **Update Header** data structure. The header contains information that identifies the target processor to which the update should be applied, as well as other information (refer to "BIOS Update Header Data Structure" on page 434).
- the 2000d byte **microcode binary image** immediately follows the header data structure.

Figure 21-1: Structure of the BIOS Update Image

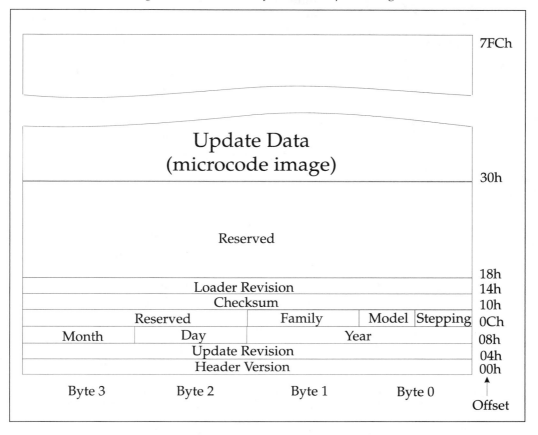

BIOS Update Header Data Structure

Refer to Figure 21-1 on page 433 and Table 21-1 on page 434.

Table 21-1: Format of the BIOS Update Header Data Structure

Field Name	Offset	Length (in bytes)	Description
Header Version	0d	4d	Version number of the update header data structure (i.e., this table). The current version number is 00000001h wherein the header data structure has the format shown in this table. Additional header data structure formats may be defined in the future. As an example, some new fields may be defined within an area currently defined as Reserved.
Update Revision	4d	4d	This represents the revision of the microcode update contained within the 2000d byte image that immediately follows this header. After the update has been loaded into the processor, this field can be compared to the signature returned by the CPUID instruction to verify a good load. For more information, refer to "The BIOS Update Loader" on page 435 and to "Determining if New Update Supercedes Previously-Loaded Update" on page 437.
Date	8d	4d	Date of creation of this update, in hex format. As an example, a creation date of 07/30/95 is represented as 07301995h.

Chapter 21: BIOS Update Feature

Table 21-1: Format of the BIOS Update Header Data Structure (Continued)

Field Name	Offset	Length (in bytes)	Description
Processor	12d	4d	Family, model and stepping of the processor that requires this update. The format of this field is identical to that returned by the CPUID instruction (see Figure 19-2 on page 413).
Checksum	16d	4d	Checksum of the entire 2048d bytes consisting of the header and the microcode update image. Checksum is correct if the sum of the 512 dwords of the image is zero.
Loader Revision	20d	4d	Version number of the loader program required to load this update. The initial version is 00000001h.
Reserved	24d	24d	Reserved for future field definition.

The BIOS Update Loader

The code fragment below is loader revision number 00000001h (see "Loader Revision" on page 435).

```
mov    ecx,79h          ;set ecx = address of BIOS Update MSR
xor    eax,eax          ;clear eax
xor    ebx,ebx          ;clear ebx
mov    ax,cs            ;set ax = start of BIOS code segment
shl    eax,4            ;add lower digit 0h to segment base
mov    bx,offset Update ;set bx = offset of Update from segment start
add    eax,ebx          ;eax = start of update in BIOS segment
add    eax,48d          ;eax = start of microcode image in segment
xor    edx,edx          ;clear edx
wrmsr                   ;issue microcode update trigger to processor
```

The loader above assumes the following:

- Update image is contained in the BIOS code segment.
- The processor is in real mode.

Actually, the update image may reside anywhere in memory that is accessible by the processor in its current operating mode (real or protected). The loader also has the following requirements:

- When the update is loaded with the processor in real mode, the update image may not cross a segment (i.e., 64KB) address boundary.
- When the update is loaded with the processor in real mode, the length of the update image may not exceed the segment limit (i.e., 64KB).
- When paging is enabled, the pages that contain the update image must be present in memory (in other words, no page faults permitted during the load process).
- The update image is not required to adhere to any byte or word boundary.

CPUID Instruction Enhanced

As already described in "Request for Version and Supported Features" on page 412, the CPUID instruction can be instructed to return the processor family, model and stepping in the EAX register. In addition to returning this information, if an update has previously been loaded into the processor the CPUID instruction also saves the ID of the update microcode image currently residing in the processor in the 64-bit MSR register residing at MSR address 8Bh. Intel refers to this as the *signature* of the loaded update. If no update has been loaded into the processor, the MSR remains unmodified. The format of the ID in MSR 8Bh is identical to that of the Update Revision field in the header data structure. The following code fragment illustrates the method used to obtain the ID of the currently-loaded update (if any):

```
mov    ecx,08Bh    ;set up address of Update ID MSR
xor    eax,eax     ;clear eax
xor    edx,edx     ;clear edx
wrmsr              ;write all zeros into Update ID MSR
mov    eax,1       ;set up request for processor info
cpuid              ;get info in eax and Update ID MSR
mov    ecx,08Bh    ;set up address of Update ID MSR
rdmsr              ;read Update ID MSR into edx
```

If the value returned in EDX from the Update ID MSR is still all zeros, then no update has been successfully loaded into the processor.

Determining if New Update Supercedes Previously-Loaded Update

Before loading a new update into a processor, follow this procedure:

1. Obtain Update Revision field from the header of the new BIOS update image.
2. Obtain the signature of the update (if any) previously loaded into the processor.
3. If the Update Revision field of the new update is greater than the signature obtained from the processor, then load the new update into the processor (see step 4). Otherwise, do not load the new image into the processor.
4. If the revision of the new update is greater, then load it into the processor, obtain the signature after the load (using the procedure described in "CPUID Instruction Enhanced" on page 436) and verify that it matches the new update's Update Revision field. Assuming that it matches, this authenticates the load as successful.

Effect of RESET# on Previously-Loaded Update

The assertion of a hard reset (RESET#) to the processor deletes any update that had previously been loaded into the processor. The assertion of INIT#, however, has no effect on a previously-loaded update.

When Must Update Load Take Place?

It is not necessary to load the update into the processor(s) immediately after RESET# is removed or early in the power-on self-test (POST) process. Intel guarantees that the boot processor can successfully execute the POST without having an update loaded. Intel recommends that the BIOS author provide a system setup option to enable or disable update loading. This implies that update loading occurs after the POST gets to the point where the user can enter system setup mode.

Updates in a Multiprocessor System

A multiprocessor system incorporates two or more processors. The system designers may choose to enforce a policy wherein all of the processors must be of the same stepping. In this case, it would only be necessary for the system software to incorporate a single update image appropriate to the supported processor stepping. The loader program must be executed by each processor and must verify, via the CPUID instruction, that the update is appropriate to the processor stepping before loading it. It must then load the update into the processor, after which it must authenticate that the load was successful.

On the other hand, the system designers may permit multiple processor steppings to coexist in the system. In this case, the system software must incorporate multiple update images, one to support each of the supported processor steppings. The loader must be executed by each processor and obtain, via the CPUID instruction, the processor's stepping information. It must then locate and load the update appropriate to the processor, after which it must authenticate that the load was successful.

Since the procedure used to initialize a multiprocessor system must verify the existence of all of the system's processors, it would be practical to include the update load process into this procedure.

22 *Paging Enhancements*

The Previous Chapter

The previous chapter described what Intel refers to as the BIOS update feature. A better name, however, might be the Microcode update feature.

This Chapter

This chapter describes the following paging-related processor features:

- The **Page Size Extension (PSE) feature** introduced in the Pentium processor. Please note that this feature was added in the Pentium processor, but was only documented with the release of the Pentium Pro processor.
- **Physical Address Extension (PAE) feature** introduced in the Pentium Pro processor. This feature permits programs to access code or data within a 64GB rather than a 4GB range. In future processors, the PAE could permit access to up to 2^{64} memory space.
- The **Global Page (PGE) feature** introduced in the Pentium Pro processor.

The Next Chapter

The next chapter describes innovations made in the Pentium Pro processor that are related to interrupts and exceptions. This includes some innovations that first appeared in the Pentium processor, but were not publicly documented until the Pentium Pro was introduced.

Background on Paging

For a detailed background on paging as implemented on x86 processors, refer to the MindShare book entitled *Protected Mode Software Architecture* (published by Addison-Wesley). Please be aware, however, that the discussion of 4MB pages in that book has been superseded by the discussion in the next section. At the time that the *Protected Mode Software Architecture* book was written, the PSE feature was still undocumented and the description in that book was based on hopefully intelligent speculation. Intel has documented the PSE feature in the Pentium Pro manuals, so we have tuned the description based on this new information.

Page Size Extension (PSE) Feature

The Problem

Consider two examples:

1. There is a rather large memory area that requires identical rules of conduct throughout. Let's say that it is a 1MB video frame buffer area. Without the ability to define large pages, the OS programmer would be forced to set up 256 page table entries, each describing the location and rules of conduct (using the entry's PCD and PWT bits) within a 4KB page, in order to cover the entire 1MB memory region. This takes a lot of housework and consumes 1KB of memory (256 entries, each 4 bytes wide) just to describe 256 contiguous 4KB memory regions, each with identical rules of conduct. In addition, since the TLB is typically fairly small, the processor can only cache a subset of these 256 page table entries in its TLB at a given instant in time. As other pages in memory are accessed, the page table entries previously-cached that describe this area are cast out of the TLB to make room for the new page table entries. This results in poor performance the next time one of these pages is accessed. The processor is forced to consult the page directory and page tables in memory in order to refetch the respective page table entry and place it back in the TLB.

2. The OS kernel code (i.e., the core of the OS), is typically kept in memory all of the time and is frequently called by other portions of the OS and by applications programs. The kernel can consume a rather large region of memory. Without large page capability, the OS programmer would have to create and maintain a large number of page table entries, each describing a 4KB area of the OS kernel. Like the previous example, as other pages in memory are accessed, the page table entries previously-cached that describe this area are cast out of the TLB to make room for the new page table entries. This results in poor performance the next time one of these pages is accessed. The processor is forced to consult the page directory

and page tables in memory in order to refetch the respective page table entry and place it back in the TLB.

The Solution—Big Pages

The Pentium and Pentium Pro processors solve this problem as follows:

1. any entry in the Page Directory can be set up as a pointer to a **4MB page** in physical memory, rather than as a pointer to a page table that describes 4KB pages.
2. the processor implements a **separate TLB to cache 4MB entries** read from the Page Directory. The first time that an access is made within the 4MB page, the Page Directory entry is cached in the 4MB page TLB. Any subsequent accesses within the same 4MB area then result in a hit in the 4MB TLB, resulting in better performance. In addition, page table entries for 4KB pages are cached in the 4KB page TLB. They therefore do not cause a castout from the 4MB page TLB (or visa vera).

How It Works

This discussion assumes that CR4[PAE] = 0 (see Figure 22-1 on page 442) and that paging is enabled (CR0[PG] = 1). The PSE feature was first implemented in the Pentium processor and was first publicly documented in the Pentium Pro processor manuals.

Normally, each entry in the Page Directory contains the base address of a Page Table and each entry in that Page Table contains the base physical address of a target page in memory. However, when CR4[PAE] = 0 and CR4[PSE] = 1, the programmer can set up some entries in the Page Directory to point to 4MB physical pages in memory rather than to Page Tables that track the location of 4KB pages. Refer to Figure 22-2 on page 442. When the PS bit (bit 7 in the Page Directory entry) = 0, the entry contains the base address of a Page Table that describes 4KB pages. However, when the PS bit = 1, the Page Directory entry contains the base address of a 4MB page in memory (see Figure 22-3 on page 443).

Figure 22-1: CR4

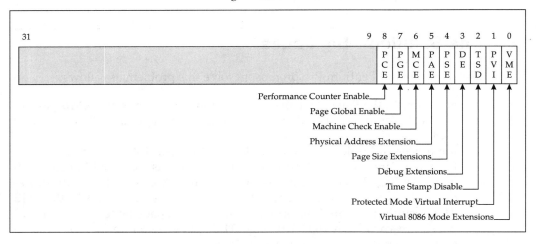

Figure 22-2: Page Directory 32-bit Entry Format (with PAE disabled)

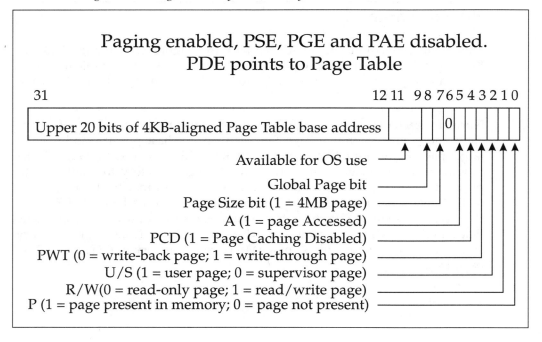

Figure 22-3: Page Directory Entry for 4MB Page

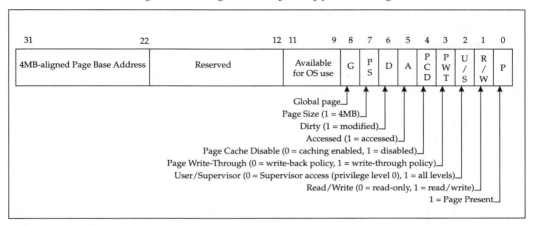

Physical Address Extension (PAE) Feature

Please note that this discussion assumes that CR4[PAE] = 1 and CR4[PSE] = 0. In other words, the PAE is enabled but the Page Size Extension (PSE) is disabled. Immediately following the discussion of the PAE, "The PAE and the Page Size Extension (PSE)" on page 456 describes how usage of the PSE alters the operation of the PAE.

How Paging Normally Works

Without the PAE feature enabled (CR4[PAE] = 0), the processor considers the overall physical memory address space as being 4GB in size, divided into 2^{20} pages of 4KB each. The program that is currently executing uses 32-bit addressing to address memory, thereby providing the program with the capability of addressing up 4GB of memory space. When a memory access is necessary (e.g., instruction fetch, or a memory data read or write caused by the execution of an instruction), the 32-bit memory address generated by adding the segment base address and the 32-bit segment offset to each other produces a 32-bit address. This is referred to as the linear, or logical, address. When paging is disabled, the linear address is the physical memory address that is actually read or written.

When the OS initially places a page of code or data related to a particular program in physical memory, it records the start location of the page in a table in memory (a page table). The program is not informed of the actual location of the page of information in memory. Whenever the currently-executing program attempts to access any location within the page, the processor's paging unit treats the program-generated 32-bit address as a logical address which it must somehow use to index into the Page Tables in memory to discover where the page of information actually resides in physical memory. In other words, it must map or translate the logical page number to the physical page number. Only then can the target physical location within the page be accessed. The paging unit views the 4GB logical address space as being subdivided into 1024 page groups, each group consisting of 1024 logical pages each of whick is 4KB in size. The paging unit therefore views the 32-bit linear (i.e., logical) address as being divided into the following fields:

- Bits [31:22] is the **target logical page group** (1-of-1024). This upper 10-bit field of the linear address is used as an index into the Page Directory, selecting an entry that points to a Page Table. The selected Page Table tracks the current physical location of the 1024 pages that make up this page group.
- Bits [21:12] is the **target page within the group** (1-of-1024). This middle 10-bit field of the linear address is used as the index into the Page Table associated with this page group. The entry selected by this bit field keeps track of the current physical location of this page in memory.
- Bits [11:0] is the **start address within the page** for the read or write (1-of-4096).

The OS sets up and maintains the Page Directory and the Page Tables to track the mapping of logical pages to physical pages:

- The OS loads CR3 with the 4KB-aligned physical base address of the Page Directory.
- Each entry in the Page Directory corresponds to a logical page group and contains the base physical memory address of the Page Table associated with that logical page group.
- There is a Page Table for each logical page group.
- Each entry in a Page Table corresponds to a logical page within that logical page group.
- Each Page Table entry contains the 32-bit base physical memory address of where the logical page of information was placed in physical memory by the OS at an earlier point in time (when the page of information was created or was loaded into memory from a mass storage device).

Using this address translation mechanism, the processor can map any access generated by the currently-executing program to any location within the 4GB physical memory area.

What Is the PAE?

The current versions of the Pentium Pro processor have 36 address lines permitting it to address up to 64GB of physical memory. The 386, 486 and Pentium processors only have 32 address lines, permitting a maximum of 4GB of physical memory to be addressed. When the PAE is disabled (CR4[PAE] = 0), the 32-bit linear address generated by the currently-executing program is translated into a 32-bit physical memory address. In other words, it's backward-compatible with the earlier processors. If things were left this way, the programmer and the processor are incapable of addressing memory over the 4GB address boundary and the upper four address lines, A[35:32]#, are always deasserted.

Once the PAE is enabled, the processor's page address translation mechanism is redefined, permitting the translation, or mapping, of a 32-bit logical memory address to any location within the processor's 64GB physical memory address range (in reality, future x86 processors with address buses up to 64-bits wide are supported by the PAE mechanism).

How Is the PAE Enabled?

The PAE is enabled by setting CR4[PAE] = 1. In addition, some changes to the paging data structures must also be made. These changes are defined in the sections that follow.

Changes to the Paging-Related Data Structures

Paging without the PAE enabled is described in the section entitled "How Paging Normally Works" on page 443 and in more detail in the MindShare book entitled *Protected Mode Software Architecture* (published by Addison-Wesley). Without the PAE enabled, the OS builds and maintains a two-level directory structure that is automatically interrogated by the processor's paging unit to determine which physical page the target logical page maps to.

Refer to Figure 22-4 on page 447. When the PAE is enabled, the OS must build and maintain a three-level directory structure. A new data structure, the Page Directory Pointer Table, or PDPT, contains the base physical memory address of up to four Page Directories. The Page Directory is still required, but, rather than acting as the level one directory, it is the level two directory and the Page Tables are the level three directories.

Figure 22-4: Paging Directory Structure when PAE Enabled

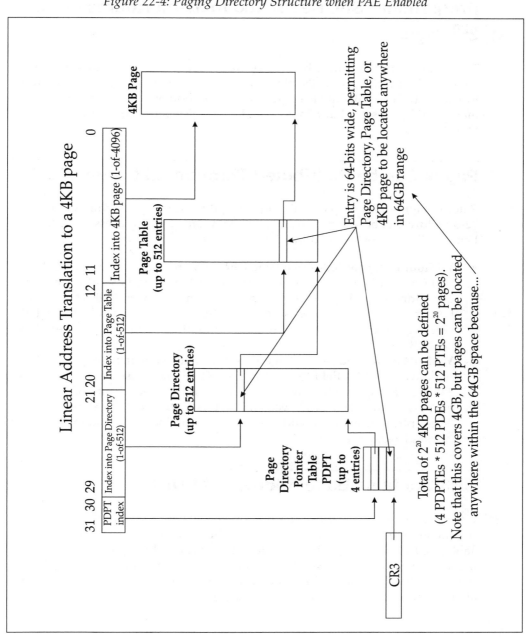

Programmer Still Restricted to 32-bit Addresses and 2^{20} Pages

The programmer can still only generate 32-bit addresses for memory data reads memory data writes, or instruction fetches. In addition, the new 3-level directory structure can still only keep track of the location of up to 2^{20} pages of information (512 pages per Page Table * 512 Page Tables per Page Directory * 4 Page Directories).

Pages Can be Distributed Throughout Lower 64GB

Refer to Figure 22-4 on page 447. However, this directory structure permits the 32-bit address to be mapped to any page within the 64GB address space that the Pentium Pro is capable of addressing:

- **Without PAE enabled**—each Page Directory and Page Table entry is 32-bits wide with a 20-bit field to identify the 4KB-aligned base physical memory address of a Page Table or a page within the lower 4GB. The lower 12 bits of the linear address is added to the lower end of this 20-bit field, creating the exact address of one of the locations within the target physical 4KB page.
- **With PAE enabled**—each Page Directory and Page Table entry is 64-bits wide with a 24-bit field to identify the 4KB-aligned base address of a Page Table or a page within the lower 64GB. The lower 12 bits of the linear address is added to the lower end of this 24-bit field, creating the exact 36-bit physical memory address of one of the locations within the target physical 4KB page.

CR3 Contains Base Address of PDPT

Figure 22-5 on page 449 illustrates the contents of CR3 when the PAE is enabled. It contains the base physical memory address of the Page Directory Pointer Table (PDPT). Notice that it is only a 32-bit register. This means that the PDPT must reside within the lower 4GB of memory. The OS programmer loads CR3 with bits [31:5] of the PDPT base address, meaning that it must be 32-byte-aligned (the entire PDPT fits in one cache line).

Chapter 22: Paging Enhancements

When the CR4[PAE] and CR0[PG] bits are set to one, or, if both are already set and CR3 is loaded with a new value, the processor automatically reads all four PDPT entries of the PDPT into an invisible register set inside the processor. These values point to the four Page Directories and will not be reloaded from memory unless a new value is loaded into CR3. The automatic read of the four entries removes the need to read the PDPT when performing address translation.

The state of the PCD (Page Cache Disable) and PWT (Page Write-Through) bits in CR3 tells the processor whether the PDPT is cacheable and, if it is, whether to use a write-through or a write-back policy in handling writes to the PDPT.

Figure 22-5: CR3 Contains Base Address of PDPT

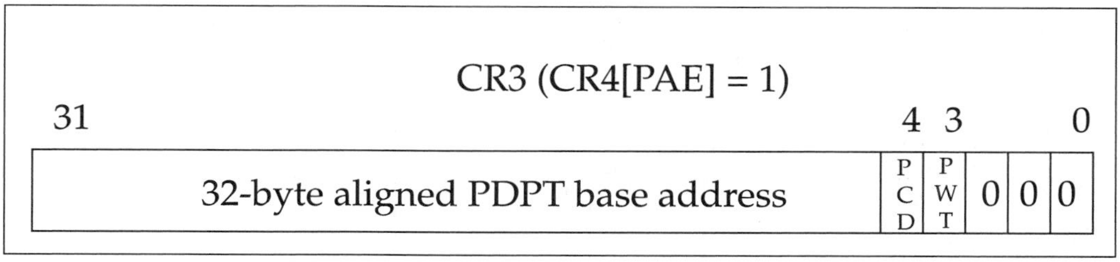

CR3 (CR4[PAE] = 1)					
31		4	3		0
32-byte aligned PDPT base address	P C D	P W T	0	0	0

Format of PDPT Entry

Figure 22-6 on page 450 illustrates the format of a PDPT entry. The reserved bits must all be zero. The programmer loads the entry with the 4KB-aligned (the upper 24-bits of the) physical memory address of the Page Directory. This permits the Page Directory to be located on any one of 2^{24} 4KB-aligned physical memory address boundaries within the lower 64GB.

The state of the PCD (Page Cache Disable) and PWT (Page Write-Through) bits tells the processor whether the Page Directory is cacheable and, if it is, whether to use a write-through or a write-back policy in handling writes to the Page Directory.

The P bit tells the processor whether the Page Directory pointed to by the entry is currently **present** in memory (or is on disk).

Figure 22-6: Format of a PDPT Entry

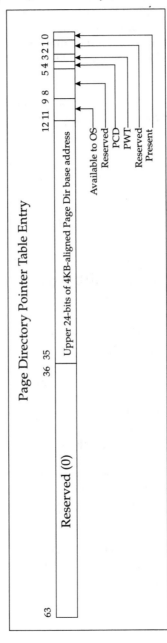

TLB Flush Necessary after PDPT Entry Change

If the programmer makes a change to one or more of the PDPT entries, those entries then point to different page directories. Up to this point in time, the processor has been caching page table entries from the current page tables in the TLB. When a change is made to the PDPT entry, a different directory is selected. This renders all of the currently-cached TLB entries stale, but they are not discarded as a result of the update to the PDPT. The programmer must invalidate the TLB by writing to CR3.

Format of Page Directory Entry

Figure 22-7 on page 453 illustrates the format of a Page Directory entry. The reserved bits must all be zero. The programmer loads the entry with the 4KB-aligned (the upper 24-bits of the) physical memory address of a Page Table. This permits the Page Table to be located on any one of 2^{24} 4KB-aligned physical memory address boundaries within the lower 64GB.

The state of the PCD (Page Cache Disable) and PWT (Page Write-Through) bits tells the processor whether the Page Table is cacheable and, if it is, whether to use a write-through or a write-back policy in handling writes to the Page Table. The remaining bits have the following meaning (in the following discussion, note that the supervisor privilege levels are 0, 1, and 2):

- P is the **Page Present** bit. The OS programmer sets P = 1 if the Page Table is currently present in memory. In addition, the programmer indicates its physical location in memory using the base address field and sets the attribute bits (PCD, PWT, R/W, U/S, and A) to the appropriate states. If the Page Table is not currently present in memory, P = 0 and bits [63:1] of the entry can be used by the OS for anything. Any memory access that selects the Page Table will then result in a page fault exception and the 32-bit linear address that caused the fault is recorded in CR2.
- R/W is the **Read/Write** bit. When R/W = 0, all of the pages pointed to by the Page Table are read-only. When R/W = 1, read/write access is permitted within those pages. Used in conjunction with the U/S bit (see next bullet in list). In addition, if CR0[WP] = 1, programs executing at supervisor privilege level must also obey this bit. If CR0[WP] = 0, programs executing at the supervisor privilege level don't have to obey this bit.
- U/S is the **User/Supervisor** bit. When U/S = 0, only programs executing at the supervisor privilege level can access the pages pointed to by the Page

Table. When U/S = 1, the pages can be accessed by programs executing at any privilege level. Note that access rights are further qualified by the R/W bit.

- A is the **Accessed** bit. Set by the processor the first time that the Page Table is accessed (for a read or a write).

Figure 22-7: Format of Page Directory Entry that Points to Page Table

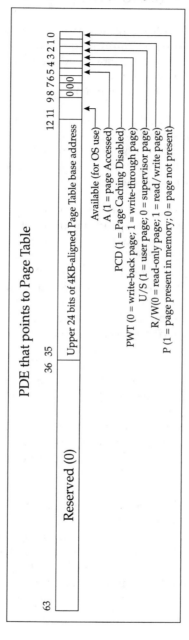

PDE that points to Page Table

63   36 35   12 11   9 8 7 6 5 4 3 2 1 0

Reserved (0)   Upper 24 bits of 4KB-aligned Page Table base address   0 0 0

Available (for OS use)
A (1 = page Accessed)
PCD (1 = Page Caching Disabled)
PWT (0 = write-back page; 1 = write-through page)
U/S (1 = user page; 0 = supervisor page)
R/W (0 = read-only page; 1 = read/write page)
P (1 = page present in memory; 0 = page not present)

Format of Page Table Entry

Figure 22-8 on page 455 illustrates the format of a Page Table entry. The reserved bits must all be zero. The programmer loads the entry with the 4KB-aligned (the upper 24-bits of the) physical memory address of a page in memory. This permits the page to be located on any one of 2^{24} 4KB-aligned physical memory address boundaries within the lower 64GB.

The state of the PCD (Page Cache Disable) and PWT (Page Write-Through) bits tells the processor whether the page is cacheable and, if it is, whether to use a write-through or a write-back policy in handling writes to the page. The remaining bits have the following meaning (in the following discussion, note that the supervisor privilege levels are 0, 1, and 2):

- P is the **Page Present** bit. The OS programmer sets P = 1 if the page is currently present in memory. In addition, the programmer indicates its physical location in memory using the base address field and sets the attribute bits (PCD, PWT, R/W, U/S, D, G and A) to the appropriate states. If the page is not currently present in memory, P = 0 and bits [63:1] of the entry can be used by the OS for anything. Any memory access that selects the page will then result in a page fault exception and the 32-bit linear address that caused the fault is recorded in CR2.
- R/W is the **Read/Write** bit. When R/W = 0, the page is read-only. When R/W = 1, read/write access is permitted within the page. Used in conjunction with the U/S bit (see next bullet in list). In addition, if CR0[WP] = 1, programs executing at supervisor privilege level must also obey this bit. If CR0[WP] = 0, programs executing at the supervisor privilege level don't have to obey this bit.
- U/S is the **User/Supervisor** bit. When U/S = 0, only programs executing at the supervisor privilege level can access the page pointed to by this Page Table entry. When U/S = 1, the page can be accessed by programs executing at any privilege level. Note that access rights are further qualified by the R/W bit.
- A is the **Accessed** bit. Set by the processor the first time that the page is accessed (for a read or a write).
- D is the **Dirty** bit. Set by the processor the first time that page is written to.
- G is the **Global** bit. When G = 1, the page is identified as a global page. The processor should retain this page table entry in its TLB when a task switch occurs (i.e., when a new value is loaded into CR3). For a more detailed discussion, refer to "Global Page Feature" on page 460.

Figure 22-8: Format of Page Table Entry

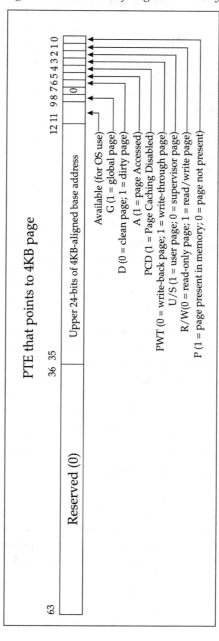

The PAE and the Page Size Extension (PSE)

Now assume that both the PAE and the PSE bits in CR4 are set to one. With one exception, everything that has been described about the PAE feature remains true. The difference lies in the format and usage of entries in a Page Directory. Normally, each Page Directory entry contains the base address of a Page Table and each entry of the Page Table contains the base physical memory address of a 4KB page in memory.

When the PSE and PAE features are both activated, however, the PS (Page Size) bit (bit 7) in a directory entry can now be set to one without causing a general protection exception. When PS = 1, the Page Directory entry doesn't point to a Page Table. Rather, it contains the 2MB-aligned physical base address of a 2MB page in memory and the attribute bits that defined the rules of conduct within that page.

Figure 22-9 on page 458 illustrates the translation of a 32-bit linear address to a 2MB page somewhere in the lower 64GB. Figure 22-10 on page 459 illustrates the format of Page Directory entry that identifies a 2MB page in memory and the rules of conduct that must be followed when performing accesses within the page.

The reserved bits must all be zero. The programmer loads the entry with the 2MB-aligned (the upper 15-bits of the) physical memory address of the page in memory. This permits the page to be located on any one of 2^{15} 2MB-aligned address boundaries within the lower 64GB.

The state of the PCD (Page Cache Disable) and PWT (Page Write-Through) bits tells the processor whether the page is cacheable and, if it is, whether to use a write-through or a write-back policy in handling writes to the page. The remaining bits have the following meaning (in the following discussion, note that the supervisor privilege levels are 0, 1, and 2):

- P is the **Page Present** bit. The OS programmer sets P = 1 if the page is currently present in memory. In addition, the programmer indicates its location in memory using the base address field and sets the attribute bits (PCD, PWT, R/W, U/S, D, G and A) to the appropriate states. If the page is not currently present in memory, P = 0 and bits [63:1] of the entry can be used by the OS for anything. Any memory access that selects the page will then result in a page fault exception and the 32-bit linear address that caused the fault is recorded in CR2.
- R/W is the **Read/Write** bit. When R/W = 0, the page is read-only. When

R/W = 1, read/write access is permitted within the page. Used in conjunction with the U/S bit (see next bullet in list). In addition, if CR0[WP] = 1, programs executing at supervisor privilege level must also obey this bit. If CR0[WP] = 0, programs executing at the supervisor privilege level don't have to obey this bit.

- U/S is the **User/Supervisor** bit. When U/S = 0, only programs executing at the supervisor privilege level can access the page pointed to by this Page Table entry. When U/S = 1, the page can be accessed by programs executing at any privilege level. Note that access rights are further qualified by the R/W bit.
- A is the **Accessed** bit. Set by the processor the first time that the page is accessed (for a read or a write).
- D is the **Dirty** bit. Set by the processor the first time that page is written to.
- G is the **Global** bit. When G = 1, the page is identified as a global page. The processor should retain this page directory entry in its TLB when a task switch occurs (i.e., a new value is loaded into CR3). For a more detailed discussion, refer to "Global Page Feature" on page 460.

Figure 22-9: Translation of Linear Address to a 2MB Page

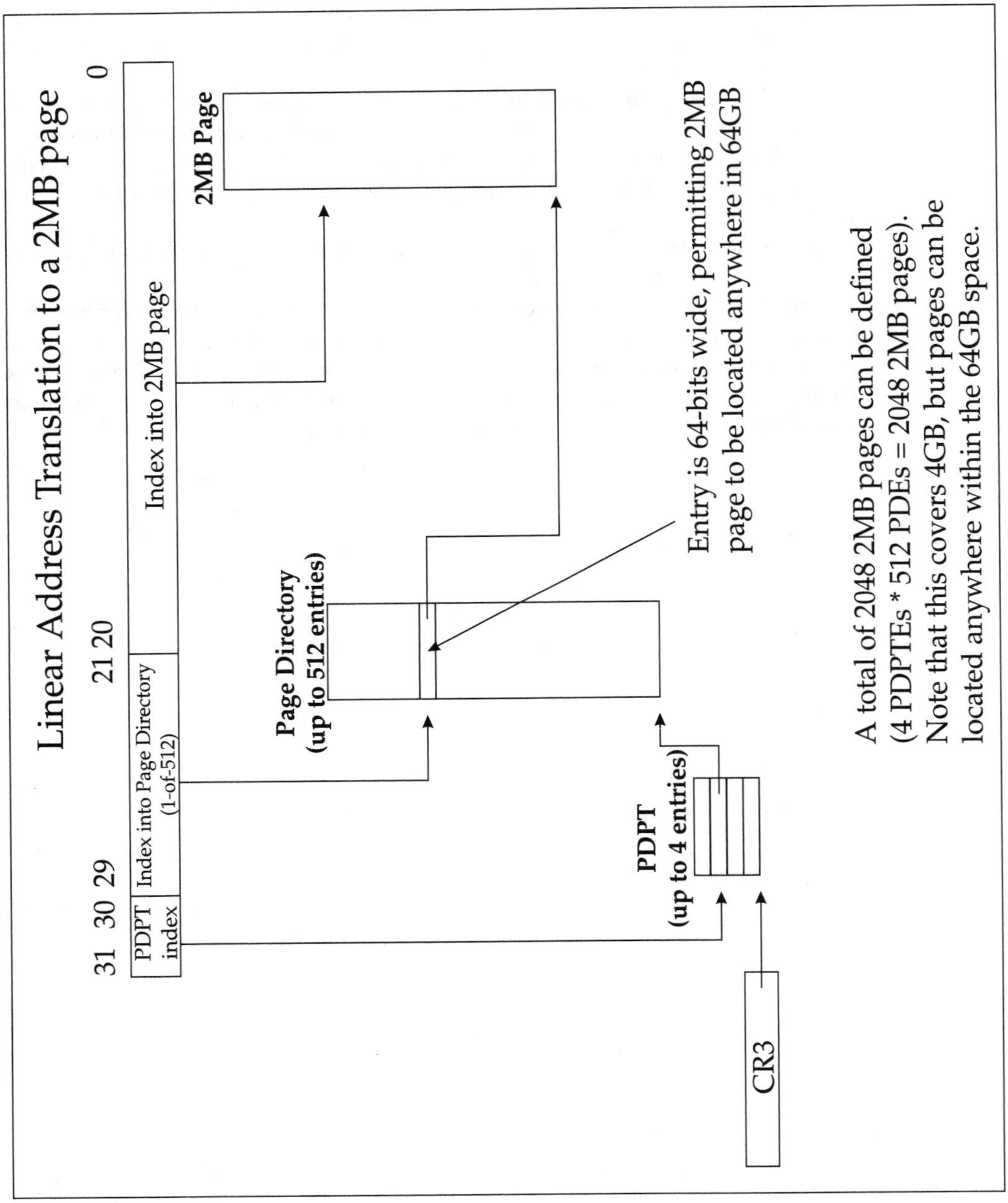

Linear Address Translation to a 2MB page

Figure 22-10: Format of a Page Directory Entry for 2MB Page

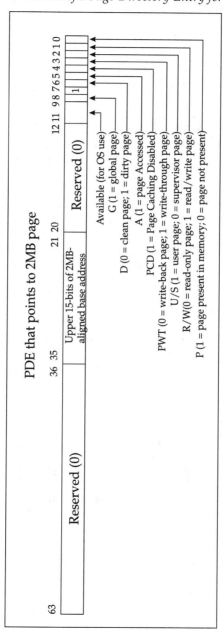

Global Page Feature

The Problem

During normal operation, the processor copies page table entries related to pages being accessed into a special cache known as the TLB (Translation Lookaside Buffer). This results in faster performance. Once the processor has placed a page's Page Table entry in the TLB, the processor has the logical-to-physical page information on-chip. It doesn't have to read the Page Directory and then the Page Table to obtain this information every time an access is made to the page.

Whenever a task switch occurs, the processor loads a new value into CR3, selecting the set of Page Directories and Page Tables that define the pages accessible by the new task. When this occurs, the processor automatically flushes all entries currently-cached in the TLB (because they were cached from the previous program's Page Tables). This causes a performance dip as the new program starts to execute because the processor will have to consult the multi-level directories in memory to obtain copies of the Page Table entries related to this program.

Quite commonly, a number of pages are shared among multiple programs. It would therefore be more efficient if the processor retained the Page Table entries related to these "global", or shared, pages in the TLB rather than discarding them along with the rest when a task switch occurs.

The Solution

The Pentium Pro processor implements a new feature referred to as the Global Page feature. It is activated by setting CR4[PGE] = 1. Once activated, any Page Table entries (or Page Directory entries for 2MB or 4MB pages) that have the G bit = 1 (see Figure 22-8 on page 455 and Figure 22-10 on page 459) are considered global. When a task switch is performed, all of the TLB entries are flushed with the exception of those marked global. The specification states that these entries will remain in the TLB indefinitely. Indefinitely is a very "fuzzy" term. It more than likely means that a global entry will remain in the TLB until it is cast out to make room for a new Page Table entry. As time goes on and accesses are made to new pages, the processor reads the Page Table entries for the newly-accessed pages and places their contents into the TLB. If the TLB entry selected by the TLB's LRU (least-recently used) algorithm is already occupied by a previously-cached Page Table entry, the older entry is cast out of the TLB to make room for the more recently accessed entry.

The specification states that the only way to deterministically (i.e., definitely) remove the global entries from the TLB is to set CR4[PGE] = 0 and then invalidate the TLB. The TLB is invalidated by clearing one of the following control bits:

- CR0[PE] to leave protected mode.
- CR0[PG] to disable paging.
- CR4[PSE] to disable the Page Size Extension feature.
- CR4[PGE] to disable the Global Page feature.
- CR4[PAE] to disable the Physical Address Extension.

Propagation of Page Table Entry Changes to Multiple Processors

It is very important that all processors in a multi-processor system utilize identical page tables to translate memory addresses from linear to physical memory addresses. When one of the processors in a multi-processor system changes the contents of one or more page table entries (PTEs), the change(s) must be propagated to all of the other processors. This process is typically referred to as "TLB Shootdown."

The change(s) may be communicated to the other processors using memory-based semaphores and/or inter-processor interrupts between processors (i.e., sending messages via the APIC bus). It is very important that one of the following approaches be taken:

- The differing page table entries are not used on different processors until the change has been communicated to all of them.
- or—the OS must be prepared to deal with the case where one or more of the other processors utilize the stale TLB entries before the update process has been completed.

23 Interrupt Enhancements

The Previous Chapter

The previous chapter described the following paging-related processor features:

- The **Page Size Extension (PSE) feature** introduced in the Pentium processor. Please note that this feature was added in the Pentium processor, but was only documented with the release of the Pentium Pro processor.
- **Physical Address Extension (PAE) feature** introduced in the Pentium Pro processor. This feature permits programs to access code or data within a 64GB rather than a 4GB range.
- The **Global Page (PGE) feature** introduced in the Pentium Pro processor.

This Chapter

This chapter describes innovations made in the Pentium Pro processor that are related to interrupts and exceptions. This includes some innovations that first appeared in the Pentium processor, but were not publicly documented until the Pentium Pro was introduced.

The Next Chapter

The next chapter describes the error logging and reporting machine check architecture first introduced in the Pentium processor and greatly expanded in the Pentium Pro processor. The machine check architecture defines an exception (the machine check exception) used to report hardware-related problems and a register set used to log both recoverable and unrecoverable errors.

New Exceptions

The Pentium Pro does not implement any new software exception conditions.

Added APIC Functionality

Either or both of the performance counters (see "Performance Monitoring and Timestamp" on page 499) may be programmed to generate an interrupt when the respective event counter overflows. The local APIC design has been enhanced by adding a fifth entry to its local vector table, or LVT (for information on local APIC operation and its LVT, refer to the chapter on the APIC in MindShare's book entitled *Pentium Processor System Architecture*, published by Addison-Wesley).

Figure 23-1 on page 465 illustrates the format of the performance counter entry in the APIC's LVT. The bit fields within the entry have the following usage:

- the **vector field** identifies the entry in the Interrupt Descriptor Table (IDT) that contains the pointer to the performance counter overflow interrupt handler routine that will be executed each time that one of the performance counters overflows.
- the **delivery mode field** specifies how the interrupt will be generated: either by jumping through the IDT entry specified in the vector field; or via the NMI entry in the IDT (entry 2) and the vector field will be ignored. Although the specification also shows ExtINT as a valid choice, it is the author's opinion this isn't so. If the processor were to generate an Interrupt Acknowledge bus transaction to obtain the performance counter vector from the 8259A interrupt controller, it would confuse the 8259A (because it did not generate the interrupt request).
- the **delivery status bit** indicates whether the interrupt has either not been generated or the interrupt has occurred and the handler has already been called (in both cases, the state would be Idle); or the interrupt has occurred, but the handler is still in the process of being called.
- the **mask bit** permits the performance counter overflow event to be ignored (mask = 1) or to be recognized (mask = 0).

Figure 23-1: Format of the Performance Counter LVT Entry

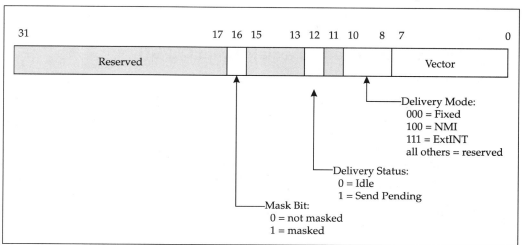

VM86 Mode Extensions

VM86 Mode Background

For a detailed description of virtual 8086 (VM86) mode, refer to the MindShare book entitled *Protected Mode Software Architecture* (published by Addison-Wesley). However, the section entitled *VM86 Mode Extensions* in that book was written based on speculation (since Intel had not yet released the documentation of the VM86 Mode Extensions). This section is based on the documentation provided by Intel in the Pentium Pro *Operating System Writer's Manual* and takes the place of that discussion.

Interrupt-Related Problems and VM86 Tasks

The sections that follow describe the problems associated with interrupt handling when the processor is executing a VM86 task (typically a DOS task) under a multitasking OS in VM86 mode (EFLAGS[VM] = 1). The software overhead imposed by the OS (and the attendant performance hit) in the following scenarios are described:

- the handling of an attempted execution of a CLI or an STI instruction when the VM86 extensions feature bit, CR4[VME], isn't enabled.
- when the VM86 task attempts to execute a software interrupt instruction (INT n) with the VM86 extensions feature bit, CR4[VME], disabled.

Software Overhead Associated with CLI/STI Execution

Attempted Execution of CLI by VM86 Task. Assume that the VM86 task has attempted to disable recognition of external hardware interrupts (because it doesn't want to be bothered by interrupts during execution of a critical piece of code). The processor did not successfully execute the instruction (it resulted in a GP exception because the VM86 task has insufficient privilege), so interrupt recognition is still enabled. The GP exception handler passes control to the VMM (Virtual Machine Monitor) program which is responsible for "baby-sitting" VM86 tasks. There are three possible cases:

1. the VMM checks the state of the IF bit in the EFlags image on the privilege level 0 stack and determines that **interrupt recognition had already been disabled (by the VMM or OS) at some earlier point in time**. In this case, the VMM adjusts the return pointer on the privilege level 0 stack to point to the instruction following the CLI that caused the exception, and then executes an IRET to **resume execution** of the interrupted VM86 task **at the instruction that follows the CLI**.
2. the VMM may know that this is a **safe time to disable interrupt recognition** (because there are no high-priority interrupts expected). In this case, the **VMM** could choose to **execute** a **CLI** instruction, adjust the return pointer on the privilege level 0 stack to point to the instruction following the CLI that caused the exception, **and** then execute an IRET to **resume execution** of the interrupted VM86 task **at the instruction that follows the CLI**.
3. the VMM may know that this is **not a safe time to disable recognition** of hardware interrupts. The text that follows provides a detailed description of this case.

The multitasking OS cannot permit the VM86 task (which doesn't know of the existence of the multitasking OS or other, currently-suspended tasks) to summarily disable interrupt recognition. At an earlier point in time, another task may have stimulated an IO device (e.g., a disk interface) to perform an operation and generate an interrupt when it has been completed. The device may complete the requested operation and generate the interrupt while the VM86 task is executing. Furthermore, the device may be quite sensitive to being serviced on a timely basis. The VM86 task is unaware of any of this.

On the attempted execution of the CLI instruction, the VMM will note (in a memory location somewhere) that the currently-executing task prefers not to be interrupted. In other words, the **VMM maintains a virtual copy of EFLAGS[IF] bit in software**. It alters the return address on the privilege level 0 stack to point to the instruction that follows the CLI and then executes the IRET to resume execution of the interrupted VM86 task at the instruction that follows the CLI.

If a hardware interrupt should subsequently occur, the VM86 task is interrupted and the hardware interrupt's protected mode handler then passes control to the VMM. If the VMM knows that the interrupting device requires fast servicing, it immediately executes the device's interrupt handler to service the device. In other words, it ignores the preference of the VM86 program that it not be interrupted. In this case, the VM86 task was interrupted even though it preferred not to be. The VMM designer should make every attempt to accomplish the check just described as expeditiously as possible and return control to the interrupted task. Otherwise, the interrupted VM86 task may not function correctly (because of the lengthy delay imposed by the VMM's software overhead necessary to determine whether to service the hardware interrupt right away or to defer servicing it until the task's timeslice has expired).

On the other hand, the VMM may determine that the interrupting device can stand some delay in being serviced and note that the state of the virtual copy of the EFLAGS[IF] bit indicates that the VM86 task prefers not to be interrupted. In this case, the VMM would set a bit in a VMM-specific data structure (let's call it the deferred interrupt data structure) indicating that the specified interrupt handler should be executed when the VM86 task completes its timeslice. It then executes the IRET instruction to resume execution of the interrupted VM86 task. Later, when the VM86 task's timeslice has expired and a task switch occurs back to the OS, the OS checks the deferred interrupt data structure (mentioned earlier) to determine if the servicing of any hardware interrupt(s) was deferred. If it was, the OS calls the respective interrupt handler(s) to service the hardware device(s).

Attempted Execution of STI Instruction. If the VM86 task attempts to reenable interrupt recognition, one of three cases is true:

1. the VMM checks the state of the IF bit in the EFLAGS image on the privilege level 0 stack and determines that **interrupt recognition is already enabled.** In this case, the VMM adjusts the return pointer on the privilege level 0 stack to point to the instruction following the STI that caused the exception, and then executes an IRET to resume execution of the interrupted VM86 task at the instruction that follows the STI.

2.   the VMM may know that this is a **safe time to enable interrupt recognition**. In this case, the **VMM** could choose to **execute** a **STI** instruction, adjust the return pointer on the privilege level 0 stack to point to the instruction following the STI that caused the exception, **and** then execute an IRET to **resume execution** of the interrupted VM86 task **at the instruction that follows the STI**.

3.   the VMM knows that this is not a safe time to reenable recognition of hardware interrupts. In this case, the VMM adjusts the return pointer on the privilege level 0 stack to point to the instruction following the STI that caused the exception, and then executes an IRET to **resume execution** of the interrupted VM86 task **at the instruction that follows the STI**.

Servicing of Software Interrupts by DOS or OS

Many VM86 tasks utilize the INT   *nn* instruction (where *nn* selects entry *nn* in the interrupt table in memory) to call the real mode OS or BIOS services. An attempt to execute an INT *nn* instruction when the EFLAGS[IOPL] field < 3 results in a GP exception (due to insufficient privilege). The processor executes the protected mode GP exception handler. The handler checks the VM bit in the EFLAGS image on the privilege level 0 stack to determine if the interrupted task is a VM86 task. If it is (VM = 1), the GP handler passes control to the VMM. The VMM must then determine what to do in response. There are two basic cases:

1.   The VMM determines that it is not legal for the VM86 task to call the target vector (i.e., routine). In this case, the VMM would be forced to terminate the VM86 task.

2.   The VMM determines that the VM86 task is attempting a legal call to a DOS or BIOS service.

In the second case, the VMM must choose one of the following options:

1.   Pass the call to the respective real mode handler.

2.   Pass the call to the protected mode OS to handle. When the OS has completed the request, the VMM then returns control to the interrupted VM86 task at the instruction immediately following the INT   *nn* instruction.

Chapter 23: Interrupt Enhancements

Solution—VM86 Mode Extensions

Introduction

The VM86 mode extensions are enabled by setting CR4[VME] = 1 (see Figure 23-2 on page 469). Once this bit is enabled, the following bits are usable:

- **EFLAGS[VIP]**. Virtual Interrupt Pending bit. See Figure 23-3 on page 470.
- **EFLAGS[VIF]**. Virtual Interrupt Flag bit. See Figure 23-3 on page 470.
- **CR4[PVI]**. Protected Mode Virtual Interrupts. See Figure 23-2 on page 469.

The sections that follow describe how these bits are used to solve the problems associated with interrupt handling in VM86 tasks.

Figure 23-2: CR4

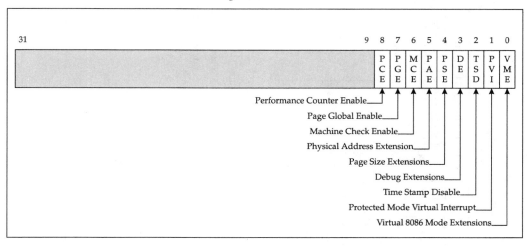

Figure 23-3: EFLAGS Register

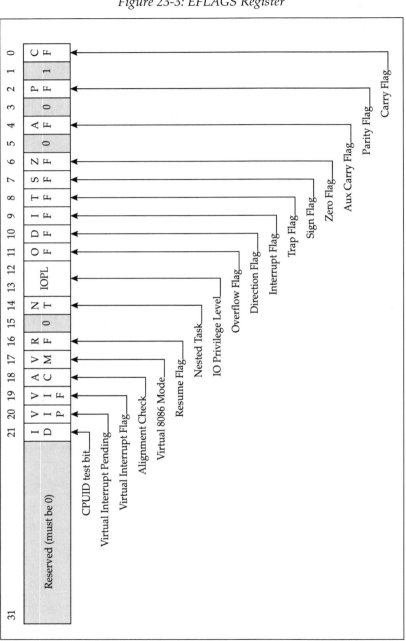

CLI/STI Solution

All VM86 tasks execute at privilege level 3. The effects of executing a CLI or STI instruction while in VM86 mode depend on a number of factors. There are three cases:

1. If EFLAGS[IOPL] = 3, the instruction is permitted to execute and is successful in changing the state of the EFLAGS[IF] bit (because privilege level 3 programs are permitted to execute CLI and STI). Execution of CLI causes recognition of external interrupts to be disabled. Execution of the VM86 task continues uninterrupted.
2. If EFLAGS[IOPL] < 3 and CR4[VME] = 0, an attempt to execute either CLI or STI causes a GP exception (due to insufficient privilege).
3. **If EFLAGS[IOPL] < 3 and EFLAGS[VME] = 1, execution of either CLI or STI changes the state of EFLAGS[VIF] rather than EFLAGS[IF]**, and execution of the VM86 task continues uninterrupted. Execution of a CLI instruction clears EFLAGS[VIF] to 0, while execution of the STI instruction sets it to one. The VMM is not called, thus avoiding the software overhead associated with CLI or STI execution. The sections that follow describe what occurs when a hardware interrupt occurs.

EFLAGS[VIF] = 1, EFLAGS[IF] = 1, Interrupt Occurs. Recognition of external interrupts is enabled (EFLAGS[IF] = 1) and the VM86 program has indicated that it doesn't mind being interrupted (as indicated by EFLAGS[VIF] = 1). In this case, any hardware interrupt will cause the processor to call the respective protected mode handler.

EFLAGS[VIF] = 0, EFLAGS[IF] = 1, Interrupt Occurs. Recognition of external interrupts is enabled (EFLAGS[IF] = 1), but the VM86 program has indicated that it wishes not to be interrupted (as indicated by EFLAGS[VIF] = 0). The following actions are taken:

1. Processor suspends the VM86 task and calls the protected mode handler associated with the interrupt vector supplied by the interrupt controller.
2. In the protected mode handler, the programmer checks the state of the VM bit in the EFLAGS image saved on the stack. If set, a VM86 task was interrupted, so the VMM program is called and provided with the vector number that corresponds to the hardware interrupt event.
3. In the VMM, check the state of EFLAGS[VIF]. In this example scenario, it is cleared, indicating that the VM86 task prefers not be interrupted.
4. The VMM sets VIP = 1 in the EFLAGS image on the stack, indicating that the interrupt request for service has been deferred until such time as the VM86 task reenables interrupt recognition (by executing an STI instruction), or the VM86 task's time slice is up.

5. The VMM makes note of which handler must be executed at a later time (VMM typically maintains a bitmap corresponding to all interrupt vectors 32d through 255d).

6. The VMM returns to the protected mode handler that called it.

7. The handler returns to the interrupted VM86 task. When the processor pops the EFLAGS image from the stack, EFLAGS[IF] = 1 (recognition of hardware interrupts is enabled), EFLAGS[VIF] is still 0 (indicating that the VM86 task prefers not to be interrupted) and EFLAGS[VIP] = 1 (indicating that servicing of an interrupt has been deferred).

8. When the VM86 task subsequently executes an STI instruction to reenable interrupt recognition (in other words, it no longer minds being interrupted), the processor takes the following actions:

   • Checks the state of EFLAGS[VIP]. If VIP = 0, indicating that no interrupts were deferred, the processor sets EFLAGS[VIF] = 1 (because STI is being executed) and continues execution of the VM86 task. If VIP = 1, this indicates that handling of one or more interrupts was deferred. The processor generates a GP exception.

   • When the GP exception handler detects VIP = 1 in the EFLAGS image on the stack, it calls the VMM (because servicing of one or more interrupts was deferred).

   • The VMM calls the handlers associated with the interrupt (or interrupts) that had been deferred.

   • When the interrupt handler(s) have all been called, the VMM sets VIF = 1 (because an STI instruction is being executed) and clears VIP = 0 in the EFLAGS image on the stack (because all deferred interrupts have been serviced).

   • The VMM then returns to the VM86 task.

Software Interrupt Redirection Solution

Hardware interrupts are always handled by the protected mode handlers, as are NMI and software exceptions. The interrupt redirection bitmap in the TSS (see Figure 23-4 on page 473) is not consulted. The **processor only consults the interrupt redirection bitmap when executing software interrupt instructions** (i.e., INT nn). Table 23-1 on page 474 assumes that a software interrupt instruction is being executed in a VM86 task. There are six different scenarios that define how it is handled.

Chapter 23: Interrupt Enhancements

Figure 23-4: Task State Segment (TSS)

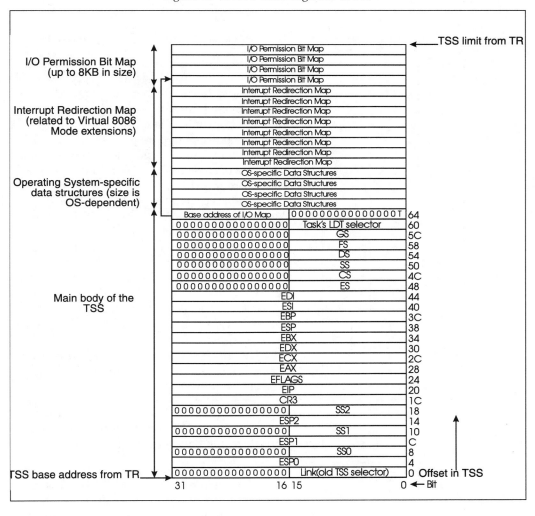

Table 23-1: VM86 Interrupt/Exception Handling

Scenario	VME Bit	EFLAGS IOPL bit field	Redir Map Bit	Description of Processor/Handler Actions
1	0	3	x	When a software interrupt occurs, the processor switches from VM86 mode to protected mode and **executes protected mode handler**. • Switches to privilege level 0 stack. • Pushes data segment registers onto level 0 stack (so they can be restored to their original values when resuming execution of interrupted program). • Clears data segment registers. • Pushes SS, ESP, EFLAGS, CS, and EIP of interrupted task onto level 0 stack. • If set, clears EFLAGS[TF], disabling single-step. • Clears EFLAGS[VM]. Processor exits VM86 mode. • If vector selects interrupt gate, clears EFLAGS[IF], disabling recognition of external interrupts. • Sets CS:EIP from interrupt gate descriptor selected by vector and begins execution of protected mode handler.
2	0	<3	x	Attempted execution of **any software interrupt instruction causes a GP exception** due to insufficient privilege. GP handler can then handle the event.
3	1	<3	1	When a software interrupt occurs, the processor consults the interrupt redirection bitmap in the task's TSS to determine whether to vector to the DOS handler or to the GP exception handler. In this case, the redirection bit = 1, indicating the **GP exception handler will be called**.
4	1	3	1	Same as scenario 1 (i.e., processor switches from VM86 mode to protected mode and **executes appropriate protected mode handler**).

Table 23-1: VM86 Interrupt/Exception Handling (Continued)

Scenario	VME Bit	EFLAGS IOPL bit field	Redir Map Bit	Description of Processor/Handler Actions
5	1	3	0	**Software interrupt is redirected to real mode handler:** • Pushes CS:IP onto current task's stack. • Clear EFLAGS[NT] and EFLAGS[IOPL]. • Push Flag onto current task's stack. • If set, clears EFLAGS[TF], disabling single-step. • If set, clears EFLAGS[IF], disabling recognition of external interrupts. • Loads CS:IP from real mode interrupt table entry selected by vector. Real mode interrupt table starts at linear address 0 in the current task's 1MB memory range. • Begins execution of real mode interrupt handler. Execution of a CLI or STI affects the EFLAGS[IF] (because privilege level 3 programs are permitted to execute CLI and STI).
6	1	<3	0	**Same as scenario 5, with the following additional effect on hardware interrupt handling.** When CR4[VME] = 1, the CPL of the DOS task is 3, and EFLAGS[IOPL] < 3, attempted execution of **CLI and STI instructions changes the state of EFLAGS[VIF] (rather than EFLAGS[IF]).** See "CLI/STI Solution" on page 471.

Virtual Interrupt Handling in Protected Mode

The CLI/STI handling mechanism (just described for VM86 mode) can also be used when executing a protected mode task (in other words, not a VM86 task). To activate this capability, CR4[PVI] = 1 and CR4[VME] = 0. This will allow privilege level 3 protected mode programs to execute CLI/STI without causing a GP exception (when IOPL < 3), and prevents the protected mode application program from successfully playing with the EFLAGS[IF] bit.

24 Machine Check Architecture

The Previous Chapter

The previous chapter described innovations made in the Pentium and Pentium Pro processors that are related to interrupts and exceptions. This includes some innovations that first appeared in the Pentium processor, but were not publicly documented until the Pentium Pro was introduced.

This Chapter

This chapter describes the error logging and reporting Machine Check Architecture first introduced in the Pentium processor and greatly expanded in the Pentium Pro processor. The Machine Check Architecture defines an exception (the Machine Check exception) used to report hardware-related problems and a register set used to log both recoverable and unrecoverable errors.

The Next Chapter

The next chapter describes the performance monitoring and time stamp counter facilities incorporated in the Pentium Pro processor. It should be noted that these facilities are also implemented in the Pentium processor, but Intel did not document them until the release of the Pentium Pro processor.

Purpose of Machine Check Architecture

The Machine Check Architecture exception and register set logs and reports hardware errors associated with:

- bus errors
- ECC errors
- parity errors
- cache errors
- TLB errors

As described later in this chapter, the Machine Check Architecture register set is implemented as a set of error logging register banks. It is Intel's intention that these registers be used in the following manner:

- The OS incorporates a utility (i.e., a daemon) that is executed on a periodic basis and is tasked with scanning the Machine Check Architecture error logging register banks. Any errors that have been logged by the processor(s) are then saved in some form of non-volatile memory. This error log can then be viewed by system maintenance personnel using a special utility program.

- Whenever a processor generates a Machine Check exception, the Machine Check exception handler scans the register banks to determine the cause of the exception. It then determines whether or not the condition can be corrected and, if it can, logs the error in non-volatile memory (see previous bullet), corrects the condition, and resumes execution of the interrupted program. Please note that as of this writing, none of the error conditions that result in a machine check exception are correctable.

Machine Check Architecture in the Pentium Processor

The Pentium processor included a very limited implementation of the Machine Check Architecture. This consisted of:

- The 64-bit Machine Check Address register, or **MCAR**, implemented as a MSR. Latches the address related to a bus cycle where a parity error is detected on a read and PEN# is asserted by the external logic. Also latches the address related to a bus cycle that is aborted by the assertion of the BUSCHK# signal to the processor.

- The 64-bit Machine Check Type register, or **MCTR**, implemented as a MSR. Latches the bus cycle type when a parity error is detected on a read and PEN# is asserted by the external logic. Also latches the bus cycle type that is aborted by the assertion of the BUSCHK# signal to the processor.

- The **Machine Check exception** (exception 18d). The processor calls the Machine Check handler if a read parity error or a BUSCHK# is detected during a bus cycle and the Machine Check exception has been enabled by CR4[MCE] = 1.

- The Machine Check exception enable bit, **CR4[MCE]** (see Figure 24-1 on page 479). When set, enables the processor to generate a Machine Check exception (exception 18d) when a read parity error or a BUSCHK# is detected during a bus cycle.

- **PEN#** (parity enable) input signal. When the processor reads one or more bytes over the data bus and detects a parity error, it asserts its PERR# output. If the chipset decides that a read from the target address should have yielded correct parity information, it asserts PEN# back to the processor. The processor latches the address and bus cycle type into the MCAR and MCTR, respectively, and, if enabled to do so (CR4[MCE] = 1), also generates a Machine Check exception.

* **BUSCHK#** (bus check) input signal. If the chipset generates BUSCHK# in response to a bus cycle generated by the processor, the processor latches the address and bus cycle type into the MCAR and MCTR, respectively, and, if enabled to do so (CR4[MCE] = 1), also generates a Machine Check exception.

Figure 24-1: CR4

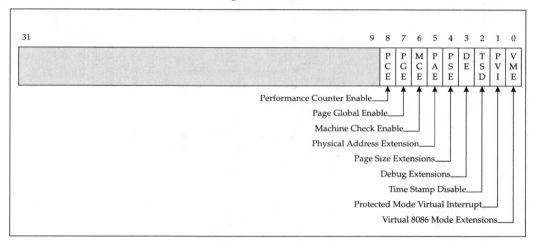

Testing for Machine Check Support

The programmer may determine if a processor supports the Machine Check exception and the Machine Check Architecture register set by executing the CPUID instruction with a request for feature support information. The information illustrated in Figure 24-2 on page 480 is returned. EDX[7] = 1 indicates that the Machine Check exception is supported, and EDX[14] = 1 indicates that the Machine Check Architecture register set is supported.

Figure 24-2: Feature Support Information Returned by CPUID

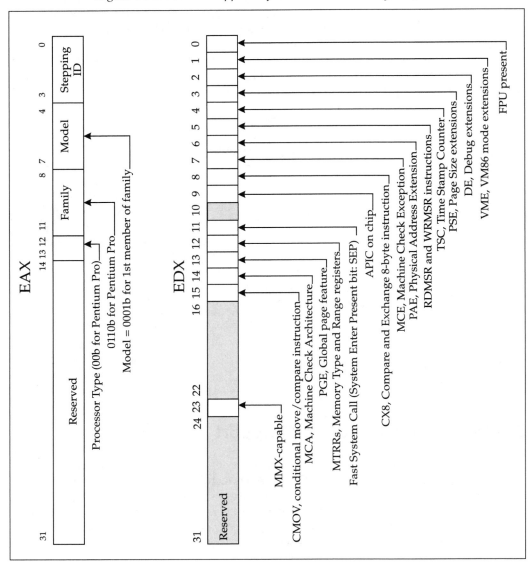

Chapter 24: Machine Check Architecture

Machine Check Exception

The Machine Check exception is enabled by setting CR4[MCE] = 1. It uses entry 18d in the interrupt descriptor table (IDT). If it is disabled and a hardware failure occurs that would ordinarily result in the generation of a Machine Check exception, the processor generates the special transaction to broadcast the shutdown message and then enters the shutdown state (in other words, it freezes).

The Machine Check exception is an abort class exception. This means that the program that was interrupted by the exception may not be reliably resumed by executing an IRET instruction at the end of the Machine Check exception handler.

Machine Check Architecture Register Set

The Machine Check Architecture (MCA) register set is implemented as a set of MSRs organized as follows:

- One set of global registers is related to all conditions that may cause a Machine Check exception.
- A separate bank of error logging registers is associated with each of the processor's units (or with a group of units). As an example, one register bank may be associated with the external bus unit, while another might be associated with the processor's caches).

The number of register banks implemented and the processor unit(s) that each bank is associated with is processor implementation-specific. As an example, the current implementation of the Pentium Pro processor implements five registers banks (pictured in Figure 24-3 on page 482). Intel does not identify the processor unit(s) that each of these banks is associated with. This bothered the author at first, until it was realized that the error code types reported in each bank reveals this information (because information embedded within the error code field identifies the guilty party).

Figure 24-3: Pentium Pro Machine Check Architecture Registers

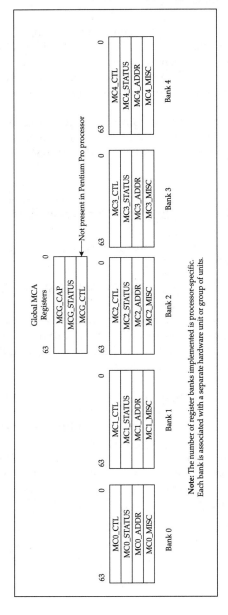

Chapter 24: Machine Check Architecture

Composition of Global Register Set

The global register set consists of the following registers:

- **MCG_CAP register.** Machine Check Global Count and Present register.
- **MCG_STATUS register.** Machine Check Global Status register.
- **MCG_CTL register.** Machine Check Global Control register.

The sections that follow describe each of these registers.

MCG_CAP Register

The Machine Check Global Count and Present register (pictured in Figure 24-4 on page 483) is a read-only register that identifies:

- the number of register banks implemented (minus one). As an example, the value 04h is returned for the current versions of the Pentium Pro processor, indicating that it implements banks 0 through 4.
- whether or not the MCG_CTL register is implemented (it is not implemented in the current versions of the Pentium Pro processor).

Figure 24-4: MCG_CAP (Global Count and Present) Register

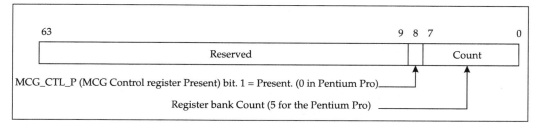

MCG_STATUS Register

The Machine Check Global Status register (pictured in Figure 24-5 on page 484) indicates the basic state of the processor after a Machine Check exception has occurred. The conditions reported are:

- The **RIPV** (**Restart Instruction Pointer Valid**) bit indicates whether or not the program interrupted by the exception can be reliably resumed at the instruction whose pointer was pushed onto the stack when the exception occurred. Most conditions that result in a Machine Check exception preclude the resumption of the interrupted program.

- The **EIPV** (**Error Instruction Pointer Valid**) bit indicates whether the instruction whose pointer was pushed onto the stack when the exception occurred is directly associated with the exception. As an example, a transaction generated on the external bus as a result of the execution of an IO read instruction (IN) might result in a Machine Check (if there's a serious problem detected during the transaction). In this case, the address of the IN instruction might be pushed onto the stack.
- The **MCIP** (Machine Check In Progress) bit is set to one by the processor when a Machine Check exception occurs. If another Machine Check occurs while this bit is still set (in other words, the Machine Check handler has not executed to the point where the programmer has cleared the MCIP bit), the processor generates a special transaction to broadcast the shutdown message and then enters the shutdown state.

Figure 24-5: MCG_STATUS Register

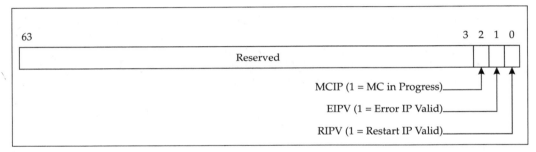

MCG_CTL Register

The Machine Check Global Control register may or may not be implemented in a processor (it's *not implemented in the current versions of the Pentium Pro processor*). Its presence (or absence) is indicated via the MCG_CTL_P bit in the MCG_CAP register (see Figure 24-4 on page 483). The current state of the 64-bits in the MCG_CTL register globally enables or disables the processor's ability to generate a machine check exception for all types of hardware failure conditions. The current specification only supports writing all ones or all zeros to this register—in other words, mass enable or disable of all errors. The control register associated with each register bank controls the generation of the machine check exception for errors related to the processor unit(s) covered by the respective bank. Future versions of x86 processors may permit selective enabling of machine check exception generation for various types of errors and disabling of others.

Chapter 24: Machine Check Architecture

Composition of Each Register Bank

General

Each of the Machine Check Architecture register banks consists of all or a subset of the following registers (where i = the number of the register bank):

- **MCi_CTL**. Control register for error logging register bank i. Each of the 64 bits in this register, referred to as EE[63:0], are used to selectively enable/disable the generation of the machine check exception for a specific error condition related to the processor unit(s) associated with register bank i. Setting a bit enables the error reporting for a specific error condition, while clearing the bit disables it. Currently, Intel does not document the error condition related to each bit and also specifies that the programmer is only permitted to write all zeros or all ones into this register. In other words, there are only two choices: enable all errors for the bank or disable all of them.
- **MCi_STATUS**. Status register for error logging register bank i. When register bank i logs an error associated with its respective processor unit(s), the error is logged in this register. For a detailed description of the MCi_STATUS register, refer to "MCi_STATUS Register" on page 486.
- **MCi_ADDR**. See Figure 24-6 on page 486. Address register for error logging register bank i. If the MCi_STATUS[ADDRV] (address valid) bit is set to one, this register contains the address of the instruction or the data item that is related to the error. If MCi_STATUS[ADDRV] bit is cleared to zero, there is no address recorded in this register and the register must not be read from. The address returned is either the 32-bit virtual, 32-bit linear, or 36-bit physical address, depending on the type of error encountered. *The author does not know what Intel means by "32-bit virtual." The term "virtual" is not used in this way anywhere else in the three-volume set of Intel Pentium Pro data books.*
- **MCi_MISC**. Miscellaneous information register for error logging register bank i. If the MCi_STATUS[MISCV] bit is set to one, this register contains additional information related to the error code. *This register is not implemented in any of the Pentium Pro processor's register banks. Do not read this register if it's not present in the processor.*

Figure 24-6: MCi_ADDR Register

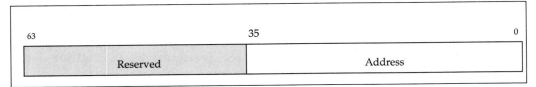

MC*i*_STATUS Register

As described in the previous section, the MC*i*_STATUS register is used to record an error code related to the unit(s) associated with this error logging register bank. The register is pictured in Figure 24-7 on page 486 and the bit fields are described in Table 24-1 on page 487. Prior to examining the other bits fields within the register, the programmer should first consult the MC*i*_STATUS[VAL] bit (1 = error logged) to determine whether or not the register has logged a valid error.

Figure 24-7: MCi_STATUS Register for Error Logging Bank i

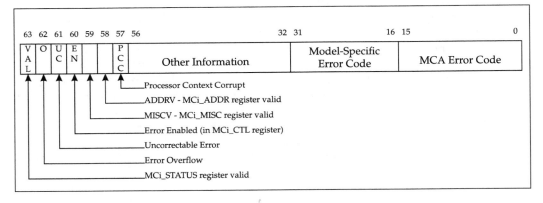

Table 24-1: MCi_STATUS Register Bit Assignment

Bit Field Name	Description
VAL	**Valid bit**. This bit is set to one when an error is logged in the MCi_STATUS register for error logging bank *i*. If another error code has been logged previously (VAL was already set to 1), the processor uses the rules stated in the description of the Overflow bit (see next row) in deciding whether or not to overwrite the previously-logged error if another error is detected before the programmer clear this register. The programmer is responsible for clearing this bit.
O	**Overflow bit**. When set, indicates that another Machine Check error occurred while a previously-logged error was still present in the status register. The processor sets this bit, but software is responsible for clearing it. The processor uses the following criteria in deciding whether or not to overwrite the previously-logged error with the new one: • **Enabled errors** (respective MCi_CTL EE bit = 1) **overwrite disabled errors** (respective MCi_CTL EE bit = 0). In other words, the assumption is made that the programmer cares more about error conditions that the programmer had previously-enabled than those that the programmer had left disabled. • **Uncorrected errors overwrite corrected errors**. Errors that the processor cannot automatically correct are consider more important than those that were detected and automatically corrected. • A **second uncorrected error does not overwrite a previously-logged uncorrected error**. Uncorrected errors are very important and will not be discarded.
UC	**Uncorrected**. When set, indicates that the processor did not correct or wasn't able to correct the error. When clear, the processor was able to clear the error condition (e.g., a corrected ECC error when reading from an internal cache).
EN	**Enabled**. When set, indicates that the programmer had enabled reporting of the error condition by setting the respective bit in the error logging bank's MCi_CTL register.

Table 24-1: MCi_STATUS Register Bit Assignment (Continued)

Bit Field Name	Description
MISCV	**MCi_MISC register valid**. When set, the MCi_MISC register contains additional information related to the error condition. When clear, it does not.
ADDRV	**MCi_ADDR register valid**. When set, the MCi_ADDR register contains an address related to the error condition. When clear, it does not.
PCC	**Processor Context Corrupt**. When set, indicates that the error left the processor in a state where it would be dangerous to resume execution of the program that was interrupted by the Machine Check exception. When clear, the error did not affect the processor's ability to reliably resume execution of the interrupted program.
Other Information	The meaning of the bits within this field is processor implementation-specific and aren't defined by the Machine Check Architecture specification. Only software that is written for a specific processor implementation can properly interpret this field.
Model Specific Error Code	As the name implies, these error codes are processor model-specific and may differ among various x86 processors. Different processors may use different model-specific error codes for the same condition.
MCA Error Code	**Machine Check Architecture-defined error code**. These error codes are strictly defined by the specification and are guaranteed to be consistent across all future x86 processors that implement the Machine Check Architecture. For a detailed description of these error codes, refer to "Machine Check Architecture Error Format" on page 491.

MSR Addresses of the Machine Check Registers

The Machine Check registers are located at the MSR addresses indicated in Table 24-2 on page 489.

Table 24-2: MSR Addresses of the Machine Check Registers

Machine Check Register	MSR Address	Notes
MCG_CAP	179h, 377d	Intel doesn't say that these addresses will remain the same for all x86 processors, but it is the author's opinion that they will (for consistency).
MCG_STATUS	17Ah, 378d	
MCG_CTL	17Bh, 379d	
MC0_CTL	400h, 1024d	This register is aliased to the EBL_CR_POWERON MSR (see Table 3-3 on page 45). Intel states that, for this reason, only platform-specific software (typically, the BIOS) should write to this register.
MC0_STATUS	401h, 1025d	
MC0_ADDR	402h, 1026d	
MC0_MISC	403h, 1027d	Not implemented in current versions of the processor.
MC1_CTL	404h, 1028d	
MC1_STATUS	405h, 1029d	
MC1_ADDR	406h, 1030d	
MC1_MISC	407h, 1031d	Not implemented in current versions of the processor.
MC2_CTL	408h, 1032d	
MC2_STATUS	409h, 1033d	
MC2_ADDR	40Ah, 1034d	
MC2_MISC	40Bh, 1035d	Not implemented in current versions of the processor.

Table 24-2: MSR Addresses of the Machine Check Registers (Continued)

Machine Check Register	MSR Address	Notes
MC3_CTL	40Ch, 1036d	Please note that the Intel documentation shows addresses 410h through 413h for bank 3 and 40Ch through 40Fh for bank 4. The author has reversed these because he believes that the banks are implemented in sequential address order.
MC3_STATUS	40Dh, 1037d	
MC3_ADDR	40Eh, 1038d	
MC3_MISC	40Fh, 1039d	Not implemented in current versions of the processor.
MC4_CTL	410h, 1040d	See note for bank 3.
MC4_STATUS	411h, 1041d	
MC4_ADDR	412h, 1042d	
MC4_MISC	413h, 1043d	Not implemented in current versions of the processor.

Initialization of Register Set

Intel recommends that the following code sequence be used to initialize the Machine Check Architecture registers to a clean state at startup time:

```
Execute CPUID instruction to obtain features support information
Test EDX[14] and EDX[7] to determine if Machine Check exception and register set implemented
    IF processor supports Machine Check exception then
        IF processor supports Machine Check Architecture register set
            IF MCG_CAP[MCG_CTL_P] = 1 (indicating that MCG_CTL present)
                Set MCG_CTL register to all ones (enable all error reporting features)
            Set variable COUNT = MCG_CAP[COUNT] field
            FOR i = 1 through COUNT DO (start at bank 1; don't write to EBL_CR_POWERON)
                Set MCi_CTL register to all ones (enable all errors for bank i)
            For i = 0 through COUNT DO
                Clear MCi_STATUS to all zeros (clear any errors)
        Set CR4[MCE] = 1 (enable Machine Check exception)
```

Chapter 24: Machine Check Architecture

Machine Check Architecture Error Format

As illustrated in Figure 24-8 on page 491, the lower 16-bits of the MC*i*_STATUS register contains the error code defined by the Machine Check Architecture specification, guaranteed to be consistent across all future x86 processors that implement the Machine Check Architecture registers. These error codes have two forms:

- **Simple error codes**. These error codes are generic in nature and are described in the section entitled "Simple Error Codes" on page 491.
- **Compound error codes**. These error codes describe errors related to the TLBs, memory, caches, the external bus, and the buses that interconnect processor units. They are described in the section entitled "Compound Error Codes" on page 492.

Figure 24-8: MCi_STATUS Register Bit Assignment

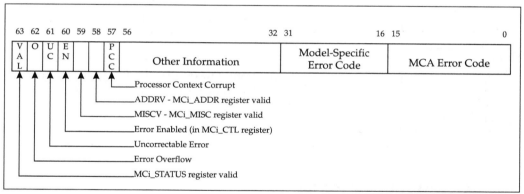

Simple Error Codes

The simple error codes defined by the architecture specification are listed in Table 24-3 on page 492.

Table 24-3: Simple Error Codes

Error	Error Value	Description
No error	0000h	No error has been logged in this register bank.
Unclassified	0001h	This error has not been classified into the architecture-defined error classes.
Microcode ROM Parity error	0002h	Intel does not specify which microcode ROM. It could be either the ROM that contains the BIST (built-in self-test) code or the ROM that contains the micro-op instructions. In either case, this is a very serious error.
External error	0003h	This processor detected BINIT# asserted by another processor, causing this processor to generate a Machine Check exception.
FRC error	0004h	The slave processor of an FRC processor pair observed an error in a transaction performed by the master processor.
Internal unclassified	0000 01xx xxxx xxxxb	Internal unclassified errors.

Compound Error Codes

As stated earlier, these error codes describe errors related to the TLBs, memory, caches, the external bus, and the buses that interconnect processor units. They take one of the three forms listed in Table 24-4 on page 493. As shown in this table, each error code form contains two or more named bit fields. Table 24-5 on page 493 through Table 24-8 on page 494 define the meaning of these bit fields.

The standard error code name defined by the architecture specification is constructed by substituting the literal text selected by the value of the respective bit field for the brace-delineated bit field within the template. The text within the template that is not enclosed in braces (including the underscore) is used as is (i.e., no substitution). As an example, when applied to the appropriate template

Chapter 24: Machine Check Architecture

from Table 24-4 on page 493, the error code value of 0000 0001 0001 0001b yields the error code name ICACHEL1_RD_ERR, indicating a level 1 instruction cache read error.

Table 24-4: Forms of Compound Error Codes

Error Type	Form (in binary)	Template
TLB errors	0000 0000 0001 TTLL	{TT}TLB{LL}_ERR
Memory hierarchy errors	0000 0001 RRRR TTLL	{TT}CACHE{LL}_{RRRR}_ERR
Bus and interconnect errors	0000 1PPT RRRR IILL	BUS{LL}_{PP}_{RRRR}_{II}_{T}_ERR Please note that the definition in the Intel manual actually reads: BUS{LL}_{PP}_{RRRR}_{II}_{TIMEOUT,}ERR but the author thinks this is incorrect and should be shown as stated above.

Table 24-5: Transaction Type Sub-Field (TT)

Transaction Type	Literal Text	Binary Value
Instruction	I	00b
Data	D	01b
Generic	G	10b

Table 24-6: Memory Hierarchy Sub-Field (LL)

Hierarchy Level	Literal Text	Binary Value
Level 0	L0	00b
Level 1	L1	01b
Level 2	L2	10b
Generic	LG	11b

Table 24-7: Request Sub-Field (RRRR)

Request Type	Literal Text	Binary Value
Generic error	ERR	0000b
Generic read	RD	0001b
Generic write	WR	0010b
Data read	DRD	0011b
Data write	DWR	0100b
Instruction fetch	IRD	0101b
Prefetch	PREFETCH	0110b
Eviction	EVICT	0111b
Snoop	SNOOP	1000b

Table 24-8: Definition of the PP, T, and II Fields

Sub-Field	Transaction	Literal Text	Binary Value
PP (Participation)	Local processor originated request	SRC	00b
	Local processor responded to request	RES	01b
	Local processor observed error as 3rd party	OBS	10b
	Generic		11b
T (Timeout)	Request timed out	TIMOUT	1
	Request did not time out		0

Table 24-8: Definition of the PP, T, and II Fields (Continued)

Sub-Field	Transaction	Literal Text	Binary Value
II (Memory or IO)	Memory access	M	00b
	Reserved		01b
	IO access	IO	10b
	Other transaction		11b

External Bus Error Interpretation

Table 24-9 on page 495 provides detailed information on the content of the architecture-defined error code, model-specific error code, and other information fields of the MC*i*_STATUS register (see Figure 24-7 on page 486) for an external bus-related error.

Table 24-9: MCi_STATUS Breakdown for Bus-related Errors

Bit	Field	Description
1:0	MCA Error Code	Undefined
3:2	"	Bit 2 = 1, then special transaction. Bit 3 = 1, then special transaction or IO transaction.
7:4	"	00WR, where W = 1 indicates write and R = 1 indicates read
9:8	"	Undefined
10	"	= 0 for all EBL (external bus logic) errors. = 1 for internal watchdog timer timeout. In this case, all other bits in the MCA error field are cleared to 0. A watchdog timer timeout only occurs if BINIT# driver enabled.
11	"	= 1 for EBL errors. = 0 for internal watchdog timer timeout.
15:12	"	Reserved
18:16	Model-Specific Error Code	Reserved

Table 24-9: MCi_STATUS Breakdown for Bus-related Errors (Continued)

Bit	Field	Description
24:19	"	Although Intel doesn't define the following terms, the author believes that they have the following meaning: • **BQ**= Bus Queue (IOQ) • **DCU** = Data Cache Unit • **IFU** = Instruction Fetch Unit. Where possible, the author has speculated on the meaning of the following error code fields. • 000000 = **BQ_DCU_READ_TYPE** error. Attempted read transaction. • 000010 = **BQ_IFU_DEMAND_TYPE** error. Attempted read line transaction generated by the Instruction Fetch Unit due to a miss on the instruction cache. • 000011 = **BQ_IFU_DEMAND_NC_TYPE** error. Attempted single-quadword read from non-cacheable memory generated by the instruction fetcher. • 000100 = **BQ_DCU_RFO_TYPE** error. Request For Ownership stands for read and invalidate transaction. • 000101 = **BQ_DCU_RFO_LOCK_TYPE** error. Locked read and invalidate transaction. • 000110 = **BQ_DCU_ITOM_TYPE** error. Attempted read with intent to modify transaction (i.e., read and invalidate). May differ from the previous two entries by virtue of being for 0 bytes. • 001000 = **BQ_DCU_WB_TYPE** error. Attempted transaction to write a modified line back to memory. • 001010 = **BQ_DCU_WCEVICT_TYPE** error. Attempted transaction to write the contents of one of the processor's write-combining buffers back to memory. In this case, all 32 bytes don't have to be written, so performed as a series of single-quadword transfers. • 001011 = **BQ_WCLINE_TYPE** error. Attempted write line transaction to write the full 32 bytes in a write-combining buffer to memory. • 001100 = **BQ_DCU_BTM_TYPE** error. Branch Trace Message error. • 001101 = **BQ_DCU_INTACK_TYPE** error. Attempted Interrupt Acknowledge transaction. • 001110 = **BQ_DCU_INVALL2_TYPE** error. Attempted to invalidate one or more entries in the L2 cache. • 001111 = **BQ_DCU_FLUSHL2_TYPE** error. Attempted to flush the L2 cache. • 010000 = **BQ_DCU_PART_RD_TYPE** error. Attempted to read a quadword (or a subset of a quadword). • 010010 = **BQ_DCU_PART_WR_TYPE** error. Attempted to write a quadword (or a subset of a quadword). • 010100 = **BQ_DCU_SPEC_CYC_TYPE** error. Attempted Special Transaction. • 011000 = **BQ_DCU_IO_RD_TYPE** error. Attempted IO read. • 011001 = **BQ_DCU_IO_WR_TYPE** error. Attempted IO write. • 011100 = **BQ_DCU_LOCK_RD_TYPE** error. Attempted locked memory read. • 011101 = **BQ_DCU_LOCK_WR_TYPE** error. Attempted locked memory write. • 011110 = **BQ_DCU_SPLOCK_RD_TYPE** error. Attempted locked memory read with Split Lock asserted.
27:25	"	• 000 = **BQ_ERR_HARD_TYPE** error. Transaction resulted in hard failure. • 001 = **BQ_ERR_DOUBLE_TYPE** error. ECC double-bit error detected on data read. • 010 = **BQ_ERR_AERR2_TYPE** error. Address parity error on 1st and 2nd transaction attempt. • 100 = **BQ_ERR_SINGLE_TYPE** error. ECC single-bit failure. • 101 = **BQ_ERR_AERR1_TYPE** error. Address parity error on 1st transaction attempt.
28	"	1 = FRCERR active.

Table 24-9: MCi_STATUS Breakdown for Bus-related Errors (Continued)

Bit	Field	Description
29	"	1 = BERR# asserted by this processor.
30	"	1 = BINIT# asserted by this processor.
31	"	Reserved
34:32	Other Info	Reserved
35	"	BINIT# sampled asserted.
36	"	Processor received a parity error on a response received from another agent.
37	"	Processor received a hard fail response from another agent.
38	"	**ROB timeout**. No micro-op has been retired for a pre-determined amount of time. Occurs when the 15-bit ROB Timeout Counter has a carry out of its high-order bit. The timer is cleared under the following circumstances: • When a micro-op retires. • When an exception is detected. • When RESET# is asserted. • When a ROB BINIT occurs. Each time that the 8-bit PIC timer has a carry, the ROB Timeout Counter is incremented by one. The PIC timer divides the bus clock by 128.
41:39	"	Reserved
42	"	This processor initiated a transaction that received a Hard Fail response.
43	"	The processor has experienced a failure that caused it to assert IERR#.
44	"	This processor initiated a transaction that received an AERR# during the request phase. Upon retrying the transaction, it again received an AERR# in the request phase.
45	"	Uncorrectable ECC error. Syndrome field is in bits 54:47.
46	"	Correctable ECC error. Syndrome field is in bits 54:47.
54:47	"	Contains the 8-bit ECC syndrome only if a correctable or uncorrectable ECC error occurred and there wasn't already a previous valid ECC syndrome in this field (indicated by bit 45 = 1). After processing an ECC error, the software must clear bit 45 to permit the logging of future ECC syndromes.
56:55	"	Reserved

25 *Performance Monitoring and Timestamp*

The Previous Chapter

The previous chapter described the error logging and reporting Machine Check Architecture first introduced in the Pentium processor and greatly expanded in the Pentium Pro processor. The Machine Check Architecture defines an exception (the Machine Check exception) used to report hardware-related problems and a register set used to log both recoverable and unrecoverable errors.

This Chapter

This chapter describes the performance monitoring and time stamp counter facilities incorporated in the Pentium Pro processor. It should be noted that these facilities are also implemented in the Pentium processor, but Intel did not document them until the release of the Pentium Pro processor.

The Next Chapter

The next chapter provides an introduction to the MMX instruction set. It should be noted that, as of this writing, MMX is not available on the Pentium Pro processor. This chapter has been included because it is well known that Intel intends to proliferate MMX throughout its processor product lines, including future versions of the Pentium Pro processor.

Time Stamp Counter Facility

Time Stamp Counter (TSC) Definition

Basically, the Time Stamp Counter (TSC) is a very accurate elapsed time measurement tool. It is a 64-bit counter that counts the number of processor clock cycles that have occurred since reset was removed (or since the programmer cleared the counter). As an example, on a processor whose internal clock speed is 200MHz, the TSC has a resolution of 5ns.

The TSC is incremented even during periods when the processor has halted or when the STPCLK# input has been asserted, causing the processor to disable the clocking of its internal units. The TSC, the local APIC, and the external bus interface still receive the clock.

When the timer reaches a count of all ones, it wraps around to all zeros and continues counting. No interrupt is generated as a result of the wraparound. Intel guarantees that the minimum time that it takes the TSC to go from a count of zero to a count of all ones will never (on future x86 processors) be less than 10 years. For the Pentium and Pentium Pro processors, the wraparound period will take several thousands of years (in other words, the current processors are pretty darn slow compared to their future cousins).

Detecting Presence of the TSC

A processor's support for the TSC counter is detected by executing the CPUID instruction (see "CPUID Instruction Enhanced" on page 409) with a request for the feature support information. If EDX[4] = 1, the processor supports the TSC.

Accessing the Time Stamp Counter

Reading the TSC Using RDTSC Instruction

The programmer may read the TSC using the RDTSC (read TSC) instruction. For more information, refer to "Read Time Stamp Counter (RDTSC)" on page 420. Please note that the RDTSC is not serializing and may therefore not yield an accurate elapsed time. For more information, refer to "RDTSC Doesn't Serialize" on page 421.

Reading the TSC Using RDMSR Instruction

On the Pentium and the Pentium Pro processors, the TSC may also be read using the RDMSR instruction (see "Accessing MSRs" on page 421). The MSR address of the TSC is 10h (16d). Note that the ability to read the TSC using the RDMSR instruction is processor-specific and may not be implemented in future processors.

Writing to the TSC

The TSC can be written to using the WRMSR instruction (see "Accessing MSRs" on page 421). The MSR address of the TSC is 10h (16d). Only the lower 32-bits of the 64-bit TSC can be written to, however. All zeros are written throughout the upper 32-bits of the TSC when the lower half of the register is written to.

Performance Monitoring Facility

Purpose of the Performance Monitoring Facility

The performance monitoring facility is invaluable when tuning, or profiling, program code to yield the best possible performance. It permits the programmer to obtain an accurate profile of how efficiently the processor and memory are utilized by a program. The Pentium and Pentium Pro processors each include two performance monitoring counters that can be programmed independently of each other to take one of two types of measurements:

*   measure the duration of a specific event type.
*   measure the number of occurrences of a specific event type.

The event types that can be measured are processor-dependent and include a large number of types such as cache hits, cache misses, TLB hits and misses, etc.

Performance Monitoring Registers

The performance monitoring facility is implemented using **four MSRs**:

*   The performance event select MSRs, **PerfEvtSel0 and PerfEvtSel1**. PerfEvtSel0 is used to control performance counter 0 (PerfCtr0), while PerfEvtSel1 is used to control performance counter 1 (PerfCtr1).
*   The performance counter MSRs, **PerfCtr0 and PerfCtr1**.

These registers are described in the sections that follow.

PerfEvtSel0 and PerfEvtSel1 MSRs

The performance event select registers are used to set up and enable or disable performance counters 0 and 1. They both have the format illustrated in Figure 25-1 on page 503. Table 25-1 on page 502 provides a detailed description of each bit field.

Table 25-1: PerfEvtSel0 and PerfEvtSel1 MSR Bit Assignment

Field Name	Description
Counter Mask	When cleared to zero and the respective event counter has been enabled, the counter increments once for each event of the selected type. When set to a non-zero value, the value is used as a threshold trigger point. When the number of events of the specified type is >= this value, the event counter is incremented by one.
INV	**Invert bit**. When set, the processor inverts the result of the counter mask comparison so that less than (i.e., <) comparisons can be made.
EN	**Enable bit**. This bit is only implemented in PerfEvtSel0. When it is set to one, both counters are enabled. When cleared to zero, both counters are disabled.
INT	**Interrupt Enable bit**. When set to one, the local APIC is enabled to generate an interrupt when the respective counter overflows.
PC	**Pin Control bit**. Assuming that the PC bit = 0, the processor toggles the PBn (where n = counter number) output pin each time that the respective counter increments. When the PC bit = 1, the processor toggles the PBn output pin when the respective counter overflows. A toggle of the PBn output pin is defined as its assertion for two BCLKs followed by its deassertion.
E	**Edge Detect bit**. When set, enables the detection of deasserted-to-asserted events of any condition that can be specified by the other fields. Note that it cannot recognize back-to-back assertions.

Table 25-1: PerfEvtSel0 and PerfEvtSel1 MSR Bit Assignment (Continued)

Field Name	Description
OS	**Operating System bit.** **OS = 1 and USR = 0**—the respective counter only counts events that occur while the processor is executing privilege level 0 code. **OS and USR = 1**—the respective counter counts events that occur while the processor is executing code at any privilege level. **OS = 0 and USR = 1**—the respective counter only counts events that occur while the processor is executing privilege level 1, 2, or 3 code.
USR	**User bit.** See the description of the OS bit.
Unit Mask	The unit mask field usage is event-specific and further qualifies the event type.
Event Select	This field is used to select the type of event to be monitored.

Figure 25-1: PerfEvtSel0 and PerfEvtSel1 MSR Bit Assignment

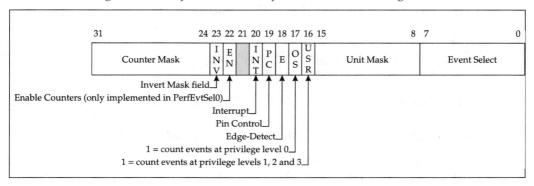

PerfCtr0 and PerfCtr1

Each of the performance counters is 40-bits wide and is independently-controlled by its respective PerfEvtSel register. For a detailed description of how to read or write the counter registers, refer to the section entitled "Accessing the PerfCtr MSRs" on page 504.

Accessing the Performance Monitoring Registers

Accessing the PerfEvtSel MSRs

The PerfEvtSel MSRs are accessed using the RDMSR and WRMSR instructions. These instructions can only be executed successfully (i.e., without causing a GP exception) while the processor is executing a privilege level 0 program or when executing in real mode. These two registers are implemented at the following MSR addresses:

- PerfEvtSel0 MSR is located at MSR address 186h (390d).
- PerfEvtSel1 MSR is located at MSR address 187h (391d).

Accessing the PerfCtr MSRs

Accessing Using RDPMC Instruction. The RDPMC (read performance counter) instruction, governed by the state of CR4[PCE], can be used to read the contents of the specified counter:

- When CR4[PCE] = 0, the RDPMC instruction can only be successfully executed (without causing a GP exception) by programs executing at privilege level 0.
- When CR4[PCE] = 1, the RDPMC instruction can successfully executed by programs executing at any privilege level.

Accessing Using RDMSR/WRMSR Instructions. The PerfCtr MSRs can be read and written directly using the RDMSR and WRMSR instructions (at privilege level 0). They are implemented at the following MSR addresses:

- PerfCtr0 is located at MSR address C1h (193d).
- PerfCtr1 is located at MSR address C2h (194d).

The 40-bit performance counters can be written to using the WRMSR instruction. However, the programmer can only directly write to the lower 32 bits of the target counter. The high-order bit is duplicated in the high-order eight bits of the counter. This allows the programmer to initialize the counters with both positive (bit 31 = 0) and negative (bit 31 = 1) values.

Chapter 25: Performance Monitoring and Timestamp

Event Types

For a detailed description of each event type, refer to appendix B in the Intel data book entitled *Pentium Pro Family Developer's Manual, Volume 3: Operating System Writer's Guide*.

Starting and Stopping the Counters

Starting the Counters

The performance counters are started as follows:

1. write valid setup information into the respective PerfEvtSel register using the WRMSR instruction.
2. the counter begins counting after the successful execution of a WRMSR instruction that sets the EN (enable counters) bit in the PerfEvtSel0 MSR.

Stopping the Counters

Both counters may be stopped by:

- clearing the EN (enable counters) bit in the PerfEvtSel0 MSR, or
- clearing all bits in the PerfEvtSel MSRs.

Just counter 1 may be stopped by writing all zeros to the PerfEvtSel1 MSR.

Performance Monitoring Interrupt on Overflow

The following steps must be taken when enabling a counter to generate an interrupt on counter overflow:

- A counter is enabled to generate an interrupt when the counter overflows by setting the INT bit in its respective PerfEvtSel MSR to one.
- The programmer must set up the local APIC's PCINT (performance counter interrupt) entry in its LVT (local vector table). For more information, refer to "Added APIC Functionality" on page 464.
- The programmer initializes the IDT (interrupt descriptor table) entry specified in the local APIC's PCINT LVT entry to point to the performance counter overflow interrupt handler routine.

26 *MMX: Matrix Math Extensions*

The Previous Chapter

The previous chapter described the performance monitoring and time stamp counter facilities incorporated in the Pentium Pro processor. It should be noted that these facilities are also implemented in the Pentium processor, but Intel did not document them until the release of the Pentium Pro processor.

This Chapter

This chapter concludes the software part of the book. It provides an introduction to the MMX instruction set. It should be noted that MMX is not available on the Pentium Pro processor. This chapter is included because it is well known that Intel intends to proliferate MMX throughout its future processor product lines, and MMX is already supported on the Pentium and Pentium II processors. For a description of the Pentium II processor, refer to the chapter entitled "Pentium II Processor" on page 379.

Please Note

This chapter is not intended to be a comprehensive reference to the MMX instruction set. Rather, it is intended to serve as a brief introduction to the concept of MMX. Intel has a comprehensive and clearly written MMX document set available on their web site.

Problems Addressed by MMX

Problem: Math on Packed Bytes/Words/Dwords

Consider the following example scenario—the programmer must add two video images in memory together to yield a resultant video image. In the example, each pixel of each of the images is represented by a separate byte in memory. In order to perform the calculation, the programmer must take the following steps:

1. Read the first byte from the first image in memory.
2. Perform the calculation with the first byte in the second image in memory.
3. Store the resultant byte into the first byte of the area of memory that will contain the resultant image.
4. Repeat steps 1 through 3 until the third image has been produced.

If it is assumed that the video subsystem is in 1024 x 768 mode, each screen image consists of 786432 pixels, or bytes. That's how many times steps 1 through 3 would have to be repeated. This will consume a tremendous amount of the processor's clock cycles and generates 786432 x 2 memory reads (one to read 1st byte from 1st image and one to get 1st byte from the 2nd image) and 786432 memory writes to update the 3rd image.

Solution: MMX Matrix Math/Logical Operations

The MMX extensions include a set of 8 MMX registers, each 64-bits wide. Using the appropriate MMX instructions and the MMX register set, the operation described in the previous section could be accomplished as follows (see Figure 26-1 on page 509):

1. Read the 1st 8 bytes from the 1st image in memory into one of the MMX registers. The MMX register then contains a packed array (or matrix) of 8 pixel bytes).
2. Read the 1st 8 bytes from the 2nd image in memory into another of the MMX registers. The MMX register then contains a packed array (or matrix) of 8 pixel bytes).
3. Execute a matrix instruction that adds the two registers together, treating bytes in the same relative position in the two MMX registers as a separate add operation. In other words, the MMX add packed-bytes instruction uses

8 separate adders to add the two registers together. The bytes that result from the 8 independent adds are stored in their respective positions in the target MMX register.

4. Perform 1 write to write the 8 packed bytes into the first 8 locations of the third image in memory.
5. Repeat steps 1 through 4 until the third image has been produced.

This operation results in only 12.5% of the activity that was generated using non-MMX operations. The MMX instruction set includes a separate version of each instruction to perform math and logical operations on packed bytes, packed words, packed dwords, or quadwords (unpacked data). Assuming the packed byte example, the processor can conclude the task 8 times more rapidly than before and generate only 12.5% of the traffic. The processor is more available to handle other tasks.

Figure 26-1: Example MMX Packed-Byte Add

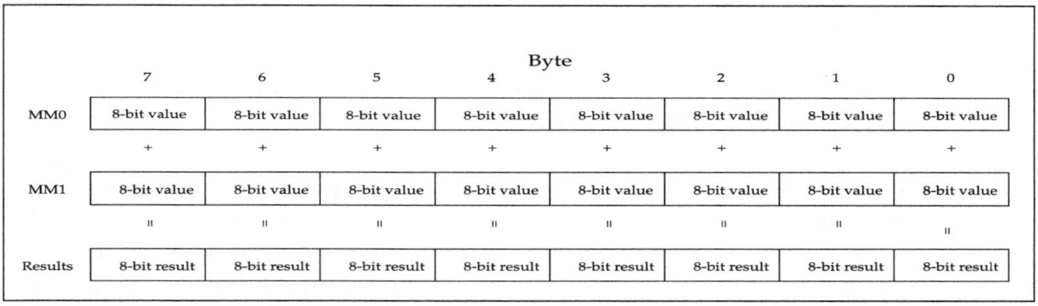

Problem: Data not Packed

The previous example assumed that the data to be operated upon already resided in memory in packed byte, word, or dword form. This is not always the case and it requires a lot of software overhead to assemble unpacked data in memory into packed form in an MMX register in preparation for a matrix math or logical operation. Likewise, after the matrix operation has been completed, the reverse operation must be performed—store the data from the MMX register back into memory in its original, unpacked form.

Solution: MMX Pack and Unpack Instructions

The MMX instruction set includes instructions that read unpacked data from memory and pack it into an MMX register. It also includes instructions that write packed data in an MMX register back to memory in unpacked form.

Problem: Math Overflows/Underflows

In the previous example, two video images were added together to produce a third, resultant image. The example, however, ignored the possibility of overflows when each pair of pixel bytes were added together. Normally, when performing calculations on pixel information, software must handle the resultant overflow and underflow conditions. This is necessary to prevent pixels from ending up the wrong color or intensity, and adds considerably to the software overhead.

Solution: Saturating Math

The MMX instruction set includes versions of each calculation type that perform saturated math: if the operation results in an overflow or underflow, the resultant value is clamped to its maximum or minimum value, respectively. This eliminates the costly software overhead normally associated with this type of operation.

Problem: Comparisons and Branches

Everyone has seen the weatherperson standing in front of the weather map. The image of the person is taken in front of a plain, blue background. The image containing the person is then combined with the map image, replacing all blue pixels in the first image with the corresponding map pixels.

Assume that each of the two images consists of 16-bits per pixel (64K colors per pixel) stored in memory as a series of packed 16-bit pixels. The image containing the person is referred to as image X and the map image as image Y.

Without MMX code, each of the 16-bit pixels would have to be handled as follows:

```
cmp   x[i], BLUE    ;check if pixel is blue
jne   next_pixel    ;if not, process next pixel
mov   x[i], y[i]    ;pixel=blue,so replace with respective map pixel
```

This code fragment would have to be executed for every pixel in the image. Not only is this code-intensive, but it involves a conditional branch based on random data (it is not predictable which pixels are blue versus those that aren't). The chances of mispredictions are high, and we know that mispredicted branches result in costly performance degradation in the Pentium Pro processor.

Solution: MMX Parallel Comparisons

The code in the previous example can be replaced with the following MMX code fragment:

```
mov   mm0, x[i]     ;put 4 packed pixels from person's image in mm0
pcmpeqwmm0, BLUE    ;compare to identify unwanted pixels
pandn x[i], mm0     ;keep person pixels, 0 blue ones in buffer X
pand  mm0, y[i]     ;keep map pixels,0 positions to place person pixels
por   x[i], mm0     ;combine map with person in buffer x
```

1. The first instruction (mov) fetches 4, 16-bit packed pixels from the image with the person on the blue background.
2. The second instruction (pcmpeqw) performs a packed word compare for words that are equal to a constant containing packed BLUE pixel values. The result is placed in MM0 (see Figure 26-2 on page 512).
3. The third instruction (pandn) performs a packed negative AND operation using the mask values created by instruction 2 on the person's image in buffer X in memory (see Figure 26-3 on page 512). The result is stored in buffer X.
4. The fourth instruction (pand) performs a packed AND operation using the mask values created by instruction 2 on the map image in buffer Y in memory (see Figure 26-4 on page 513). The result overwrites the mask value in MM0.
5. The fifth instruction (por) performs a packed OR operation to combine the four pixels of the person with the four pixels of the map (see Figure 26-5 on page 513).

This routine will be faster (it simultaneously operates on two arrays of four pixels each) and also eliminates the conditional branches and therefore the possibility of mispredicts.

Figure 26-2: Results of PCMPEQW (Packed Compare If Words Equal) Instruction

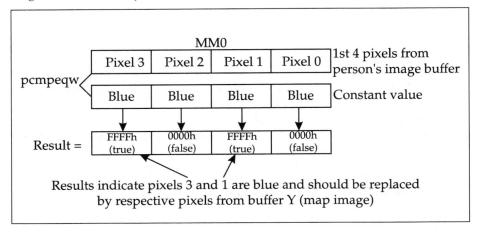

Figure 26-3: Results of PANDN (Packed Logical AND NOT) Instruction

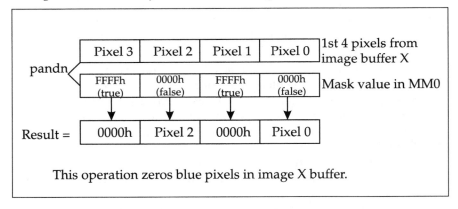

Figure 26-4: Result of PAND (Packed Logical AND) Instruction

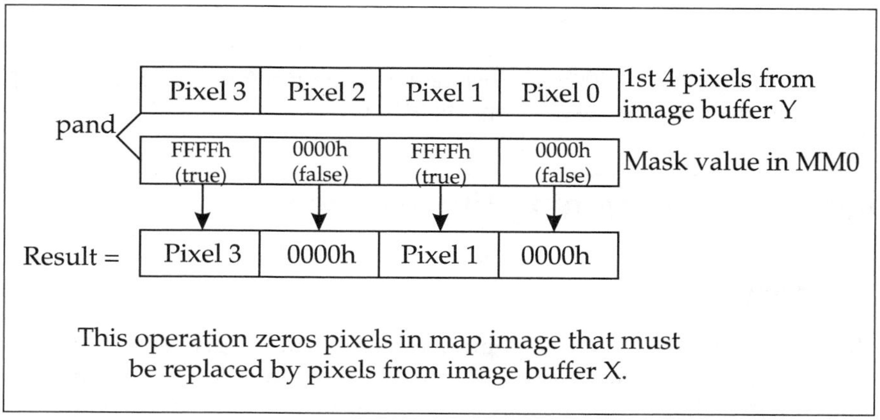

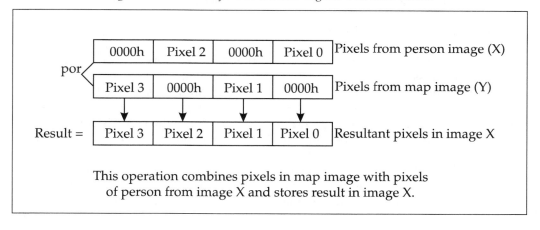

Figure 26-5: Result of POR (Packed Logical OR) Instruction

Single Instruction, Multiple Data (SIMD)

Intel uses the term SIMD to describe the fundamental premise underlying the MMX instruction set: a single instruction capable of operating on multiple, packed data items.

Pentium Pro and Pentium II System Architecture

Detecting Presence of MMX

The MMX extensions can be detected by executing the CPUID instruction with a feature request (see "CPUID Instruction Enhanced" on page 409). EDX[23] = 1 indicates that the processor supports MMX.

Changes to Programming Environment

General

In a word: none. No new exceptions, modes, interrupts, etc. There are 8 new MMX registers, MM[7:0], each 64-bits wide, but Intel took pains to ensure that the new registers didn't add to the number of registers that would have to be saved and reloaded on a task switch—the MMX registers are mapped right over the FPU registers (see Figure 26-6 on page 515) which are already saved and reloaded on a task switch (see "Handling a Task Switch" on page 515).

- The MM[7:0] registers are aliased on the 64-bit mantissa portion of the FP registers.
- When a value is written to one of the MMX registers, it also appears in the mantissa portion of the respective FP register. The reverse is also true—a value written to a FP register also appears in the respective MMX register. In other words, the lower 64-bits of each FP register has two separate names that it responds to—the MMX register name and the FP register name.
- When a value is written to an MMX register, bits [79:64] of the corresponding FP register are all set to ones.
- The FP registers are addressable as stack locations. Pushes and pops are used to put a value onto the FP register that is currently at the TOS (top-of-stack) position and pops are used to read the value from the FP register that is currently at the TOS position. The MMX registers, on the other hand, are each explicitly addressed by name.

Figure 26-6: MMX Registers are Mapped Over FP Registers

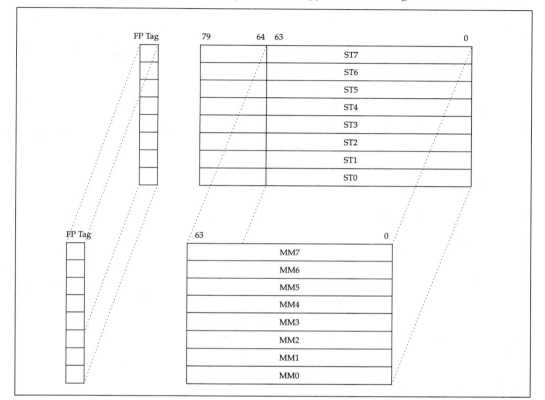

Handling a Task Switch

When a task switch occurs, the processor saves most of its register set contents in the current tasks's TSS (Task State Segment data structure) and automatically sets CR0[TS] = 1 as it enters the next task. However, the processor doesn't automatically save the state of the FPU registers on a task switch (the TSS data structure that a task's register image is stored in doesn't contain entries for the FPU registers).

It is possible that the task just suspended was using the FPU or the MMX registers, and they must be saved before the current task starts using the FPU or MMX registers. If the CR0[TS] (task switch) bit is set and a FP or MMX instruction is executed, this results in a Device Not Available exception (INT 7). The

OS's `INT 7` handler can use the same code that it uses to save the FPU state to save the MMX state. Both the FSAVE and FRSTOR instructions are used to save and restore either the FP or MMX state, whichever register set is currently in use (because they are one and the same). After the `INT 7` handler saves the FPU or MMX register set and clears the CR0[TS] bit, the handler can then execute a return instruction, causing the processor to reattempt execution of the FPU or MMX instruction. The instruction now executes successfully (because CR0[TS] is no longer set).

When Exiting MMX Routine, Execute EMMS

As stated earlier, the MMX register set consists of 8 registers, MM[7:0], each 64-bits in width. They are mapped onto the FPU register set, FP[7:0]. The moment that the first MMX instruction is executed, two things occur:

- the FPU registers are renamed as the MMX registers.
- the FPU tag word is marked valid.

Because the FPU tag word is marked valid (indicating that the FPU registers contain valid data—something that is not true), it is imperative that an EMMS (Empty MMX State) instruction be executed after completion of the MMX code and before any FPU code is executed.

MMX Instruction Set

Instruction Groups

The MMX instruction set is divided into the following groups:

- Arithmetic instructions
- Comparison instructions
- Conversion instructions
- Logical instructions
- Shift instructions
- Data transfer instructions
- Empty MMX State (EMMS) instruction

Chapter 26: MMX: Matrix Math Extensions

Instruction Syntax

Each MMX instruction is built from the following elements:

- Optional P (**prefix**) indicating that it deals with packed data.
- Instruction **operation**—e.g., ADD, CMP, or XOR.
- Optional data-type **Suffix**:
  - US—Unsigned Saturation.
  - S—signed saturation.
  - B—packed byte.
  - W—packed word.
  - D—packed dword.
  - Q—quadword.

As an example, the PADDUSW instruction mnemonic represents a packed add using unsigned saturated addition operating on packed words.

Some instructions that have different input and output elements have two data-type suffixes. As an example, the conversion instruction converts from one data type to another and has two suffixes: one for the original data type and one for the converted data type.

Instruction Set

Table 26-1 on page 517 defines the MMX instruction set.

Table 26-1: MMX Instruction Set

Instruction Group	Mnemonic	Description
Data Transfer, Pack, Unpack	MOV[D,Q]	Move dword or quadword to/from MMX register.
	PACKUSWB	Pack words into bytes with unsigned saturation.
	PACKSS[WB,DW]	Pack words into bytes, or dwords into words, with signed saturation.
	PUNPCKH[BW,WD,DQ]	Unpack (interleave) high-order bytes, words, or dwords from MMX register.
	PUNPCKL[BW,WD,DQ]	Unpack (interleave) low-order bytes, words, or dwords from MMX register.

Table 26-1: MMX Instruction Set (Continued)

Instruction Group	Mnemonic	Description
Arithmetic	PADD[B,W,D]	Packed add on bytes, words, or dwords.
	PADDS[B,W]	Saturating add on bytes or words.
	PADDUS[B,W]	Unsigned saturated add on bytes or words.
	PSUB[B,W,D]	Packed subtract on bytes, words, or dwords.
	PSUBS[B,W]	Saturating subtraction on bytes or words.
	PSUBUS[B,W]	Unsigned saturating subtract on bytes or words.
	PMULHW	Multiply packed words to get high bits of product.
	PMULLW	Multiply packed words to get low bits of product.
	PMADDWD	Multiply packed words to get pairs of products.
Shift and rotate	PSLL[W,D,Q]	Packed shift left logical on words, dwords, or quad-words.
	PSRL[W,D,Q]	Packed shift right logical on words, dwords, or quad-words.
	PSRA[W,D]	Packed shift right arithmetic on words or dwords.
Logical	PAND	Bit-wise logical AND.
	PANDN	Bit-wise logical AND NOT.
	POR	Bit-wise logical OR.
	PXOR	Bit-wise logical XOR.
Compare	PCMPEQ[B,W,D]	Packed compare if equal on bytes, words, or dwords.
	PCMPGT[B,W,D]	Packed compare if greater than on bytes, words, or dwords.
Miscellaneous	EMMS	Empty MMX state.

Chapter 26: MMX: Matrix Math Extensions

Pentium II MMX Execution Units

MMX is not implemented on the Pentium Pro processor. However, the Pentium II processor (and most likly all future Intel x86 processors) supports MMX. The MMX execution units are connected to the Reservation Station (RS) as illustrated in Figure 26-7 on page 520:

- Port 0: MMX ALU Unit and MMX Multiplier Unit
- Port 1: MMX ALU Unit and MMX Shifter Unit.

The MMX execution units have the following characteristics:

- The Reservation Station can simultaneously (i.e., in the same clock) dispatch MMX instructions through ports 0 and 1.
- Since there is an MMX ALU unit on each of these two ports, two MMX ALU instructions can be executed simultaneously.
- MMX multiply and shift instructions can simultaneously be dispatched and begin execution.

Figure 26-7: Pentium II MMX Execution Unit Distribution

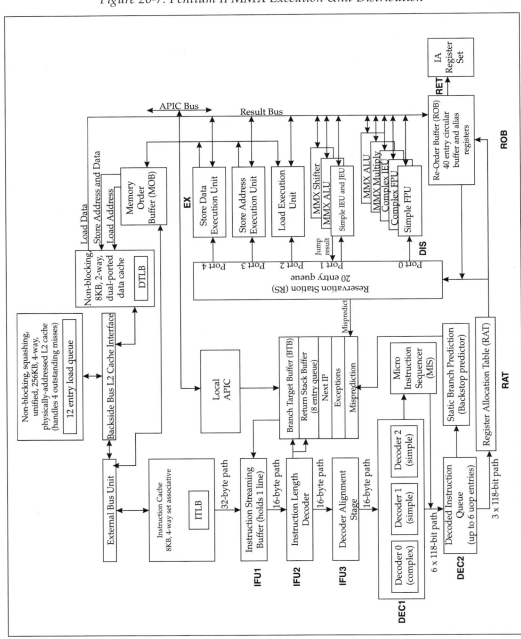

Part 5:
Overview of Intel
Pentium Pro
Chipsets

The Previous Part

Part 4 provided a description of the enhancements to the software environment.

This Part

Part 5 provides an overview of the Intel 450KX, 450GX, and 440FX chipsets (the chipsets that had been released as of this writing). It consists of the following chapters:

- "450GX and KX Chipsets" on page 523.
- "440FX Chipset" on page 559.

27 *450GX and KX Chipsets*

This Chapter

This chapter provides an overview of the Intel 450GX and 450KX Pentium Pro chipsets.

The Next Chapter

The next chapter provides an overview of the Intel 440FX Pentium Pro chipset.

Processor Bus Operation

For a detailed description of the Pentium Pro processor bus operation, refer to:

- "Hardware Section 2: Bus Intro and Arbitration" on page 197
- "Hardware Section 3: The Transaction Phases" on page 259
- "Hardware Section 4: Other Bus Topics" on page 325

PCI Bus Operation

For a detailed description of PCI bus operation, refer to the MindShare book entitled *PCI System Architecture* (published by Addison-Wesley).

450GX Chipset

Overview

Refer to Figure 27-1 on page 526. The 450GX chipset supports up to a total of eight devices on the processor bus:

- a cluster of up to four processors.
- one or two host/PCI bridges. They are referred to as the compatibility and the auxiliary PBs (PCI bridges).
- one or two memory controllers, each capable of controlling up to 4GB of memory. Each memory controller consists of a DC (DRAM controller), a DP (data path unit), and four MICs (memory interface components). Collectively, they place one load on the processor bus.

As a variation, Figure 27-2 on page 527 illustrates two processor clusters interconnected by a cluster bridge. This model still meets the limit of eight devices on the processor bus, even if each processor bus each incorporates two PBs.

Major Features

The 450GX chipset incorporates the following major features:

- Supports 60 or 66MHz processor bus speed and 30 or 33MHz PCI bus speed.
- In addition to performing parity checking on the address and the REQ[4:0]# signal groups, ECC checking on the data bus is supported.
- Compatibility PB supports the boot ROM and the ISA bus beyond the bridge. In other words, it acts as the response agent for processor-initiated accesses to ISA devices and to the boot ROM.
- The two PBs share usage of the BPRI# signal when PCI masters require access to main memory. Only one device may assert BPRI# at a time, however. In the event that both PBs require access to main memory simultaneously, the compatibility PB acts as the arbiter between the two. The two sideband signals IOREQ# and IOGNT# are used by the aux PB to request ownership of the BPRI# signal.
- The main memory controller can be configured to handle either 1-way, 2-way, or 4-way interleaved memory, up to a maximum of 4GB in size.
- If there are two memory controllers implemented, they can be configured to occupy contiguous or non-contiguous memory ranges.
- The memory controller and the PBs are highly configurable regarding the memory and/or IO ranges that they recognize when acting as the target of a transaction originated on either side of the PBs.
- The memory controller can be programmed to control access to System Management memory.
- Both the PBs and the memory controller can be programmed with different accessibility attributes relative to the address ranges that they are configured to recognize.
- When acting as the target of processor-initiated transactions that target PCI

devices, each PB can accept up to four transactions in its outbound transaction queue.

- Each PB can accept up to four inbound PCI-to-main memory transactions in its inbound transaction queue.
- Each memory controller can handle up to four transactions that target main memory.
- Each PB contains four, 32-byte outbound data buffers that handle processor-to-PCI memory writes and PCI reads from main memory.
- Each PB contains four, 32-byte inbound data buffers that handle PCI-to-main memory writes and processor-initiated reads from PCI memory.
- The memory controller contains four, 32-byte outbound data buffers that handle writes to main memory.
- The memory controller contains four, 32-byte inbound data buffers that handle reads from main memory.

Figure 27-1: Block Diagram of Typical System Designed Using Intel 450GX Chipset

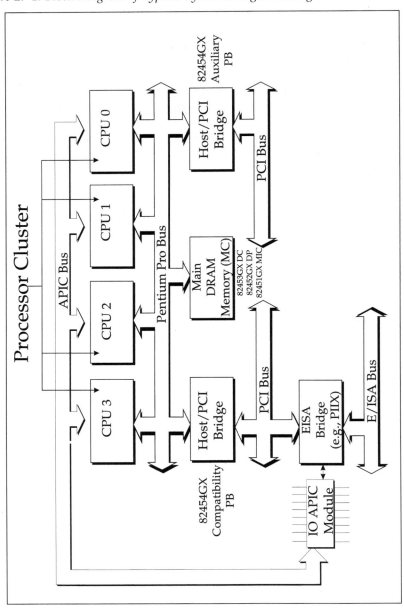

Figure 27-2: Two Pentium Pro Clusters Connected by a Cluster Bridge

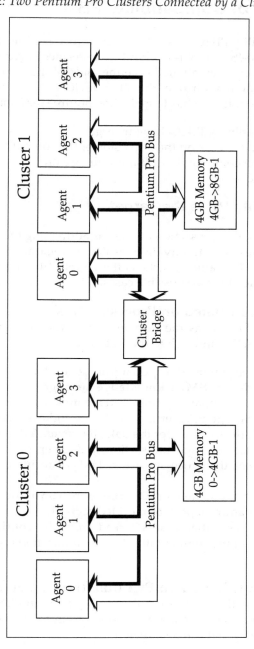

Overview of Compatibility PB

The compatibility PB resides between the processor bus and a PCI bus. In addition, the PCI-to-ISA or PCI-to-EISA bridge resides beyond the compatibility PB. When a transaction is initiated on either side of the compatibility PB, the compatibility PB, along with all of the other devices on that bus, latches the transaction information. It then has to make one of three decisions:

1. The compatibility PB itself is the target.
2. The target device is on the other side of the compatibility PB.
3. Neither the compatibility PB nor a device on the other side is the target of the transaction.

Compatibility PB is the Target

In other words, the transaction initiator is addressing the compatibility PB itself. In this case, the compatibility PB doesn't pass the transaction through to the bus on the other side. Rather, it acts as the target of the transaction. The next two sections describe the two possible cases.

Transaction Initiated on Processor Bus. In the following cases, the compatibility PB acts as the response agent for the transaction, but does not pass the transaction through to the PCI bus:

- Processor has initiated a special transaction that issues a **flush, sync, flush acknowledge, or SMI acknowledge message**.
- Processor has initiated a **branch trace message** transaction. The PB acts as the response agent, asserting TRDY# to indicate when it's ready to accept the data. It does not accept the data, however. A debug tool monitors for the branch trace message transaction and accepts (using snarfing) the data when it sees the processor assert DRDY# to indicate the presence of the data.
- Processor has initiated an **IO write to** the **configuration data port**, the **configuration address port,** or the **TRC** register.
- Processor has initiated an **IO read from** the **configuration data port** (to access one of the compatibility PB's configuration registers) **or the TRC** register.

Transaction Initiated on PCI Bus. There are **no cases** where a transaction initiated on the PCI bus is targeting the compatibility PB itself. There are no IO ports within the PB that are accessible from the PCI side and the PB has no internal memory that can be targeted.

Target on Other Side of Compatibility PB

The transaction initiator is addressing a device that resides on the other side of the compatibility PB. In this case, the PB must arbitrate for ownership of the bus on the other side and must re-issue the transaction on that side. Since the target resides on the opposite side of the PB, the PB must act as the surrogate for the target on the other side. The next two sections describe the two cases:

Transaction Initiated on Processor Bus. The compatibility PB acts as the response agent for the following transactions and must pass the transaction through to the PCI bus:

- Processor-initiated **interrupt acknowledge** transactions are passed onto the PCI bus as a PCI interrupt acknowledge transactions. When the ISA bridge returns the interrupt vector, it is passed back to the processor.
- Processor-initiated special transactions that issue the **shutdown, halt, or stop grant acknowledge message** are passed to the PCI bus as a PCI special cycle transaction. The message is broadcast on the PCI bus during the PCI transaction's data phase.
- Processor-initiated **IO read or write that targets** a **PCI or** an **EISA device, or** that addresses an IO port that falls within the range that may be used by an **ISA device** (IO addresses 0100h through 03FFh or any address that aliases to this range).
- Processor-initiated memory read or write that targets a **PCI or** an **EISA device, or** that addresses memory that falls within the range that may be used by an **ISA device** (memory addresses 000000000h through 000FFFFFFh).

Transaction Initiated on PCI Bus. The only PCI-initiated transactions that are passed through to the processor bus are memory transactions that target main memory. The PB acts as the target of the PCI transaction and acts as the request agent on the processor bus.

Neither Compatibility PB nor Device on Other Side Is Target

In this case, the compatibility PB ignores the transaction.

Overview of Aux PB

The aux PB resides between the processor bus and a PCI bus. Unlike the compatibility PB, however, the PCI-to-ISA or PCI-to-EISA bridge doesn't reside beyond the aux PB. When a transaction is initiated on either side of the aux PB, the aux PB, along with all of the other devices on that bus, latches the transaction information. It then has to make one of three decisions:

1. The aux PB itself is the target.
2. The target device is on the other side of the aux PB.
3. Neither the aux PB nor a device on the other side is the target of the transaction.

Aux PB is the Target

In other words, the transaction initiator is addressing the aux PB itself. In this case, the aux PB doesn't pass the transaction through to the bus on the other side. Rather, it acts as the target of the transaction. The next two sections describe the two possible cases.

Transaction Initiated on Processor Bus. There is only one case where the aux PB acts as the response agent of a processor-initiated transaction where the aux BP itself is the target of the transaction. This is the case where the processor is **accessing the aux PB's configuration registers** through the configuration data port.

Transaction Initiated on PCI Bus. There are **no cases** where a transaction initiated on the PCI bus is targeting the aux PB itself. There are no IO ports within the PB that are accessible from the PCI side and the PB has no internal memory that can be targeted.

Target on Other Side of Aux PB

The transaction initiator is addressing a device that resides on the other side of the aux PB. In this case, the PB must arbitrate for ownership of the bus on the other side and must re-issue the transaction on that side. Since the target resides on the opposite side of the PB, the PB must act as the surrogate for the target on the other side. The next two sections describe the two cases:

Transaction Initiated on Processor Bus. The compatibility PB acts as the response agent for the following transactions and must pass the transaction through to the PCI bus:

• Processor-initiated **IO read or write that targets** a **PCI device**.
• Processor-initiated memory read or write that targets a **PCI device**.

Transaction Initiated on PCI Bus. The only PCI-initiated transactions that are passed through to the processor bus are memory transactions that target main memory. The PB acts as the target of the PCI transaction and acts as the request agent on the processor bus.

Neither Aux PB nor Device on Other Side Is Target

In this case, the aux PB ignores the transaction.

Overview of Memory Controller

The memory controller (MC) consists of the following components:

- a DC (DRAM controller)
- a DP (data path unit)
- four MICs (memory interface components).

Collectively, they place one load on the processor bus. When a transaction is initiated on the processor bus, the memory controller latches the transaction along with all other bus agents. It must then make one of four decisions:

1. Main memory is the target.
2. SMM memory is the target.
3. The memory controller's configuration registers are the target.
4. The transaction has nothing to do with main memory or SMM memory.

In the first three cases, the memory controller acts as the response agent in the transaction. In the fourth case, it ignores the transaction.

Startup Autoconfiguration

Introduction

When the platform is first powered up, the PBs sample input pins to determine what their agent IDs are and what their PCI configuration device numbers are.

Autoconfiguration of PBs

On the rising-edge of the PWRGD signal, both of the PBs sample their IOREQ# and IOGNT# pins to determine which one is the compatibility PB and which is the aux PB. Table 27-1 on page 532 shows the resultant bridge type and ID assignments based on the values sampled from the pins. Note the following:

- The PBs require an agent ID assigned because they initiate transactions on the processor bus and a request agent is required to supply its agent ID during the transmission of request packet B.
- The PBs' configuration registers are accessed using the same mechanism used to access the configuration registers associated with PCI devices. For more information, refer to "How Chipset Members are Configured by Software" on page 539.

As a result of the powerup assignment, the two PBs have the default responsibilities indicated in Table 27-2 on page 532 and Table 27-3 on page 533.

Table 27-1: PB Powerup ID Assignment

IOREQ#	IOGNT#	Bridge Type	Agent ID	PCI Configuration Device Number
0	1	Compatibility PB	9	19h (25d)
1	0	Aux PB	Ah (10d)	1Ah (26d)

Table 27-2: Default Startup Responsibilities of Compatibility PB

Responsibilities
Acts as the response agent for writes to the configuration address port.
Passes accesses for boot ROM to PCI bus (because the boot ROM is located on the ISA bus).
Turbo Reset Control (TRC) register can be accessed. For more information, see "Processor Bus Agent Configuration" on page 535.
Acts as the response agent for branch trace message (but does not latch data) and special transactions issued with the halt, stop grant, and shutdown messages.

Table 27-2: Default Startup Responsibilities of Compatibility PB (Continued)

Responsibilities
Acts as the response agent for the special transaction issued with the SMI acknowledge message. When the first SMI acknowledge message is detected (with SMMEM# asserted in request packet B), the PB asserts the SMIACT# signal and keeps it asserted until the second SMI acknowledge message is detected (with SMMEM# deasserted in request packet B). It then deasserts SMIACT#. While asserted, SMIACT# tells the memory controller that it must enable the SMM memory decoder.
Provides the arbiter for use of BPRI# when both PBs require access to main memory.
Deturbo Counter Control (DCC) register can be accessed.
IO decoders enabled, causing this PB to act as the response agent for all processor-initiated IO transactions. All IO transactions other than those directed at the configuration address and data ports and the TRC register are passed onto the PCI bus.
CONFVR register is accessible. For more information, refer to "Processor Bus Agent Configuration" on page 535.

Table 27-3: Default Startup Responsibilities of Aux PB

Responsibilities
Doesn't act as the response agent for writes to the configuration address port. Snarfs data written to it. Compatibility PB acts as the response agent.
Doesn't pass accesses for boot ROM to PCI bus (because the boot ROM is located beyond the compatibility PB on the ISA bus).
Turbo Reset Control (TRC) register cannot be accessed. For more information, see "Processor Bus Agent Configuration" on page 535.
Ignores the branch trace message and special transactions issued with the halt, stop grant acknowledge, SMI acknowledge, and shutdown messages.
Issues IOREQ# to the compatibility PB when it requires ownership of BPRI# to access main memory. It then waits for the other PB to assert IOGNT# before it asserts BPRI# to obtain ownership of the request signal group.
Deturbo Counter Control (DCC) register cannot be accessed.

Pentium Pro and Pentium II System Architecture

Table 27-3: Default Startup Responsibilities of Aux PB (Continued)

Responsibilities
IO space range registers aren't active, causing this PB to ignore all processor-initiated IO transactions other than those directed at the configuration address and data ports.
CONFVR register isn't accessible. For more information, refer to "Processor Bus Agent Configuration" on page 535.

Autoconfiguration of Memory Controller

Refer to Table 27-4 on page 534. The memory controllers sample the state of the OMCNUM (Orion memory controller number) input on the rising-edge of the PWRGD signal to determine which is the primary memory and which the secondary memory controller. In addition, the value sampled also determines the memory controller's PCI device number. Note the following:

- The memory controller doesn't need an agent ID assigned because it never initiates transactions.
- Although the memory controller doesn't reside on the PCI bus, its configuration registers are accessed using the same mechanism used to access the configuration registers associated with PCI devices. For more information, refer to "How Chipset Members are Configured by Software" on page 539.

As a result of this powerup assignment, the two memory controllers have the default responsibilities indicated in Table 27-5 on page 535 and Table 27-6 on page 535.

Table 27-4: Memory Controller Powerup ID Assignment

OMCNUM	Memory Controller Number	PCI Device Number
0	0	14h (20d)
1	1	15h (21d)

Table 27-5: Default Startup Responsibilities of Memory Controller 0

Responsibilities
Snarfs processor IO writes performed to the configuration address port. For more information, refer to "How Chipset Members are Configured by Software" on page 539.
Base address set to 000000000h.
Responds to accesses within first 512KB of memory (000000000h through 00007FFFFh) and in the 1MB through 4MB minus one range (000100000h through 0003FFFFFh).
DRAM architecture set to non-interleaved (i.e., 1-way).
DRAM timing set to reasonable values for a 66MHz bus and slow memory.

Table 27-6: Default Startup Responsibilities of Memory Controller 1

Responsibilities
Snarfs processor IO writes performed to the configuration address port. For more information, refer to "How Chipset Members are Configured by Software" on page 539.
Base address set to 100000000h (4GB).
Responds to accesses within first 512KB of memory above the 4GB boundary (100000000h through 10007FFFFh) and in the 3MB range from 100100000h through 1003FFFFFh.
DRAM architecture set to non-interleaved (i.e., 1-way).
DRAM timing set to reasonable values for a 66MHz bus and slow memory.

Processor Bus Agent Configuration

As described in the chapter entitled "Automatically Configured Features" on page 35, each processor bus agent samples a series of its pins on the trailing-edge of reset. The values sampled are used to select some of the device's basic operational characteristics.

The compatibility PB implements a register, CONFVR (configuration value register), that, in conjunction with the TRC (turbo reset control) register, permits the BIOS programmer to provide a different set of configuration settings to the bus agents after reset has already been removed. This is accomplished in the following manner:

1. After program execution has been initiated, the programmer writes the desired new configuration settings to the CONFVR register.
2. The programmer then performs an IO write to the TRC register in the compatibility PB (see Figure 27-4 on page 538) with the CPU Reset bit set to one.

In response, the compatibility PB takes the following actions:

1. Asserts RESET# to all processor bus agents.
2. Drives the contents of the CONFVR register onto the signal lines specified in Figure 27-3 on page 537 that correspond to the bits in the CONFVR register.
3. Removes the reset signal.
4. After at least two BCLKs (minimum autoconfiguration signal hold time), ceases to drive the configuration signal lines.

Figure 27-3: Pins Sampled on Trailing-edge of RESET#

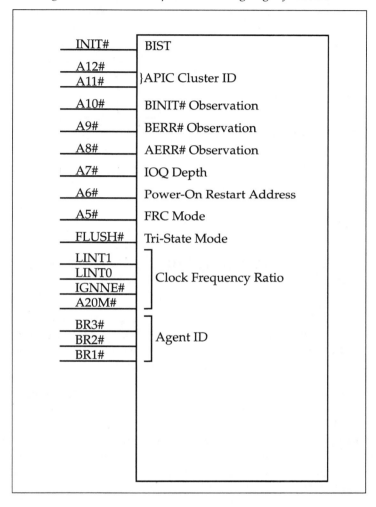

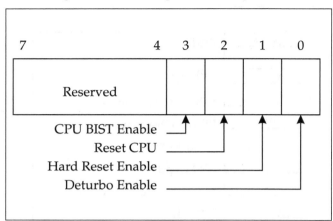

Figure 27-4: TRC Register Bit Assignment

Transaction Deferral Not Implemented—Retry Used Instead

The 450GX PBs do not support transaction deferral when acting either as request or response agents. Rather, when a processor initiates a transaction that targets a device on the PCI side of the bridge (i.e., either PB), the bridge takes the following actions described in the following text.

When a processor initiates a transaction that targets a device beyond the host/PCI bridge, the bridge stretches the snoop phase (via snoop stalls) while it tries to acquire PCI bus ownership. If the host/PCI bridge cannot acquire PCI bus ownership within a reasonable amount of time (we don't know the limit the bridge uses, but let's say around 400ns), it ends the snoop phase (indicating a miss) and terminates the transaction with a retry response. It does not memorize the transaction. The bridge will issue a retry to the processor each time that it retries the transaction until it can get PCI bus ownership within the window. It then starts the PCI transaction, stretching the snoop phase until the PCI device is ready to transfer the data (TRDY# asserted). It then indicates the normal data response (assuming that it's a read) and transfers the data across the bridge to the processor. We asked HP Instrument Division to take some measurements using their Pentium Pro preprocessor and have included an example in table x that shows an attempt to read from a CMOS RAM location (IO port 71h). On the first two attempts, the snoop phase was stalled for 352ns and 376ns, respectively, after which the retry response was delivered to the processor (because the PCI bus could not be acquired quickly). On the third attempt, the PCI bus was acquired within the window, the PCI transaction initiated, and the snoop phase stretched for 1.256us while the ISA read took place. The snoop phase was then terminated with a clean snoop and the normal data response was then received and the data transferred.

Table 27-7: Example IO Access Crossing Host/PCI Bridge

IO Port	Operation	Snoop Phase Duration	Response Type	PCI Transaction Initiated?
71h	IO Read	352ns	Retry	No
71h	IO Read	376ns	Retry	No
71h	IO Read	1.256us	Normal Data	Yes

How Chipset Members are Configured by Software

Each of the PBs and the memory controllers implements a set of configuration registers that are programmed by the BIOS. The sections that follow define the manner in which the configuration registers are accessed and the usage of these registers.

Chipset Configuration Mechanism

The PBs and the memory controllers are configured using the configuration mechanism that is used to configure PCI devices. This may seem puzzling in the case of the memory controllers because they don't reside on the PCI bus. It's always a processor that performs device configuration for devices located on both the processor and PCI buses. The fact that the memory controllers don't truly reside on a PCI bus doesn't mean that the same method can't be used to access their configuration registers.

For a detailed description of the PCI device configuration mechanism and registers, refer to the MindShare book entitled *PCI System Architecture* (published by Addison-Wesley).

Each of the PBs and memory controllers implement the PCI configuration address port and configuration data port. Both are implemented as 32-bit IO ports. The address port occupies IO locations 0CF8h through 0CFBh (pictured in Figure 27-5 on page 541), while the data port occupies IO locations 0CFCh through 0CFFh (each of the four IO locations corresponds to a location with a dword of the selected PCI device's configuration space). To access any PCI device's configuration registers, the programmer performs the following process:

1. Perform a 32-bit IO write to the address port setting the enable bit and specifying the target PCI bus, physical PCI device, PCI function number (i.e., logical device within the physical device), and the target dword (1-of-64) within the logical device's configuration space. The only information that's missing is whether it's a configuration read or write and which bytes within the selected dword of the target device's configuration space.

2. The PBs and the memory controllers all consider themselves as residing on PCI bus 0 and each has a unique PCI physical device number that is automatically assigned to it on machine powerup (see Table 27-1 on page 532 and Table 27-4 on page 534). Each of them considers itself to be a single-function PCI device with a PCI function number of 0. Remember that both PBs and both memory controllers implement the address port at the same IO locations. It would therefore seem that there will be a contention problem with possibly four devices simultaneously acting as the response agent of the transaction. Only the compatibility PB, however, acts as the response agent and actively participates in the transaction. The aux PB and the memory controllers, on the other hand, quietly snarf the data as it is accepted by the compatibility PB. At the conclusion of the IO write, therefore, both PBs and both memory controllers have accepted the write data into their address port.

3. At the conclusion of the IO write, both PBs and both memory controllers then compare the target bus, device, and function number to their own to determine which, if any of them, is the target of the soon to be performed access to the configuration data port.

4. The programmer then performs a one, two, or four byte read from or write to the configuration data port (which, once again, is implemented at the same IO locations in all of the devices). Only the device which had a match on its bus, device, function number acts as the response agent of the read or write. The other devices ignore the access to the data port. The access to the data port tells the selected device whether this is a configuration read (if it's an IO read from the data port), or a configuration write (if it's an IO write). In addition, the processor's byte enables identify which of the four locations within the selected dword are being accessed.

Now that the method for accessing a device's configuration registers has been identified, the sections that follow provide a description of the configuration registers that are implemented in the PBs and the memory controllers.

Figure 27-5: PCI Configuration Address Port

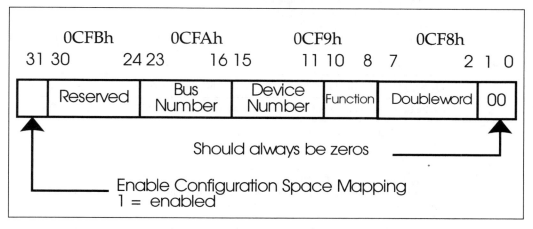

PB Configuration Registers

Figure 27-6 on page 551 illustrates the PB's configuration registers, while Table 27-8 on page 541 provides a description of each of them. This table describes the PB configuration registers for both the 450GX and 450KX PB chips.

Table 27-8: PB Configuration Registers

Offset	Description
00h-01h	**Vendor ID**. Intel vendor ID = 8086h
02h-03h	**Device ID**. PB device ID = 84C4h.
04h-05h	**PCI Command**. Implements all PCI spec-defined bits except: Fast Back-to-Back Enable, Palette Snoop Enable, and Special Cycle Monitoring. • IO Enable bit enables/disables PCI IO accesses on host bus. Default is enabled. • Memory Enable bit enables/disables PCI memory accesses on host bus. Default is enabled. • Bus Master Enable bit is hardwired to the enabled state. • Memory Write and Invalidate bit is disabled at startup. • Parity Error Response is disabled at startup. • Stepping is never used. • SERR# Enable is disabled at startup. For more information, refer to the MindShare book entitled "PCI System Architecture."

Table 27-8: PB Configuration Registers (Continued)

Offset	Description
06h-07h	**PCI Status**. Implements all PCI spec-defined bits except: 66MHz Enable. • The bridge is not fast back-to-back capable. • Status bit are all cleared at startup. • Bridge is a medium-speed PCI target. For more information, refer to the MindShare book entitled "PCI System Architecture."
08h	**Revision ID**.
09h-0Bh	**Class Code**. Hardwired to value 060000h, indicating that it's a host/PCI bridge.
0Ch	**Cache Line Size**. Hardwired to 08h, indicating a cahe line size of 32 bytes (8 * 4 = 32).
0Dh	**Latency Timer**. Default value set to 20h, indicating a maximum burst length of 32 PCI clocks. Can be changed. For more information, refer to the MindShare book entitled "PCI System Architecture."
0Eh	**Header Type**. Hardwired to 00h, indicating that the bridge is a single-function device with header type 0. For more information, refer to the MindShare book entitled "PCI System Architecture."
0Fh	**Built-In Self-Test**. Bridge does not implement a BIST. Although register is read/write, writes have no effect.
10h-3Fh	Reserved. Bridge **does not implement**: any BARs, CardBus CIS Pointer, Subsystem Vendor ID, Subsystem ID, Expansion ROM BAR, Interrupt Line, Interrupt Pin, Min_Gnt, or Max_Lat registers.
Remainder of registers are device-specific, outside the scope of the PCI specification.	
40h-43h	**Top of System Memory**. If enabled, defines the top of main memory (with a granularity of 1MB). Any processor memory accesses above this address (up to the 64GB end of memory space) are forwarded to the PCI bus. Any PCI memory accesses between the top of main memory and the 64GB boundary are ignored by the bridge.
44h-47	Reserved.
48h	**PCI Decode Mode**. Performs two functions with regard to processor-initiated IO transactions: • **Enable/disable masking of A[31:16]** before comparing IO address to the ranges defined in the two IO Space Range registers. In some cases, the processor places a one on A[16] when performing an IO transaction (referred to as IO address wraparound). This feature permits A16 to be forced to 0 by the bridge before the IO address is passed to the PCI bus. • **Enable/disable ISA IO aliasing**. When enabled, the bridge masks A[15:10] before comparing the IO address to the ranges defined in the two IO Space Range registers. In a dual-PB GX system, both PBs must have the ISA IO Alias bit set the same. Otherwise, both may respond to the same IO address.

Table 27-8: PB Configuration Registers (Continued)

Offset	Description
49h	**Bridge Device Number.** This read-only register provides the bridge's PCI physical device number. Established at powerup when both PBs sample IOREQ# and IOGNT# at the leading-edge of PWRGD. • KX, value always 19h (25d). • GX, value for compatibility PB = 19h (25d), while value for aux PB = 1Ah (26d).
4Ah	**PCI Bus Number.** Read/write register. Number of PCI bus immediately on the other side of the PB. Default value is 00h in both PBs. Programmer must change number in aux PB before attempting to access device configuration registers for devices on PCI bus 0. For more information, refer to the MindShare book entitled "PCI System Architecture."
4Bh	**PCI SubOrdinate Bus Number.** Read/write register. Number of highest-numbered PCI bus that resides beyond the PB. Default value is 00h in both PBs. Programmer must change number in aux PB before attempting to access device configuration registers for devices on PCI bus 0. For more information, refer to the MindShare book entitled "PCI System Architecture."
4Ch	**PB Configuration.** This register controls various PB features: • If the Host Bus Timeout feature bit is enabled in the PB Extended Error Reporting Command register, a timeout of either 1.5ms (default) or 30ms may be selected in this register. • If a PCI-to-PCI bridge is present beyond the bridge, programmer must enable (default = disabled) the Lock Atomic Reads feature bit. Any reads that cross a dword boundary are then issued as locked reads. • If the Branch Trace Message Response Enable bit is enabled (default = enabled) in the compatibility PB (in a GX system) or a KX bridge, the bridge acts as the target of the Branch Trace Message transaction (but it does not latch the address delivered on the data bus). Disable this bit if a development tool needs to act as the target. In a dual-bridge GX system, the aux PB ignores this bit. • If enabled to do so (default = enabled), bridge responds to Shutdown Special transaction by asserting INIT# to the processor, typically resulting in a reboot of the OS. In a dual-bridge GX system, the aux PB ignores this bit. • **PB arbiter selection.** The two PBs both use the BPRI# signal to request ownership of the Pentium Pro request bus. Since it's obvious that both can't use BPRI# simultaneously, there must be a BPRI# arbiter. Possible selections are: *no arbitration* (single-bridge system); *this PB provides arbiter* (default); or *other PB provides arbiter*. In a KX system, use default. In a GX system with only one PB, select *no arbitration*. In a dual-bridge GX system, select default for compatibility PB and *other PB provides arbiter* for aux PB.
4Dh-50h	Reserved.

Table 27-8: PB Configuration Registers (Continued)

Offset	Description
51h	**DeTurbo Counter.** If enabled (via a bit in the TRC register), value in this register is compared to the value in an 8-bit free-running counter running at the host bus clock/8. While the counter value > this register, BPRI# is kept asserted by PB. BPRI# is deasserted while the value is =< this register. Default = 80h. Provides a draconian method of making the system appear to run slower (by keeping the processors from using the host bus for periods of time). Used in KX system. Only used in compatibility PB in GX system.
52h	Reserved.
53h	**CPU R/W Control.** Permits the programmer to enable/disable posting of host-to-PCI writes in the PB. Default = disabled.
54h-55h	**PCI R/W Control.** Controls following features: • Whether a PCI-initiated memory read line command is passed to main memory as a line read or as a series of single-beat transfers. Additionally, a memory read line can be converted into main memory line read followed by a prefetch of 3 or more lines from main memory. Default = disabled. • Whether a PCI-initiated memory read multiple command is passed to main memory as a line read or as a series of single-beat transfers. Additionally, a memory read multiple can be converted into main memory line read followed by a prefetch of 3 or more lines from main memory. Default = disabled. • Whether a PCI-initiated memory read command is passed to main memory as a line read or as a single-beat transfer. Additionally, a memory read can be converted into main memory line read followed by a prefetch of 3 or more lines from main memory. Default = disabled. • Whether or not back-to-back line writes by processor(s) can be converted to one, continuous PCI burst write transaction (referred to as write-combining in the PCI spec). Default = disabled. • Whether or not PCI-to-main memory writes can be posted in the PB. Default = disabled.
56h	Reserved.
57h	**SMM Enable.** When enabled, PB does not discriminate between accesses to locations in SMRAM range and PCI memory that occupies the same range. If a processor initiates a memory read or write to SM memory (SMMEM# asserted in request packet 2) and the address is within a range also assigned to PCI memory beyond the bridge, the transaction will be passed to the PCI bus. When disabled (default) and a processor initiates a memory read or write of SM memory, the address is compared to the range specified in the SM Range register. If within range, the PB ignores the transaction, even if it compares to one of the normal memory ranges defined in the other PB configuration registers.
58h	**Video Buffer Area Enable.** When enabled, processor accesses to the video frame buffer (0000A0000h through 0000BFFFFh) are passed to the PCI bus. When disabled, they are ignored. Default in the KX and the compatibility PB is enabled, and disabled in the aux PB.

Table 27-8: PB Configuration Registers (Continued)

Offset	Description
	General info on PAM registers: PAM registers 0 through 6 define the PCI read/write attributes for 14 memory ranges between 512KB (000080000h) and 1MB-1 (0000FFFFFh). Each of the ranges can be designated as disabled, read-only, write-only, or read/write. If enabled for read or write and a processor access of that type is detected within the range, the access is passed to the PCI bus. Conversely, if a PCI access of that type is detected, it is ignored. Each PAM register controls the access rights within two regions. Default for aux PB is all ranges disabled. Default for KX and compatibility PB is all areas (except 512KB-1MB) enabled.
59h	**PAM (Programmable Attribute Map) 0.** Controls the regions 000080000h through 00009FFFFh (512KB through 640KB -1), and 0000F0000h through 0000FFFFFh (the BIOS area).
5Ah	**PAM 1.** Controls the regions 0000C0000h through 0000C3FFFh, and 0000C4000h through 0000C7FFFh. This is part of the ISA expansion ROM area.
5Bh	**PAM 2.** Controls the regions 0000C8000h through 0000CBFFFh, and 0000CC000h through 0000CFFFFh. This is part of the ISA expansion ROM area.
5Ch	**PAM 3.** Controls the regions 0000D0000h through 0000D3FFFh, and 0000D4000h through 0000D7FFFh. This is part of the ISA expansion ROM area.
5Dh	**PAM 4.** Controls the regions 0000D8000h through 0000DBFFFh, and 0000DC000h through 0000DFFFFh. This is part of the ISA expansion ROM area.
5Eh	**PAM 5.** Controls the regions 0000E0000h through 0000E3FFFh, and 0000E4000h through 0000E7FFFh. This is part of the BIOS extension area.
5Fh	**PAM 6.** Controls the regions 0000E8000h through 0000EBFFFh, and 0000EC000h through 0000EFFFFh. This is part of the BIOS extension area.
60h-6F	Reserved.
70h	**Error Reporting Command.** Controls following features: • Enable/disable assertion of SERR# when the PB is acting as the PCI initiator and receives a target abort. • Enable/disable assertion of SERR# when the PB is acting as the PCI initiator of a write transaction and a parity error is detected by the target (it asserts PERR#) when it receives the write data. • Enable/disable assertion of SERR# when PB is acting as PCI initiator of a read transaction and a parity error is detected by the PB (it asserts PERR#) when it receives the read data. • Enable/disable assertion of SERR# when the PB detects PCI address phase parity error. • Enable/disable assertion of PERR# when the PB receives a bad data item on a read, or when being written to by another PCI master.

Table 27-8: PB Configuration Registers (Continued)

Offset	Description
71h	**Error Reporting Status**. Writing a 1 to 1 clears a set status bit. These bits report the following events: • Parity error detected when writing data to a target. • Parity error detected when reading data from a target. • When another PCI master initiated a transaction, an address phase parity error detected. • Shutdown Special transaction detected on host bus. This bit only used in KX and compatibility PB.
72h-77h	Reserved.
78h-79h	**Memory Gap Range**. In combination with the *Memory Gap Upper Address* register, defines a memory address range defined as a "hole" in main memory space. Host accesses within this range are to be directed to the PCI bus. PCI accesses within the hole are not passed to the host bus. The hole may be from 1MB to 32MB in size (in powers of two) and may be enabled or disabled. Default = disabled.
7Ah-7Bh	**Memory Gap Upper Address**. See *Memory Gap Range*.
7Ch-7Fh	**PCI Frame Buffer**. Default = disabled. Use to define the following: • Frame buffer start address (aligned on 1MB boundary). • Enable/disable assignment of frame buffer's attributes (defined in this register) to the VGA video buffer (resides in 0000A0000h through 0000BFFFFh). • Enable/disable frame buffer decoder in PB. • Enable/disable locked accesses to PCI frame buffer. • Flush/do not flush inbound data buffer on non-deferred frame buffer reads. • Frame buffer size.
80h-87h	Reserved.
88h-8Bh	**High Memory Gap Start Address**. In combination with the High Memory Gap End Address register, defines a memory address range defined as a "hole" in main memory space. Host accesses within this range are to be directed to the PCI bus. PCI accesses within the hole are not passed to the host bus. The hole may be any size and may be enabled or disabled. Default = disabled.
8Ch-8Fh	**High Memory Gap End Address**. See *High Memory Gap Start Address*.
90h-97h	Reserved.

Table 27-8: PB Configuration Registers (Continued)

Offset	Description
98h-9Bh	**KX** - Reserved. The KX PB passes all processor-generated IO transactions to the PCI bus except for accesses to the configuration address and data ports and the TRC register. No PCI-initiated IO transactions are passed to the host bus.
	GX - IO Space Range #1. In a **single PB GX system**, the compatibility PB passes all processor-generated IO transactions to the PCI bus except for accesses to the configuration address and data ports and the TRC register. No PCI-initiated IO transactions are passed to the host bus. In a **dual-PB GX system**, the IO Space Range registers have opposite effects in the two PBs: • The compatibility PB **passes all** processor-initiated IO transactions to the PCI bus *except* those that fall within either of the two programmed ranges, and those that target the configuration address and data ports and the TRC register. • The aux PB **ignores all** processor-initiated IO transactions *except* those that fall within either of the two programmed ranges.
9Ch	**PCI Reset**. Permits the programmer to assert the PCI RESET signal under program control.
9Dh-9Fh	Reserved.
A0h-A3h	**KX** - Reserved. See definition of IO Space Range #1.
	GX - IO Space Range #2. See definition of IO Space Range #1.
A4h-A7h	**IO APIC Range**. Each PB may have one or more IO APIC modules residing beyond the bridge. The processors use memory accesses to access the registers within the IO APICS. Each PB must therefore be programmed to recognize the range of memory addresses associated with the IO APICs that reside beyond the bridge. This register is used to specify: • IO APIC base address (defaults to FEC00000h). • Lowest IO APIC unit number (in the range 0h through Fh). • Highest IO APIC unit number. • Enable/disable this range.
A8h-AFh	Reserved.

Table 27-8: PB Configuration Registers (Continued)

Offset	Description
B0h-B1h	**Configuration Values Driven on Reset**. The Pentium Pro processor (and other host bus agents) sample a number of the lower address lines on the trailing-edge of reset to determine a number of their operational characteristics. When the system is first powered up, reset forces all zeros into this register. The programmer can then write the desired value into this register and then use the TRC register to assert host bus RESET# under program control. The KX or compatibility PB asserts RESET#, drives the contents of this register onto the appropriate host bus signal lines, and then deasserts RESET#. It should be noted that the programmed reset does not clear this register. The *Captured System Configuration Values register* latches the values from the host bus on the trailing-edge of RESET# and can be read at any time to determine startup configuration options. The operational characteristics that can be programmed via this register are: • APIC cluster ID • BINIT# input enable (i.e., BINIT# observation policy). • BERR# input enable (i.e., BERR# observation policy). • AERR# input enable (i.e., AERR# observation policy). • In-Order Queue depth of 1 or 8. • POST entry point of 0FFFFFFF0h or 0000FFFF0h. • FRC mode enable or disable.
B2h-B3h	Reserved.
B4h-B5h	**Captured System Configuration Values**. See description of *Configuration Values Driven on Reset* register.
B6h-B7h	Reserved.
B8h-BBh	**SMM Range**. See description of *SMM Enable* register.
BCh	**High BIOS**. Allows the programmer to enable/disable PB's ability to pass processor-initiated memory accesses within the 0 through 512KB and the high BIOS area (2MB area from 0FFE00000h through 0FFFFFFFFh) to the PCI bus. In reality, the high BIOS area is typically only 128KB in size, but the Pentium Pro processor's internal MTRR register that covers this range has 2MB granularity.
BDh-BFh	Reserved.

Table 27-8: PB Configuration Registers (Continued)

Offset	Description
C0h-C3h	**PB Extended Error Reporting Command**. Use this register to: • have PB report errors associated with host bus initiated transactions via either a Hard Fail response in the response phase, or by asserting SERR# on the PCI side (typically causes the E/ISA bridge to assert NMI to processor). Defaults to SERR#. • report master aborts, or don't. If programmer set up the PB not report master aborts, the PB returns all Fs for a read that master aborts. For a write, it reports good completion. Defaults to not report master aborts. • enable/disable reporting (via BERR#) of uncorrectable host bus data errors. Default is disable. • enable/disable correcting of single-bit data errors on host bus. Default is disable.Default is disable. • enable/disable reporting of host bus timeouts (due to no target claiming transaction. Default is disable. • enable/disable host bus timeout. If enabled, PB claims host transactions that are not claimed within either 1.5ms or 30ms (programmed via *PB Configuration* register). Default is disabled. • enable/disable assertion of SERR# on detection of AERR# during error phase of host transaction. Default is disabled. • enable/disable assertion of SERR# on detection of BERR# during error phase of host transaction. Default is disabled. • enable/disable assertion of BINIT# on detection of BERR# during error phase of host transaction. Default is disabled. • enable/disable assertion of BINIT# on detection of host bus protocol error. Default is disabled. • enable/disable assertion of AERR# (during error phase) due to host request phase parity error. Default is disabled on aux PB, enabled on KX and compatibility PB.
C4h-C7h	**PB Extended Error Reporting Status**. Used by the PB to report the following error conditions: • Received Hard Failure response during host bus transaction. • Detected an address parity error when another agent issued a request on the host bus. • Detected an parity error on REQ[4:0]# when another agent issued a request on the host bus. • Detected a correctable data error on the host bus (not implemented in KX PB). • Detected a protocol error on the host bus. • Detected an uncorrectable data error on the host bus (not implemented in KX PB). • Timeout detected on host bus (not implemented in aux PB). • Detected BINIT# asserted on host bus. • Detected AERR# asserted on host bus. The programmer clears a one bit by writing a one to it.

Table 27-8: PB Configuration Registers (Continued)

Offset	Description
C8h–CBh	**PB Retry Timers**. Permits programmer to set up both host bus and PCI bus retry counters. • **Host Retry Counter**. 16-bit field to program host retry count in host clocks. A count of 0000h disables it. If a PCI master attempts to read from system memory and is retried by the PB, the PB suspends posting of PCI-to-main memory writes. The PB will reenable posting of PCI-to-main memory writes until either the retried master successfully retries the transaction or this count expires, whichever comes first. • **PCI Retry Counter**. If the PB attempts a PCI transaction for a host bus agent and is retried, posting of processor memory writes to PCI is suspended until either the transaction is successfully retried or this counter expires, whichever comes first. Counter can be set up for from 0, 16, 32, 64, or 128 PCI retry attempts.
CCh–FFh	Reserved.

Figure 27-6: PB Configuration Registers

3	2	1	0	Dword Number
\(\leftarrow\)	Byte		\(\rightarrow\)	
Device ID		Vendor ID		0
PCI Status		PCI Command		1
Class Code			Rev. ID	2
BIST	Header Type	Latency Timer	Cache Line Size	3
Reserved				4
Reserved				5
Reserved				6
Reserved				7
Reserved				8
Reserved				9
Reserved				10
Reserved				11
Reserved				12
Reserved				13
Reserved				14
Reserved				15
Top of System Memory				16
Reserved				17
SubOrd Bus Num	Bus Number	Device Number	PCI Decode Mode	18
Reserved			PB Configuration	19
CPU R/W Control	Reserved	DeTurbo Counter Control	Reserved	20
SMM Enable	Reserved	PCI R/W Control		21
PAM2	PAM1	PAM0	Video Buffer Area Enable	22
PAM6	PAM5	PAM4	PAM3	23
Reserved				24
Reserved				25
Reserved				26
Reserved				27
Reserved		Error Reporting Status	Error Reporting Command	28
Reserved				29
Memory Gap Upper Address		Memory Gap Range		30
PCI Frame Buffer				31
Reserved				32
Reserved				33
High Memory Gap Start Address				34
High Memory Gap End Address				35
Reserved				36
Reserved				37
IO Space Range #1 in GX, Reserved in KX				38
Reserved			PCI Reset	39
IO Space Range #2 in GX, Reserved in KX				40
IO APIC Range				41
Reserved				42
Reserved				43
Reserved		Configuration Values Driven on Reset		44
Reserved		Captured System Configuration Values		45
SMM Range				46
Reserved			High BIOS	47
PB Extended Error Reporting Command				48
PB Extended Error Reporting Status				49
PB Retry Timers				50
Dwords 51-63 Reserved				63

Memory Controller Configuration Registers

Figure 27-6 on page 551 illustrates the PB's configuration registers, while Table 27-9 on page 552 provides a description of each of them.

Table 27-9: MC Configuration Registers

Offset	Description
00h-01h	**Vendor ID**. Intel vendor ID = 8086h
02h-03h	**Device ID**. PB device ID = 84C5h.
04h-05h	**PCI Command**. MC's PCI Command register is hardwired to all zeros.
06h-07h	**PCI Status**. Hardwired to value 0080h, indicating that the MC supports fast back-to-back transactions.
08h	**Revision ID**.
09h-0Bh	**Class Code**. Hardwired to value 050000h, indicating that it's a RAM memory controller.
10h-3Fh	Reserved. Bridge **does not implement**: Cache Line Size, Master Latency Timer, Header Type, BIST, any BARs, CardBus CIS Pointer, Subsystem Vendor ID, Subsystem ID, Expansion ROM BAR, Interrupt Line, Interrupt Pin, Min_Gnt, or Max_Lat registers.
	Remainder of registers are device-specific, outside the scope of the PCI specification.
40h-43h	**MC Base Address Register**. Only implemented in the GX MC. The default base address for MC 0 is 000000000h, while that for MC 1 is 100000000h (4GB). Each MC samples its respective OMCNUM pin on the leading-edge of PWRGD to determine whether its MC 0 or 1.
44h-48	Reserved.
49h	**Controller Device Number**. This read-only register provides the MC's PCI physical device number. Established at powerup when both MCs sample OMCNUM at the leading-edge of PWRGD. • KX MC, value always 14h (20d). • GX MCs, value for MC 0 = 14h (20d), while value for MC 1 = 15h (21d).
4Ah-4Bh	Reserved.

Table 27-9: MC Configuration Registers (Continued)

Offset	Description
4Ch-4Fh	**Command**. Controls DRAM configuration, memory controller operations, and reports In-Order Queue depth (captured from A[7]# on trailing-edge of reset. Features controller include: • KX MC permits selection of 1- or 2-way interleaved memory architecture. This bit field reports current selection. Default = none. • GX MC permits selection of 1-, 2-, 3-, or 4-way interleaved memory architecture. Default = none. • Hold DRAM page open or close it (default). • Enable/disable of common CAS feature. Default is disabled. • Enable/disable read-around-write feature. Default is disabled. • Enable/disable memory address bit permute feature. Default is disabled. • KX MC permits selection of 1- or 2-way interleaved memory architecture. This bit field used to make selection. Default = 1-way. • GX MC permits selection of 1-, 2-, 3-, or 4-way interleaved memory architecture. This bit field used to make selection. Default = 1-way. • Select number of wait states to be inserted in each beat of multi-beat read. Default = 3 wait states per beat.
50h-56h	Reserved.
57h	**SM RAM Enable**. Enables/disables the SM memory range specified in the *SM Memory Range* register. Default is disabled.
58h	**Video Buffer Region Enable**. Enables/disables video buffer region (0000A0000h through 0000BFFFFh). Default is disabled.
General info on PAM registers: PAM registers 0 through 6 define the MC read/write attributes for the 14 memory ranges between 512KB (000080000h) and 1MB-1 (0000FFFFFh). Each of the ranges can be designated as disabled, read-only, write-only, or read/write. If enabled for read or write and an access of that type is detected within the range, the access is passed to main memory. Each PAM register controls the access rights within two regions. Default for MC is all ranges disabled except for the BIOS area.	
59h	**PAM (Programmable Attribute Map) 0**. Controls the regions 000080000h through 00009FFFFh (512KB through 640KB -1), and 0000F0000h through 0000FFFFFh (the BIOS area).
5Ah	**PAM 1**. Controls the regions 0000C0000h through 0000C3FFFh, and 0000C4000h through 0000C7FFFh. This is part of the ISA expansion ROM area.
5Bh	**PAM 2**. Controls the regions 0000C8000h through 0000CBFFFh, and 0000CC000h through 0000CFFFFh. This is part of the ISA expansion ROM area.
5Ch	**PAM 3**. Controls the regions 0000D0000h through 0000D3FFFh, and 0000D4000h through 0000D7FFFh. This is part of the ISA expansion ROM area.
5Dh	**PAM 4**. Controls the regions 0000D8000h through 0000DBFFFh, and 0000DC000h through 0000DFFFFh. This is part of the ISA expansion ROM area.

Table 27-9: MC Configuration Registers (Continued)

Offset	Description
5Eh	**PAM 5**. Controls the regions 0000E0000h through 0000E3FFFh, and 0000E4000h through 0000E7FFFh. This is part of the BIOS extension area.
5Fh	**PAM 6**. Controls the regions 0000E8000h through 0000EBFFFh, and 0000EC000h through 0000EFFFFh. This is part of the BIOS extension area.
60h-63h	**DRAM Row Limits for Rows 0 through 3**. Implemented in KX and GX MC. Used to specify the lower and upper addresses for each of the first four RAM rows.
64h-67h	**DRAM Row Limits for Rows 4 through 7**. Only implemented in GX MC. Used to specify the lower and upper addresses for each of the last four RAM rows.
70h-73h	Reserved.
74h-77h	**Single-Bit Correctable Error Address**. Contains the memory address that experienced the error. Permits identification of failing SIMM package. Valid only if the corresponding error status bit is set in the *Memory Error Status* register.
78h-79h	**Memory Gap**. In combination with the *Memory Gap Upper Address* register, defines a memory address range defined as a "hole" in main memory space. Host accesses within this range are to be directed to the PCI bus (the PBs must be programmed accordingly). The hole may be from 1MB to 32MB in size (in powers of two) and may be enabled or disabled. Default = disabled. Must reside between the ranges defined by the Low Memory Gap register, and the range defined by *High Memory Gap Start Address* and *High Memory Gap End Address* registers.
7Ah-7Bh	**Memory Gap Upper Address**. See description of the *Memory Gap* register.
7Ch-7Fh	**Low Memory Gap**. Defines a memory address range defined as a "hole" in main memory space. Host accesses within this range are to be directed to the PCI bus (the PBs must be programmed accordingly). The hole may be from 1MB to 32MB in size (in powers of two) and may be enabled or disabled. Default = disabled. Must reside below the range defined by the *Memory Gap* and *Memory Gap Upper Address* registers, as well as that defined by *High Memory Gap Start Address* and *High Memory Gap End Address* registers.
80h-87h	Reserved.
88h-8Bh	**High Memory Gap Start Address**. Defines a memory address range defined as a "hole" in main memory space. Host accesses within this range are to be directed to the PCI bus (the PBs must be programmed accordingly). The hole may be any size and may be enabled or disabled. Default = disabled. Must reside above the ranges defined by the *Low Memory Gap, Memory Gap* and *Memory Gap Upper Address* registers.
8Ch-8Fh	**High Memory Gap End Address**. See description of *High Memory Gap Start Address* register.
90h-A3h	Reserved.

Table 27-9: MC Configuration Registers (Continued)

Offset	Description
A4h-A7h	**IO APIC Range**. Each PB may have one or more IO APIC modules residing beyond the bridge. The processors use memory accesses to access the registers within the IO APICS. Each PB must therefore be programmed to recognize the range of memory addresses associated with the IO APICs that reside beyond the bridge. The MC must be programmed to ignore accesses within this range. This register is used to specify: • IO APIC base address (defaults to FEC00000h). • Lowest IO APIC unit number (in the range 0h through Fh). • Highest IO APIC unit number. • Enable/disable this range.
A8h-ABh	**Uncorrectable Error Address**. Contains the memory address that experienced the error. Valid only if the corresponding error status bit is set in the *Memory Error Status* register. Permits identification of failing SIMM package
ACh-AFh	**Memory Timing**. Used to program the MC for RAM refresh timing and memory access timing.
B0h-B7h	Reserved.
B8h-BBh	**SM RAM Range**. Defines the address range associated with SM memory.
BCh	**High BIOS Gap Range**. Used to enable or disable the MC's ability to recognize addresses within the 2MB high BIOS range (0FFE00000h through 0FFFFFFFFh).
BDh-BFh	Reserved.
C0h-C1h	**Memory Error Reporting Command**. Used to enable/disable correction of single-bit memory errors, as well as enable/disable of correctable and uncorrectable memory errors.
C2h-C3h	**Memory Error Status**. Indicates whether a correctable or uncorrectable memory error has occurred.
C4h-C5h	**System Error Reporting Command**. Used to: • control the generation of ECC data • control logging of ECC errors • read startup configuration information regarding AERR#, BERR#, and BINIT# observation. • enable/disable MC's ability to drive AERR#, BERR#, and BINIT#.
C6h-C7h	**System Error Status**. Reports following error conditions: • parity error on address latched in request packets 1 or 2 of a transaction's request phase. • parity error on REQ[4:0]# latched in request packets 1 or 2 of a transaction's request phase. • correctable error logged. • uncorrectable error logged. • host bus protocol error
C8h-FFh	Reserved.

Figure 27-7: MC Configuration Registers

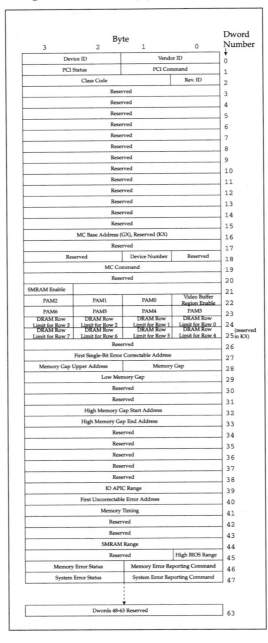

450KX Chipset

Overview

Refer to Figure 27-8 on page 558. The 450KX chipset is a diminished-capability version of the 450GX chipset that supports up to a total of six devices on the processor bus:

- one or two processors.
- one host/PCI bridge.
- one memory controller that support up to 1GB of non-interleaved or 2-way interleaved memory.

Major Features

The 450KX chipset supports the following features:

- 60 or 66MHz processor bus speed and 30 or 33MHz PCI bus speed.
- Up to 1GB of 2-way interleaved or 512MB of non-interleaved memory with optional ECC capability.
- Single-bit memory error correction, double-bit or nibble error detection capability.
- Generates parity on the address and REQ[4:0]# signal groups, but not on the data bus.
- Supports 64-bit PCI memory addressing.
- Supports EISA/ISA bridge behind the host/PCI bridge (PB).
- No support for a second PB.
- The memory controller and the PB is highly configurable regarding the memory and/or IO ranges that they recognize when acting as the target of a transaction originated on either side of the PB.
- The memory controller can be programmed to control access to System Management memory.
- Both the PB and the memory controller can be programmed with different accessibility attributes relative to the address ranges that they are configured to recognize.
- When acting as the target of processor-initiated transactions that target PCI devices, the PB can accept up to four transactions in its outbound transaction queue.
- The PB can accept up to four inbound PCI-to-main memory transactions in its inbound transaction queue.
- The memory controller can handle up to four transactions that target main memory.

- The PB contains four, 32-byte outbound data buffers that handle processor-to-PCI memory writes and PCI reads from main memory.
- The PB contains four, 32-byte inbound data buffers that handle PCI-to-main memory writes and processor-initiated reads from PCI memory.
- The memory controller contains four, 32-byte outbound data buffers that handle writes to main memory.
- The memory controller contains four, 32-byte inbound data buffers that handle reads from main memory.

Figure 27-8: Typical Platform Designed Around 450KX Chipset

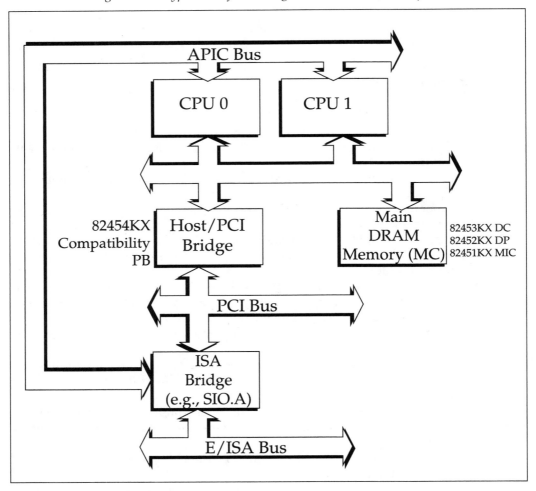

28 *440FX Chipset*

The Previous Chapter

The previous chapter provided an overview of the Intel 450GX and 450KX Pentium Pro chipsets.

This Chapter

This chapter provides an overview of the Intel 440FX chipset.

Processor Bus Operation

For a detailed description of the Pentium Pro processor bus operation, refer to:

- "Hardware Section 2: Bus Intro and Arbitration" on page 197
- "Hardware Section 3: The Transaction Phases" on page 259
- "Hardware Section 4: Other Bus Topics" on page 325

PCI Bus Operation

For a detailed description of PCI bus operation, refer to the MindShare book entitled *PCI System Architecture* (published by Addison-Wesley).

ChipSet Overview

Refer to Figure 28-1 on page 566. The Intel 440FX chipset consists of the following components:

- PIIX3 bridge.
- 82441FX PCI and memory controller (PMC).
- 82442FX Data Bus Accelerator (DBX).

It supports three devices on the processor bus: one or two processors, the PMC, and the DBX. Note that the PMC and DBX together place one device load on the processor bus.

Major Features

The 440FX chipset incorporates the following major features:

- Reduced chip count for low-cost system design.
- Support for one or two processors.
- From 8MB to 1GB of memory.
- Supports 32-bit addressing (not 64-bit addressing).
- Unlike the 450GX and KX chipsets, supports deferred transactions.
- Supports bus frequencies up to 66MHz.
- Supports 5V or 3V DRAMs.
- The PMC incorporates the PCI bus arbiter. The arbitration is hardwired such that it rotational between the processors, a PCI master (other than the PIIX3), and the PIIX3. Within the PCI masters, it is rotational.
- Complies with the revision 2.1 PCI specification.
- The PIIX3 incorporates the ISA bus bridge, the USB controller, an IDE interface and a link to the IO APIC module.
- When a PCI master accesses main memory, the memory address is supplied to the processors for a snoop.
- The DRAM controller autodetects the DRAM type and size and autoconfigures itself.
- DRAM controller supports ECC or parity (programmable) in memory.
- Supports up to five PCI masters (in addition to the PIIX3).
- The PCI clock is synchronous, divide-by-two with reference to the processor BCLK speed.
- The PMC asserts INIT# to the processor(s) when a shutdown message is received from a processor (via a special transaction). INIT# can also be asserted under program control by writing the appropriate value to the PMC's TRC register.
- BNR# is used by the PMC to throttle the processor(s) from overrunning its IOQ (which can be set a depth of 1 or 4 via strapping option).
- PMC cannot generate the PCI dual-address command (i.e., 64-bit memory addressing isn't supported).
- PMC can be programmed to assert SERR# for: main memory single-bit ECC error; main memory parity error; or main memory multiple-bit ECC error.
- The PMC can be programmed to assert SERR# when it receives a PCI target abort or when PERR# is asserted.
- The DBX asserts BREQ0# during reset to assign agent IDs to the proces-

sor(s) (for more information, see "Processor's Agent and APIC ID Assignment" on page 42).

- The PMC implements two IO ports: the PCI configuration address and data ports (at IO locations 0CF8h through 0CFBh, and 0CFCh through 0CFFh, respectively).
- Relative to accessing its configuration registers, the PMC is on PCI bus 0, physical device 0, function 0.
- The IDSEL-to-AD line mapping is AD11 asserted for device 0 (this never occurs because the PMC never passes configuration accesses to the PCI bus when it is the targeted device), AD12 for device 1, etc., up to AD31 asserted for device 20.

PMC Configuration Registers

Table 28-1 on page 561 describes the PMC's configuration registers.

Table 28-1: PMC Configuration Register

Offset	Description
00-01h	**Vendor ID** = 8086h
02-03h	**Device ID** = 1237h

Table 28-1: PMC Configuration Register (Continued)

Offset	Description
04-05h	**PCI Command register**. Bits assigned as follows: • Bits [15:10] reserved. • Bit [9] is the fast back-to-back enable bit. Not implemented and hard-wired to 0. • Bit [8] is the SERR# enable bit. • Bit [7] is the Stepping control bit. Not implemented and hardwired to 0. • Bit [6] is the PERR# enable bit. • Bit [5] is the VGA Palette Snoop enable bit. It is hardwired to 0. • Bit [4] is the Memory Write and Invalidate enable bit. Not implemented and hardwired to 0. • Bit [3] is the Special Cycle enable bit. Not implemented and hardwired to 0. • Bit [2] is the Bus Master enable bit. This bit is hardwired to 1, permitting the PMC to initiate PCI transactions when necessary. • Bit [1] is the Memory Access enable bit. This bit is hardwired to 1, permitting the PMC to act as the target of PCI memory transactions that target main memory. • Bit [0] is the IO Access enable bit. This bit is hardwired to 0, because the PMC never acts as the target of PCI-initiated IO transactions.
06-07h	**PCI Status register**. Bits assigned as follows: • Bits [15] is the Detected Parity Error bit. • Bit [14] is the Signaled SERR# bit. • Bit [13] is the Received Master Abort bit. • Bit [12] is the Received Target Abort bit. • Bit [11] is the Signaled Target Abort bit. • Bit [10:9] is the DEVSEL# timing field. Hardwired to 01b, indicating that the PMC is a medium decode speed PCI device. • Bit [8] is the Data Parity Reported bit. • Bit [7] is the Fast Back-to-Back Capable bit. Hardwired to 1, indicating that the PMC supports fast back-to-back transactions with different targets. • Bit [6] is the UDF Supported bit. Hardwired to 0, indicating that no diskette is necessary to complete the configuration of the PMC. • Bit [5] is the 66MHz Capable bit. Hardwired to 0, indicating that the PMC cannot operate properly on a PCI bus that runs faster than 33MHz. • Bits [4:0] are reserved and are hardwired to 0.

Table 28-1: PMC Configuration Register (Continued)

Offset	Description
08h	**Revision ID** = the rev level (i.e., the stepping) of the PMC silicon.
09-0Bh	**Class Code register** = 060000h, indicating that the PMC is a host/PCI bridge (class code 06, subclass 00).
0Ch	**Cache Line Size** register is hardwired to 0 because the PMC "knows" the cache line size (32 bytes).
0Dh	**Master Latency Timer register**. Must be programmed with the PMC's timeslice when performing a PCI transaction. Lower three bits are hardwired to 0, forcing the programmed value to a value divisible by eight.
0Eh	**Header Type** register = 00h, bits [6:0] = 0 indicating that the layout of configuration dwords 04d through 15d follows the header type 0 template. Bit [7] = 0 indicating that the PMC is a single-function PCI device.
0Fh	**BIST** (built-in self-test) register. Hardwired to 00h, indicating that the PMC doesn't implement a BIST.
10-3Fh	Hardwired to 0. The PMC doesn't implement the following registers: Base Address registers, CardBus CIS Pointer, Subsystem Vendor ID, Subsystem ID, Expansion ROM Base Address register, Interrupt Line, Interrupt Pin, Min_Gnt, Max_Lat.
Device-Specific Configuration Registers	
40-4Fh	Hardwired to 0. The PMC doesn't implement device-specific configuration dwords 16d through 19d.
50-51h	**PMC Configuration register** (PMCCFG). Allows configuration (or read) of such features as write buffer flushing on interrupts, number of RAS (Row Address Strobe) lines to address DRAM, processor bus frequency, selection of ECC or parity checking for memory accesses, IOQ depth selected.
52h	**Deturbo Counter Control (DCC)** register. After enabling the Deturbo feature in the TRC register (IO port 93h), this register is programmed with a value that defines how long the PMC keeps BPRI# asserted to keep the processor(s) from using the bus. This features permits the emulation of running the program on a slower machine.

Table 28-1: PMC Configuration Register (Continued)

Offset	Description
53h	**DBX Buffer Control register (DBC).** Permits configuration of such features as: • retrying a PCI-to-main memory transaction to permit a processor-to-PCI transaction to use the PCI bus. • enable/disable the PMC's ability to post IO writes to the IDE controller (in the PIIX3). • USWC write posting enable/disable. • enable/disable PMC's ability to retry any PCI transaction that takes longer than 32 PCI CLKs. • enable/disable processor-to-PCI memory write posting. • enable/disable pipelining of PCI-to-main memory writes. • enable/disable combining of individual processor-to-PCI memory writes into a PCI burst memory write transaction. • enable/disable ability in the PMC of a main memory read to pass previously-posted main memory writes.
54h	**Aux Control register (AXC).** Permits selection of: DRAM RAS precharge duration and DRAM address buffer drive strength.
55-56h	**DRAM Row Type register (DRT).** Used to identify the type of DRAM that populates each row and also identifies empty rows.
57h	**DRAM Control register (DRAMC).** Select following features: • DRAM refresh queuing. • DRAM EDO auto-detect mode enable/disable. • DRAM refresh type: RAS-only, or CAS-before-RAS. • DRAM refresh rate.
58h	**DRAM Timing register (DRAMT).** Used to select such features as: • (for BEDO DRAM) usage of toggle-mode or linear mode data transfer sequence. • select DRAM read data delivery rate at 2-2-2, 3-3-3, or 4-4-4. • select DRAM write data acceptance rate at 2-2-2, 3-3-3, or 4-4-4. • selection of RAS-to-CAS delay.
59-5Fh	**Programmable Attribute Map registers (PAM[6:0]).** Allows selection of memory R/W attributes within 13 individual ranges within the 640KB-to-1MB range.

Table 28-1: PMC Configuration Register (Continued)

Offset	Description
60-67h	**DRAM Row Boundary registers (DRB[7:0]).** Used to define the start and end addresses occupied by each row of DRAM modules.
68h	**Fixed DRAM Hole Control register (FDHC).** Permits the programmer to enable/disable two holes in system memory within the 512KB-640KB and 15-16MB range. When the holes are enabled, processor accesses within these regions are passed to the PCI bus.
69-6Fh	Reserved.
70h	**Multi-Transaction Timer register (MTT).** Controls the amount of time that a PCI master is permitted to perform back-to-back PCI transactions within a guaranteed time slice programmed into this register.
71h	**CPU Latency Timer register (CLT).** Permits the PMC to defer a transaction whose snoop phase has been stalled for the amount of time specified in this counter.
72h	**SMM RAM Control register (SMRAM).** Controls accesses to SMM memory.
73-8Fh	Reserved.
90h	**Error Command register (ERRCMD).** Controls the PMC's response to various error conditions: • enable/disable SERR# assertion on receipt of target abort. • enable/disable SERR# assertion on detection of PERR# asserted. • enable/disable SERR# assertion on multiple-bit or parity error. • enable/disable SERR# assertion on single-bit ECC error.
91h	**Error Status register (ERRSTS).** Used to report the following error conditions: • records row that first multi-bit ECC error occurred in. • records if an uncorrectable ECC error was detected. • records row that first single-bit ECC error occurred in. • records if a correctable single-bit ECC error was detected and corrected.
92h	Reserved.

Table 28-1: PMC Configuration Register (Continued)

Offset	Description
93h	**Turbo Reset Control (TRC) register**. Controls the following features: • enables/disables processor BIST execution at startup. • permits programmed hard (RESET#) or soft (INIT#) processor reset. • enable/disable of deturbo mode (see "52h" on page 563).
94-FFh	Reserved.

Figure 28-1: Typical Platform Designed Around 440FX Chipset

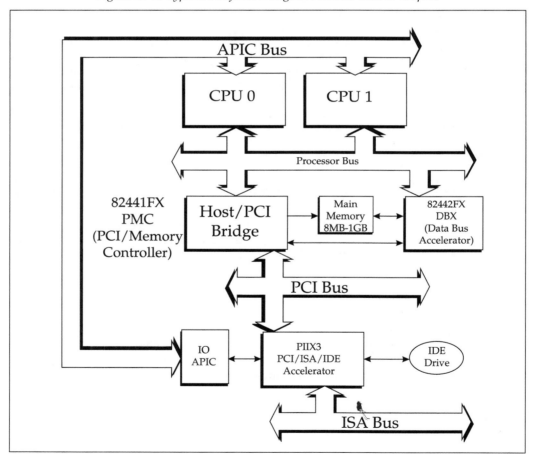

Appendix A

The MTRR Registers

Introduction

The subject of the Memory Type and Range registers (MTRRs) was introduced in the chapter entitled "Rules of Conduct" on page 133. This appendix includes more detail on the MTRRs. All of the MTRRs are implemented as MSRs.

Feature Determination

Use the CPUID instruction with the feature request to determine if the MTRR registers are supported by a processor. EDX[15] = 1 indicates that the MTRRs are supported. Additional information regarding the MTRR registers is obtained by reading the MTRRcap register (MTRR Count and Present register; see Figure 1 on page 568):

- WC = 0 indicates that the WC memory type is not supported, while WC = 1 indicates that it is.
- FIX = 0 indicates that the fixed-range MTRRs aren't supported, while FIX = 1 indicates that they are.
- VCNT = the number of variable-range MTRRs that are supported.

Figure A-1: MTRRcap Register

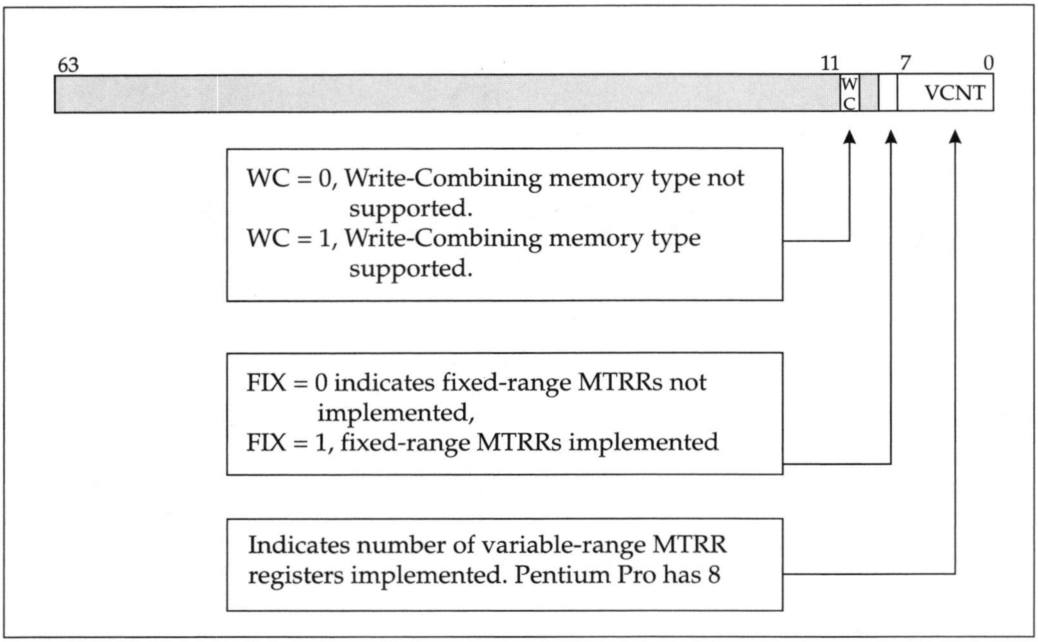

```
63                                    11   7      0
                                      |W|   | |VCNT|
                                      |C|   | |    |
```

WC = 0, Write-Combining memory type not
    supported.
WC = 1, Write-Combining memory type
    supported.

FIX = 0 indicates fixed-range MTRRs not
    implemented,
FIX = 1, fixed-range MTRRs implemented

Indicates number of variable-range MTRR
registers implemented. Pentium Pro has 8

MTRRdefType Register

As described in "Rules of Conduct" on page 133, the MTRRdefType register (see Figure 2 on page 569) defines the memory type for regions of memory not covered by the currently-enabled MTRRs (or for all of memory if the MTRRs are disabled). Reset clears the MTRRdefType register, disabling all MTRRs and defining all of memory as the UC (uncacheable) type.

Figure A-2: MTRRdefType Register

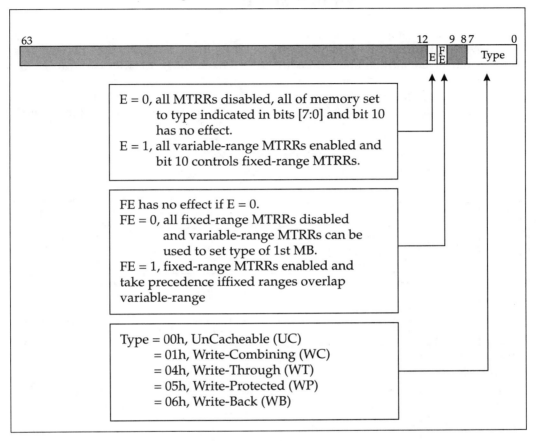

Fixed-Range MTRRs

Enabling the Fixed-Range MTRRs

The fixed-range MTRRs are enabled by setting the E and the FE bits = 1 in the MTRRdefType register (see Figure 2 on page 569).

Define Rules Within 1st MB

When present and enabled, the fixed-range MTRRs define the rules of conduct within the first MB of memory space (see Figure 3 on page 571). This region is subdivided into 88 subregions by the 11 fixed-range MTRRs (see Table 1 on page 570). Note that each of the fixed-range MTRR registers is 64-bits wide and is subdivided into 8 fields of 8 bits each. The 8-bit value placed in each field defines the memory type (same values as indicated in the TYPE field in Figure 2 on page 569) for the area defined by the bit field.

Table A-1: Fixed-Range MTRRs

63 56	55 48	47 40	39 32	31 24	23 16	15 8	7 0	Register
70000- 7FFFF	60000- 6FFFF	50000- 5FFFF	40000- 4FFFF	30000- 3FFFF	20000- 2FFFF	10000- 1FFFF	00000- 0FFFF	MTRRfix64K_00000 8, 64KB regions
9C000- 9FFFF	98000- 98FFF	94000- 97FFF	90000- 93FFF	8C000- 8FFFF	88000- 8BFFF	84000- 87FFF	80000- 83FFF	MTRRfix16K_80000 8, 16KB regions
BC000- BFFFF	B8000- BBFFF	B4000- B7FFF	B0000- B3FFF	AC000- AFFFF	A8000- ABFFF	A4000- A7FFF	A0000- A3FFF	MTRRfix16K_A0000 8, 16KB regions
C7000- C7FFF	C6000- C6FFF	C5000- C5FFF	C4000- C4FFF	C3000- C3FFF	C2000- C2FFF	C1000- C1FFF	C0000- C0FFF	MTRRfix4K_C0000 8, 4KB regions
CF000- CFFFF	CE000- CEFFF	CD000- CDFFF	CC000- CCFFF	CB000- CBFFF	CA000- CAFFF	C9000- C9FFF	C8000- C8FFF	MTRRfix4K_C8000 8, 4KB regions
D7000- D7FFF	D6000- D6FFF	D5000- D5FFF	D4000- D4FFF	D3000- D3FFF	D2000- D2FFF	D1000- D1FFF	D0000- D0FFF	MTRRfix4K_D0000 8, 4KB regions
DF000- DFFFF	DE000- DEFFF	DD000- DDFFF	DC000- DCFFF	DB000- DBFFF	DA000- DAFFF	D9000- D9FFF	D8000- D8FFF	MTRRfix4K_D8000 8, 4KB regions
E7000- E7FFF	E6000- E6FFF	E5000- E5FFF	E4000- E4FFF	E3000- E3FFF	E2000- E2FFF	E1000- E1FFF	E0000- E0FFF	MTRRfix4K_E0000 8, 4KB regions
EF000- EFFFF	EE000- EEFFF	ED000- EDFFF	EC000- ECFFF	EB000- EBFFF	EA000- EAFFF	E9000- E9FFF	E8000- E8FFF	MTRRfix4K_E8000 8, 4KB regions
F7000- F7FFF	F6000- F6FFF	F5000- F5FFF	F4000- F4FFF	F3000- F3FFF	F2000- F2FFF	F1000- F1FFF	F0000- F0FFF	MTRRfix4K_F0000 8, 4KB regions
FF000- FFFFF	FE000- FEFFF	FD000- FDFFF	FC000- FCFFF	FB000- FBFFF	FA000- FAFFF	F9000- F9FFF	F8000- F8FFF	MTRRfix4K_F8000 8, 4KB regions

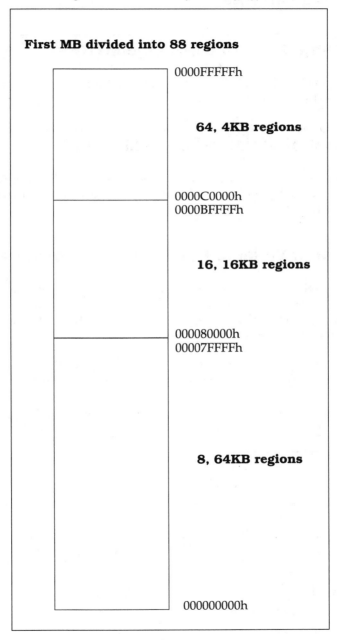

Figure A-3: First MB of Memory Space

First MB divided into 88 regions

0000FFFFFh

64, 4KB regions

0000C0000h
0000BFFFFh

16, 16KB regions

000080000h
00007FFFFh

8, 64KB regions

000000000h

Variable-Range MTRRs

Enabling the Variable-Range MTRRs

The variable-range MTRRs are enabled by setting the E bit in the MTRRdefType register = 1 (see Figure 2 on page 569).

Number of Variable-Range MTRRs

The number of variable-range MTRRs supported by the processor can be read from the MTRRcap register (see Figure 1 on page 568). The current implementations incorporate eight registers.

Format of Variable-Range MTRR Register Pairs

Each variable-range register actually consists of a register pair—the base and mask registers. The format of a register pair is illustrated in Figure 4 on page 572 and Figure 5 on page 572. Note that the letter n indicates the number of the register pair (0-7 for the current processors).

Figure A-4: Format of Variable-Range MTRRphysBasen Register

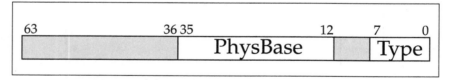

Figure A-5: Format of MTRRphysMaskn Register

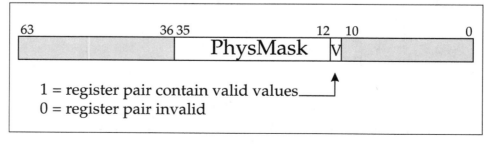

MTRRphysBase*n* Register

The base register (Figure 4 on page 572) is used to set the base address of the memory region whose memory type is defined by the lower 8 bits of the base register. The minimum granularity of the base address is 4KB-aligned (can't use the lower 12 bits to set the base). The base address assigned must be aligned on an address divisible by the range size defined in the MTRRphysMask register's PhysMask field (see next section).

MTRRphysMask*n* Register

The mask register (Figure 5 on page 572) is used to define the size of the memory range (using the PhysMask field). In addition, the V bit = 0 indicates that the register pair hasn't been set up, while V = 1 indicates that the pair contains valid information.

When 000h is appended to the 6-digit (hex) value in the PhysMask field, the binary-weighted value of the least-significant 1-bit in the mask indicates the size of the memory region defined by the register pair. Note that the PhysMask field must contain all 1-bits from the least-significant 1-bit through bit 35.

Examples

Here are two examples for the variable-range MTRRs:

1. Base = 0000000A20000006h, Mask = 0000000FFF000800h. Indicates that the base address = A20000000h, the memory type = writeback (WB), and the size = 16MB.
2. Base = 0000000549200004h, Mask = 0000000FFFFE0800h. Indicates that the base address = 549200000h, the memory type = write-through (WT), and the size is 128KB.

Index

Index

Index

Index

Index

Index

Index

PCI Device Number 534
PCI frame buffer 546
PCI master 231
PCI R/W control 544
PCI reset 547
PCI retry counter 550
PCI specification 292, 330, 560
PCI status 542
PCI subordinate bus number 543
PCI/ISA bridge 357
PCINT 505
PCI-to-EISA 528, 529
PCI-to-ISA 528, 529
PCLK 374
PCMPEQ 518
pcmpeqw 511
PCMPGT 518
PDPT 428, 446, 448
PDPT entry 449
PEN# 478
Pentium 27, 122, 134, 154, 209, 212, 411, 418,
    420, 421, 423, 441, 465, 477, 478, 499,
    501
Pentium II 379
Pentium II servers 395
Pentium, dual-processor 27
PerfCtr registers 503
PerfCtr0 501
PerfCtr1 501
PerfEvtSel registers 502, 504
PerfEvtSel0 501
PerfEvtSel1 501
performance counter enable 428
performance counter interrupt 505
performance counter overflow interrupt 464, 505
performance counters 503
performance counters, starting 505
performance counters, stopping 505
performance monitoring 54, 419, 423, 424, 464,
    499, 501
performance monitoring counter 420
performance monitoring counters 501
performance monitoring or breakpoint 424
PERR# 560, 565
PGE 428, 439, 463
phase-locked loop 41
Phase-Locked Loop decoupling pins 374
physical address extension 412, 428, 439, 463
physical memory address 156
PhysMask field 573
PIC timer 497

PICCLK 371, 404
PICD[1:0] 371, 404
PICD1 58
PIIX3 560
pin control bit 502
pin grid array 380
pipeline stages 171
pipelined 151, 152
pipelining 27
pixel bytes 508
PLL 41, 374, 390, 400, 401
PLL[2:1] 374
PMADDWD 518
PMC 559, 560
PMCCFG 563
PMULHW 518
PMULLW 518
point-to-point transaction 353
pop 514
por 511, 518
port F0h 369
POST 13, 40, 56, 59, 73, 99, 137, 359
posted write 121, 138, 140, 167, 246
Power conservation 392
power conservation 398
POWERGOOD 212, 373
Power-on restart address 47
power-on self-test 13, 99
PowerPC 248
PRDY# 370
prefetch 494
prefetch streaming buffer 52, 55, 78, 99, 157, 192
prefetcher 78, 149, 192
prefix 245
PREQ# 370
priority 222
priority agent 231, 256
priority request agent 211
priority scheme 211
Probe Ready 370
Probe Request 370
processor context corrupt 488
Processor Signature 388
processor type 414
processor version information 411
programmable attribute map 545
programmable attribute map registers 564
protected mode handler 471, 474
protected mode task 475
protected mode virtual interrupt 427
protected mode virtual interrupts 469

Index

Rt 202
rules of conduct 133, 270
RWITM 248

S

S state 14
saturated math 510
SBB 245
SD 107
SEC 380
segment descriptor 245, 296
segment register 130
segment registers 393
self-modifying code 129, 140, 191
self-snooping 193, 288
semaphore 242, 296
SEP (System Enter Present) feature bit 389
serializing 129, 139, 245, 246, 500
serializing instruction 417, 420, 421
SERR# 560, 565
setup time 203
shadow RAM 140
shared memory buffer 241
shared resource 242
shared state 160
shutdown 272, 359, 481, 484, 529, 533, 560
signal groups 213
signature 388
SIMD 513
single-bit correctable error address 554
single-bit memory error correction 557
Single-Edge Cartridge 380
single-quadword, 0-wait state data transfer 321
single-step debug exception 426
single-step exception on branches 424
SIO.A 354
SIPI 59
Sleep 392, 396
Sleep State 400
Slot 1 380, 386, 401
Slot Occupied 392
slot occupied 401
SLOTOCC# 392, 401
SLP# 392, 396, 399, 400
SM RAM enable 553
SM RAM range 555
SMI acknowledge 272, 360, 528, 533
SMI interrupt 398
SMI# 360, 372
SMIACT# 360, 533
Smith algorithm 125
SMM enable 544

SMM handler 360
SMM memory 565
SMM RAM control 565
SMM range 548
SMMEM# 273, 360, 533
SMP 222
SMP OS 13
SMRAM 565
snarf 311, 363, 528, 533, 535, 540
snoop 15, 152, 184, 375, 494, 560
snoop agent 208, 215, 262, 277, 280
snoop event 399
snoop events 398, 400, 401
snoop phase 212, 215, 217, 277
snoop phase, non-memory transactions 288
snoop ports 151, 159, 188
snoop result 188, 280, 282, 284, 293
snoop stall 280, 287, 288, 565
snooper 15
socket 1 380
socket 7 380
socket 8 380
socket, PGA 380
Soft reset 371
software features register 52
software interrupt 475
software interrupt instruction 472
special 288
special transaction 18, 264, 267, 272, 301, 354, 496, 532, 533, 560
speculative code execution 129, 131, 393
speculative execution 32
speculative reads 134, 138, 139, 140
SPLCK# 247, 273, 336
split lock 247, 273, 496
squashed 152
SRAMs 382
SS 53
stack 53, 466, 514
stall 130
stall, partial 130
stalled 253
stalled/throttled/free indicator 251, 253
stalling 173
startup inter-processor interrupt 59
startup IPI 14
startup message 56
static branch prediction 99, 123, 129
static branch predictor 126
status 542, 552, 562
STI 466, 467, 471, 472, 475